COMMUNICATION SATELLITES

COMMUNICATION SATELLITES

———————————— ○ ————————————

Their Development and Impact

HEATHER E. HUDSON

THE FREE PRESS
A Division of Macmillan, Inc.
NEW YORK

Collier Macmillan Publishers
LONDON

The Free Press
A Division of Macmillan, Inc.
866 Third Avenue, New York, N. Y. 10022

Collier Macmillan Canada, Inc.

Printed in the United States of America

printing number
1 2 3 4 5 6 7 8 9 10

Library of Congress Cataloging-in-Publication Data

Hudson, Heather E.
    Communication satellites: their development and impact/Heather
E. Hudson.
        p.   cm.
    Includes bibliographical references.
    ISBN 0–02–915320–4
    1. Artificial satellites in telecommunication.   I. Title.
TK5104.H83   1990
384.5'1—dc20   89–16918
                                                                              CIP

This book is dedicated to the memory of Wilbur Schramm, whose many interests and talents, prolific writing, and commitment to development are a constant inspiration.

"We have now reached the stage when virtually anything we want to do in the field of communications is possible. The constraints are no longer technical, but economic, legal, or political."

ARTHUR C. CLARKE,
United Nations Telecommunications Day, 1983

Contents

Foreword

In the fall of 1957, I was one of millions of people throughout the world who watched in fascination as humankind's first artificial satellite, Sputnik, flashed across the sky. Less than a month earlier I had started my first term as a graduate student in a communication studies program. Throughout my graduate studies and later academic and business career, the fascination remained.

Over the years I learned that the exciting technical potential didn't automatically result in the social benefits that many of us thought could flow from the new technology. Instead, the story of communication satellites is largely the story of institutional power struggles over control of the technology and its applications.

Communication satellites have two major technical and cost advantages over land-based communication technologies. One is the ability to broadcast signals—whether television, radio, or data—over the entire coverage area of the satellite, which can be as large as one-third of the world. The other is to provide reliable communication connecting any pair of points in the coverage area with costs independent of distance or intervening oceans or terrain. Despite much progress since 1957, there are still many parts of the world that have yet to benefit from these technical advantages.

The first commercial applications of satellites were to provide international telephone and television transmission, primarily between the United States and Europe. Satellites permitted a dramatic increase in the number of transoceanic telephone channels and made possible transoceanic television. The story of the development of those first applications is not a story of technology, however, but of the international institutional power struggles that led to the organization of Intelsat and a competing Soviet system.

In the United States, despite a substantial U.S. technical lead over the rest of the world, long political and institutional struggles delayed the advent of satellites for domestic communication until after two other countries, the Soviet Union and Canada, already had domestic satellite networks. The outcome of the struggle was an "open skies" policy that permitted competitive entry and was a harbinger of the later U.S. telecommunications competition that led to the break-up of AT&T.

The competitive U.S. satellite environment can be given significant credit for the growth of cable television in the United States. Pay television and other national cable channels distributed by satellite to cable headends led to a healthy video industry as well as stimulating a backyard satellite television reception industry for rural areas not served by cable.

The open U.S. institutional environment also permitted the emergence of data networks using low-cost satellite earth stations, called very small aperture terminals, or VSATs. As a cofounder and later president of the first VSAT company, Equatorial Communications Company, I was fortunate to be able to help bring into being some of the technical possibilities that were intrinsic to satellite technology. In other countries the institutional barriers would have been too great to permit the entry of such a competitor to established telecommunications institutions.

Elsewhere in the world, with minor exceptions and some hints of future change, the ongoing story of satellites continues to be one of established institutional power defending traditional turf, whether in broadcasting, in telephone communications, or in industrial policy.

Professor Hudson's book provides a welcome, readable summary of the interplay that results when new technical opportunities are met by established institutions. The fascination with the technology and its social potential remains, but the need to focus on the institutional linkages between the technology and the possible social benefits is made abundantly clear in the following pages. I commend them to you.

EDWIN B. PARKER
Gleneden Beach, Oregon
April 1989

Acknowledgments

Many people and organizations contributed to this book. Douglas Parkhill and Richard Gwyn, then of the Canadian Department of Communications, sent me to the Canadian north, where I learned a great deal about the process of communication planning and about development. At Stanford, Edwin Parker encouraged me to work on the Alaska ATS-1 satellite project, where I first saw the potential of satellites realized. Clifford Block of the U.S. Agency for International Development enthusiastically supported projects to harness the potential of satellites for developing countries. The International Telecommunication Union, The Organization for Economic Cooperation and Development, and the World Bank supported my field research on the role of telecommunications in rural development. George Codding, Donna Demac, Dennis Foote, John Gilbert, Douglas Goldschmidt, Michel Guite, Gerry Kenney, Emile McAnany, Bella Mody, Donna Pace, Walter Parker, Joe Pelton, Walther Richter, T.V. Srirangan, Bjorn Wellenius, Florence Woolner, and many others contributed insights about the social, economic, political, and cultural contexts that shape the role and impact of new technologies.

The users themselves taught me a great deal about the benefits of satellite communications. They include native health aides in Alaska; Cree, Ojibway, and Inuit people in northern Canada; aborigines in the Australian Outback; educators in the South Pacific, the West Indies, India, Indonesia, and China; as well as numerous representatives of large corporations, small businesses, nonprofit organizations, and social-service agencies who have harnessed satellites to help achieve their organizations' goals. They are the pioneers. I hope that the countless other individuals and organizations around the world who need this technology will reap similar benefits in the coming decade.

1

Realizing the Dream

In 1957, Sputnik astounded the world with its beeps from space. Seven years later, a geostationary satellite called Syncom transmitted live television coverage of the Tokyo Olympics across the Pacific. In the quarter-century since the first commercial transmissions, we have come to take communication satellites for granted. Live global television coverage of the Olympics and World's Cup reaches hundreds of millions of viewers; our nightly news carries stories from around the world and may even be anchored from abroad. Reporters arrive to cover earthquakes, floods, and political upheavals with satellite antennas packed in suitcases. The links between the financial markets of New York, London, Tokyo, and Hong Kong have created a global stock market. We can pick up a telephone and dial directly to more than seventy countries. In our homes, we can receive dozens of television channels delivered by satellite to cable systems or directly to our backyards. Rooftop antennas link corporate offices, insurance agencies, manufacturing plants, bank branches, and convenience stores.

But perhaps the change has been greatest in those parts of the world that did not have reliable communications before the satellite era. Twenty-five years ago, most developing countries were linked to each other and the outside world only by high-frequency radio. Today their Intelsat earth stations enable them to communicate reliably with their neighbors as well as with the rest of the world. Satellites have been a means of overcoming isolation for people in remote areas around the world, from Alaska and northern Canada to Brazil, the South Pacific, and the Australian Outback.

Although we have come to take satellite technology for granted, we have yet to fully understand its impact. How does the ability to share information globally affect our outlook? Satellites have carried foreign news reports out of Poland, Panama, the Philippines, and China that were then transmitted back to the people in those countries—also via satellite. Globally televised fundraising concerts demonstrate how the shared perception of a problem such as famine in Africa can now evoke a worldwide response. International "space bridges" between East and West can help people with very different traditions and cultures to understand each other. The financial networks linking stock markets around the world, as we have seen, can set off global chain reactions. Basic telephone service via satellite to isolated communities can help to link producers to markets, coordinate logistics and project management, and, most importantly, save lives.

The operative word in the above description is "can." Satellites can do these things and more. But whether they will be used in these or other ways is a question not of technology but of a myriad of other factors that could best be summarized as "policy." We must look at the political, economic, and sociocultural environment to understand not only what the impact of communication satellites has been, but also the reasons for that impact. Why was there an international satellite system, for instance, before there were domestic systems? Why do more than 100 Alaskan villages have telephone service via satellite? Why are several Western European nations making heavy investments in broadcasting satellites? Why are Arabsat, Brasilsat, Mexico's Morelos, and Indonesia's Palapa operating at only partial capacity? Why is there as yet no satellite for sub-Saharan Africa, a developing region that because of its size and geography might benefit from satellites perhaps more than any other?

This book reviews the major developments and consequences of satellite communications over the past quarter-century. In doing so, it attempts to shed some light on a crucial but complex area of contemporary communications. It is hoped that this analysis will contribute to our understanding both of communication satellites and of the social, economic, and political issues surrounding the introduction of new technologies.

VOICES FROM SPACE

In 1945, Arthur C. Clarke, in an article in *Wireless World*, described a system of "extra terrestrial relays," or repeaters, in space. Now best known for his science fiction, Clarke is a physicist, who at that time was secretary of the British Interplanetary Society. He calculated that an object put into orbit 22,300 miles (36,000 kilometers) above Earth would revolve around the planet in 24 hours, the same time it takes for Earth to rotate once on its axis. Thus the repeater would appear motionless from Earth. He pointed out that three such repeaters located 120 degrees apart above the equator would cover the entire globe.[1]

Clarke's concept of a geostationary satellite led to the communication satellites we use for domestic and international communications today. Clarke noted wistfully in his book *Voices from the Sky* that "it is with somewhat mixed feelings that I can claim to have originated one of the most commercially viable ideas of the twentieth century, and to have sold it for just $40."[2] Clarke did not patent his idea, because he thought satellites would not be technically or economically feasible until the next century. He imagined they would have to be operated as space stations with on-board technicians to replace burned-out radio tubes. Clarke had not anticipated the development of the transistor (and later the integrated circuit), which would result in quantum leaps in the reliability and miniaturization of electronic components.[3]

In fact, it took less than twenty years for Clarke's idea to become a reality. In 1957, the Soviet Sputnik showed the world that people could communicate using space satellites. Sputnik was not a geostationary satellite; it was in a low earth orbit and had to be tracked across the sky, and it simply beeped! But it spurred U.S. scientists and engineers to develop more sophisticated satellites for commercial use. In the early 1960s, the American Syncom series of satellites was built; in 1964, the world saw the results of the research, as Syncom 3 transmitted television coverage of the Tokyo Olympics. In 1965, just twenty years after Clarke's article was published, the first commercial international satellite, known as Early Bird or Intelsat 1, was launched to link North America and Europe.

Satellites have changed dramatically since 1965. Early Bird had 480 voice channels; the latest international satellites, the Intelsat 6 series, each have 80,000 voice channels. The satellites themselves are much larger and more sophisticated. Multiple spot beams can be pointed at high-traffic areas and moved if necessary. Several different frequency bands can be used on the same satellite. Commercial satellites now carry supplies of hydrazine fuel for station keeping that have extended their useful lifetimes from a few months in the early days to at least ten years.

EARLY VISIONARIES

The idea of placing objects in space is linked with the history of firepower and rockets. According to Chinese legend, the first astronaut rode a grid of fireworks into the sky. Sir Isaac Newton envisioned launching projectiles by firing a cannon with sufficient firepower at the correct angle. In 1869, the *Atlantic Monthly* published a story called "The Brick Moon" by Edward Everett Hale, about an artificial moon that was to be launched by water-powered flywheels as a navigational aid to sailors. The brick moon was accidentally launched prematurely, carrying with it workers, engineers, and their families who were living inside it. Somehow the space travelers survived; they were spotted by telescope doing "short leaps and long leaps," apparently trying to approximate the dots and dashes of Morse code—perhaps the first communication from space.[4]

Others before Clarke had the idea of a stationary orbit. A Russian theorist, Konstatin Tsiolkovsky, noted that a geostationary orbit existed but did not identify practical applications. In 1928, an Austrian scientist, Hermann Noordung (the pseudonym of a scientist named Potocnik), suggested that the geostationary orbit might be a good location for a manned space station.[5] Meanwhile, the notion of communicating using space was gaining interest. A German scientist and rocket expert, Hermann Oberth, suggested in 1923 that crews of orbiting rockets could communicate with earth by signaling with mirrors. George O. Smith wrote in *Astounding Science Fiction* in 1942 and 1943 about Venus Equilateral, a fictitious artificial planet that functioned as a relay station between Venus and Earth when direct communication was blocked by the sun.[6]

SATELLITE ORBITS

The geostationary orbit is sometimes referred to as the Clarke orbit or Clarke belt, for Arthur Clarke, who first wrote about its benefits for communications. In geosynchronous orbit, the period of revolution of the satellite is equal to the period of rotation of the Earth about its axis. A geosynchronous orbit can be circular or elliptical, and inclined at various angles to the plane of the equator. The geostationary orbit is unique. In addition to being geosynchronous, it is circular and lies in the equatorial plane; the satellite follows the same direction of rotation as the Earth. At this orbit, the angle of view of the satellite is 18 degrees, covering about 42.3 percent of the Earth's surface. The maximum allowable distance between earth stations is about 11,000 miles.[7]

Other orbits can be used for satellites. Low earth orbit (500 km, or less than 300 mi, from Earth) is used for reconnaissance, localized weather and resource imaging, and space manufacturing. The U.S. space shuttle (Space Transportation System, or STS) can launch and retrieve satellites in low earth orbit. Space stations can be deployed at this distance.

In medium earth orbit (12,000 km, or 7,000 to 8,000 mi, above Earth) satellites are typically launched in a polar orbit, allowing one pass every 90 minutes. These satellites are used for navigation, remote sensing, weather monitoring, and sometimes for communications. The Molniya system, for example, uses several polar orbit satellites to transmit television throughout the Soviet Union.

Finally, the supersynchronous, or cislunar, orbit would occupy locations between the geosynchronous and lunar orbits. Not now in use, this orbit may be used in the future for military or scientific purposes.[8]

FEATURES OF SATELLITES

Communication satellites have several properties that make them particularly appropriate for many telecommunications applications. Three features in particular stand out. First, geostationary satellites can cover as much as one-third of the Earth's surface. Domestic satellites are designed to cover large nations such as the United States, Canada, and the U.S.S.R., while regional satellites can serve the entire Arab world or Western Europe, for example. Second, earth stations placed anywhere in the satellite's beam are linked with each other through the satellite, so that the cost of communicating across 500 or 5,000 miles is the same. In contrast, the cost of building and maintaining terrestrial facilities is directly proportional to the length of circuit or transmission route. Third, satellite earth stations can be installed wherever they are needed, without relying on the extension of terrestrial wire, cable, or microwave. Thus, earth stations can be installed according to national or organizational priorities regardless of location: for example, on customer premises, in isolated villages, on trailers or ships, or at disaster sites.

— Satellites are particularly appropriate for point-to-multipoint services such as broadcast television (to cable systems or directly to viewers) and broadcast data (e.g., wire services, financial news services, weather reports, and the like). Satellites with twenty-four or more wideband transponders can transmit enormous amounts of information. Intelsat's latest generation of satellites can carry 40,000 telephone circuits, for example, or 200 television channels. Satellites can also carry data at high transmission speeds over continuous long-distance paths. Optical fiber is now challenging satellites in available bandwidth, but is at present appropriate primarily for high-volume point-to-point (versus point-to-multipoint or multipoint-to-multipoint) service.

— The flexible capacity of satellites makes it possible to start small and then add on more or different capacity. For example, an isolated village might start with a few voice circuits and then later add television and more voice circuits. Some terrestrial technologies such as copper wire have very limited capacity; others such as microwave must be designed initially for the maximum eventual traffic, because expanding capacity later would require overbuilding the entire network. Satellites also offer flexibility for allocation of traffic such as traffic overloads from undersea cables.

— Satellite networks are extremely reliable. If a problem occurs in an earth station, only that site is affected, whereas all sites beyond the trouble point in a terrestrial network will be knocked out of service unless fully redundant routing is built into it. Furthermore, satellite earth stations generally can be located near the people they serve, so that they are readily accessible for maintenance. In contrast, microwave repeaters on mountaintops and undersea cables can be very difficult and costly to repair. Once in orbit, satellites are generally highly reliable throughout their expected lifetimes.

— Traveling at the speed of light, a bit of information takes about 270 milliseconds to complete the one-way trip of 44,600 miles from Earth to satellite and back to Earth; allowing for processing on board the satellite and at the earth terminals, the total transmission delay is about 320 milliseconds. Terrestrial transmission delays are negligible. The satellite's transmission delay has significant, although varying, impact on different types of users. For speech, a user has to wait 640 milliseconds to hear the reply of his respondent. In data transmission, the delay affects response time for interactive types of application, and throughput efficiency and error rates in high-volume applications.[9]

The echo effect, in which the speaker hears the echo of his or her own voice—a feature of terrestrial telephone channels—is caused by the presence of both two-wire and four-wire circuits and the transition between the two.[10] Over short distances, the effect is negligible. For longer terrestrial links, as well as satellite links that are accessed by terrestrial circuits, echo suppressors must be built into the network.

Because they use radio frequencies transmitted over a wide area, satellite transmissions can be intercepted. Business data networks, pay-television channels, and military users now encrypt their signals using advanced digital techniques. Some users have expressed concern that communication satellites could be destroyed by hostile forces. Satellites at low earth orbit are much more vulnerable than geostationary satellites, just as terrestrial facilities are more accessible than transmitters in space.

Satellite signals degrade gradually, so that signals may spill over outside the intended coverage areas. Newer satellites use much tighter beam shaping than older ones, but signals may still reach far beyond national borders. Signals from U.S. domestic satellites, for example, can be picked up throughout the Caribbean and Central America and as far south as Colombia.

Satellite frequencies and orbit locations must be coordinated in order to avoid interference between adjacent satellites and to ensure that all satellite systems can be accommodated in the geostationary orbit.

SATELLITES TODAY

By the late 1980s approximately 3,300 satellites have been launched into orbit. The direct and related revenues generated from communication satellites currently amount to more than $10 billion per year.[11] The first major service on U.S. commercial satellites was pay television. In 1975, Home Box Office (HBO) began transmissions to cable stations around the country on RCA's Satcom 1. HBO's management realized that the satellite could be used to bring feature movies to every cable system in the country. Satellites helped to spur the growth of cable television in major markets as they carried programming that was unavailable on broadcast channels. And they led to the development of "narrowcasting," or programming aimed at specific target audiences, no matter where they live. Today, the Satcom, Galaxy, Westar, and Telstar satellites deliver specialized news, sports, music, movie, and educational channels to cable systems nationwide.

The television networks use satellites to distribute their programming to affiliates, and independent distributors also transmit syndicated programs to subscribing stations. Satellites play an increasingly important role in news programming. Intelsat's international satellites transmit eyewitness coverage of foreign news, sports events such as the Olympics and World's Cup, and special events such as fundraising concerts to viewers worldwide. Even small television stations can now transmit stories using portable antennas for satellite news gathering (SNG).

Satellites also transmit data for business users. Wire services and stock market reports are received by satellite at newspapers and brokers' offices around the country. Large corporations use rooftop antennas to transmit data from one office to another. Others transmit their data to large teleports in major cities which are equipped to communicate with many satellites. Now smaller users can also communicate via satellite with very small aperture terminals (VSATs), which can transmit and receive data from microcomputers and individual computer terminals.

Organizations also turn to satellites for video teleconferencing, or "business television." Some companies have in-house networks for communicating from headquarters to field staff. Others use portable antennas (uplinks) for occasional conferences. Hotels, public television stations, and many universities now offer teleconferencing facilities.

The Intelsat system, which began offering international satellite services in 1965, now provides 110 member countries with international telephone, data, and video communications. More than twenty-five countries now also use Intelsat for domestic communications, to bring telephone and television services to cities and towns that would be too difficult and expensive to serve with terrestrial networks.

In addition to the United States, several other countries have their own satellite systems. Canada, the U.S.S.R., and Australia use satellites to reach remote communities as well as for national networks. Japan, France, and West Germany are beginning to use satellites for direct broadcasting to homes and for business communications. Because of their reliability, flexibility, and cost-insensitivity to distance, satellites may offer a particularly appropriate solution for developing countries' communication problems. The first developing country to have its own satellite was Indonesia in 1976; its Palapa satellite now covers other Southeast Asian nations as well. India, Mexico, and Brazil operate their own domestic satellites, and twenty-two Arab countries are members of the regional Arabsat system. China intends to procure its own communication satellite, and several other countries are at various stages of planning.

FUTURE DIRECTIONS

The future promises many new developments in satellite technology. Intersatellite links will enable one satellite to communicate directly with another, without retransmitting its signals to earth. Multiple antennas with switchable spot beams may make possible the equivalent of global cellular telephone service. High-powered satellites at higher frequencies will make rooftop and suitcase antennas commonplace, and someday we may even see Dick Tracy–style wristwatch communication by satellite as well.

Several new satellite services will be available by the early 1990s. "Mobile satellites" will allow trucking companies to keep track of their fleets through satellite links direct to antennas on each truck. Automatic teller machines and point-of-sale terminals in stores will transmit data from the consumer's credit card via satellite to national host computers. Broadcasters will use satellites for on-the-spot coverage from anywhere in the world.

Meanwhile, developments in other technologies will give users more choices in selecting the most appropriate and least expensive means of transmitting information. Fiber-optic networks will link major cities, but satellites will still retain their importance for communication among large numbers of sites (multipoint networks) and for service to remote areas. "Smart buildings" designed for voice and data communications will communicate with other smart buildings through rooftop antennas or fiber-optic links to city teleports.

OTHER SERVICES

The focus of this book is on civilian and commercial applications of communication satellites. Military systems for communications, control, command, and intelligence also include both geosynchronous and nonsynchronous satellites. Satellite technology can also be used for purposes other than communications. Meteorological satellites transmit data back to earth for weather forecasting. Remote-sensing satellites transmit high-resolution images used in surveillance, mapping, land management, and identification of geological formations and vegetation. These applications are briefly discussed in Chapter 16.

The Early Years

POSTWAR U.S. ACTIVITIES IN SPACE RESEARCH

In order to understand the U.S. response to Sputnik, it is important to note the developments in U.S. space research and policy in the decade following Clarke's article. Technological advances during the period included the invention of the transistor, which made possible the miniaturized electronic components necessary for lightweight space objects; the resulting development of high-speed computers to calculate and track orbits; solar cells to power the satellites; and high-powered rockets resulting from the cold war race to develop delivery capability for intercontinental ballistic missiles (ICBMs).

The United States was shocked out of its postwar complacency by the escalation of the cold war. While the development of early liquid-fuel rockets resulted from World War II, long-range rockets were a product of the cold war. In 1949, the Soviet Union exploded an atomic bomb; in 1950, the Korean War renewed military competition, now not with Germany (many of whose rocket scientists, including Wernher von Braun, were now in the United States) but with the Soviet Union. In response to cold war hostilities, President Harry S Truman initiated a research and development program for large liquid-fuel rockets, which was expanded under President Dwight D. Eisenhower. The call for intercontinental missiles led to the development of the Atlas, Jupiter, and Thor rockets.[1]

The advances in rocketry during and after World War II and the invention of the transistor paved the way for more realistic thinking about communicating from space. Bell Laboratories' John R. Pierce

11

wrote (under a pseudonym) in 1952 that communication with the moon and other planets was within the reach of current technology. He suggested transmission of transatlantic television using a base on the moon. In 1955, writing under his own name, Pierce published an article entitled "Orbital Radio Relays," in which he stated that it seemed possible to achieve broadband transoceanic communications with any one of three types of repeaters: spheres at low altitudes, a plane reflector, or an active repeater in 24-hour orbit. Pierce noted that the launching capability for such a satellite did not yet exist and urged the scientific community to develop rockets capable of launching communication satellites.[2] (Pierce went on to play a major role in NASA's first passive communication satellite experiment, Project Echo, and, in collaboration with Rudolph Kompfner, invented the traveling-wave tube, a wideband amplifier that made possible the transmission of television signals.)[3]

The military began classified feasibility studies of Earth-orbiting satellites after World War II. However, these studies did not progress beyond the planning stage because the various agencies involved were not able to cooperate in a successful joint effort, and the satellite program lacked a clear-cut military objective.[4]

The first public discussion in the United States of the potential social impact of communication satellites appears to have taken place at a conference hosted by the Rand Corporation in 1949 which noted that "the paramount utility of a satellite probably resides in its potentialities as an instrument for the achievement of political/psychological goals." The participants concluded that "radio signals or voice messages from a satellite would probably have initial arresting and mystifying effects," but the effects "would soon wear off and be adjusted to psychologically." Thus "signals or messages from a satellite could be used as attention getters, but other communications techniques . . . would probably prove more effective for disseminating propaganda."[5]

Scientific and military interest in rocketry after World War II resulted in the development of rockets necessary to launch satellites. Between 1946 and 1952, the U.S. Army launched more than sixty V-2 rockets that had been captured from the Germans at the end of World War II. The military invited scientists to participate in a research program on the upper atmosphere, using data collected from the rockets. The Naval Research Laboratory sponsored the development of the Viking rocket, which was used to collect data on seismic ray emissions and solar radiation and, according to Delbert Smith, gave credence to the notion that it was possible to launch a satellite within a few years' time.[6]

Indeed, the activity of the scientific community led to the first U.S. efforts to launch a satellite for the International Geophysical Year (IGY), which lasted from July 1957 to December 1958. The purpose of the research satellite was to collect geophysical data in and above the upper atmosphere. President Eisenhower endorsed the proposal for the satellite put forth by the National Academy of Sciences in July 1955. The Academy and the National Science Foundation were responsible for the design and selection of the scientific experiments to be conducted on the satellite, and the Department of Defense (DOD) was to supply the launch vehicle. After reviewing submissions from the Army, Navy, and Air Force, the Defense Department selected the Navy's Viking rocket for what became known as Project Vanguard.[7] During an era of technological complacency, Project Vanguard received a much lower priority than the ballistic missile program.

SPUTNIK AND THE U.S. RESPONSE

Then came Sputnik. Sputnik was launched on October 4, 1957, as part of the Soviet program for the IGY. With its two radio transmitters sending continual beeps, Sputnik had the psychological and political impact predicted but discounted by the Rand seminar eight years before. The image of the United States as the world's technological and scientific leader was shaken. Its assumed military superiority was also called into question. Wernher von Braun stated: "Overnight it became popular to question the bulwarks of our society, our public education system, our educational strength, international policy, defense strategy and forces, the capability of our science and technology. Even the moral fiber of our people came under searching examination."[8]

Sputnik was nearly nine times as heavy as the proposed U.S. satellite and was orbiting at 560 miles above the earth, nearly twice the altitude proposed for the U.S. satellite.[9] The implication was that the Soviet Union was far ahead in both satellite and rocket technology. Ironically, the United States could have orbited a satellite in 1956. However, government policy dictated that satellite development was to be perceived as a peaceful activity; thus, satellite experimentation was linked to the International Geophysical Year.

The first U.S. satellite was to be launched by the Navy's Viking rocket, which had no military uses. However, after Sputnik, the Army's Jupiter launcher was selected, despite its role in the development of U.S. deterrent forces. Thus, the first U.S. satellite, Explorer 1, was launched by a Jupiter rocket on January 31, 1958, less than four months after Sputnik.[10]

Because of Sputnik, U.S. prestige had become integrally tied to success in space, with the result that both the president and Congress turned their attention to increasing the resources and visibility of the space program. In November 1957, President Eisenhower created the position of special assistant to the president for science and technology, and established the President's Science Advisory Committee by moving the Office of Defense Mobilization's Science Advisory Committee to the White House. The secretary of defense created a new agency responsible for research on satellites and space which became the Advanced Research Projects Agency (ARPA).

In Congress, Sen. Lyndon B. Johnson, chairman of the Preparedness Investigating Subcommittee of the Armed Services Committee, ordered hearings on the missile and satellite program in November 1957. The Senate then established the Special Committee on Space and Astronautics, also chaired by Lyndon Johnson, in February 1958, while the House established its own Committee on Astronautics and Space Exploration in March.

The president's new Science Advisory Committee listed four factors important to a national space program: the compelling urge of man to explore the unknown; the military potential of outer space; the effect upon national prestige; and opportunities for scientific observation and experimentation.[11] The president sent his recommendation to Congress in April 1958 for a civilian space science and exploration program under a new agency, the National Aeronautics and Space Administration (NASA).

In July 1958, Congress passed the National Aeronautics and Space Act, which established NASA as the civilian vehicle for U.S. space research and development, and declared that "it is the policy of the United States that activities in space should be devoted to peaceful purposes for the benefit of all mankind." However, "activities peculiar to or primarily associated with the development of weapons systems, military operations, or the defense of the United States (including the research and development necessary to make effective provision for the defense of the United States) shall be the responsibility of, and shall be directed by, the Department of Defense."[12] In addition to its emphasis on peaceful and scientific activities (while leaving the door open for military involvement in space), the Act limited aeronautical and space activities to research, thus leaving operational activities to the private sector.[13]

EARLY U.S. SATELLITES

In 1954, the Naval Research Laboratory transmitted the first voice message through space, successfully using the moon to reflect radio signals. These experiments led to the development of the Moon Relay System, which became operational for communications between Hawaii and Washington, D.C., in 1959 and remained in use from 1959 to 1963. The principle of the moon relay was used in NASA's first communication satellite, Echo I, launched in August 1960 (after two failures). Echo I was a sort of inflatable space balloon; the vaporization of a bag of water that was opened in space unfolded and inflated the sphere. Earth stations across the United States and in Europe picked up its signals. Echo I was visible to the naked eye, and was followed with great interest during its eight-year life. Leonard Jaffe of NASA stated: "Echo I had more to do with the motivation of following communications satellite research than any other single event."[14]

Echo I was followed by another passive satellite, Echo II, in 1964. With Echo II, U.S. and Soviet scientists collaborated for the first time on international space experiments, under an agreement between NASA and the Soviet Academy of Sciences. Signals were transmitted between the University of Manchester for NASA and the Gorki State University. These passive satellites simply reflected radio signals like a mirror, and were launched to an altitude of more than 600 miles. The disadvantages of passive satellites were (1) that the earth stations required high power (10 kw) to transmit signals strong enough to produce an adequate return echo, and therefore would have to be large and expensive, and (2) that a global system would have required twenty-four passive spheres, which would have been very expensive to launch.[15] The advantages of active satellites, which amplify and retransmit signals from Earth, were that they were directly controlled by their operators and that they required less costly, lower-power earth stations. However, the active satellites carried electronic components that could fail, needed an on-board power supply, and required larger more powerful rockets to achieve orbit.

The military considered a number of passive options, including a "needle belt" proposal, called Project West Ford, that involved launching millions of small wire dipoles into orbit around the Earth to reflect microwave signals.[16] However, it chose to develop active satellites for space communications. The world's first active communication satellite was SCORE (Signal Communication by Orbiting Relay Equipment), launched by the Air Force in 1958. It was called active because it had its own energy source on board and transmitted a prerecorded message of Christmas greetings from President Eisenhower. However, the satellite did not function as a true repeater because it did not receive and retransmit a signal from Earth. SCORE lasted only twelve days.

Although SCORE was launched by the military, President Eisenhower spoke of peace: "This is the President of the United States speaking. Through the marvel of scientific advance, my voice is coming to you from a satellite circling in outer space. My message is a simple one. Through this unique means, I convey to you and to all mankind America's wish for peace on earth and good will towards men everywhere."[17]

The world's first fully active satellite was Courier, launched by the Department of Defense in 1960. Courier, like all satellites today, received signals from earth, translated their frequencies, amplified them, and retransmitted them to Earth. Courier carried twenty-two teletype and four voice channels, operated at higher speed, and was the first satellite to use solar cells rather than batteries. It functioned for only seventeen days.

These two satellites launched by the military were the only active satellites launched by the United States until 1962, despite the fact that active rather than passive satellites were required for commercial applications of voice and video transmission.

THE NEXT PHASE: PRIVATE SECTOR INVOLVEMENT

In 1959, NASA officials stated that "the government must lead the way and . . . later, commercial concerns [will be] prepared to invest large sums in proven techniques and hardware."[18] NASA was to facilitate the development of an operational system and to coordinate the activities of government and industry. President Eisenhower confirmed and strengthened NASA's role in a December 1960 statement that cited as a national objective the establishment of a commercial satellite system and directed NASA to advance the needed research and development, and to encourage private industry to apply its resources for commercial civilian communication requirements.[19]

President John F. Kennedy accelerated the move toward commercial satellite communications. Several events apparently prompted him to make a public commitment to the space program. A government advisory committee had criticized the record of NASA and the Defense Department, and stated that the government should make available the required facilities "as well as any extraordinary financial support to make the undertakings successful."[20] When the Soviet astronaut, Yuri Gagarin, became the first person to orbit the Earth in April 1961, questions were again raised about U.S. technological vulnerability. The Bay of Pigs incident a few days later added to concerns about U.S. prestige and security. In May, Kennedy wrote to NASA that he was "most interested in having facilitated early development of communication satellites" and added $50 million to NASA's budget. He soon appointed Vice President Lyndon Johnson as chairman of the National Aeronautics and Space Council, "to undertake to make the necessary studies and government-wide policy recommendations for bringing into optimum use at the earliest practicable time operational communication satellites."[21]

In 1959, John Pierce of Bell Laboratories told Congress that four technological advances were contributing to increased commercial interest in satellites: better microwave antennas, broadband transistors, higher-frequency transistors, and the development of a microwave amplifier called a maser.[22] Bell Laboratories were investigating the requirements of a passive satellite system. ITT was concentrating on active satellites because it was concerned about the high cost of the powerful transmitters needed for passive satellite transmissions. General Electric and Lockheed also indicated that operational satellites were not far off.

Thus by 1960, the major communication and aviation companies were conducting research and competing for NASA contracts to develop satellites. Several studies, including one by the U.S. Senate, estimated the potential demand based on the increase in the number of telephones and in telephone traffic. NASA involved the private sector in shaping its policies through a series of industry conferences in 1960 attended by, among others, AT&T, ITT, RCA, GE, GTE, Philco, and the Douglas Aircraft Company.[23]

Engineers at Hughes Aircraft developed plans for three active satellites that were presented to Hughes management in 1959. Estimated cost for the project was $5 million. Hughes was sufficiently unsure of the prospects that it approached NASA for support, but NASA rejected the proposal. Hughes then decided to begin development of the spacecraft without NASA's commitment for launch, on the assumption that if another company got into orbit first, Hughes would forfeit a great deal of publicity and prestige and would have to compete for traffic. Further, Hughes was committed to a low-cost program, and delays would only increase cost.

AT&T also had shown an early interest in satellites. In 1959 and 1960, it investigated a passive satellite system, and in 1960, it proposed to the Federal Communications Commission (FCC) a low-altitude passive system consisting of fifty satellites in polar orbit at an altitude of 3,000 miles. In July 1961, NASA announced arrangements with AT&T to develop and test two to four satellites in 1962. AT&T was to design and construct the satellites at its own expense and to reimburse NASA for launch facilities, launching, and tracking.

AT&T's Telstar, the nation's first active satellite and the first developed and funded by the private sector, was launched in July 1962. Telstar was placed in elliptical orbit, circling the earth in 2 hours and 40 minutes. It was visible simultaneously from two earth stations for only about 10 minutes. The transmission of live transatlantic television had a wide impact. Voice, television, facsimile, and data were transmitted between various sites in the United States and Great Britain, France, Brazil, and Italy. Telstar I's command system was affected by the radiation from a high-altitude nuclear test.[24] Telstar II, with an improved command element, was launched in May 1963 to continue its forerunner's experiments and demonstrations.

Several factors led NASA to shift its focus from passive to active satellites. Active satellites were more reliable in orbit, could be controlled from the ground, and were not open to random use; their earth stations needed less power to receive them. Other factors included growing commercial and military interest in active satellites and the beginnings of International Telecommunication Union (ITU) interest in allocating frequencies for satellite communications.[25] Relay I, built for NASA by RCA and launched in December 1962, was the first satellite to include redundancy, or backup systems, in case of system failure. In fact, one transponder did fail, but the satellite continued to function for three years. Relay I transmitted telephone and television signals to Europe, South America, and Japan, thereby demonstrating the global market for broadband communications and setting the stage for exporting U.S. technology to nations that would later join Intelsat. (See chapter 3.) Relay II, launched in July 1964, employed improved solar cells, traveling-wave tubes, and radiation-shielding and power-regulating mechanisms, and operated until mid-1967.

THE FIRST GEOSTATIONARY SATELLITES

Telstar and Relay proved the technical viability of active low-orbit satellites and demonstrated the commercial potential of international voice and video links. However, because they operated at a low orbit, up to twenty-four satellites were needed for a global system. A 1960 agreement between NASA and the Department of Defense provided that the department and not NASA would work on geosynchronous satellites. By 1961, the Defense Department's geosynchronous satellite program, known as Advent, was behind schedule and experiencing difficulties. The Defense Department then agreed to NASA's undertaking a research program in synchronous satellites.

NASA awarded a contract to Hughes to develop a geosynchronous satellite to be called Syncom, proposed by the visionary engineer Harold Rosen. Syncom was launched in February 1963 and successfully achieved geosynchronous orbit, although its electrical equipment failed soon after. Syncom II was launched in July 1963 and was used for many experiments, the most notable of which was transmission to the 1963 Extraordinary Administrative Radio Conference (EARC) of the ITU in Geneva, where the delegates were working on allocation of frequencies for satellite communications.

The most famous of the series, Syncom III was launched in 1964 and used to transmit the Olympic games from Tokyo to the United States, demonstrating the commercial market for the technology. Interestingly, both Syncom II and Syncom III were turned over to the Defense Department for military use, to compensate for the termination of the Advent program. Nonetheless, they marked a turning point in the development of satellite communications, because all commercial satellites that followed were designed to operate from geostationary orbit.[26]

THE NEED FOR FREQUENCIES

The ITU's Atlantic City Radio Regulations of 1947 made no mention of space services. Until 1959, experiments in space had to be carried out so as not to cause harmful interference to services operating in accordance with the table of frequency allocations. This restriction was a serious handicap to activities scheduled for the IGY and to further experimentation by the United States. The United Nations established an Ad Hoc Committee on the Peaceful Uses of Outer Space in December 1958 to build on the success of the space experiments of the IGY and to attempt to direct space research toward peaceful ends. The lack of frequencies allocated for space services led the United Nations' Outer Space Committee to call for the ITU to allocate frequencies for space services at its 1959 World Administrative Radio Conference (WARC).[27]

At the 1959 WARC, only the United States, the U.S.S.R., and the United Kingdom expressed interest in frequencies for space communications. However, the conference delegates, recognizing the rapid progress in space research and the potential of satellite communications, decided to hold a special conference in 1963 to consider frequency allocations for space communications. Within the United States, there was also growing concern about the lack of available frequencies. In 1960, AT&T urged the FCC to allocate or plan for frequencies for satellite communications, but the FCC decided not to do so at that time.[28]

The transmissions of Syncom II to the delegates assembled in Geneva for the 1963 EARC dramatized the potential of the new technology and the need to identify frequencies for space communications. The U.S., Soviet, French, and British delegations all had somewhat differing proposals for frequency allocations. A compromise resulted in the allocation of 2,800 megahertz for space communications, enough to handle 8,000 to 9,000 telephone calls and about four duplex television channels. Since there were only 550 overseas telephone circuits in 1961, with a demand for 8,000 not projected until 1980, the 1963 allocations appeared quite adequate.[29]

The Beginning of International Satellite Communications

BEGINNINGS OF U.S. INTERNATIONAL INITIATIVES

By the early 1960s, communication satellites had been recognized as an important vehicle for international cooperation and the advancement of U.S. foreign policy. In his State of the Union message on January 30, 1961, President Kennedy invited "all nations—including the Soviet Union—to join with us in developing . . . a new communications satellite program."[1] Kennedy's special presidential message, "On Urgent National Needs," transmitted to Congress on May 25, 1961, not only contained the much publicized goal of landing a man (sic) on the moon and returning him safely to earth by the end of the decade, but also asked Congress to "make the most of our present leadership" by accelerating the development of space satellites for worldwide communications. Kennedy thus integrated communication satellites into his administration's space and foreign policy programs, in contrast to the Eisenhower administration's more commercially oriented approach.[2]

On July 24, 1961, Kennedy invited "all nations to participate in a communication satellite system, in the interest of world peace and a close brotherhood among peoples throughout the world."[3] In this statement of national satellite policy, Kennedy declared that a communication satellite system should be established at the earliest practicable date, with provisions for private ownership and operation of the U.S. portion of a global system, provided certain criteria were met. These included nondiscriminatory access to the system by all authorized carriers and competition through bidding and ownership structure. The government's role would include continued research and development by NASA, the results of which were to be available to private enterprise. The government would provide technical assistance to developing countries and require that the system be truly global, even if this meant extending service to unprofitable areas.[4] Kennedy thus foreshadowed the role and posture of the United States in establishing Intelsat.

The State Department under President Kennedy was concerned with four goals in satellite communications: U.S. leadership, rapid implementation of the system, the establishment of a truly global system, and the benefits to all mankind from satellite communications.[5] Edward R. Murrow, then director of the United States Information Agency (USIA), stated that an operational satellite system would be "a dramatic demonstration of our concern for the peaceful uses of outer space and our willingness and indeed our eagerness to use that communications system in the tradition of free reporting in this country."[6] (In the 1980s, USIA implemented a satellite-based network called Worldnet that transmits U.S. programming to embassies around the world. See chapter 6.)

Congress also recognized the international benefits of satellite communications. The Senate Space Committee's Communications Satellite Report called space communications "an entirely new concept of worldwide communication . . . that would afford a unique potential as an instrument of international affairs."[7] The report's authors foresaw the greatest growth in demand for satellite links to Europe, followed by the Caribbean and Latin America. Ironically, demand for communication with Asia was predicted to grow much more slowly. The Senate Space Committee also saw an opportunity for the United States to take the lead in assisting with Third World development:

> These new nations are certain to desire independent communications systems as part of their program of self-government. A single space relay over Africa has entertaining possibilities as a link between all African nations and may prove attractive regardless of purely economic considerations. The United States may thus have a unique opportunity to assist these nations in their goals of self-realization.[8]

At the United Nations in December 1961, U.S. Ambassador to the U.N. Adlai Stevenson proposed a five-point program for cooperation in outer space, including endorsement of the desirability of a global system of communication satellites. Stevenson said that this fundamental breakthrough could affect the lives of all human beings because it could

- forge new bonds of mutual knowledge and understanding between people everywhere;
- offer a powerful tool to improve literacy and education in developing areas;
- support world weather services by speedy transmittal of data;
- enable leaders of nations to talk face-to-face on a convenient and reliable basis.[9]

The United Nations unanimously adopted General Assembly Resolution 1721 (XVI), which stated that "communications by means of satellite should be available to the nations of the world as soon as practicable on a global and nondiscriminatory basis." This resolution internationally codified a main tenet of U.S. satellite policy eight months before the passing of the Communications Satellite Act.[10]

THE ROLE OF THE PRIVATE SECTOR

President Eisenhower strongly encouraged private-sector leadership in U.S. space initiatives: "We have achieved communication facilities second to none among the nations of the world. Accordingly, the Government should aggressively encourage private enterprise in the establishment and operation of satellite relays for revenue-producing purposes."[11] President Kennedy was concerned that an operational satellite system be established at the earliest possible time, and wanted to beat the Soviets at this new endeavor in space. However, Kennedy, although a supporter of private enterprise, viewed Eisenhower's policy as "turning control of space communications over to AT&T."[12] Thus Kennedy included provisions for maximum competition in ownership and control of the system, with government participation in the form of research and development by NASA that would be available to the private sector.

On May 24, 1961, the day before Kennedy's special presidential message, the FCC issued its First Report and Order on satellites, in which it concluded that some sort of joint-venture ownership by the international common carriers warranted consideration, and that the commission had the authority to authorize such a system. The commission also claimed to assume policy jurisdiction for the new technology:

It is recognized that this new technology of communication may present numerous unique and difficult problems which may involve several approaches and solutions of a type and nature different from those which have been used heretofore in the field of international communications. However, we are satisfied that any such new problems can be resolved by working within the existing framework of our international common carrier industry.[13]

This policy effectively limited participation to AT&T, ITT, RCA, and Western Union. The manufacturers argued that since many of the common carriers were themselves equipment manufacturers, it would be unfair for the government to exclude noncarrier manufacturers. However, the FCC responded:

We fail to see why ownership participation by the aerospace and communication equipment industries will be beneficial or necessary to the establishment of a satellite communication system to be used by the common carrier industry. On the other hand, such participation may well result in encumbering the system with complicated and costly corporate relationships, disrupting operational patterns that have been established in the international common carrier industry, and impeding effective regulation of the rates and services of the industry.[14]

On October 12, 1961, the FCC's Ad Hoc Carrier Committee Report proposed the establishment of a nonprofit corporation to develop, operate, and manage the proposed satellite communication system. The corporation would act as a carriers' carrier, leasing circuits to authorized carriers, which would own the ground stations and satellites. The board of directors would include representatives of the carriers, plus three public directors appointed by the president.[15] However, some members of Congress and industry representatives expressed concern that AT&T might dominate in this arrangement. Various safeguards were proposed. Some members of Congress also raised the issue of monopoly: "a bill authorizing recently competing private corporations to get together and do the same thing that they are doing, constitutes an exception to the Sherman Antitrust Act."[16]

Industry leaders expressed various views. There was disagreement over whether satellite technology was evolutionary or revolutionary. Some, such as David Sarnoff, chairman of the board of RCA, considered the technology to be revolutionary and unlimited in its potential. Sarnoff advocated an international monopoly of all U.S. voice and record carriers, regardless of technology, to strengthen the U.S. position relative to that of other countries, which typically operated a national and international telecommunications monopoly.[17] Others, including AT&T and ITT officials, saw satellites as just another transmission medium, which should therefore be controlled by the international carriers. Several manufacturers—for example, GE, Bendix, and Philco—regarded satellites as a revolutionary breakthrough and stated that this unique technology should not be limited to international carriers. Philco officials sought government direction: "We would urge that the government establish a grand strategy to utilize these achievements to lessen world conflicts and to ease world tensions."[18]

There was no consensus within the government on public versus private ownership of the system. Congress was split on the role of the private sector in 1962. Senator Kerr of Oklahoma favored private ownership with minimal government regulation; Senator Kefauver of Tennessee favored government ownership at least initially, and Senator Pastore of Rhode Island wanted private ownership with strong government control specified in the enabling legislation.[19] The State Department was split between those favoring government ownership and those advocating broad-based private ownership, although all agreed on the policy goals. The State Department finally agreed to support a private corporation under government regulation.

During the debate, Telstar was successfully launched, receiving widespread favorable response from abroad and strengthening the argument for private-sector participation in international satellite communications.

COMSAT: THE "CHOSEN INSTRUMENT"

After lengthy debate in Congress, the satellite bill was passed by the Senate and the House, and President Kennedy signed the Communications Satellite Act into law on August 31, 1962. Kennedy stated of the Communications Satellite Act: "By enacting this legislation, Congress has taken a step of historic importance. It promises significant benefits to our own people and to the entire world. Its purpose is to establish a commercial communication system utilizing space satellites which will serve our needs and those of other countries and contribute to world peace and understanding."[20]

The Communications Satellite Corporation (Comsat) was created as a "chosen instrument" to "establish as expeditiously as practicable a commercial communications satellite system as part of an improved global communications network" and to "direct care and attention toward providing . . . services to economically less developed countries and areas as well as those more highly developed."[21] McGeorge Bundy noted the benefit to the United States in seizing the initiative: "Comsat was created for the purpose of taking and holding a position of leadership for the United States in the field of international global commercial satellite services."[22]

It appeared that there were three options for the structure of the new satellite entity: government ownership, private ownership by carriers, and broad-based private ownership. In the end a unique hybrid of all three was chosen. Comsat was to be owned half by the carriers and half by the public through shares; the board was to be composed of six representatives elected by the carriers, six elected by the public stockholders, and three appointed by the government. (Twelve of the fifteen board members are now elected by the public stockholders.)

The public/private nature of the corporation was unprecedented; never had public representatives been appointed to the board of a private corporation in which the government had no financial interest. The public offering was set at $100 per share to encourage broad participation. The carriers could not own more than 50 percent of the stock. Initially, AT&T, ITT, GTE, and RCA purchased more than 90 percent of the available nonpublic stock series, of which AT&T held 57.9 percent. A subsequent amendment to the act and FCC pressure decreased carrier ownership to 20 percent; AT&T and ITT divested themselves completely of their investment in Comsat.[23]

Section 305 of the Communications Satellite Act authorized the corporation to carry out the following:

1. plan, initiate, construct, own, manage, and operate, itself or in conjunction with foreign governments or business entities, a commercial communication satellite system;

2. furnish for hire channels of communication of United States communications carriers and to other authorized entities, foreign and domestic; and

3. own and operate satellite terminal stations when licensed.[24]

NASA was to provide reimbursable satellite launching and associated services. Research and development from NASA was to be undertaken only at the request of Comsat and also on a reimbursable basis, to prevent government subsidy of a private corporation.[25]

POLICY IMPLICATIONS
OF THE "CHOSEN INSTRUMENT"

The decisions embodied in the Communications Satellite Act set important precedents in U.S. satellite policy. Especially significant was the choice of a single system for international communications. The State Department in 1963 stated that "economic, technical, and political considerations all point to the desirability of a single system":

> From the *economic* point of view a single system would avoid wasteful duplication of expensive satellite and ground facilities.
>
> From the *political* point of view a single system would enhance the possibility of fruitful exchange of communication between all countries and would avoid destructive competition to tie different countries into the communication system of political blocs.
>
> From the *technical* point of view a single system would facilitate technical compatibility between satellites and ground terminals, would assure the best use of scarce frequency spectrum, and would promote operational efficiency and flexibility in routing.[26]

A decade later, U.S. policymakers rejected these arguments after prolonged deliberations on the structure of a domestic satellite industry, choosing instead open competition. (See chapter 4.) Two decades later, in the early 1980s, the debate on the "chosen instrument" was reopened when American companies wanted to launch satellites to compete with Intelsat. This time, again after lengthy negotiations pitting the State Department against the FCC, among others, competition (with some restrictions) finally won the day. The State Department found it difficult to explain to Intelsat signatories, especially from the developing world, why the arguments it had made apparently in their interests as well as on behalf of the U.S. were now to be discarded. (See chapter 14.)

The Communications Satellite Act also focused attention on the roles of the government and the private sector in the provision of satellite capacity. Once again, during the debate on the establishment of domestic systems, the advantages of government involvement, private-sector initiatives, and a combination of public and private development were considered. A recurring question in the debate involved the role of the carriers: Should they extend their services to embrace these new "evolutionary technologies," or should they compete with new entrants, who argued that satellites were a "revolutionary technology" that deserved an innovative approach? Finally, the legislation raised questions about the private sector's role in foreign policy, as it became difficult in later decades to distinguish between international business negotiations and foreign policy initiatives. While in the 1960s Comsat acted as the spokesman for both the U.S. international satellite industry and U.S. foreign policy in satellite communications, by the 1980s other private U.S. interests were arguing that what was best for Comsat was not necessarily best for the industry and, by extension, for users of international satellite services. (See chapter 14.)

INTELSAT: THE INTERIM ARRANGEMENTS

By the mid-1960s, transoceanic cables were carrying a limited amount of traffic between North America and Europe and across the Pacific. In 1956, the first transatlantic cable was laid between Newfoundland and Scotland, with an original capacity of 36 telephone circuits. This cable was jointly owned by AT&T; its Canadian subsidiary, Eastern Telephone Company; the British Post Office; and the Canadian Overseas Telecommunications Commission (now Telecom Canada). In 1957, AT&T and Hawaiian Telephone laid a 36-circuit cable between the U.S. mainland and Hawaii. In 1959, a similar cable was laid under the Atlantic under joint ownership of AT&T, the French ministry of posts, telegraph, and telephones (PTT), and the German Bundespost. Cable capacity increased in the 1960s, with the laying of a 128-circuit cable by AT&T and the British Post Office in 1963. In 1964, a similar cable was laid to Japan by AT&T; Hawaiian Telephone; the Japanese overseas telecommunications authority, Kokusai Denshin Denwa Ltd. (KDD); and RCA Global Communications. The British

Commonwealth also laid the CANTAT and COMPAC transoceanic cables during this period, linking Canada with the United Kingdom, and with Australia and New Zealand. In 1965, AT&T and the French laid another transatlantic cable.[27]

Given this growth of cable capacity, what was the attraction of communication satellites? First, for the developing world, satellites offered a means of catching up in international telecommunications without waiting for undersea cables and terrestrial microwave to link them to the industrialized world and to each other. Most communication traffic within Africa, for example, was still transmitted using high-frequency radio and routed through the former colonial capitals of London, Paris, and Brussels. Satellites offered greater capacity than cables: Intelsat I (Early Bird) had a total capacity of 480 telephone channels, while the largest transoceanic cable carried only 256 channels.[28] The leaders of industrialized countries felt the attraction of a new technology and worried about being left behind in the technological competition between the superpowers.

The difference in ownership structure between transoceanic cables and Intelsat was important to the participants. A cable owned by the participants (PTTs and private companies) could generate both profits and depreciation, directly affecting the participants' bottom line. Intelsat, on the other hand, was a cooperative rather than a partnership or corporation; its members shared expenses and revenues, but did not actually obtain the benefits of ownership.

The Communications Satellite Act provided for foreign participation "in the establishment and use" of a communication satellite system, and the corporation was authorized to operate the system "itself or in conjunction with foreign governments or business entities." Central issues to be resolved in establishing the international satellite system were how Comsat and foreign entities should participate. A two-level approach involving participation by both governments and their telecommunications administrations was adopted, for it was assumed that other nations would be unwilling to join a venture whose political and economic consequences were completely removed from their influence.[29]

In December 1962, the Europeans formed CEPT (European Conference of Posts and Telecommunications Administrations). The CEPT members formed the European Conference on Satellite Communications (ECSC) in July 1963 in order to be able to negotiate as a bloc with Comsat. In February 1964, U.S. officials began meeting with the Europeans to plan implementation, and found themselves negotiating with a group rather than individuals, since the Europeans had eliminated the possibility of bilateral agreements.[30]

The Europeans proposed an international consortium, which the Americans reluctantly accepted (the United States had hoped to rely on a series of bilateral agreements to avoid setting up a new international entity).[31] At later meetings the parties agreed to appoint Comsat as manager of the consortium, with two separate agreements, one between governments and another more detailed between operating entities, regulating their activities.

Developing countries and the U.S.S.R. were not included in these meetings. The U.S. delegates stated that the countries included represented 90 percent of the world's international traffic and that the goal was to expedite the agreement. The Soviet Union was approached, but at first Soviet officials called exploratory talks premature, and later did not express much interest since they felt that the plans were basically U.S.-inspired and experimental in nature. Some analysts think that the Soviets did not want to expose their lack of technical competence. The United States had launched Syncom in 1963, whereas the Soviet Molniya, launched in 1965, was in a lower elliptical orbit.[32] However, the Soviets may have indirectly played a major role in the formation of Intelsat by spurring the United States to accelerate its space program and to enlist global participation.

In July 1964, the final negotiations for the international satellite system were completed, and nineteen nations became the founding members of the International Telecommunications Satellite Organization (Intelsat): Australia, Austria, Belgium, Canada, Denmark, France, West Germany, Ireland, Italy, Japan, the Netherlands, Norway, Portugal, Spain, Sweden, Switzerland, the United Kingdom, the United States, and the Vatican City. Comsat was to serve as manager of the organization. The agreements entered into force on August 20, 1964.

The basic five-year interim agreement stated that the space segment should be owned by the signatories in proportion to their respective capital contributions. The main decision-making body was the multilateral Interim Communications Satellite Committee (ICSC); each signatory with an ownership share of 1.5 percent or more could be represented. The ICSC was given responsibility for the design, development, construction, maintenance, and operation of the space segment. This committee was to issue a report either one year after the initial system became operational or at the latest by January 1, 1969. The committee would then recommend continuation of the interim arrangements or organizational and administrative changes, with an international conference to be convened within three months to consider them. Definitive arrangements were to be formulated at the earliest possible date, tentatively by January 1, 1970.[33]

Voting was by majority, except for "important or substantive issues," which had to be concurred in by representatives having a combined total of 12.5 percent over and above the representative having the largest vote. Initial ownership was based on international usage: the United States 61 percent, Western Europe 30.5 percent, and Canada, Japan, and Australia 8.5 percent. These quotas could be adjusted to enable developing countries to participate in up to 17 percent of the total, although the U.S. share would never fall below 50.6 percent.[34]

THE EUROPEAN RESPONSE

Some European officials felt that the United States was placing them in a "no win" situation by forcing the implementation of an international satellite organization. A British member of Parliament stated that "there is now a growing feeling that . . . we shall finally end by starving the transatlantic cable of telegraphic communications from America and assisting Comsat to get off the ground, and that Britain will merely end up by renting a line from the Americans." The British postmaster general replied: "the Government's view is that the only way of preventing an American monopoly in this sphere is to join a partnership with the U.S. and other countries and so secure the right to influence the course of events."[35]

The space age put smaller industrialized nations at a great disadvantage compared to the superpowers. Early on, the Western Europeans saw the advantage of building multilateral organizations to pool their resources and develop a technological base independent of the United States. In 1961, 146 European aerospace companies had formed Eurospace as a nongovernmental, nonprofit organization to create a Western European industrial complex capable of providing governments, supranational bodies, and private interests with expert assistance and advice on space programs. In several instances, European industries chose to develop the relevant electronic and aerospace technologies on their own, rather than waiting for the United States to release restricted information.

In response to the U.S.-led Intelsat initiative, the Europeans created two additional multilateral organizations in 1964: the European Space Research Organization (ESRO) and the European Space Vehicle Launcher Organization (ELDO). The purpose of ESRO was "to provide for, and to promote, collaboration among European states in space research and technology exclusively for peaceful purposes." Its founding members were Belgium, Denmark, France, Italy, the Netherlands, Spain, Sweden, Switzerland, the United Kingdom, and West Germany. ELDO planned to develop operational programs in meteorology, navigation, and telecommunications as well as generating data for pure scientific research. Its founding members were Belgium, France, Italy, the Netherlands, the United Kingdom, West Germany, and Australia.[36] (The European launcher experienced several failures and was discontinued in 1971. In 1973, ELDO and ESRO were consolidated into the European Space Agency. European activities in space are discussed in chapter 8.)

During the interim period the Europeans became increasingly concerned about U.S. domination of Intelsat as they strove to protect their cable investments and win Intelsat procurement contracts. The United States heightened their alarm by placing controls on the export of technology that was likely to be utilized in communication satellites. European signatories also expressed dissatisfaction over hardware contracts, perceiving that the U.S. proposal of the best quality for the best price would guarantee the United States the lion's share of the procurement contracts. Instead, they advocated geographic distribution of contracts. For example, for the Intelsat III series, Europe received only 4 percent of the hardware contracts while providing 25 percent of the capital for the system.[37] At the European Space Telecommunications Conference in 1967, the Europeans agreed on the desirability of removing Comsat as the system manager and restricting its voting power, and developing separate regional systems.[38]

THE DEFINITIVE ARRANGEMENTS

The ICSC draft report of December 1968 recommended replacing Comsat with a management entity accountable to the governing body of Intelsat, giving the consortium a legal personality, negotiating a voting formula that reduced the influence of the United States and the other major users of the system, and drafting two agreements, one between participating nations and the other between their authorized telecommunication agencies.[39]

Ninety-eight delegations attended the first Plenipotentiary Conference in 1969, including sixty-seven of the sixty-eight members (as well as the U.S.S.R., several Eastern European countries, the United Nations, and the ITU as observers). During the negotiations Yugoslavia became the first Communist country to join. The negotiations for the definitive arrangements continued until the final draft was approved by seventy-three national delegations in May 1971. (France, Mexico, Monaco, and the Malagasy Republic abstained.)[40]

The future role of Comsat and U.S. voting strength were issues of major contention. Changes in the 1964 agreements included:

- creation of two plenary organs;
- restructuring of voting and membership roles in the changeover from the ICSC to a board of governors;
- shift in managerial arrangements over a six-year period;
- a narrow and restrictive interpretation of how Intelsat might provide specialized services;
- an increase in the capitalization limit to $500 million.[41]

The definitive arrangements thus shifted from strictly technical and operational considerations to include political and institutional considerations. To meet the demand of smaller nations for a voice in decision making, the consortium was restructured into four bodies:

The *Assembly of Parties* and *Meeting of Signatories* were to operate on a one-nation–one-vote basis, with a simple majority required on procedural questions and an affirmative vote by two-thirds of the participants for subtantive matters.

Effective power rested with the *Board of Governors*, the successor to the ICSC, which was to be responsible for the "design, development, construction, establishment, operation and maintenance of the Intelsat space segment" and for the adoption of plans and programs "in connection with any other activities which Intelsat is authorized to undertake." The board was to be composed of approximately twenty signatories, with voting weighted in proportion to use of the satellite system. To assuage concerns over potential U.S. dominance, the agreement stated that an individual member could not "cast more than forty percent of the total voting participation of all signatories and groups of signatories represented on the Board of Governors." If unanimity could not be achieved, a decision required an affirmative vote by at least four governors with two-thirds of the weighted vote or an affirmative vote by all but three of the governors.

The *Executive Organ* was to be phased in as a replacement of Comsat management over a six-year period. A director general appointed by the Board of Governors and confirmed by the Assembly of Parties was to be in place by December 31, 1976.[42]

The Europeans won the concession that any party had the right to set up a competing system, providing that it informed Intelsat and sought to ensure technical compatibility and to avoid economic harm. The "significant economic harm" article (14D) became a major issue as both industrialized and developing regions began to launch their own satellites in the 1970s and 1980s. (See chapter 14.)

ISSUES CONCERNING DEVELOPING COUNTRIES

During the negotiations of the definitive arrangements, developing countries found themselves at times aligned with European nations against the United States, and at times at odds with all of the industrialized countries. For example, most Europeans wanted to curtail U.S. control of Intelsat, but not to the extent that decisions could be made that would adversely affect their own investments in Intelsat. Some less developed countries (LDCs) wanted more control of the organization and less U.S. influence, but not to the extent that European nations could subsidize their industries by awarding contracts to themselves at higher prices. Some developing countries realized that expanding the number of Intelsat organizations, although increasing the LDCs' relative power, would add to their own and Intelsat's administrative costs. Some Europeans and most LDCs were uncertain about whether the internationalization of Intelsat management and granting Intelsat a legal identity as a fully constituted international organization would decrease the efficiency of the organization or adversely affect the technical design and reliability of the satellite system.[43]

While the advent of communication satellites appeared to widen the technological gap between developed and developing contries, it is significant to note that the developing countries were now assured direct nondiscriminatory access in terms of usage and ownership, whereas before they had had to rely on foreign-owned cables. One analyst found U.S. sponsorship of this latter concept "revolutionary in terms of this nation's traditional telecommunications behavior."[44]

However, not everyone in the U.S. space community favored this policy. Leonard Jaffe, director of communication systems for NASA, stated in 1963:

Communication satellites will aid the less developed countries only to the extent that those areas possess or acquire telecommunications networks, educational plants and socieconomic systems capable of distribution and gainfully using the telecommunications made available by communications satellites. All nations will not benefit equally from participation in a world-wide communications satellite system; indeed, some nations perhaps should not participate at all. Clearly, only a small number of countries should have satellite ground stations.[45]

Jaffe correctly anticipated some of the problems developing countries would face but was overly pessimistic. Developing countries were early users of Intelsat for international telecommunications, but slower to adopt satellites for domestic use. (See chapters 11, 12, and 13.)

U.S. FOREIGN POLICY ISSUES

Two of the principal objectives of early U.S. foreign policy in the sphere of satellite communications were to further international cooperation and to protect the national interest. Developing a strategy that would harmonize these goals created tension between Comsat and the State Department: "the government believed that Comsat, as a creation of Congress and the chosen instrument of U.S. satellite policy, should be held accountable to governmental processes; whereas the individuals from private industry directing Comsat perceived it primarily as a profit-oriented organization."[46] The State Department wanted a multilateral organization that would own and operate the system, whereas Comsat wanted to own and manage the system itself. Furthermore, Comsat wanted to conduct its own international negotiations, rather than leaving satellite diplomacy to the State Department.

In 1970, the State Department defended Intelsat on the basis of U.S. self-interest: 92 percent of the total spent since 1964 had gone to U.S. contractors, and it was estimated that U.S. manufacturers had supplied more than 50 percent of the hardware for earth stations. A State Department document added: "The Intelsat system has also brought modern and direct communications to many areas of the world which previously had none, thus enabling American business to better utilize its operations in many countries."[47]

The Interim Arrangements appeared to be a victory for U.S. foreign policy, demonstrating that an operational system could be established in a very short time by implementing the United States' proposed organizational model for Intelsat. NASA had predicted in 1962 that an operational system would not be possible until 1967, but Early Bird, also known as Intelsat I, was launched in 1965. To avoid confrontation, the United States' negotiating position had evolved from propositions dedicated to the supremacy of Comsat to proposals giving Comsat the primary role for an interim period. Thus, the necessary institutional steps had been taken through the Interim Arrangements, while the technical issues of frequency allocations had been resolved, at least for the short term, at the ITU's Extraordinary Administrative Radio Conference (EARC) in 1963.

The U.S. approach created a system that was flexible, open-ended, and inclusive rather than exclusive. The international carriers considered satellite communications as just another means of international communications, while the aerospace industry and government agencies in the United States and Europe rushed to seize the opportunity offered by the new technology to introduce major changes in the institutional environment of international telecommunications. In the process, earlier "international subculture" of common carriers and government departments was transformed.[48]

If time had been of no concern, the United States might have waited until the market could support multiple independent private systems or joint ventures limited to parties without vested communications interests.[49] However, the United States' creation of Comsat introduced a new order of domestic complexity, raising several thorny issues. Comsat was established as a carriers' carrier. Users wanted to go directly to Comsat and bypass the carriers. (Later, they wanted to go directly to Intelsat, bypassing Comsat.) The carriers played many conflicting roles in Comsat as stockholders, customers, competitors with stakes in cable, and equipment suppliers. Comsat saw itself as a chosen instrument, not only for U.S. foreign communicators, but for domestic satellite services. Struggles developed over earth-station ownership, authorized users, and the control and ownership of domestic satellites. (Domestic issues are addressed in the next chapter.) The tensions surrounding Comsat's role in international communications and U.S. foreign communications policy simmered until the

1980s, when they boiled over during deliberations on U.S. policies concerning competitive international satellite systems. (See chapter 14.)

INTERSPUTNIK: THE SOVIET RESPONSE

Sputnik in a sense started it all: Soviet advances in space propelled the United States toward a commitment to a civilian space program, which in turn stimulated the commercialization of satellite communications. But Sputnik itself was very primitive; it simply beeped. In 1957, the year Sputnik was launched, a Soviet scientist predicted that the Soviet Union would develop the capability to broadcast television signals internationally via satellite. In 1961, the president of the Soviet Academy of Sciences stated that a high priority was being given to space communications, writing that "the use of communications, and satellites, and of satellites for relay services would revolutionize communications and TV services."[50]

Chairman Nikita Khrushchev and President Kennedy exchanged letters that discussed cooperation in applying space technology for the benefit of mankind, and an agreement between NASA and the Soviet Academy of Sciences was signed in 1963. Soviet scientists participated in experiments on Echo II. A decade later agreements were made to exchange technical information (for example, lunar, environmental, and meteorological data, and medical information on man's reaction to working in space), but no proposal was put forth for cooperation in the field of communications. A NASA spokesman stated: "We were unable to achieve an understanding of the need for structuring an experiment to achieve mutual benefits."[51]

Meanwhile, the Soviet Union developed a position critical of Comsat and Intelsat. U.S. and Soviet officials met in Geneva in 1964, but the Soviets thought operational arrangements were premature and expressed little interest. At the United Nations in 1964, the Soviet Union and other Communist countries expressed strong opposition to Intelsat. They felt that its intent was to transfer the control of space communications to the U.S. private sector, and to establish a profit-oriented system for the benefit of the industrialized countries at the expense of the developing countries. They also criticized the weighted voting procedures of the Interim Arrangements as violations of the principle of sovereign equality, and objected to the attempt to place Intelsat outside the organizational frameworks of the U.N. and the ITU.[52]

The Soviets eventually decided to establish their own international satellite system, known as Intersputnik. In 1968, the U.S.S.R., Bulgaria, Cuba, Czechoslovakia, Hungary, Mongolia, Poland, and Romania submitted a draft agreement for Intersputnik to the U.N. A final treaty was deposited with the U.N. in 1971, but Intersputnik did not begin operation until 1974.

4

United States Domestic Policy
Toward Open Skies

DOMESTIC OPPORTUNITIES

In the early 1960s, policymakers were divided on whether satellites represented a revolutionary new technology that would change the world of telecommunications or an evolutionary technology to supplement existing terrestrial facilities. They also disagreed as to how the technology should be owned, operated, and applied. Should it be operated by the common carriers, as the FCC and the carriers proposed? Should it be publicly funded but privately owned and operated for the benefit of all mankind, as advocated by NASA spokesmen? Or should satellites be operated as a government-owned enterprise, as some liberal members of Congress advocated?

As we have seen in the previous chapter, international decisions came first. In 1962, Congress enacted the Communications Satellite Act, which established Comsat as the "chosen instrument" to "establish as expeditiously as practicable a commercial communications satellite system as part of an improved global communications network" and to "direct care and attention toward providing . . . services to economically less developed countries and areas as well as those more highly developed."[1] Comsat was to be owned half by U.S. international carriers and half by the general public. In 1964, Intelsat was established, with Comsat acting as its U.S. representative.

In April 1965, NASA launched the Early Bird satellite (also known as Intelsat I), inaugurating commercial international satellite services. Five months later, the American Broadcasting Company (ABC) applied to the FCC to establish a domestic broadcast distribution service via satellite. However, opinions concerning domestic services were much more divided. A decision on the structure of the U.S. domestic satellite industry took seven years to emerge from Washington, and the first U.S. domestic satellite was not launched until 1974, nearly a decade after ABC's proposal.

ABC applied to the FCC for authority to launch and operate a geosynchronous satellite (to be built by Hughes) to transmit its programming from New York and Los Angeles to 268 network affiliates in the continental U.S., Alaska, Hawaii, Puerto Rico, and the Virgin Islands. ABC also proposed to provide satellite facilities without charge to the National Educational Television network, which would distribute noncommercial television to educational stations in those areas. At that time ABC was paying AT&T nearly $12 million per year for microwave distribution; it estimated that it would save $5 million over five years with the satellite system.[2] ABC may have been using its satellite option merely to put pressure on AT&T, by threatening defection if AT&T increased its rates; the broadcasters may not have really have wanted to be in the satellite business.

After six months of deliberation, the FCC returned the application without prejudice because of the novel legal and political questions it raised, and initiated instead formal hearings to determine whether the FCC could inaugurate such systems, and if so under what terms and conditions. Thus the ABC proposal precipitated an FCC Notice of Inquiry in 1966 into alternative institutional arrangements for domestic satellites, which invited comments on the ABC proposal and general comments as to whether the FCC "may promulgate policies and regulations, looking toward the authorization of nongovernmental entities to contract and operate communications satellite facilities for the purpose of meeting their private or specialized domestic communications requirements."[3] Nineteen parties responded, including four entities that proposed their own domestic systems: COMSAT, ABC, AT&T, and the Ford Foundation.

THE COMSAT DILEMMA

The key to opening the domestic market was the development of the geostationary satellite. In 1962, scientists at Bell Laboratories thought a geostationary satellite was still a decade away. However, in February 1963, NASA began to launch the Syncom series, and the success of Syncom II, III, and Early Bird established the technical feasibility of geostationary satellites.[4] Comsat quickly adopted the technology for international use, but geostationary systems also made the provision of domestic services attractive because of a decrease in space segment costs and simpler earth-station technology.

The Communications Satellite Act stated: "It is not the intent of Congress by this Act to preclude the use of communications satellite systems for domestic communications services where consistent with the provisions of this Act nor to preclude the creation of additional communications satellite systems, if required to meet unique governmental needs or if otherwise required by the national interest."[5] Apparently, the act was drafted on the assumption that at least for the near future, operational systems would employ low- or medium-altitude spacecraft on the Telstar model. Since nearly fifty satellites would be required for an operational global network, an international consortium seemed to be the most efficient means of building and operating the system. Medium-altitude satellites did not appear suitable for domestic use. When a market for domestic satellites developed sooner than expected, it raised a new set of policy questions.

In its FCC filing, Comsat claimed exclusive right to the domestic market, arguing that the Communications Satellite Act gave it monopoly over both domestic and international communications, and that the FCC was without authority to license any other entity to own and operate a domestic system. Comsat proposed a domestic system to begin operation in 1969, with expansion over a nine-year period. Comsat's system was to carry voice, data, and television, in contrast to the other proposals that were simply for television. (Comsat had surplus capital to invest in the project because its 1964 stock offering of $196 million was based on projected costs for a medium-altitude rather than a geostationary satellite system.)[6] Questions about Comsat included whether its claim to domestic monopoly was valid, whether it planned to operate the domestic network separately from the global network, whether it could do so without a conflict of interest, and whether its domestic revenues would have to be shared with Intelsat members.[7]

AT&T'S PROPOSAL

AT&T's basis for arguing that satellites had no application for domestic communication was that low-orbit satellites could never compete economically with cable and microwave. However, AT&T recognized the threat to its business posed by proposals from the networks to bypass its terrestrial facilities by using geostationary satellites. AT&T's strategy was to protect its investment in terrestrial technology and at the same time develop its own share of the new satellite market. AT&T questioned the technical and economic feasibility of authorizing noncarriers to own and operate satellite systems, preferring instead a multipurpose system operated by a single common carrier. (This was essentially also the position taken by other carriers including Comsat, Hawaiian Telephone, ITT World Communications, and Western Union.)[8] AT&T proposed a multipurpose system to be integrated with its existing cable and microwave facilities. It planned to start with two twelve-transponder spacecraft and two major uplinks near New York and Los Angeles, plus seventy-three downlinks, and to expand satellite capacity and earth stations throughout the decade to meet U.S. domestic communication requirements through 1980.

AT&T proposed that Comsat own and operate the space segment. AT&T would still have enjoyed a dominant stake in the entire enterprise, as AT&T then owned 29 percent of Comsat stock and would have retained ownership of the earth segment, which represented nearly 55 percent of the capital cost of the system.[9]

THE FORD FOUNDATION PROPOSAL

The Ford Foundation was a major funder of educational television in the 1960s. The foundation saw in satellites a means of using profits from commercial television to subsidize educational broadcasting. It proposed the establishment of a Broadcasters Non-Profit Satellite Corporation (BNSC) to own and operate a geosynchronous satellite for distributing commercial and educational television programs. The Ford proposal, developed by experts from Hughes, IBM, Rand, and several universities, included six channels for commercial television plus five noncommercial channels in each of four time zones.

The satellite would distribute network television around the country for $44 million per year less than the broadcasters were paying AT&T. BNSC would pass $15 million on to the networks, while leaving $30 million available for educational programming as a "people's dividend" from the taxpayers' investment in space research. Educational broadcasters would also receive free program distribution via satellite, instead of having to "bicycle" their tapes (i.e., by mail or courier) around the country because they could not afford microwave links. McGeorge Bundy, the president of the foundation, stated that the people of the United States were to be the direct beneficiaries, by receiving a valuable social return on the millions of dollars in public funds invested in the space program.

The first potential public network service mentioned in the Ford satellite proposal was "full and live coverage of significant hearings and debates." Second was "interpretation of news." It should be noted that Fred Friendly had joined the Ford Foundation after quitting as head of CBS news because CBS refused to carry Sen. William Fulbright's hearings on the Vietnam War. More than a decade later, Congress established the C-SPAN channel to bring live congressional coverage to U.S. viewers via cable television. (See chapter 5.)

The Ford proposal met with resistance from several quarters. AT&T, for example, argued that the BNSC would actually be functioning as a common carrier, and under the Communications Act of 1934 could not discriminate by offering free service to educational broadcasters.[10] Others thought that the proposal was too great a threat to the established relationship between the commercial broadcasters and the carriers. In 1967, the Ford Foundation proposed that NASA be asked to carry out a demonstration using its Applied Technology series of experimental satellites in cooperation with federal agencies and interested private parties in order to gain practical experience in satellite applications upon which to base a definitive policy decision.

In a related development, Congress established the Carnegie Commission on Educational Broadcasting, which proposed in 1967 the establishment of a Corporation for Public Broadcasting and recommended preferential treatment for public broadcasting when satellite distribution services became available.

OTHER PROPOSALS

An unanticipated consequence of the Ford Foundation proposal was its catalyzing effect in generating competitive counterproposals for attractive television interconnection rates. The Ford plan served as a credible competitive alternative to conventional terrestrial television interconnection and to multipurpose systems, and elicited cost-saving proposals from Comsat and AT&T. Just three days before Ford filed its plan, AT&T had asked the FCC for permission to raise its television transmission rates. Five months later, in response to the Ford proposal, AT&T proposed a combined satellite–terrestrial system that would cut distribution costs by $19 million (more than 25 percent) in 1969.[11]

Comsat also proposed a pilot project, with two high-capacity satellites for voice, data, and television transmission. Comsat officials thought that the long-distance market was sufficiently large to permit new entrants: "Because the bulk of communications traffic in these two western time zones is handled by General Telephone and Electronics and a small number of independents, there is a larger market for long-haul communications available without creating competition for American Telephone and Telegraph."[12]

Comsat offered to supply the capital and operate the system under government supervision. Under the proposal's terms, any common carrier could participate in joint ownership of the earth segment and have access to channel capacity. Comsat proposed to make transponders available to educational broadcasters at no charge. Hawaiian Telephone, GTE, and AT&T were most strongly in favor of the Comsat pilot program; CBS, NBC, and Western Union gave qualified support, but warned against the possibility of Comsat's gaining an unfair advantage; ABC and Ford opposed the Comsat plan and proposed that NASA conduct the demonstration.

In 1969, CBS proposed a satellite financed by the networks and providing distribution to public television at no charge. This proposal was seen as another threat to AT&T, as well as making it more difficult for newcomers (such as cable television distributors) to enter the market. Comsat then proposed a domestic system of forty-eight channels for television distribution only, for the networks and all other video customers.[13]

THE ROSTOW TASK FORCE

In August 1967, President Johnson sent a special message on global communications to Congress in which he stated: "man's greatest hope for world peace lies in understanding his fellow man. . . . So the challenge is to communicate."[14] Johnson considered satellites an important instrument for global communications: "The communications satellite knows no geographic boundary . . . [and] owes allegiance to no single language or political philosophy. Man now has it within his power to speak directly to his fellow man in all nations."[15]

In his message, the president announced the establishment of the Rostow Task Force (after Eugene Rostow, undersecretary of state for political affairs) to prepare a report with recommendations for a national telecommunications policy. Meanwhile, before the report was completed, Johnson announced his intention not to seek reelection, and the Soviet Union proposed its own international Intersputnik system.

Among the questions the task force was to answer were (1) How soon would a domestic satellite system be economically feasible? (2) Should a domestic satellite system be general-purpose or specialized? and (3) Should there be more than one system?[16] The National Academy of Engineering's Committee on Telecommunications was established in 1968 to advise the Rostow Task Force on technical matters. The committee compared satellites and cable, based on demand projections in the Atlantic Basin for 1968–85. It found that all new demand could be met with satellites, that such a system could be a minimum-cost system, that a premium would be paid for the use of cables, and that cable could be used to temporarily postpone an investment in satellites for a year or two in certain cases.[17]

The authors of the Rostow Report concluded that a blending of satellite and existing technology was the best course, based on their calculations that there would not be substantial savings "in the very near term from the substitution of satellite facilities for the terrestrial equivalent." They endorsed the multipurpose satellite approach and proposed a "modest operational pilot domestic program . . . with Comsat playing the lead role," although they noted that the choice of Comsat as trustee of the program did "not reflect a judgment that it is entitled to such ownership as a matter of 'right' under the 1962 Communications Satellite Act."[18]

However, domestic satellite policy developed not from the Rostow Task Force recommendations (which favored a monopoly multipurpose system) but from the White House itself. When the final report of the Rostow Task Force was made public by the Nixon administration, it carried no formal endorsement by either the Nixon or Johnson administration.

NIXON ADMINISTRATION PROPOSALS

The only major recommendation of the Rostow Report that was implemented was the establishment within the executive branch of a permanent office for the development and coordination of national policy. In April 1970, the Office of Telecommunications Management, formerly under the Office of Emergency Planning, was reorganized into the Office of Telecommunications Policy (OTP) under Director Clay T. Whitehead "to formulate the executive branch policies and programs pertaining to communications matters and seek to implement them through various means, including proposals of legislation."[19]

The Nixon administration intended to formulate guidelines that defined the public interest because it felt that the FCC had been unable to find a workable solution through the hearings process. In January 1970, one month before OTP was established, the Nixon administration issued a memorandum to the FCC urging that it adopt an interim policy allowing any entity with the requisite financial and technical resources to launch and operate a satellite system:

> Subject to appropriate conditions to preclude harmful interference and anti-competitive practices, any financially qualified public or private entity, including Government corporations, should be permitted to establish and operate domestic satellite facilities for its own needs; join with related entities in common-user, cooperative facilities; establish facilities for lease to prospective users; or establish facilities to be used in providing specialized carrier services on a competitive basis. Within the constraints outlined below, common carriers should be free to establish facilities for either switched public message or specialized services, or both.[20]

In March 1970, the FCC issued its First Report and Order on the domestic satellite docket it had initiated four years earlier, outlining a policy of open entry which was eventually delineated in a 1972 Memorandum Opinion and Order. Noting that there was "substantial reason" to expect that satellites would play a role in domestic communications, the FCC concluded that rather than subject the domestic satellite question to further study or filings, the critical consideration appeared to be "what persons with what plans, are presently willing to come forward to pioneer the development of domestic communications satellite services according to the dictates of their business judgment, technical ingenuity, and any pertinent public interest requirements laid down by the Commission." The FCC concluded that it had the power to authorize "any entity, either common carrier—including Comsat—or non-carrier" to own and operate a domestic satellite system.

Eight system applications were filed in response to this policy of "open entry":

Hughes Aircraft with GTE: two satellites, to be used by GTE to interconnect local telephone services in Pennsylvania, Florida, Indiana, and California, and by Hughes for cable TV;

Western Tele-Communications: one satellite to be built by North American Rockwell to be used for data, cable TV, and broadcast TV;

MCI and Lockheed: MCI to use a satellite built by Lockheed for cable TV, broadcast, telephone, and private line services;

Fairchild Industries: two 120-transponder satellites to carry AT&T's telephone traffic (based on Fairchild's ATS-6 design);

Western Union: three satellites for record traffic, message service to Alaska and Hawaii, and TV to all states;

RCA Globcom and Alascom: a range of services to the continental U.S. (CONUS) and Hawaii, plus service to the Alaska bush (see chapter 5);

Comsat: procurement, launch, and operation of three geosynchronous satellites for AT&T, with the entire capacity leased to AT&T, which would own the earth stations and could sublease satellite capacity;

Comsat: a multipurpose, three-satellite system to serve all users and carriers except AT&T; to distribute network and public TV, cable, and message service to and within Alaska.[21]

The Justice Department then submitted comments to the FCC endorsing the entry of AT&T into the domestic satellite industry, but noting that special conditions would have to be attached to AT&T's participation to prevent it from engaging in anticompetitive or monopolistic practices. The Justice Department also stated that applicants with manufacturing experience (e.g., Hughes, RCA, Fairchild) or carriers (RCA, Western Union) should not be barred from owning and operating a domestic satellite system, because the entry of such companies would not create a competitive danger. OTP again pressured the FCC in October 1971 to adopt its "open skies" recommendation and remove the indecisiveness that was blocking the introduction of commercial satellites: "There are customers waiting for satellite services and prospective suppliers with the capital and the will to offer them on a commercial basis. . . . We see no reason for the government to continue keeping these groups apart."[22]

In March 1972, the FCC released a Proposed Rule Making known as "Open Entry Option II," drafted by its Common Carrier Bureau, which proposed "limited open entry" because completely open entry "presents a danger . . . of fragmenting the market . . . to such an extent that most carrier entrants would fail to come even remotely close to covering their costs."[23] Applicants with similar technologies were to be required or at least encouraged to share ownership and operation of a common space segment to lower the total investment and overhead of the participants and prevent the failures and mergers that the staff felt would result from authorization of all proposals. It suggested that the eight proposals be grouped into four systems. Regulations were proposed to protect the smaller companies, such as restricting AT&T to using satellites only for monopoly services such as message toll and wide-area telephone services. In response, OTP's Whitehead stated that he was prepared to go to Congress to seek legislation to support the open-entry recommendations. The Justice Department also argued against "Open Entry Option II" on the grounds that multiple competing systems would encourage techno- logical innovation.[24]

OPEN SKIES

Finally, the FCC introduced what amounted to a new era in satellite communications when it announced its "Open Skies" policy in June 1972, authorizing any qualified entity, subject only to specified tech- nical and antitrust criteria, to launch and operate a domestic satellite system, thus ending the seven-year controversy. The commissioners, however, remained divided; the proposal passed by a 4-to-3 vote.

There were some restrictions. AT&T was limited to using satellites for provision of its two basic switched services, message toll and Wide Area Telephone Service (WATS), and for its AUTOVON system (oper- ated for the Department of Defense for emergency restoration of communication facilities in the event of a temporary outage of terres- trial facilities). The FCC also ruled that the joint proposal of Comsat and AT&T was contrary to the public interest. AT&T could build and operate its own satellite system or lease from any carrier who elected to operate solely as a carrier's carrier. Comsat could choose either to launch a multipurpose system or provide space segment to AT&T and any other carrier under the same tariffed rates (i.e., it was to operate as a wholesaler). Comsat was required to form an independent subsidiary to implement either of these options. The order also endorsed GTE's proposal to compete in message toll service, provided it could show that its system would serve the public interest in terms of its effects on the efficiency and economy of the interstate public network.

The commissioners in the minority objected to the restrictions placed on the participation of Comsat and AT&T. For example, Dean Burch (who was later to become director general of Intelsat in the Reagan administration), felt that the commission's rejection of the Comsat-AT&T lease arrangement was foolish because it did not allow Comsat to build on the guaranteed traffic of the Bell System.[25]

The FCC reviewed six petitions and numerous reply comments during the remainder of 1972. On December 22, 1972, the commission issued a unanimously supported Memorandum Opinion and Order (actually the third report and order), ending seven years of deliberations. The order modified the earlier Comsat-AT&T restrictions. Comsat was still required to form a separate subsidiary to engage in domestic satellite ventures. The FCC endorsed a plan whereby Comsat, MCI, and Lockheed would jointly own and operate a multipurpose system. This decision freed Comsat also to pursue a satellite for the exclusive use of AT&T. AT&T, however, was precluded from entering the specialized service markets until three years after the commencement of its operations. The FCC made all its concessions to Comsat and AT&T contingent upon AT&T's selling out its 29 percent interest in Comsat and removing itself from the Comsat board.[26] Accordingly, AT&T divested itself of its Comsat holdings, and Comsat formed Comsat General for domestic operations.

THE TELECOMMUNICATIONS POLICY ENVIRONMENT

The Open Skies decision must be viewed within the telecommunications policy context of the 1960s and early 1970s, in which several steps were taken to introduce competition. For example, in 1959, the FCC's "Above 890" decision removed all significant barriers to the installation and operation of private microwave systems. The FCC felt that the opportunity to introduce competition outweighed the small social loss due to diseconomies of scale and nominal adverse impacts upon carrier revenues.[27] After "Above 890," if an organization had a requirement for its own private communications but could not afford its own system, the only option was service from the common carrier.

However, in 1969, the FCC gave MCI permission to build a microwave system between Chicago and St. Louis, and to sell circuits to large users. This precedent-shattering decision created the special common carrier industry, and was cited by Whitehead of OTP and by the FCC in its 1970 order.[28] In its Specialized Carrier decision of 1971, the FCC permitted virtually free entry to all financially and technically qualified applicants in the specialized carrier service. Meanwhile, in 1969, in its Carterfone decision, the FCC found AT&T's tariff requirements to use carrier-supplied attachments only to be "unreasonable, unlawful, and discriminatory," thus beginning the movement toward an open market for customer premises equipment.

The rapid advances in technology during the 1960s forced policymakers to realize that telecommunications and computers were becoming more interdependent. The FCC's First Computer Inquiry, launched in 1966, was going on throughout most of the domestic satellite proceedings. The combination of rapidly advancing technology and vigorous competition in the computer industry decreased the cost of computer time, thereby making communication costs more and more significant. It is estimated that the crossover point at which the cost of using computers to allocate bandwidth for time-sharing became cheaper than the costs of communications themselves was reached in 1969.[29] The commission concluded that the regulation of data processing was unwarranted, but that it would treat hybrid services on a case-by-case basis. (These issues continued to be addressed by the FCC throughout the 1970s and 1980s.)

Thus new technologies provided both the incentive and the opportunity to introduce innovative policies. Old restrictions against competition made little sense for technologies and services that no longer appeared inherently monopolistic. Yet satellites were not only a new technology but a very capital-intensive one. Stakes were high, as the carriers sought to protect their interests not only from each other, but from new entrants, including broadcasters and manufacturers. President Nixon's Office of Telecommunications Policy and eventually the FCC endorsed competition in the satellite industry, rejecting the "chosen instrument" international satellite policy developed by Congress to establish Comsat a decade earlier.

POLICY PRESSURES

At Senate subcommittee hearings in 1973, FCC Commissioner Richard Wiley stated: "I think that there are more issues yet to be resolved is simply a reflection of the fact that the technology of the industries that we regulate is running far ahead of the policy and the law."[30] Yet other factors besides technological change influenced the "Open Skies" decision. FCC Commissioner Nicholas Johnson stated at the same hearings: "The idea of the FCC as an independent agency established as 'an arm of Congress' and responsible to it is a creed to which the FCC genuflects on all appropriate occasions before the Congressional committees. But it is a creed that no one seriously believes any longer, because it is not true. . . . [T]he Executive Branch can and does exercise control over the FCC."[31] The Office of Telecommunications Policy established in the White House by the Nixon administration exerted continuous pressure on the FCC during the domestic satellite proceedings.

The industry also pressured the FCC, either to preserve the status quo by favoring the existing carriers or to create new opportunities by opening the domestic satellite field to new entrants. Some critics at the time felt that cooperation between business and all levels of government "has tended to thwart rather than to nurture technological advance, and to deny the benefits of satellite technology to the taxpayers whose investment in outer space made it possible."[32] Ralph Nader's opinion was reminiscent of views expressed during the Communications Satellite Act hearings a decade earlier: "the U.S. taxpayers paid and still pay for most of the development of outer space and the return on their investment is coming instead to AT&T and all the other communication carriers such as ITT and RCA Global Communications."[33]

The vested interests of Comsat and AT&T bear closer scrutiny. In their joint proposal, they planned two satellites; Comsat would own the satellites and AT&T would own the earth stations (five costing $96 million!). AT&T would also manage the system and handle all sales to customers. AT&T said it proposed to use satellites because "[i]n spite of the unfavorable economics, . . . it is possible that a domestic satellite system closely integrated with the terrestrial network could provide offsetting advantages by providing circuits on a time shared basis to relieve peak traffic demands or as a backup facility."[34] AT&T said it should be allowed to use satellites for any services because there was no advantage to doing so! While it is commonly argued that an advantage of satellites is their cost-insensitivity to distance, AT&T stood this argument on its head: "Indeed, from one perspective, satellite costs do not decline as distances become shorter—a fact which is particularly pertinent with respect to service between the

Mainland and Puerto Rico, the cost of which would be no less than for service between the Mainland and points of Europe."[35] As Michael Kinsley points out, an effective commission would then have required AT&T to lower its rates to Europe to equal those for calls to Puerto Rico!

The FCC made approval of the Comsat-AT&T proposal contingent upon AT&T divesting itself of Comsat stock and giving up its seats on the Comsat board. According to Kinsley, "Worse than shutting the barn door after the horse has escaped, this is allowing her to escape, so long as she agrees to shut the door on her way out."[36] "Comsat was left as nothing more than a source of capital and good will for the telephone company, owning the pieces of metal in the sky, but having no control over their use or nonuse. Furthermore, AT&T made clear from the start that this association was disposable any time it was no longer needed."[37] The fact that Comsat would agree to an arrangement like this was widely regarded, according to Kinsley, even by the FCC as proof of ATT's anticompetitive influence with Comsat. AT&T also apparently used pricing as a means of staving off the threat of competition from satellites when it lowered its rates to the television networks by $18 million per year in 1973.[38]

Thus, "the domestic communications interests . . . succeeded for almost a decade in preventing the use of satellites for communications within the United States."[39] Yet, in the end, the result was a bold decision to create a competitive satellite industry that has led the world in introducing innovative technologies and services.

The Evolution of Domestic Satellite Services in the United States

THE EXPERIMENTAL ERA

The experimental era in the United States may be considered to extend from about 1971 to 1977. During this period, there were numerous experiments and demonstrations of satellite applications for education and training, health services, community development, and cultural exchanges. These projects were conducted on the U.S. Applied Technology Satellite series (ATS-1, ATS-3, and ATS-6) and the joint Canadian-U.S. Communications Technology Satellite (CTS, or Hermes).

NASA's Applied Technology Satellites

In 1966, NASA launched the first of its Applied Technology Satellite series, ATS-1. These satellites were designed for technical experiments to test and evaluate new technologies. ATS-1 was designed with a two-year life span; as it was still functioning in 1970, the state of Alaska requested time on the satellite for experiments to determine whether satellites could improve telecommunications services to its hundreds of remote villages. Like other remote areas, including northern Canada and many developing countries, Alaska had very poor communications, primarily by high-frequency radio, which was subject to outages depending on the weather, the season, and the sunspot cycle. In addition, the radios in villages were owned by a variety of government agencies and private organizations, such as missions and merchants, so that there was no publicly accessible telecommunications system. Most of the sets were not well maintained.

The National Library of Medicine supported a project implemented by the University of Alaska to determine whether satellite communications could improve the quality of health care of Alaska natives. Satellite earth stations were installed in regional hospitals, the Alaska Native Medical Center in Anchorage, and in several villages in the Tanana region of central Alaska. An evaluation by Stanford University found that the number of patients treated with a doctor's advice more than tripled in the year after the installation of the first experimental satellite network. Health aides also found that they learned from listening in to the doctor's consultations with other aides on the shared channel.[1]

The University of Alaska also conducted educational experiments to link village schools and to produce radio programs about village life. Microphones and speakers in the classroom allowed students to talk to their counterparts in other villages. Children and adults came to the schools in the evenings to hear programs about native topics, including whaling in Barrow, a stick-dancing festival, Arctic winter games, keeping healthy dogs, and native land claims.[2]

The ATS-1 satellite was situated far enough west to cover all of Alaska as well as the continental United States. As a result of its position and its global beam, its signal also covered much of the Pacific. In 1972, the University of Hawaii established a project known as PEACESAT (Pan Pacific Education and Communication Experiments via Satellite) that established a network of homemade ATS-1 terminals throughout the South Pacific and as far away as Australia and New Zealand. The University of the South Pacific, based in Fiji, also set up USPNET to link its extension centers in island nations across the South Pacific. (See chapter 13.) Many of its centers also participated in PEACESAT. Over the years until ATS-1 began to drift out of orbit in 1985 (nearly twenty years after its launch), there were several exchanges between the South Pacific and Alaska; occasionally, physicians in the South Pacific gave advice to Alaskan heath aides! ATS-1 was followed by several other experimental satellites. ATS-3 was also used for educational projects in the continental United States, Alaska, and the Caribbean. After the moonwalk in 1969, public pressure increased to apply the advances of space technology to problems on earth. One of the results was that future NASA satellites were planned to include social experiments.

NASA's ATS-6 experimental satellite, launched in May 1974, was equipped with global and spot-beam antennas, using C band (4–6 GHz) and S band (2.5 GHz). Using ATS-6 in conjunction with two earlier NASA satellites, ATS-1 and ATS-3, for interactive voice (talk-back) and data links, the then Department of Health, Education, and Welfare, NASA, and the Corporation for Public Broadcasting sponsored the Health Education and Telecommunications (HET) experiments, a series of six projects in twenty-three states including Alaska, the Rocky Mountain states, and Appalachia. The goals of HET were:

1. to demonstrate a satellite TV distribution system that could be implemented commercially at a cost that [would] ensure its usefulness to such public services as health and education;
2. to explore technical and organizational mechanisms for dealing simultaneously with the need for high-quality audio-visual materials at low per capita cost and the desire to individualize services to meet specific local needs;
3. to develop several technology-based system models in service areas where public commitment is evident but no developed institutional response exists.[3]

The Indian Health Service conducted telemedicine experiments in Alaska using ATS-6. Interactive video and data links for remote diagnosis and patient treatment included two-way video between two village clinics, a regional hospital, and the Alaska Native Medical Center. Patients could be examined remotely from the village, and training materials could be transmitted over the network. The evaluators found that, although useful in most cases, the video was not cost-effective. Given the limited facilities in the villages, there was little that could be done for patients without evacuation, and reliable audio communication seemed adequate to assist the heath aides in diagnosis and treatment. However, consultations from the regional hospital to the medical center seemed to benefit more from the video link.[4]

The ATS-6 biomedical experiments included medical curriculum, administration, computer-aided evaluation, community health consultation, and instruction among medical practitioners and students in Washington, Alaska, Montana, and Idaho. Interactive video was also used for consultations with physicians in Seattle and for links between the medical school at the University of Washington and premedical students in Alaska, Montana, and Idaho. A separate education experiment used ATS-6 to deliver culturally relevant educational, community health, and native news programming to Alaskan villages, and to distribute public television programs.

A second cluster of projects involved enrichment programs for rural schools in the Rocky Mountain region. The Satellite Technology Demonstration (STD) managed by the Federation of Rocky Mountain States delivered career education programs to rural junior-high-school students. In addition, educational programs of general interest were distributed via satellite for community viewing at the schools in the evening, and a Materials Distribution Service transmitted programs selected from a special catalog to the schools for viewing or recording on videocassette. STD also arranged teleconferences among students, as well as among teachers and parents using interactive audio.

In a third experimental region, Appalachia, both medical and educational experiments attempted to overcome the isolation of small scattered communities. The Veterans Administration used ATS-6 to link major medical centers with hospitals in Appalachia for consultation and continuing education. The Appalachian Educational Satellite Project (AESP), under the direction of the Appalachian Regional Commission, was an experiment in the delivery of training programs in elementary reading and career education to Appalachian teachers, counselors, and administrators. Materials prepared at the University of Kentucky were delivered via ATS-6 to terminals at community colleges and other centers in the region, and fed into local cable systems.

The Communications Technology Satellite

The last of the experimental satellites was the Communications Technology Satellite, or CTS (known in Canada as Hermes), jointly sponsored by NASA and the Canadian Department of Communications. In 1971, Canada and the United States agreed to establish a joint Communications Technology Satellite (CTS) program. Canada undertook to design and build the spacecraft, while the United States provided the launch and supplied several of the components, including a high-power traveling-wave tube amplifier. The European Space Research Organization (ESRO) also supplied some of the satellite components.

Canada and the United States carried out several technical and applications experiments on CTS, which was launched in 1975. The principal technical objectives were to conduct experiments using the 12- and 14 GHz bands (Ku band) and low-cost, transportable ground terminals; develop and flight-test a 200-watt amplifier, a lightweight extendible solar array, and a three-axis stabilization system.[5] CTS was also used for telemedicine and tele-education experiments, some of them continuations or refinements of experiments begun on ATS-6, and a few experiments linking organizations in both countries, such as an exchange of engineering courses between Stanford University in California and Carleton University in Ottawa, Ontario. (See chapter 7.)

THE END OF THE EXPERIMENTAL ERA

By the late 1970s, Congress decided that NASA had fulfilled its experimental mission in satellite communications, and that the technology had been successfully transferred to the private sector. A tiny budget was reserved to keep the ATS series of satellites operating. ATS-1 and ATS-3 in particular refused to quit, and a lobby from the Pacific reversed NASA's plans to turn them off and remove them from orbit. It is interesting to note that NASA is back in the experimental satellite field, with plans for a high-powered Ka-band satellite (Advanced Communications Technology Satellite, or ACTS) to be launched in 1990. Industry representatives led the lobby for renewed NASA involvement, stating that the private sector would not be able to invest in the necessary research and development to field-test technology using frequencies above 20 GHz.

SUCCESSFUL TRANSITIONS TO OPERATIONAL SERVICE

Many of the experiments carried out on the ATS and CTS satellites did not continue once free satellite time was no longer available. In some cases, the experiments were a low-cost way of testing an idea that turned out not to be viable or to be premature. For example, two-way interactive video proved of limited use for consultation in Alaskan villages and would have been far too expensive to consider using commercial satellites. However, much less costly freeze-frame video has now been introduced in the North Slope Borough of Alaska for medical consultation and continuing education.

In some cases, an experiment was evaluated positively but not continued. Often factors outside the scope of the project itself limited its lifetime. For instance, experiments and pilot projects in telemedicine demonstrated the applications of telecommunications technologies for the transmission of X rays and electrocardiograms, and for the remote examination and monitoring of patients.[6] Many of these projects were promoted on the basis of their potential for improving rural health services through teleconsultations with urban specialists while limiting the number of referrals to hospitals. However, telemedicine projects that allowed patients to be treated by a local general practitioner or paraprofessional with remote consultation from a specialist were not popular with specialists or with hospitals that needed revenue from occupied beds. As Maxine Rockoff pointed out, the U.S. medical system provides few incentives to reduce the number of referrals from general practitioners to specialists or to fill fewer hospital beds.[7] Perhaps the insurance industry will eventually provide the incentives needed for these technologies to become more widely adopted in patient treatment and monitoring.

Similarly, in tele-education projects rural teachers would use materials delivered by satellite for occasional enrichment, but not rely on them as long as they had the knowledge and training to cover all the subjects they were required to teach. By the late 1980's, with states requiring all high schools to offer several foreign languages and advanced science courses, satellites have become a means of sharing high-quality instruction. They are also used to deliver graduate courses to employees at their workplace. Employers can now use satellite courses as an incentive in hiring and retaining high-quality professionals.

The artificial nature of a satellite experiment can also obscure issues that must be addressed if the experiment is to become an operational service. The experimenters on NASA satellites had to supply their own equipment and personnel; NASA supplied free satellite time. Most experimenters received grants from government agencies to cover staff and equipment costs. To make the transition to operational service meant finding ongoing financial support. Commercial satellite time had to be paid for. Staff could not be borrowed indefinitely from other positions. Operating costs would have to become line items in agency budgets. For many experimenters these obstacles were simply too high. Those who did continue invariably had planned experiments to meet important unmet needs that were recognized by their agencies. In many other cases, experimenters demonstrated the successful applications of satellite technology but did not consider the realities of priorities, agency politics, and budget constraints in planning their experiments.

Two projects that did turn into viable ongoing services were two-way voice communications for Alaskan villages and television for continuing education of teachers and other professionals and para-professionals in Appalachia. Both of these projects filled previously unmet needs in their regions. Both required carefully planned strategies to make the transition to operational service that took into consideration the need for financial and political support.

The Alaska Village Satellite System

Alaskan policymakers were determined that all villages should benefit from the reliable satellite communications demonstrated by ATS-1. A film made about the project included footage of both Alaska senators (a Democrat and a Republican) stating that a way had to be found to bring reliable communications to all Alaskan communities. RCA had purchased the military's "White Alice" communications network in 1971 and had made a commitment to provide telephone service to 143 villages. However, by 1974 when RCA was planning to launch its first Satcom satellite, fewer than 50 villages had received service. RCA stated that the villages were too expensive to serve by terrestrial means and that satellite earth stations were too expensive to be cost-effective.

The state hired its own consultants to develop and demonstrate small satellite earth stations that could operate with the Satcom satellite. It also pressured RCA to modify the footprint of the first Satcom to include coverage of Alaska and to change the transponder gain settings on the satellite to make it possible to use small earth stations with 4.5-meter antennas. The state legislature then appropriated $5 million to purchase more than 100 small earth stations that were to be installed and operated by RCA Alascom. Each earth station was to have a minimum of two circuits—one for public telephone service and one audioconference circuit for medical communications.

More than 100 Alaskan villages now have satellite earth stations to provide a health communications network and public telephone service. Telephone service was initially provided via a public long-distance telephone in the village, usually in the village store. However, local exchanges were later installed in many villages so that people could have telephones in their homes. Additional channels in the earth stations were activated to accommodate the growth in traffic. Existing Alaskan telephone companies expanded into some villages to provide these services; in other locations cooperatives and new private companies were formed to deliver local telephone service and interconnect with Alascom. The local exchange not only enables residents to make long-distance calls from their homes, but also provides an information network in the village. Local telephone service is a greatly appreciated way of keeping track of children, organizing meetings, and checking on the elderly and disabled in communities where the temperature may drop below minus 40 degrees for weeks at a time.

The medical network consists of conference channels linking clusters of villages with their regional hospital, and is based on the ATS-1 model in which health aides shared a single common channel with a regional hospital. The ATS-1 evaluation showed that the health aides learned from listening to the doctor's advice to their colleagues and that the audioconference circuit could also be used for more structured continuing education. Consultation with the doctor makes it possible to treat some patients in the villages who would previously have had to be evacuated to a hospital, as well as to check on the aides' diagnoses and treatment plans. The ratio of benefits of using the satellite network to treat a patient in the village, compared to costs in travel and hospitalization expenses, ranges from 21 to 1 in rural zones in general to more than 40 to 1 in the most isolated areas.[8] The system can also be used for continuing medical education, by offering a course from one location to health providers throughout the state who tune in on the same channel. A computerized record-keeping system allows medical staff to access and update patient records from any location, and to monitor patients who need special attention (e.g., patients with pacemakers, children requiring vaccinations, TB patients, and others). This record system was first implemented as part of the ATS-6 experiments, and was very positively evaluated by all health care providers.

Once the earth stations were installed, new applications of the satellite system were developed. Another pioneering service for rural and isolated Alaskans is the Legislative Teleconferencing Network (LTN), which brings government and the people closer together. People living in towns with legislative information offices can use their facilities—which include audioconferencing, a computer network, and facsimile—to get information on the status of a bill, to track down legislation, or to talk to their elected representatives. Teleconferencing for legislative hearings has been perhaps the most successful LTN service. Residents who cannot afford to travel to Juneau to testify in hearings can contribute their views from their home communities. LTN staff say that the system has enabled constituents to participate who have never testified before. Legislators are also able to hold committee meetings from their home districts when the legislature is not in session.[9]

Experiments using ATS-6 to deliver educational television to Alaskan villages demonstrated the value of video both for enrichment of classroom instruction and for adult education. Following the ATS-6 experiments, the Alaska Public Broadcasting Commission (APBC) worked with the communities to install satellite earth stations for television reception that were licensed as affiliates of all four major networks. A statewide committee selected network programs, which were assembled and transmitted on a single channel from Anchorage. The satellite delivery system was designed to replace the circulation of videotapes from village to village, and to eliminate the circulation of pirated tapes from Seattle. Mail service to the villages tends to be very unreliable because mail is delivered by small bush planes that cannot fly in bad weather. APBC found that the tapes they sent out spent most of their time in mailbags.

Once the video network was in place, it could be used for instructional programming during the daytime. A project called Learn/Alaska was established to use telecommunications to reach virtually every student in the state, whether at a village school or regional college, whether studying at home or at work. Instructional programs were selected in consultation with teachers to supplement the curriculum in village schools, which often have only one room or only a handful of high-school students. The programs could be viewed live or taped for later use.

An electronic mail system connects the school boards throughout the state so that they can receive messages from the Department of Education in Juneau and share information with each other electronically. Audioconferencing also enables students to communicate with distant faculty and with each other. Students may use conferencing equipment in schools, colleges, and community centers; they may also dial into an audio bridge in Anchorage from their home telephones.[10]

Unfortunately, state budget cuts in Alaska due to the decline in the price of oil, on which the state is largely dependent, resulted in severe cutbacks in state-funded telecommunications projects. However, the health communications network continues to operate, as does the public telephone system, which is operated by small telephone companies at the local level and Alascom[11] for long-distance service. Many villages have installed their own television-receive earth stations, as well as local cable systems or retransmitters to receive cable television channels distributed by satellite.

Appalachian Community Services Network: The Learning Channel

Another telecommunications service designed particularly for rural residents was the Appalachian Educational Satellite Project (AESP), which developed the Appalachian Community Services Network (ACSN). ACSN originated as an experiment sponsored by the Appalachian Regional Commission in 1975, using NASA's ATS-6 satellite to distribute courses primarily for continuing and career education to small centers in Appalachia. The project was continued on the CTS satellite (see below); ACSN was finally launched as a cable network with a transponder on the commercial RCA Satcom satellite. ACSN's directors planned to make it easy for cable operators to pick up their programs by using the same satellite that delivered HBO. Their constituency expanded beyond Appalachia to include the whole nation.

No longer a regional entity, the network changed its name to the Learning Channel. Now the Learning Channel uses a commercial satellite to disseminate adult education courses to households throughout the country via local cable systems, exemplifying the "narrowcasting" function of satellites to reach audiences with specialized interests throughout the country. Residents of small communities without postsecondary educational institutions are perhaps the major beneficiaries of satellite-distributed educational narrowcasting. ACSN/The Learning Channel is clearly one of the success stories of the experimental era.

EARLY U.S. COMMERCIAL SATELLITES

Unfettered by the debate that delayed the introduction of U.S. domestic satellites, Canada proceeded with the construction of its domestic satellite, Anik, launched by NASA in November 1972. (See also chapter 7.) To gain an edge on the competition before their own satellites were launched, U.S companies leased capacity on Telesat Canada's backup satellite, Anik A2 launched in April 1973. American

Satellite Corporation and RCA used Anik for U.S. domestic service until U.S. domestic satellites were available. RCA used Anik A2 for links between New York and California, and between Alaska, the "lower forty-eight" states, and Canada. TelePrompTer used Canada's Anik satellite with a transportable 8-meter (25-foot) antenna at many locations around the United States to assess and demonstrate the feasibility of television reception for cable system use. Reception from Anik was possible even in the southern states, although its antenna pattern had been shaped to provide coverage of Canada.[12]

The first commercial domestic satellites in the United States were built by Hughes Aircraft and operated by Western Union. They were followed by the Comstar series, built by Hughes and owned by Comsat General, with earth stations owned and operated by AT&T. RCA's Satcom I, a three-axis stabilized satellite with twenty-four transponders, was launched in 1976. Western Union's Westar I was launched in April 1974, followed by Westar II in October 1974. The satellites each had the capacity for 7,200 voice circuits or twelve television channels. Western Union planned to use the satellites for its own data and record services and private line services, and to lease transponders to the American Satellite Corporation for a network serving government and commercial users. Fairchild and Western Union International had formed American Satellite, which planned to purchase three satellites from Hughes in 1973. However, American Satellite instead decided to lease space on Westar.

The first Comsat satellite, Comstar, was launched in 1976 for use by AT&T. Comsat established a separate subsidiary, Comsat General, for its non-Intelsat activities. Comsat also was the first company to design a satellite solely for business communications. MCI and Lockheed had formed MCI Lockheed Satellite Corporation and applied for two forty-eight-transponder satellites. They proposed to charge distance-insensitive rates.[13] Comsat offered to merge its proposal with MCI/Lockhead and form a new corporation called CML. The proposed CML system was reorganized into what became Satellite Business Systems. IBM proposed to purchase the majority share of CML; IBM and Comsat General would organize a new joint enterprise, of which 55 percent would be owned by IBM and 45 percent by Comsat General. IBM was the first major communications user with no previous stake in the industry to invest in satellites. However, the FCC required the participation of at least one more partner and stipulated that no partner should control more than 49 percent or less than 10 percent of the enterprise. As a result, Aetna Life and Casualty joined Comsat General and IBM in a new venture called Satellite Business

Systems (SBS). The FCC authorized the SBS system in 1977, and its first satellite was launched in 1980.[14] (See chapter 6.)

The satellite operators expected that the television networks would be their first major customers. However, the networks already had long-term contracts with AT&T for microwave links to their affiliates, AT&T had lowered its rates apparently as a result of the threat of competition from satellites, and broadcasters were reluctant to abandon the proven system for the new technology. Furthermore, it was not clear who would pay for the earth stations if satellites were used; the networks did not want to install earth stations at each affiliate, and the affiliates were unwilling to bear the cost. (This issue remained unresolved until the 1980s, by which time the cost of earth station technology had decreased and the networks were willing to enter into agreements with the affiliates for cooperative financing of the facilities.) Instead, a pay-television service called Home Box Office (HBO) became the system's most important customer. HBO had begun to offer movies to cable systems locally and through limited microwave distribution. HBO officials realized that satellites would permit them to reach every cable system in the country. And pay television was the attraction that cable needed to attract urban customers who already had several over-the-air program choices.

RCA's Satcom series became the early success of the industry, as Satcom carried HBO signals and soon other cable channels to cable companies across the country. Hughes wanted to create a satellite-to-cable television network; it owned part of a Manhattan cable system and was a large stockholder in TelePrompTer, the largest cable system at the time.[15] However, Hughes abandoned its plan (although in the mid-1980s it launched a series of satellites called Galaxy that have become the most popular choice for distribution of cable television programs). Satellite-delivered pay TV and cable turned out to be a synergistic combination that fueled the growth of the cable industry and its penetration of the major urban markets that had been opened by the FCC for cable franchising. Thus, for the next decade, cable television networks became the major customer of domestic satellite companies.

CABLE TELEVISION DISTRIBUTION VIA SATELLITE

Satellites have transformed the cable industry in the United States from mom-and-pop operations bringing in distant over-the-air signals into a major business with annual revenues of $10 billion. The availability of nonbroadcast signals has transformed cable into a primarily urban enterprise. Currently there are thirty-seven million cable subscribers in the United States, out of a total of eighty-seven million television households, with some fifty channels available. Video users of domestic satellites include thirty-four basic channels, four superstations (WTBS-Atlanta, WGN-Chicago, WOR-New York, and WIPX-New York), and eleven pay-television services: HBO, Showtime, Cinemax, the Movie Channel, the Disney Channel, the Playboy Channel, Home Theatre Network, Bravo, American Movie Classics, ON Satellite TV, and Galavision.[16]

Foremost among the types of programming delivered via satellite to cable subscribers are movies, for which viewers pay a surcharge each month in addition to monthly cable charges. The major movie channels are HBO, Cinemax, Showtime, and the Movie Channel. News is offered 24 hours a day on Cable News Network (CNN) based in Atlanta, with headline news on CNN 2. The Financial News Network provides stock market and futures quotations and advice from financial analysts. Full-time coverage of Congress is carried on C-SPAN; National weather channels provide around-the-clock forecasts, with many cable systems adding their own local weather channel. All-sports channels cover everything from college football and hockey to Australian-rules football, with the flagship channel being ESPN. Regional sports channels specialize in sports of local interest such as college football.

Various local stations in cities such as Atlanta, New York, and Chicago are now transmitted nationwide. These "superstations" tend to feature movies and syndicated programs. High-quality children's programs are offered on the Disney Channel, Nickelodeon, and Discovery Channel. The advent of music channels has spurred the growth of music videos, particularly for rock. MTV (Music Television) is the leading service of this kind, although competitive channels are being introduced; the Nashville Network specializes in country and western music.

At least six religious channels offer sermons, spiritual music, and religious education. The "electronic church" raises huge amounts from solicited donations. In addition, the Mormon church has an extensive closed-circuit network and the Catholic church runs a national educational network. The Learning Channel offers adult education courses for enrichment and credit, while Lifetime transmits health programming. Other channels offer continuing education for professionals.

The Spanish International Network (SIN) offers Spanish language programming, mostly from Mexico, to major Hispanic markets nationwide. Galavision is a Spanish-language, pay-television movie network. Other ethnic channels include Black Entertainment Television (BET) and National Jewish Television (NJT).

The Home Shopping channel and others display products that can be ordered over the telephone with major credit cards; local shopping channels feature residential real estate and used cars. Specialized entertainment is provided by the Nostalgia Channel, Caribbean Super Station, regional entertainment networks, the Home Theater network (for family viewing), and the Daytime channel, which carries specialized programming for women. "Restricted" pay channels include the Playboy Channel and American Extasy (sic).

The economics of these new television services are complex. Some networks make their programming available to the cable operators free of charge. The religious broadcasters have turned satellite television into a major source of revenue by soliciting donations from their viewers. Another group of networks offer their programs free but also carry paid advertising. Financial News Network, which reaches more than twenty-five million subscribers, is an example of such a channel. Pay-television services such as HBO charge a monthly fee per subscriber which is collected by the cable operator.

Most channels charge the cable system operator a fee per month per subscriber. The cable operator recovers these charges by packaging the channels, generally as "tiers." The lowest tier includes local channels (that had to be carried until recently according to FCC regulations), local access channels, and a few others such as news and sports channels. More popular channels are placed on higher tiers, for which there are additional monthly charges. A converter may be required to receive these channels. Movie channels are generally packaged separately with an additional monthly charge.

Pay-per-view channels charge for individual events such as boxing matches. On two-way systems equipped with addressable decoders, subscribers can order such services. However, these systems are not widespread, and most subscribers must rent a decoder from the cable operator. These programs are often also shown in clubs and bars with their own satellite receivers.

BROADCASTING SERVICES VIA SATELLITE

Satellites are an ideal technology for delivering broadcast services because any site within the satellite's beam can be equipped to receive the signal. No point-to-point terrestrial links or switching are required. Satellites also offer substantial cost savings over terrestrial microwave leased from AT&T. The first network to interconnect its affiliates via satellite was the Public Broadcasting Service in 1978–79. The commercial broadcasters did not adopt satellite distribution to their affiliates until the mid-1980s, partly because of disputes over whether the networks or the affiliates would pay to equip the stations with satellite-reception facilities. NBC contracted with Comsat General for a Ku-band system on SBS in 1985, while ABC and CBS use AT&T's Telstar satellite.

American radio networks have also switched to satellites because of their flexibility, high-quality sound system, and cost advantage. Between 1978 and 1979, Mutual, National Public Radio, RKO Radio, and the AP Radio networks began to offer their affiliates satellite-distributed programming. The ABC, NBC, and CBS radio networks moved more slowly but are now also satellite-distributed. More than 3,500 radio stations have antennas pointed at RCA's Satcom satellite.[17]

Most programmers use digital transmission, which results in transmission of very high quality and better discrimination against adjacent satellite interference than analog, making it possible to reduce the size of receiving antennas. The national radio networks are using satellites not only to feed news and special programs to affiliates, but also to create a new type of automated radio station. These stations typically offer one format of music (e.g., classical, hard rock, or easy listening), with breaks for local advertising. The listener may not even realize that the program does not come from a local studio. Some broadcasters have found the satellite package a low-cost way of competing with more established stations without hiring well-known announcers or building extensive recording libraries. In smaller cities and towns, these satellite-fed stations have introduced specialized formats such as classical music and jazz, that were not offered by local stations.

For example, Satellite Radio Network, based in Dallas, offers eight "full-service live [radio] formats" via satellite to nearly 1,000 radio stations in all fifty states plus Bermuda and the Caribbean.[18] Other full-time networks include SuperRadio Network, based in Boston, and SUN Radio Network (news and talk format), while numerous others deliver specialized programming such as Spanish-language programs, football, opera, business news, health news, motor racing, and truckers' programs. Radio stations may choose to affiliate with several networks. Approximately 83 percent of U.S. AM radio stations and 92 percent of FM stations have satellite antennas; about 30 percent of these are affiliated with a satellite-delivered programmer.[19] The networks achieve economies of scale by centralizing production and taking advantage of the satellites' suitability for narrowcasting. "Radio stations historically have been operated as little, stand-alone Mom-n-Pop businesses—11,000 stations each with its own philosophy, systems, departments. . . . Today, whether it's hamburgers or hotels, product distribution with centralized planning, packaging, and resources wins in every competitive situation. Thanks to the technology and economics of satellite broadcasting, the radio industry has moved into this realm."[20]

Satellites deliver programming not only to radio stations but to stores and offices. Several music networks, including Muzak, 3M Sound Products, Music Network (AEI), and Seeburg Satellite Music Network, transmit background music, primarily via Ku-band satellites. Retailers such as Safeway and K-Mart use satellite audio networks for in-store music, advertising, and promotional announcements. Muzak also provides in-store messaging, one-way data transmission, and occasional one-way video transmission primarily for retail chains.

Digitalized satellite audio is now available to home audiophiles. The Digital Music Network offers eight "100 percent compact disk standard digital music channels"via satellite for distribution to listeners over cable television systems. Digital Radio Laboratories (DRL) will uplink up to sixteen encrypted compact disk–based audio formats also for distribution over local cable systems.[21] The advent of digital audiotape (DAT) cassette recording equipment may increase the market for high-quality satellite- and cable-distributed music to households.

BACKYARD ANTENNAS

U.S. satellites are designed for fixed rather than broadcasting services, that is, to transmit to television stations and cable headends that then retransmit the signal to viewers. However, since 1980, approximately two million backyard antennas have been installed in the United States, primarily in rural areas without cable service.[22] In the early days, these home antennas became popular not only because they brought cable channels to homes in areas without cable, but because the programming was free. Owners simply pointed their antennas and tuned in up to 150 channels. Program distributors at first wanted to deal only with cable systems that would collect revenues from subscribers, not with individuals themselves. However, the proliferation of the antennas and pressure from their owners resulted in a requirement that individuals be allowed to subscribe to pay services.

In order to end the piracy of signals, HBO and other premium channels have encrypted their signals. Viewers must now buy a decoder for approximately $400 and pay a monthly fee for each channel. However, as many as half of all consumer descramblers may be illegally modified, using pirate computer chips designed to break the scrambling codes that protect satellite-delivered television.[23] The FBI is trying to crack down on illegal reception through well-publicized raids on entrepreneurs selling the illegal descramblers, but a thriving industry operates offshore in Canada and in the Caribbean. Descramblers there are used to pick up channels from U.S. satellites, and the illegal chips are shipped back into the United State.

Program distributors would clearly prefer to deal only with cable operators. One concern the distributors have raised is the complexity and overhead of billing individuals. A strategy to facilitate access to satellite television by rural subscribers has been devised by the National Rural Telecommunications Cooperative (NRTC), which is owned by approximately 425 utility cooperatives. NRTC has negotiated with the distributors on behalf of their customers for a package of satellite channels. They collect monthly fees using the billing system already in place for rural electrical services, thus sparing the distributors the chore of billing individuals.

SATELLITE MASTER ANTENNA TELEVISION

Another way of delivering additional channels of television is via satellite master antenna television (SMATV), which uses satellite antennas to deliver cable programming to hotels and apartment houses. A satellite antenna on the roof or adjacent to the building receives the programming, which is distributed via cable throughout the building. About 800,000 to 1 million people in the United States subscribe to SMATV, or "private cable"; another 800,000 watch SMATV-delivered programs at the 3,000 hotels that use the system.[24]

Cable system operators tend to consider SMATV operators as competitors because the latter, unlike cable operators, do not need a city franchise. Cable companies resent the loss of some of their most profitable high-density areas. Some pay-television networks have refused to be redistributed over SMATV systems, and SMATV operators are charged 15 to 20 percent more than cable operators for programming. However, this niche service is quite profitable and is attracting investment by cable operators and telephone companies.

THE SYNERGY OF SATELLITES AND CABLE

In the United States, cable television began as a rural phenomenon. Entrepreneurs built cable systems to bring television to communities that could not get over-the-air signals from distant urban transmitters. Cable in cities was primarily used to eliminate the "ghosts" and other distortion caused by interference from high-rise buildings. City dwellers were not particularly interested in additional channels imported from other cities because they usually could receive the network affiliates and several independent stations in their own area. In the early 1970s, experiments and pilot projects demonstrated the potential of cable television for education and community participation, but without innovative new entertainment services that viewers would be willing to pay for, cable was not attractive enough to city dwellers to offset the installation costs. However, when HBO decided to put its movie channel on RCA's Satcom satellite, the cable industry had a product to offer that was not available on urban television.

Cable systems now deliver a wide range programming nationwide via satellite. While some channels, such as sports and headline news, are aimed at a fairly wide audience, others, such as ethnic and educational programs, are examples of narrowcasting. Satellites make nationwide narrowcasting possible because their breadth of coverage allows programmers to reach special-interest audiences across the country. Graduate engineering students, country-music fans, and Spanish-speaking viewers can all receive specialized programming that could not be affordably delivered before the advent of satellites.

Satellites and cable have made possible the formation of numerous new specialized networks. Yet the diversity of programming may be less than meets the eye. We certainly have more news, sports, and movies on television than ever before; religious broadcasters and the music industry have unquestionably found cable television a profitable vehicle. Although some channels are devoted to continuing education, the variety of cultural programming predicted for cable in the 1970s had not materialized, despite some early efforts that did not demonstrate short-term profitability. Cable has, however, enabled programmers to target specific subaudiences, and, coupled with the growth in the market for videocassette recorders, has reduced the audiences of the major networks and fragmented the viewing public. Satellites have also facilitated syndication, so that both independent stations and network affiliates can now choose from a varied menu of additional news feeds, features, and reruns.

The proliferation of channels available via satellite and cable has been used to justify a transition from communication regulation based on scarcity to deregulation based on abundance. The Communications Act of 1934 justifies government intervention on the basis of allocation of scarce resources. Once scarcity is no longer a problem, the rationale for regulation vanishes. The FCC has assumed that all groups who wish to use television to spread their message can find some channel capacity available. However, many organizations have found that although they may be able to find some channel time, they are relegated to electronic ghettos of unpopular times or unwatched channels, or forced to find time on several channels, so that their target audience may not know that programming for them exists or where to find it. While retaining a reduced role in regulating over-the-air broadcasters but exerting no authority over "nonbroadcast" cable networks, the FCC has drawn a technological distinction that is irrelevant to the viewer. Television today includes any program seen on a television screen, whether delivered by satellite, cable, over the air, or on a cassette. Communication policymakers need to rethink the government's public-interest role in relation to the electronic media, regardless of the delivery system.

6

Specialized Services in the United States Today

CURRENT STATUS OF THE SATELLITE
INDUSTRY IN THE UNITED STATES

In 1988, nine companies owned and/or operated eighteen C-band, ten Ku-band, and four hybrid (C-and-Ku-band) commercial U.S. domestic satellites. These companies include Alascom (Aurora 1; Alascom formerly leased capacity on an RCA Satcom satellite); AT&T (Telstar series); Comsat (Comstar series); Contel ASC (ASC-1); GE Americom (Satcom series; GE purchased RCA, including its satellite subsidiary, RCA Americom), GTE Spacenet (GSTAR and Spacenet series); Hughes Communications (Galaxy series); MCI Communications (SBS series, purchased in 1985 from IBM); and Western Union (Westar series).[1] This list does not include companies that lease transponder capacity in bulk or own one or more transponders.

Approximately 40 percent of the transponders in use, both C-band and Ku-band, are devoted to satellite television service, and the majority of these distribute channels to cable systems. The networks have shifted their delivery of programming to affiliates from microwave to satellite, and also use satellites for program feeds, remote coverage, and special coverage. Syndicators and specialized and regional networks transmit their programming by satellite as well. Private television networks for in-house teleconferencing and business television also contribute to video use. Satellites now carry radio broadcast transmission too. (See chapter 5.)

Voice traffic, including voice circuits that have been conditioned to handle data traffic, is the third largest user of satellite capacity after cable and broadcasting services. Applications include light- and heavy-route trunks between switching centers and long-haul circuits for private networks. Annoying echoes that plagued early voice networks have largely been eliminated, although the delay caused by the transmission distance of more than 44,000 miles makes satellite voice transmission inferior to terrestrial means. However, in remote areas such as Alaska, satellite communication will continue to be the only viable means of long-distance communication.

Satellites are also used for data transmission, ranging from very-high-speed transmission for high-volume users to low-speed transmission of alphanumeric data, often on voice circuits conditioned for data transmission. As the number of VSATs and teleports increases, and as fiber-optic telephone networks proliferate, data communication will surpass voice as a percentage of satellite traffic. Point-to-point terrestrial circuits will carry large volumes of data, but satellites will be used for data broadcasting and interactive communications between large numbers of dispersed users.

In many cases, specialized programming and business services use only limited time periods on a transponder and may be shared with other users. Satellite brokers find transponder time for such customers who need access to satellites on an occasional or part-time basis. Applications include distribution of sports and other special-events programming, syndicated program distribution, occasional news feeds, and teleconferences. The main brokers are Bonneville Satellite Systems, Hughes Television Network, Netcom, Public Service Satellite Consortium, Group W's Television Videotape Satellite Communications (TVSC), Videostar Connections, and Wold Communications.

BROADCAST SERVICES

Whatever Happened to DBS?

The FCC began accepting applications for direct-broadcast satellites (DBS) for transmission directly to households in 1981, when Comsat established a subsidiary called Satellite Television Corporation (STC) and applied for permission to establish a DBS service. Without waiting to examine the policy issues raised by the proposed new service, the FCC responded by opening the door for proposals to all groups interested in entering the DBS market. By 1982, nine DBS construction permits had been awarded, and thirteen other companies had also applied to provide DBS service. Yet more than five years later, there is no DBS service in the United States.

The FCC had accepted a dozen applications and approved one (STC's) before deciding on its own policies for the new service. In 1982, it adopted a set of interim rules, essentially the proposals drafted by the staff twenty months earlier without any public hearings.[2] The FCC's treatment of cable in the 1970s may be contrasted with its approach to DBS in the 1980s: "A Commission that only a decade ago had spent seven years to develop 'modern' television rules had in this case selected its DBS applicants within a year of the time it began its inquiry and issued rules for those licenses to be issued to these applicants only eight months after they had been selected."[3]

The FCC's hasty and cursory approval of DBS policies may also be contrasted with the slow and tortuous path to the "Open Skies" decision described in chapter 4. However, the FCC could also rationalize that, having devoted so much time and effort to the decision to open the fixed service satellite market to competition, it needed little additional analysis to come to a similar conclusion for DBS. Yet the terms for DBS entrants were far more lenient than the requirements imposed on domestic fixed satellite service providers. There were no restrictions on the number of channels or systems that could be owned by a single entity or on cross-ownership, no content guidelines, no technical standards except basic interference criteria, and no requirements imposed on broadcasting entities or common carriers, except for adherence to the equal-opportunity hiring policies required of broadcasters.[4]

The first step toward U.S. DBS service was taken by United Satellite Communications Incorporated (USCI), with backing from General Instruments and Prudential Insurance. In November 1983, USCI began DBS service to Indianapolis and the Washington, D.C., area, using leased transponders on a Canadian Anik C-2 satellite with medium-powered Ku-band coverage. USCI eventually expanded coverage throughout the Northeast, offering five channels of movies, general entertainment, children's programs and sports for about $40 per month and a one-time $150 installation charge. After eight months USCI was near bankruptcy, with just 15,000 customers in twenty-six states.

STC had accelerated its DBS plans by opting to lease capacity on an SBS satellite rather than waiting for its own DBS "bird," and planned to begin competing with USCI in late 1984. Then USCI and STC merged in August 1984, proposing to follow STC's original plan to launch its own satellites in 1986. However, in late 1984, the Comsat Board voted against entering into a DBS partnership with Prudential Insurance and USCI, despite having invested $40 million in DBS. The other applicants have since fallen by the wayside, deterred by the high capital costs and apparent limited market at this point for DBS.

Whether DBS will become established in the United States, as predicted in the early 1980s, remains an unanswered question. It appears unlikely that DBS will reach the penetration of cable, since the major markets are already heavily cabled. The current high-powered satellite technology required to transmit television signals to very small antennas cannot offer as many channels as are available on most cable systems. In addition, DBS has not been able to show a price advantage over cable. Initially, DBS operators proposed selling antennas that would allow owners to pick up future programming at no monthly charge. However, unmet projections on penetration and insufficient advertiser support soon made promoters realize that they would have to charge a monthly fee. Only if DBS operators can find a means to undercut cable fees significantly or to offer alternative programming so attractive that it lures viewers from cable, will urban penetration take off.

Direct satellite reception may be adopted only in areas where cable distribution is uneconomical, that is, in approximately fifteen million to twenty million households (or about 20 percent of U.S. television households). Although DBS operators originally planned to offer programming not available through other sources, there does not seem to be a niche that has not been filled by other media, including broadcast television, cable television, pay television, and VCRs. One industry analyst states that the financial incentive needed to make DBS a success is the additional revenue that program suppliers would generate by delivering their programs to households without cable.[5] Whether this revenue would be sufficient to cover the actual cost of DBS operation remains to be seen.

While it appears that DBS is attractive for noncabled rural areas, more than two million rural viewers have already installed C-band antennas to pick up the channels being fed to cable systems. Even if more of these channels are scrambled, it is still likely to be more economical for program providers to offer their programming for direct reception using the same transponders that are leased for distribution to cable systems, rather than to pay for duplicate satellite capacity for DBS subscribers. Medium-powered DBS, such as Canada has provided on its Anik C satellites and some European systems have chosen, may represent an attractive compromise between higher power and smaller antennas, compared to the extremely expensive, high-power systems originally proposed for DBS.

Some recent technical developments may eventually make direct-to-home satellite transmission more workable. In 1988, Comsat and Matsushita introduced a flat plate antenna 15 inches square, similar to antennas now being used with Japan's DBS satellite (see chapter 9). An advantage of these small, unobtrusive antennas is that they are generally not subject to zoning ordinances. However, they are designed to be used with high-powered Ku-band satellites and not with the C-band or even medium-powered Ku-band satellites currently available in the United States. In late 1987, Hughes Communications announced that it was interested in talking with programmers, equipment suppliers, and others with the intent of forming a DBS consortium. Hughes then announced that it would offer for the first time two three-axis stabilized high-powered Ku-band satellites in the early 1990s. The design of these satellites, each of which is to be equipped with sixteen transponders, as compared with the four to six transponders in earlier DBS designs, may make DBS-type services much more economical.[6]

Some DBS proponents see high-definition television (HDTV) as the savior of the DBS industry. HDTV requires enormous bandwidth to deliver the volume of digital information necessary to create a high-quality moving picture. Terrestrial frequencies for broadcasting are scarce, so satellites may become the source of bandwidth for HDTV delivery to the home. DBS-delivered HDTV is now being offered experimentally in Japan. (See chapter 9.) Alternatively, HDTV may be nationally distributed by satellite, but then delivered to the home via optical fiber, if the cable television and/or telephone companies install new fiber networks.

Satellite News Gathering

Another recent satellite service is satellite news gathering (SNG), the use of portable satellite uplinks to cover news from the field. Satellite news-gathering vehicles (SNV) carry satellite antennas mounted on a truck chassis for mobile uplinking. SNVs can provide live coverage of events outside the range of terrestrial microwave and can transmit from anywhere within a satellite's footprint. Approximately 15 percent of commercial television stations own SNVs. Flyaway antennas are portable satellite earth stations capable of delivering live broadcasts from anywhere in the world. The networks have used flyaway antennas that can be packed in several suitcases to cover fast-breaking stories around the world, such as the "people's revolution" in the Philippines and the 1985 earthquake in Mexico City.

SNG makes possible fast real-time coverage of disasters and events such as airplane crashes, forest fires, and state visits; it also provides a means of covering parts of the United States with limited microwave facilities, such as the Rocky Mountain region and west Texas. The impact of this equipment is already evident on national newscasts; networks can now ask their affiliates to cover a story and to transmit footage for insertion in the national news. The flexibility of satellites in allowing transmission from any point, now from suitcase-size units, guarantees that this technology will continue to make an important contribution to news gathering.

Satellite-Based "Virtual Networks"

The flexibility of satellite technology, coupled with the ability of stations across the United States to cover and transmit news stories using SNG equipment, has created the possibility of establishing "virtual networks" composed of local television stations that cooperate in producing certain programming such as newscasts. CONUS is an example of such a network. CONUS (the acronym in the satellite industry stands for "continental U.S.," as in CONUS coverage) is an independent national news network composed of member television stations from almost every major news market that exchange stories via satellite. CONUS has the largest satellite news-gathering network in the nation, with more than eighty SNV-owning members.

CONUS offers local television stations an alternative to the major networks for national news. The major networks soon realized not only that their affiliates had another source of news footage, but also that satellites offered a way for affiliates to contribute to the networks by providing live coverage of major events and feature stories. As a result, ABC, NBC, and CBS have implemented their own satellite news-gathering projects to better serve their affiliates. ABC's Absat was the first, offering a partial reimbursement plan for the purchase of SNVs, as well as coordinating transponder usage and providing logistical support. NBC followed with Skycom and CBS with Newsnet, also offering funding for SNV purchases.

REMOTE PRINTING AND PUBLISHING

In the 1970s, futurists predicted that newspapers would disappear, and we would "read all about it" (or as much as we wanted to know) on our television screens or computer monitors. However, newspapers are still with us, although many now rely on satellites for distribution. The advantages of satellites for distributed printing include:

- page composition at a central location, with simultaneous transmission to a number of printing plants;
- creation of special editions by inserting local copy or advertisements into the centrally edited paper;
- same-day delivery of newspapers and magazines, rather than slower delivery by mail;
- shorter deadlines, allowing the incorporation of the latest news.

In fact, satellites have helped to expand newspaper markets, as editions can be printed simultaneously across the country or around the world. Examples of newspapers or periodicals printed this way in the United States are the *Wall Street Journal* (fourteen sites), *USA Today* (twenty-two sites), the *New York Times*, and *Time* Magazine (nine sites). Toronto's *Globe and Mail*, which is transmitted via satellite to regional printing plants for early-morning delivery to subscribers and coin boxes, has become Canada's national newspaper. Several regional newspapers have used satellites to become global, including the *International Herald Tribune*, printed in several locations around the world; the *Wall Street Journal*, with editions printed in Europe; the *Asian Wall Street Journal*, printed in Hong Kong; and the *Financial Times*, now printed in Europe and the United States as well as the United Kingdom. Japan's *Asahi Shimbun* is now printed in the United States for U.S. distribution, as are the *Economist* and *Guardian Weekly*.

Satellite printing not only saves time and money, but also gives publishers a competitive advantage either because they are able to beat the competition to the newsstands or because the shorter deadline periods allow them to print more up-to-date information. Before printing via satellite, the *Economist* sent the plates for the entire magazine via courier on the Concorde to New York and then by road to the printers in Connecticut. Part of the time saved by switching to satellite printing came from avoiding the customs clearance required for courier-carried film.[7] Satellite printing allows the print run to begin between eight and twelve hours earlier.

Digitized color graphics now make it possible for covers and color pictures to be transmitted electronically. However, a single color page requires 30 megabytes of data for high-quality print production. Data-compression techniques are now being used to reduce the volume of data by a ratio of 8 to 1.[8] Thus, not only magazines but color catalogs can be printed remotely using digital data transmission.[9]

BYPASSING THE PUBLIC SWITCHED NETWORK

Advances in technology as well as the deregulation of the telecommunications industry and the breakup of AT&T have resulted in opportunities to bypass the public telephone network. Once entrepreneurs sensed that the field was no longer exclusively dominated by the telephone companies or other major carriers, the bypass industries, including VSATs and teleports, were born. Customers can now bypass the network entirely, for example, by installing their own dedicated satellite networks for premises-to-premises communications. Such networks can operate in a mesh configuration, in which one site is able to communicate directly with any other site, or a star configuration, in which traffic goes through a central hub, which may be owned by the customer or provided by the satellite carrier or a teleport. (See p. 85.) Some customers may opt to bypass only local telephone company, using alternative facilities such as optical fiber, microwave, or digital radio to reach a teleport.

Perhaps the most important innovation in satellite technology in the 1980s was the very-small-aperture terminal, or VSAT, also known as a micro earth station. VSATs were designed for inexpensive low-volume data transmission, although versions have now been developed that transmit higher volumes of data and video. The receive-only version is generally less than 1 meter in diameter and is used for point-to-multipoint data transmission, also called data broadcasting. There are now more than 60,000 VSATs installed in the United States. Approximately 40 percent of VSAT applications are for one-way data broadcasting and 25 percent are for interactive data services. Broadcast video, for both business and educational uses, represents 35 percent of the applications.[10]

VSAT technology is attractive because the service provider can guarantee high quality and fixed user costs. Since deregulation, terrestrial networks have become more complex: several telephone companies may be involved in the transmission, local loop charges are increasing, and significant delays are being encountered in installing and modifying facilities. The benefits of VSATs include high network quality, flexibility in capacity, ease of configuration in adding and changing sites, and the ability to control and predict costs. In contrast, terrestrial telephone networks with many switching nodes are often less reliable for data transmission. Since several telephone companies are involved for local and long-distance service, response times for installation and maintenance may vary. VSAT operators are able to control costs by either owning the network or obtaining long-term leases, as opposed to having to pay telephone company charges, which may change frequently. One-way point-to-multipoint networks save about 50 percent over land lines; for interactive two-way networks the savings are about 30 percent.[11]

VSATs are used primarily to replace terrestrial circuits for private data networking between a central hub and many distant sites. VSAT transmissions employ packet-switching to maximize the amount of data exchanged between multiple and the central hub. A packet is a block of data containing all the information required to send it through the network and combine it with other packets at destination.[12] In a star network, intelligence is centralized at the hub station. Circuits routed through the hub switch require a double-hop satellite connection: VSAT to hub, hub to VSAT. This configuration can be used for file transfers, batch processing, and some interactive data applications. For mesh-connected VSAT-to-VSAT transmission, the hub station can operate as a transit switching center. Eventually, higher-powered satellites with on-board switching should facilitate direct VSAT-to-VSAT communication.[13]

VSATs for data broadcasting are used by news services to deliver stories to newspapers nationwide, by the National Weather Service to distribute weather maps and forecasts, and by the financial industry to deliver market data to brokers and commodities traders. More recently, interactive VSATs have been introduced for data communications from field offices to headquarters, and client transactions such as car rentals, credit-card verifications, and automatic-teller transactions.

The Agricultural Marketing Service (AMS) of the U.S. Department of Agriculture (USDA), which reports on prices, availability, and quality of goods, is linked by a network combining VSATs and electronic mail. AMS offices in state capitals and near farm markets pick up information and pass it to one another. Using personal computers, office staff dial into Telenet's Telemail electronic mail network. Telemail's store-and-forward system sends a message to the VSAT network hub operated by Contel ASC in Mountain View, California, where it is beamed to all 130 VSAT-equipped offices. A data selector at each site recognizes the alphanumeric codes of each message's address and blocks irrelevant messages, so that offices in Minnesota do not receive cotton prices and offices near citrus growers do not receive wheat prices.[14]

The oil industry has also devised a use for VSATs. Schlumberger Well Services companies engage in geophysical exploration in the continental United States and Gulf of Mexico. Field engineers used to fly their computer tapes backs to their headquarters' data-processing centers for analysis. In the meantime, data collection would start at another site, even though the results of the analysis might require further work at the first site. Now data can be transmitted directly from remote sites or drilling platforms via transportable VSATs. Instead of the work crew having to revisit the site after receiving the results of the data analysis, data can be analyzed and sent back while work is still in progress. VSATs can also be used to monitor remote installations such as power stations, reservoirs, and forest fire lookouts. For Niagara Mohawk Power, which users VSATs to monitor its power grid in New York State, control over communications was the most important issue, because the phone companies no longer offered the reliable services needed by the energy management system.[15]

Farmers Insurance Group is the third largest insurer in the United States, with sixteen regional service offices and 14,000 agents. Many agents now use VSAT terminals to access the data base at the Los Angeles home office. For Farmers, the issue "was not transmission quality; there is no difference to us in having a phone company or a satellite vendor handle our data. We wanted to cut operating expenses, reduce turnaround time for agent inquiries, and find a better—and faster—way to add agents to the network."[16] Agents use the system principally to inquire about clients' driver's records, changes of address, and policy status; pricing quotes; coverage verification; and claims processing.

VSATs can be combined with point-of-sale technology for credit verification and inventory control. For example, Walmart sweeps each of its stores for inventory twelve times a day with its VSAT network, instead of twice a day using the old terrestrial technology. Service Merchandise, the largest catalog retailer in the United States, uses VSATs for credit-card verification, nighttime file transfers of sales data back to headquarters, and pricing updates to stores. Customer profiling allows the chain to collect data on new customers which can then be updated with subsequent purchases for marketing purposes.[17] K-Mart has installed a VSAT network linking headquarters and more than 2,100 stores, regional offices, and distribution centers for authorizing credit-card purchases and tracking buying trends.[18] McKesson, a pharmaceuticals supplier, promises next-day delivery to 14,000 drugstores throughout the country using a dedicated VSAT network. Small earth stations relay drugstore orders to local distribution centers.[19]

Reducing response time, faster installation of new sites, and fixed costs are important considerations for VSAT users. Caterpillar's investment in about 175 VSATs has increased network availability and control of the system, and will result in estimated cost savings of $3 million over the first five years. Holiday Inn has replaced the leased lines used in its reservation system with VSATs to cut costs and reduce response time, as well as to provide up-to-the-minute information on room reservations, guest arrivals, inventory control, and all aspects of property management. Some businesses use satellites for other purposes. Walmart uses video to enable its president to communicate directly with his managers. Days Inns' satellite network offers transmission that is ten times faster than the company's old dial-up network. Applications include credit-card processing and verification, teleconferencing, and in-room entertainment.[20] Holiday Inns, Chrysler, Walgreen's, Walmart, and Toyota Motor Sales USA all operate their own dedicated VSAT hubs.[21] Others use hubs provided by a full-service company, sharing leased facilities with other companies.

NEW DATA SERVICES

A new technology dubbed TSAT (T-carrier small-aperture terminals) has modified small earth stations to carry higher-speed data at T1 data rates (1.544 megabits per second). Ku-band earth stations of about twice the diameter of low-data-rate VSATs (2.4 meters in diameter, as opposed to 1.2 meters) can be configured in mesh networks for voice, data, or video.[22]

Specially packaged satellite data services are also available internationally. British Telecom offers SatStream services to North America via Intelsat. Intelsat V-B satellites allow cross-strapping, that is, links between Ku-band spot beams covering major commercial centers and hemisphere or zonal beams operating in C band.[23] Cross-strapping allows users to access virtually any transmitting or receiving site. Similar services for Europe are offered on ECS satellites and France's Telecom-1.

VIDEO TELECONFERENCING

Another specialized application of satellites is teleconferencing. Video teleconferencing for business use has become known as "business television." Several types of video teleconferencing are now common. Private teleconferencing systems link several branches of an organization for regular meetings and consultations. These systems may be full duplex, with two-way video (and associated audio and data), or one-way video with only audio and data return links. Small in-house networks may be full duplex, for example, to permit regular meetings between corporate headquarters and regional centers, or between engineers at different locations working on the development of a single product.

Some companies operate their own dedicated systems for the exclusive use of their staff. Hewlett Packard, ARCO, and Aetna Life and Casualty have corporate video teleconferencing networks for consultation, administration, and training. Others may use rented facilities, for example, teleconferencing rooms located in hotels, business parks, or downtown office buildings available to users on a reservation basis.[24] Examples include Holiday Inns' HI-NET, which is available for video teleconferences in the daytime and delivers cable television programming to hotel rooms in the evening, and Conference Express, a network of teleconferencing rooms in several cities owned by U.S. Sprint.

More common are point-to-multipoint systems that provide video transmission from one location to numerous sites, each of which may have only an audio return link. Since Chrysler installed a network to distribute training and marketing information to its plants and dealers in 1983, at least sixty business television networks have been installed by such diverse concerns as the Army School of the Air, Computerland, Domino's Pizza, and K-Mart.[25] In order to stay abreast of the latest developments in the computer industry, Micro-Age Computer Stores and Computerland have installed networks for distribution of video programming about vendors' products and for training. Domino's Pizza has established its own Domino's Pizza Satellite Network (DPSN) for training and motivating its employees. The network can transmit pep talks from the president, tips on improving recipes and customer service, and contests to boost morale. A transportable uplink is used for transmissions from Domino's outlets around the country.[26]

Some corporations have adopted satellite teleconferencing as a regular management tool. A specialized business television industry has emerged to operate videoconferencing facilities for corporate clients. Merrill Lynch transmits information every morning to its brokers around the United States, using facilities operated by the Private Satellite Network, based in New York City. Videostar, operating out of Atlanta, provides videoconferencing services for Eastman Kodak, MONY Financial Services, Coca Cola, and American Express, among others.

Other enterprises use satellite facilities for ad hoc teleconferencing, that is, single or infrequent video meetings. Trade associations can offer special seminars or short training courses to members around the country. Car manufacturers can introduce their new product line to their dealers. For example, Ford can reach audiences as large as 20,000, using dedicated and leased facilities.[27] Unions and political parties may hold strategy sessions with their members nationwide. Both the Democratic and Republican parties used satellite teleconferences to plan and mobilize supporters for the 1988 presidential campaign. Typically, these groups will rent the facilities they need for both transmission and reception. For example, they may rent transportable uplinks to transmit from a convention center, or use the studios of a television station. Viewers can gather at locations with television receive-only antennas (TVROs) and meeting facilities. Several hotel chains now offer this service, using the same equipment that receives pay television for guests in the evening. Intercontinental Hotels even offer a transatlantic link to London. Public television stations also rent out their facilities, and universities with satellite equipment may also act as sites for teleconferences.

An innovative use of satellite teleconferencing for education is the National Technological University (NTU). Established in 1985, NTU is an outgrowth of the Association for Media-Based Continuing Engineering Education (AMCEE), whose members are universities that use television in engineering instruction. Many of these schools operate Instructional Television Fixed Service (ITFS) networks that transmit courses to students in industries in their surrounding area. The companies pay a fee to participate in the program as well as the tuition for their employees, who are able to take graduate courses at work without taking the time to travel to a campus. These universites videotape their courses and make them available as packages for group instruction through AMCEE, with credit being offered by the originating institution.

NTU takes this concept several steps further by offering courses via satellite direct to the workplace anywhere in the country. Again, corporate members pay a fee to join the network, plus tuition for each student. Students are able to interact with the instructor earlier during live classes through telephone links or by calling at other times to consult with the instructor. NTU has recently granted its first graduate engineering degrees and now offers courses in 123 subject areas.[28]

A satellite network called TI-IN was established in 1984 to deliver courses to rural schools in Texas. The state had required its high schools to include more instruction in foreign languages and advanced science and mathematics. Many school districts could not afford or could not find teachers with the necessary qualifications to teach the courses. TI-IN now reaches 500 school districts and education agencies in twenty-seven states with more than 100 hours per week of live and interactive high-school credit courses. TI-IN provides an additional 400 hours of in-service training for teachers and administrators. The TI-IN network features a talkback system using a cordless telephone that automatically dials the teaching studio, so that remote students can talk with their instructors.[29]

TELEPORTS

A teleport is "a communications facility or center that switches voice, video, and data communications to and from destinations, primarily using steerable and frequency-agile antennas."[30] A teleport offers shared access to communication satellites and to other transmission media, such as fiber-optic networks, for local, regional, national, and international communications. Teleports divide the high cost of network construction and maintenance among many customers. Most teleports provide end-to-end service (full connectivity); however, some rely on the local telephone company, cable television operator, other carrier to make the "last mile" connection to the customer.

There are two basic types of teleports: stand-alone and real estate–based. Stand-alone teleports are sometimes referred to as antenna farms or gateways, and serve customers in their area through local distribution systems. Many are used primarily for video, such as uplinks for television networks, cable feeds, and business television. New York, Chicago, and Washington, D.C., were among the first cities with stand-alone teleports. Real estate–based teleports are located in or adjacent to business parks, and offer additional telecommunications services to park tenants on a shared basis, for example, through shared electronic switches (PBXs) and specially wired "smart buildings." The teleport serves as an amenity to attract customers to the business park; and the tenants in turn form a customer base for the teleport. The Bay Area Teleport in Alameda, California, near San Francisco, is an example of a real estate–based teleport.[31] This approach has also been used in Western Europe (e.g., Amsterdam, Rotterdam, Cologne, London Docklands) and Japan (e.g., Tokyo, Osaka, Kobe, Nagoya, Yokohama).[32]

The first formally designated teleport was the New York Teleport built on Staten Island in 1982, a joint venture of the Port Authority of New York and New Jersey; Merrill, Lynch, Pierce, Fenner and Smith; and Western Union Telegraph Company. The project includes an antenna farm and office park with a shared telecommunications system. A key feature of the New York teleport is its fiber-optic network which links the teleport with Manhattan, looping through the city to connect such locations as the World Trade Center, the Empire State Building, and the Fisk Building. Cable extensions tie the teleport to Queens, Brooklyn, and several cities in New Jersey.[33] The franchise granted by the Port Authority to pull fiber through Manhattan is the teleport's most important asset, making it more like a specialized second telephone company than a teleport. The local network is more profitable than the satellite-transmission part of the teleport's business.

Another interesting example is the National Teleport in Washington, D.C., which is located on top of the National Press Building and owned by Pyramid Video Communications of Washington, D.C., and Videostar of Atlanta.[34] Using Ku-band technology, the teleport can transmit television feeds for coverage of Washington news directly from downtown. Pacific Telecom, based in Vancouver, Washington, owns a group of teleports, including the Bay Area Teleport and UpSouth and National Gateway teleports that border both oceans so that it can pursue both Pacific and Western European expansion strategies. (Pacific Telecom is involved in several other international ventures including the North Pacific cable and the proposed Pacstar satellite in the South Pacific.) The Chicago Teleport is owned by United Video, a major cable television systems operator. The Los Angeles Teleport was financed by public offerings. The Dallas Teleport, an example of the real estate model, is operated by Trammell Crow, the nation's largest real estate developer, as an amenity to its tenant base, and is playing a growing role as a hub for business television in Dallas.[35]

The heaviest users of teleports are radio and television broadcasters, followed by the financial services industry, videoconferencing, and others. An emerging growth industry for teleports is VSATs because teleports can serve as shared hubs for VSAT networks. Fifty-one teleports are in operation, under construction, or in the planning stages in the United States, out of a total of seventy-one to date worldwide.[36] There are many models for financing and operating U.S. teleports, including telephone companies, cable television operators, investment firms, and real estate developers. Despite optimistic projections for growth in U.S. teleports (Frost and Sullivan estimate a potential U.S. market for 200 teleports),[37] many already in existence are not yet profitable. The most successful are those with revenues from local bypass networks, such as the New York Teleport, and with substantial existing demand for their services, such as the teleport located at Washington, D.C.'s National Press Building. Teleports in other markets and those tied to real estate developments are more dependent on creating a demand for their services.

THE IMPACT OF DEREGULATION

Several changes in U.S. regulatory procedures were significant in facilitating the development and expansion of new satellite services. Initially, the FCC required applicants for both transmitting and receiving satellite earth stations to go through a three-step process: frequency coordination, construction permit, and licensing. Frequency coordination is the process used to avoid potential interference from other sources such as terrestrial microwave systems. Deregulation of receive-only earth stations occurred in 1979, spurred by the cable television industry. The FCC instituted nonmandatory licensing, permitting the installation and operation of receive only earth stations with no filings with the FCC. Receive-only earth stations were no longer required to meet any technical standards because they could not cause interference. The risk of interference shifted to the earth station operator; an unlicensed station was afforded no protection from existing or planned terrestrial systems.[38]

Transmitting stations continue to require licensing. In 1983, the FCC announced its objective of achieving 2-degree orbital spacing between satellites. To meet this objective, transmitting earth stations must demonstrate that they will not cause interference with adjacent satellites.[39] VSATs with antenna diameters as small as 1.2 meters were permitted if manufacturers could demonstrate that they could meet the new 2-degree spacing interference objectives.[40]

An important change for the VSAT industry was the introduction of blanket licensing. Previously, each new VSAT site required a separate license, and delays by the FCC in processing the paperwork made VSAT networks unattractive compared to terrestrial systems that were not subject to regulatory delays. VSAT operators may now obtain blanket licenses for entire networks rather than having to file for each additional site. A Ku-band network is defined as consisting of a master hub antenna of at least 5 meters in diameter and remote sites with antennas of at least 1.2 meters in diameter. An applicant whose network meets the FCC's technical criteria and who files the necessary forms describing the network, the equipment, and the number and location of sites will receive a ten-year operating license.[41] Ku-band networks are charged $5,000 for a blanket network authorization. C-band networks, which require coordination with other satellite and microwave users of C-band frequencies, are charged $3,000 for the master station and $30 for each remote VSAT location.[42]

Changes in satellite tariff regulations have also influenced the growth of the U.S. satellite industry. In 1980, Western Union wrote to the FCC stating its intention to sell ownership rights, on a noncommon carrier basis, to transponders on its Westar V satellite. In 1982, the FCC ruled that transponder sales were consistent with FCC policies fostering multiple satellite entry. The FCC said transponder sales would encourage additional entry, additional facility investment, and more efficient use of the orbital and frequency spectrum, and would allow for technical and marketing innovation. The rates for transponder sales were left entirely to the marketplace.[43]

The movement toward deregulation of common carriers has also affected satellites. In 1983, the FCC ruled that satellite carriers would no longer be considered "dominant," that is, possessing the power to affect rates in the marketplace and subject to traditional regulation. As "nondominant" carriers, domestic satellite carriers could file tariffs on fourteen days' notice with no supporting cost data. In addition, the FCC found that allowing the rates of domestic satellite carriers and resellers to equal market-clearing prices would promote the public interest.[44] Another major regulatory issue still facing satellite carriers is the deregulation of AT&T, which is the last dominant carrier. If and when AT&T becomes completely deregulated, it may challenge the satellite industry by lowering its rates on services that compete with satellite-based bypass systems. Terrestrial fiber-based networks may then be competitive with satellites in terms of price and quality for many interactive applications.

MARKET MISCALCULATIONS

As noted in the discussion of DBS above, not every application of satellite technology has been successful. Satellite Business Systems (SBS), a joint venture of COMSAT, IBM, and Aetna Life and Casualty, was the first satellite system designed for business communications, primarily for data and video teleconferencing. SBS 1 was launched in 1980, followed by SBS 2 in 1981 and SBS 3 in 1982. Perhaps SBS was ahead of its time, as its transponder capacity was far from fully utilized. IBM eventually took over all of SBS, and, in 1985, MCI Communications acquired SBS from IBM. MCI now uses the SBS satellites as backup to its optical-fiber network for data and digital voice services in both private and public switched networks.

In 1985, Federal Express announced a "big, big network. It will be the largest in the world."[45] The proposed VSAT network was designed for a service called ZapMail that was to enable Federal Express to transmit documents via facsimile and satellite. The idea was that Federal Express would pick up documents and then fax them to the nearest Federal Express office, with guaranteed two-hour delivery, or communicate directly with major customers via facsimile. However, Federal Express cancelled its ZapMail project because of limited demand, as more and more potential customers started buying their own facsimile machines. Federal Express also planned to procure two satellites to be called Expresstars, but these plans were shelved. Federal Express does, however, have a large in-house satellite network for logistics coordination and training.

Changes in technology, regulatory policy, and demand for services may all affect the future of the satellite industry in the United States. Satellites are likely to maintain their lead in point-to-multipoint services, such as data broadcasting and video transmission for broadcast, cable, and business television. The flexibility of satellite capacity and the ability to add nodes to a network will continue to make the technology attractive for interactive data and video services, but the cost of satellite services will need to remain competitive with that of terrestrial networks. Satellites will continue to provide service to isolated and remote areas, whether through direct VSAT links for the smallest users or to regional hubs with the "last miles" covered by terrestrial radio technologies such as BETRS (Basic Exchange Telephone Radio Service), cellular radio, or digital microwave.

7

Canada's
"Magic from the Sky"

THE BEGINNING

Canada is a geographical and cultural anomaly. Eighty percent of its twenty-four million inhabitants live within 100 miles of the U.S. border. These Canadians have long been exposed to U.S. television, which can often be received over the air and for more than twenty years has been available on Canadian cable systems. This majority is approximately one-third francophone, and Canada is officially bilingual. But many other languages and cultures (European and, increasingly, Asian) are represented in the mosaic. The remaining 20 percent are scattered over Canada's 10 million square kilometers and seven time zones. This geographical minority includes native Indians and Inuit (Eskimos), many of whom live in isolated communities.

Canada was one of the earliest members of the global satellite community, launching its first satellite in 1962. As in the United States, the major impetus for space communication research in Canada came from the military. The first Canadian satellite, Alouette, was funded and designed by the Defence Research Telecommunications Establishment and launched for Canada by NASA. Interestingly, its purpose was not to test satellite communications, but to collect data on the ionosphere from above. The propagation effects of the ionosphere were important for high-frequency radio communications used by the military and also at that time for civilian communications in the remote north. Alouette I was followed by two other experimental satellites, Isis I and II, both designed and built in Canada and launched by NASA, to continue research on the ionosphere.

CANADIAN SATELLITE POLICY

Telesat Canada was established by the Telesat Canada Act in 1969 to own and operate Canada's communication satellites. The act stipulates that the corporation is to be owned by the carriers, the government, and the public. However, public shares have yet to be offered. Hence, at present, Telesat is owned half by the government and half by the carriers (of which Bell Canada is the largest shareholder, with a 24.6 percent interest).[1] As a result of its ownership and structure, Telesat has never been able to compete aggressively with the established carriers as satellite companies have in the United States, but rather supplements their terrestrial facilities.

In 1975, Telesat decided that it should become a member of the Trans-Canada Telephone System (TCTS), now Telecom Canada, which is a consortium of Canadian telecommunications carriers, to facilitate the integration of facilities and obtain additional financial resources for planning and construction of its next generations of satellites. In early 1976, the federal government endorsed the plan, subject to the approval of the Canadian Radio-Television and Telecommunications Commission (CRTC). However, after extensive hearings, the CRTC rejected the plan, believing that an independent Telesat might better serve the public interest in fostering competition in long-haul data, video, and other private line services.[2] Under intense lobbying from the carriers, the Governor-in-Council, however, varied (i.e., reversed) the decision, stating that the public interest would be better served by providing Telesat with access to the carriers' financial resources and encouraging the carriers to use the system. Thus, unlike in the United States, where an FCC decision would be appealed through the courts, in Canada a "political appeal" of a regulatory decision may be made directly to the Cabinet.[3]

The CRTC once more attempted to foster competition in 1981 by ordering Telesat to offer service to end users and to lease less than full transponders in order to meet the needs of smaller carriers and end users. However, once again the Governor-in-Council varied the decision in order to maintain Telesat's "carrier's carrier" role, but allowed

Telesat to deal directly with broadcasters.[4] In 1985, Telesat amended its definition of "customer" so that it could deal directly with end users, but it remained firmly entrenched in the Telecom Canada family.

CANADIAN SPACE POLICY

In 1967, the Science Council of Canada published a report entitled *A Space Program for Canada* that advocated a national effort to develop space facilities because of their importance for Canada's "political and economic future."[5] In the next two decades, Canada established a national satellite system and created a domestic space industry. In 1985, the Canadian government spent about $150 million on space, placing eighth among Organization for Economic Cooperation and Development (OECD) countries in terms of space expenditures as a percentage of GNP.[6] The current objectives of the Canadian Space Program are:

    a. to ensure that the potential of space technology for meeting practical applications to meet Canadian needs is fully developed;
    b. to encourage the development of competitive space industries;
    c. to ensure that Canada maintains a position of excellence in the worldwide scientific exploration of space.[7]

Canada's approach to space research has been to use federal funds to foster development of a Canadian space industry. Telesat's charter requires it to provide telecommunications services on a commercial basis and to utilize Canadian industry to the extent practicable. A major thrust of Canadian space policy has been the development of a prime contractor for satellites.[8] When the first Anik satellite was procured, no Canadian company had the resources and experience to be the prime contractor. However, the government required that the U.S. contractor include "Canadian content" through subcontracts with Canada's embryonic space industry.

Today, the industry is still small (a total of 3,800 people are employed in the entire space industry),[9] but one company has been a prime contractor for recent Anik satellites and for the Brazilian domestic system, and several supply earth stations and components. The first three Anik systems were built in the United States (Anik A and C by Hughes Aircraft and Anik B by RCA), with subcontracts to Canadian firms. The prime contract for Anik D, however, was awarded to Spar Aerospace, a Canadian firm nurtured by the earlier subcontracts.

THE ANIK SYSTEM

Canada became the first country to use a geostationary satellite for domestic communications with the launching of Anik A-1 in 1972 and its backup, Anik A-2, in 1973. (The Soviet Union was already using satellites in nongeosynchronous polar orbits for domestic telecommunications. See chapter 9.) The name Anik, which means "brother" in Inuktitut (the language of the Inuit, or Eskimos), was chosen to symbolize the government's commitment to use satellites to improve communications in the far north, although several years passed before that promise was fulfilled. There appeared to be two other major reasons behind Canada's decision to establish a communication satellite system as proposed in 1967 in a cabinet white paper. The first was to stimulate the development of a Canadian space industry. The second was to secure optimal orbital locations before the United States claimed them. At the time, the United States had put a freeze on the commercialization of satellite communications until it could be determined how the industry would be structured: i.e., publicly or privately owned; monopolistic or competitive. (See chapter 4.)

The early days of satellite service in Canada were noteworthy primarily for the absence of use of the system. As with many new technologies, institutional rather than technological barriers stood in the way. The telephone companies had no incentive to expand service into the remote north because of the low volume of traffic and projected high costs. Where required by regulators to provide or extend service, they preferred to use terrestrial technologies such as microwave because they could own the equipment and put it in the rate base. Satellite transponders and earth stations were leased from Telesat Canada, and thus could not go in the rate base, although the actual costs could be passed through to the customer. And although the cost of using satellites is independent of distance, Canadian tariffs continued to be based on point-to-point distance, despite pressure for flat rates for intra-north calling.[10]

The only broadcaster to use the satellite was the CBC, which is required under the Broadcasting Act to provide service to all Canadians "as funds become available." The private broadcasters, having no such mandate and finding markets small and satellite transponder lease charges high, stayed away from Anik for nearly a decade.

NORTHERN BROADCASTING

Before Anik, the CBC relied on several rudimentary means of reaching the north. Radio, in the form of the CBC Northern Service, was produced in Montreal and transmitted via shortwave from transmitters in New Brunswick designed for international broadcasting. The signal was variable according to season, time of day, and ionospheric conditions, and generally reached only northern Quebec and the eastern Arctic.[11] Five local CBC radio stations in the north produced programs for their immediate area. Vast areas of the north, especially the central Arctic and the northern parts of the provinces had no CBC radio service (nor from any other source). CBC television distribution was even more limited. The five northern communities with CBC radio, plus a few other towns, received the Frontier Coverage Package of CBC videotapes played over local low-powered transmitters.

With the advent of Anik came the first live television transmissions to the far north. CBC network programming, most of which originated in Toronto, was transmitted to the Arctic on two transponders in Atlantic and Pacific time (the Arctic actually stretches across five time zones). Regional news from St. John's, Newfoundland, or Vancouver was inserted, but there was no northern-oriented or native-language programming.

Television quickly became popular among native and nonnative northerners alike. Indeed, the primary beneficiary was likely the Hudson's Bay Company, with general stores (the modern equivalent of the fur-trading post) throughout the north. Early Hudson Bay advertisements proclaimed: "Magic from the sky! Television from Anik! Get your TV set at the Bay." As early as 1970, native leaders expressed concern about the likely impacts of "southern" television and demanded programming about the north and in native languages.[12] A decade passed before the CBC took the first steps to include indigenous programming.

Despite this beginning, perhaps the greatest success of the Canadian satellite experience to date has been achieved in native broadcasting. It took many years for native people in the north to obtain the benefits promised by the government in the late 1960s. However, during that period, a solid foundation for native broadcasting, in the form of community radio and a development-oriented approach to the media, was built. One strong influence was the National Film Board's Challenge for Change program, which used film as a participatory, community development tool. The French community development approach of using an "animateur," or animator, was applied to media projects from urban video and cable access to remote community radio.

The Department of Communications funded a pilot project in northern communications with a community development approach in the early 1970s. The CBC supported community radio by facilitating access to CBC radio transmitters. Pilot projects with federal and provincial support explored a range of community media models from local access to TV transmitters to portable video to community radio. Thus, when native people began to gain access to satellites (at first through experiments and pilot projects on Hermes and Anik B), the community-oriented developmental model was already well in place. This decentralized, participatory, and developmental use of satellites is being adopted by aborigines in Australia and may be a useful model for other developing regions.

Although Canadian network television was beamed to the north, where it was both popular and largely irrelevant, radio by satellite was treated quite differently. From the earliest days, the CBC Northern Service used the satellite to feed programming, including native-language content, to isolated communities. The difference was that CBC radio was already established in the north, with five radio stations across the Arctic. These were local stations that produced much of their own content and rebroadcast network and other programs received by shortwave before the satellite era. With the advent of Anik, these stations were able to receive the CBC network to add to their own local production. But in the process, they were transformed into regional network hubs, redistributing their signals out to the villages in their region.[13] Thus northerners received a mixture of national and regional content with a significant native-language component. Under an innovative CBC community radio project, each local community could contract with the CBC to produce a limited amount of local programming which could be substituted for network programs. In many cases, the CBC trained local people and provided a small studio placed in a building supplied by the community. Most stations were run by volunteers, with operating expenses covered by locally raised funds.

Northern television took much longer to evolve, despite continued protests from native leaders about the negative cultural and linguistic impact of CBC network television. The opportunity to test an alternative approach came with the experimental Hermes satellite and Anik B, which soon succeeded it.

EXPERIMENTAL SATELLITES: CTS AND ANIK B

The Communications Technology Satellite (CTS), or Hermes, was a joint project of the Canadian Department of Communications and NASA. Its high-powered Ku-band transponder provided the first opportunity to experiment with direct broadcasting to very small antennas (less than 1 meter in diameter). CTS was followed by Anik B, a dual-frequency C- and Ku-band satellite. The Department of Communications leased much of the satellite's capacity to continue experimentation and demonstrations begun on Hermes. (The third generation of Anik satellites, Anik C, is a Ku-band system, whereas the fourth generation, Anik D, is again C-band, replacing the now aging Anik A.)

At the time of its launch in 1976, CTS was the most powerful satellite ever built. During its four years of operation, thirty-seven experiments and demonstrations were conducted in telemedicine, teleconferencing, distance education, and direct broadcasting to northern rural and remote communities. In retrospect, CTS was considered a "concept tester."[14] During the Anik B program, which lasted from 1978 to 1984, thirty-two pilot projects were conducted, of which twelve involved tele-education.[15] A few of these have made the transition to operational services on a commercial Anik satellite. The Department of Communications viewed CTS's successor, Anik B, as a vehicle for preoperational trials to determine the viability of new services.

One successful experiment involved TV Ontario (TVO), officially the Ontario Educational Communications Authority. TVO used the Anik B satellite to deliver educational programs previously available only in southern and eastern Ontario to forty-six underserved communities, transmitting directly to schools, libraries, cable TV systems, master antenna systems, and low-power TV transmitters. TVO now provides province-wide coverage by satellite, using Anik C to deliver its programs throughout Ontario and to replace the costly microwave system that previously linked major centers.

The TVO network also delivers native-language radio programming throughout remote northern Ontario. A pilot project on Hermes demonstrated the feasibility of producing and delivering native-language radio programming from a production center in Sioux Lookout, Ontario, to remote Indian settlements with their own community radio stations. The remote stations would rebroadcast the programs to their communities and originate programs themselves on a rotating basis. Listeners were very enthusiastic about the regional programming, and the sponsoring organization began to search for the funds to continue and expand it. However, the tariffs set by Telesat and Bell Canada were far beyond the means of the organization. Eventually an agreement was reached with TVO that enables the native broadcaster, Wawatay, to piggyback its audio signal on a TVO transponder. At the community, the signal is split, with the TV component being rebroadcast over a low-power transmitter and the radio signal being delivered to the community radio station, where it is retransmitted.

In British Columbia, educators undertook an experiment in distance education on Hermes, which was extended on Anik B and is now an ongoing service on Anik C. The Knowledge Network delivers educational programs to isolated communities, where they are retransmitted over cable systems or viewed at community centers and colleges. An audioconferencing link enables students to interact with their instructors based in the Vancouver-Victoria area.

The educational applications of satellite broadcasting have been slower in expanding than might have been expected, given the number of small and isolated communities that could benefit from distance education. The major obstacle to the growth of tele-education is that education is a provincial responsibility in Canada; there is no standardization in educational content or accreditation at the national level. The Knowledge Network in British Columbia has developed a successful model, but it has not been emulated or extended to other provinces. TV Ontario's programs are now available throughout Ontario and can be received elsewhere, although they are used more for enrichment than formal instruction. There is as yet no national educational channel or university channel as is found in the United States.

Inuit have also participated in experiments to test and implement new broadcasting services for the north. Inuit Tapirisat of Canada, the national Eskimo organization, carried out a pilot project on Anik B which linked communities and produced programs. Another experiment on CTS linked eight Inuit communities in Arctic Quebec with an audioconferencing network. The network was used to broadcast two hours of Inuktitut-language programming every other night for two months in 1978. All of the communities (none of which at that time had television service) could take part through the conferencing link.

ITC's Inukshuk project (named for the stone cairns that serve as guideposts in the Arctic) linked six Inuit communities in three Arctic regions (with different dialects and time zones) in a one-way video, two-way audio teleconferencing network. The video signal was viewed in each community on a large screen in a meeting room, and in five communities it could be rebroadcast to reach people at home. Interaction from each site was facilitated by coordinators. During a nine-month period, the project produced more than 320 hours of programming, of which approximately half took the form of live, generally interactive teleconferences.[16] The project not only fostered communication among Inuit across three regions about issues of land claims, education, and cultural identity, but also demonstrated to all—including the federal government, the Northwest Territories government, and the CBC—that the Inuit were capable of producing their own programs.

In 1981, the Inuit established the Inuit Broadcasting Corporation, which now broadcasts five hours of Inuktitut programming each week using time on the CBC Northern Television Service channels. Uplinks are located in Frobisher Bay (on Baffin Island) and in Arctic Quebec. In 1983, the federal government recognized the importance of native broadcasting in its Northern Broadcasting Policy, which established the Northern Native Broadcast Access Program (NNBAP). This program has provided more than $40 million (Canadian) to enable thirteen northern native communications societies to establish production facilities, train broadcasters, and produce and distribute native-language and native-oriented programming. Many of the organizations distribute their programs via satellite.

SATELLITES AND CABLE TELEVISION

Approximately 98.1 percent of all Canadian households have at least one television set, with 87 percent of television households owning at least one color set. Satellite broadcasting in Canada is intertwined with cable television. Canadians adopted cable technology early on as a means of receiving U.S. channels. By 1961, there were already

200,000 subscribers and 260 cable systems. By 1982, there were 564 operating cable systems with about five million subscribers. About 80 percent of Canadian homes are passed by cable, and most of the rest are too scattered or isolated to be economically reached. About 75 percent of the homes passed by cable subscribe to the service. Penetration rates in some cities are extremely high. For example, in Toronto, 77 percent of households are subscribers, while in Vancouver, 91 percent of households are cable subscribers.[17]

Canadian cable systems are federally licensed and regulated by the Canadian Radio-Television and Telecommunications Commission (CRTC), which sets policies on ownership, fees, and content. Canadian cable systems must carry local CBC and other local educational and commercial channels, regional CBC (unless it duplicates local CBC programming), all other regional programming, extraregional CBC, extraregional educational channels, community programming, and any other extraregional stations that do not duplicate higher-priority stations. Once these priorities are met, the cable systems may carry foreign stations according to a 3-plus-1 import limit of three commercial signals and one noncommercial signal. Thus, until recently, Canadian cable subscribers received only the four U.S. networks, generally picked up from U.S. over-the-air broadcasts at the border and retransmitted by microwave to the cable system.

The first satellite-delivered special program available to Canadian cable subscribers was coverage of the House of Commons, transmitted via Anik and now carried live on cable systems across Canada. While the Commons debates are not tops in the ratings, they do give citizens, and students in particular, an opportunity to see their representatives in action, and provide footage that is often inserted in network and local newscasts. Another well-established service is a package of programs received from the French TDF satellite and retransmitted to cable systems in Quebec by a consortium of cable operators called "La Sette."

Canadian broadcasters have apparently concluded that their future is tied to cable. Under Canadian must-carry rules, their signals are included on the basic tier of cable systems; however, if Canadians find direct reception from U.S. satellites more attractive than cable, they may not even be exposed to Canadian programs. Thus, even broadcasters have endorsed a CRTC decision to allow Canadian cable systems to carry up to five U.S. advertiser-supported channels. Now urban Canadians can see what their rural counterparts have been watching for several years.

SATELLITES ACROSS THE BORDER

Although Canadian satellites were used to bring services to the north, traffic growth for other services was very slow because of the costs of leasing facilities and transponder time from Telesat. However, Canadians devised ways to benefit from satellite services available not via Anik but via U.S. domestic satellites. With the advent of pay TV on U.S. satellites, small earth stations began to pop up all over Canada, from Arctic villages to hotel roofs. At first the government tried to shut down these "pirate operations," but public reaction was very strong. (In an extreme case, northern loggers armed with chain saws chased Royal Canadian Mounted Police who had arrived in their logging camps with arrest warrants to shut down the pirate systems.) Bowing to public pressure, the government legalized ownership of receive-only earth stations. By the early 1980s, a policy anomaly had developed in that owners of individual backyard and community earth stations were receiving (and in some cases redistributing) U.S. satellite channels, whereas the cabled urban areas received only the U.S. networks, because CRTC regulations prohibited cable operators from carrying these signals.

One of the most visible "video pirates" was the British Columbia Minister of Universities, Science, and Communications, who installed a satellite antenna behind his office in the Parliament buildings in Victoria in 1980. Backyard dishes became popular in the Canadian north, where choices for television viewing were generally limited to at most one or two channels, if television reception was available at all. These antennas were used not only for reception in individuals' homes and farms, but also for redistribution over low-power rebroadcast transmitters. Northern communities often bought the system with residential contributions. For example, the town of Fort St. John, British Columbia, raised $95,000 in voluntary membership fees with which it purchased two satellite receive stations and four VHF 10-watt transmitters.[18] Decision making on what programming to receive was also a community affair. Fort St. John decided to pick up BCTV (a regional private network) from the Anik satellite and two pay-TV channels plus the Chicago superstation from the RCA Satcom satellite.

Remote Indian communities were equally innovative. Many villages, especially those too small to qualify for CBC service, purchased satellite receivers and local transmitters with community funds. Decision making on what programs to air often followed traditional patterns. For example, in one Indian community, the chief set up a committee to select programming for the single-channel system. The committee members divided the program week into time blocks, studied the program guide of what was available on the RCA Satcom satellite, and chose a mixture of movies, sports, and religious programs from various sources for their one community channel. The chief reserved the right to turn off the system if, for example, there was a death in the community. Satellite television does not seem to have supplanted radio; many native communities also operate community radio stations that broadcast several hours per day, primarily in native languages.

EARTH-STATION OWNERSHIP

Although originally only Telesat was allowed to own satellite earth stations, which it then leased to customers, this policy has gradually changed in recent years. In 1979, broadcasters and common carriers were allowed to license receive-only earth stations, and common carriers could obtain licenses for their own 14 GHz transmit stations. Not until 1983 could individuals and small commercial establishments own their own receive-only stations without a license (long after thousands of Canadians had purchased TVROs to pick up U.S. satellite television). In 1984, the Department of Communications announced a two-step process to liberalize uplink ownership for broadcasters and business users.[19] The result has been a dramatic reduction in the cost of earth stations for users and a decline in equipment-leasing revenues for Telesat.

SATELLITES AND PAY TELEVISION

The federal government authorized the first Canadian pay-TV service in order to offer northern viewers a Canadian alternative. CANCOM carries four Canadian commercial channels, three English and one French. Its licensing agreement requires CANCOM to provide time for native-language programming as well. Individuals may now legally own their own downlinks, and reception and even redistribution of programming from U.S. satellites in remote areas is unofficially sanctioned. However, the recent scrambling of U.S. pay-TV services will restrict access to them.

In 1980, the CRTC adopted a policy of authorizing Canadian pay-television channels as a means of countering the threat of programming delivered by U.S. satellites not only in remote areas, but across the country. The first of these channels began operation in 1983. The CRTC chose a form of "controlled competition," authorizing a limited number of Canadian-owned pay-TV channels. The policy initially amounted to allowing U.S. content to be offered via a Canadian satellite, as most of the movies, sports, and music come from the United States.

In order to prevent excessive market fragmentation, the CRTC limited the number of pay services in any region to four. The licenses were awarded to First Choice Canadian Communications to provide 24-hour movie and entertainment channels in English and French; Lively Arts Market Builders for a national cultural channel ("C-Channel") of performing arts, films, quality children's programs, and so on; five regional film and entertainment channels; and one regional multilingual channel.

The CRTC placed conditions on the license in order to ensure the delivery of Canadian content. For example, First Choice was required to devote 60 percent of its programming budget to Canadian material and 50 percent of that to drama. In order to protect Canadian broadcasters, C-Channel was not allowed to fill more than 40 percent of its schedule with films, and not more than 5 percent with films that had been among the top thirty grossing films in Canada in the past three years.

Operating under these constraints, pay-television floundered. C-Channel folded five months after it began operation. (Two cultural channels in the United States were also cancelled in 1982–83.) Promoters stated that the market was much smaller than they had predicted; perhaps more significantly, a longer-term commitment was needed to test the viability of national cultural networks. The specialized entertainment channels have also suffered bankruptcies and mergers. One major English-language and one French-language movie channel and a music channel have survived. Cable operators are now allowed also to offer U.S. cable channels (such as CNN, Cable News Network, Financial News Network and ESPN sports) on higher tiers.

DBS VERSUS CABLE

Although proposals for DBS in Canada were originally based on the CTS/Hermes model, with very-high-power transmission to terminals of 2 feet or less in diameter, a modified version of "medium-power" DBS that was implemented on Anik B and Anik C appears to be more cost-effective for North American applications. It appears that satellite broadcasting in Canada is to be limited to distribution to cable systems (and low-power transmitters in small communities), despite the attention given to direct household reception a decade ago. The investment in cable in Canada has made it the standard delivery system for multiple channels. High-powered direct-broadcast satellites could not deliver as many channels and would require replacing the cable infrastructure with individually owned antennas.

In most cases, the signal is retransmitted over existing cable television or broadcasting transmitters, or a low-power transmitter is installed to cover the immediate community. Individual receivers can also be installed where required, such as on farms and ranches where the population density is too low to justify community redistribution, as well as in schools or hospitals or on oil rigs. However, the community redistribution model is generally the least expensive solution.

LESSONS FROM THE CANADIAN EXPERIENCE

The Challenge of New Technologies

New technologies challenge the existing framework of regulation and policy-making. For example, in Canada, individuals and communities installed satellite antennas to pick up signals from U.S. satellites. To them the signals were a broadcasting service, with the signals literally there for the taking (although some groups offered to pay the U.S. originators). To the federal Department of Communications this reception was piracy, because individuals were receiving signals from fixed service satellites that were intended only for redistribution and not direct reception. The courts did not resolve the issue, and the government was forced to turn a blind eye to the politically vociferous (and primarily rural and isolated) antenna owners.

The government could keep most urban Canadians from watching U.S satellite channels by refusing to allow licensed Canadian cable systems to carry them. However, individual reception and the growing numbers of VCRs were already undermining the Canadian content policies. Thus, the CRTC acted to introduce Canadian pay television before the government's policy arm (the Department of Communications) was ready with a pay-TV policy. This was one in a series of cases in which the policymakers accused the regulators of preempting their function. However, the regulators felt obliged to deal with the realities of the communication world and to respond to public and industry pressure to authorize new services.

Culture Versus Choice

In 1982, nearly 75 percent of all English-language viewing time by Canadians was spent watching U.S. programs (primarily entertainment and drama) on U.S. and Canadian channels. Some 96 percent of entertainment drama—films, soap operas, detective series, plays, and so on—was produced in the United States and Great Britain. The Canadian policy dilemma was summarized in 1983 by then Minister of Communications Francis Fox, who stated that "within a healthy and viable Canadian broadcasting system Canadians are entitled to as much choice in programming as possible." He added: "I also firmly believe that 'choice' for Canadians is meaningless unless it also includes programming which reinforces the cultural heritage of all Canadians."[20] Yet Canadians do watch domestic news, sports, current affairs, and documentaries, and this behavior (which was first studied by the author in 1969)[21] has continued even though more foreign programming has become available through pay TV.

Tax incentives and the devalued Canadian dollar have resulted in a boom in "made-in-Canada" movies, for both theater and pay-television release. Several of these have been coproductions involving Canadian and U.S. pay-TV services. While creating some jobs and a new source of revenue, most of these productions have not been recognizably Canadian in theme or setting. Indeed, Canadian cities, university campuses, and even wilderness are often disguised to look like their U.S counterparts for these films. In 1983, the CRTC established a tax on cable operators to create a program development fund. Canadian producers must match each dollar from the fund with two from private sources.

Implications for Other Countries

The Canadian case may be illustrative for policymakers elsewhere, particularly in Europe, who are in the process of authorizing new satellite and cable services. "As it has elsewhere, the growth of satellite distribution has mitigated toward new forms of economic and cultural domination in Canada. In broadcasting, satellites have contributed to more foreign programming, less Canadian content, and fewer opportunities for local participation. But satellites can, of course, also be used to counteract this trend."[22]

Canada's Federal Cultural Policy Review Committee has stated that "if Canada is to retain a programming presence in its own broadcasting and telecommunications system, it must use satellites' technological and creative resources to provide Canadian programs and services that Canadians want to see and hear, programs that are competitive in quality with those from other countries."[23] However, U.S. entertainment programming has remained overwhelmingly popular. Thus, rather than declaring the reception of U.S. satellite–delivered channels illegal, Canadian policymakers have sought to use them to keep subscribers happy, while encouraging the delivery of as much Canadian-produced programming as they can find means to support.

Canada's dilemmas concerning satellite broadcasting may soon be shared by other nations as satellites and new video technologies proliferate. The channel capacity of cable and satellite delivery systems is enormous. National producers may find that they lack the resources to produce sufficient content to fill the channels or to attract an audience to pay for the production and delivery systems. The demise of several Canadian pay channels and the demonstrated preference of Canadians for American entertainment programming either on cable, backyard satellite antennas, or videocassettes may indicate future trends in other countries attempting both to introduce new technologies and to foster their own cultures and production industries.

Western Europe

Industrial, Technological, and Cultural Policies Collide

Western Europe has been the scene of much rhetoric and many confusing initiatives in satellite communications. This chapter examines Europe's early experimental satellite activities and the establishment of the European Space Agency and Eutelsat, and then turns to the current status of satellite planning and operations in France, West Germany, the United Kingdom, Luxembourg, Belgium and the Netherlands, the Nordic countries, and Italy. As with other countries and regions, it is important to place European satellite developments in their institutional context. Unlike the situation in the United States, the market forces have not provided the primary impetus for the development of European satellite systems. The apparent contradictions of European satellite initiatives serve as a case study in conflicting industrial, technological, and communication policies.

THE ALLURE OF BROADCASTING SATELLITES

The European nations have shown a preference for high-powered or direct-broadcasting (DBS) type satellites over the multipurpose telecommunications satellites that have been favored in the United States. One reason for this tendency may be the influence of the PTTs, which have little interest in using satellites to replace or even complement their terrestrial networks. Another is related to the strong stand that Western European nations took at the 1977 Regional Administrative Radio Conference, where they succeeded in promoting a technical plan for broadcast satellite services in Europe. The RARC plan, which will remain in effect for fifteen years, gave every nation on the continent, regardless of size, five DBS channels. Yet the European interest in DBS cannot be attributed exclusively to strong pressure from European broadcasters, who recognize that DBS can import signals not only from other European countries but also from the United States. It appears that the major motivation for adopting DBS service was to prove that Europe could build and launch satellites, and that European technology could leap one step ahead of U.S. systems.

THE TECHNOLOGICAL ENVIRONMENT

The introduction of cable and satellite technology has resulted in pressures toward deregulation of audiovisual communications. The extension of cable brings with it the promise of an easily accessible pan-European market. With DBS "the pan-European market will become even more accessible, and effective regulation will become more difficult to achieve by nations acting independently."[1] Yet cable is not the only system competing to deliver video in Europe. The VCR, which has become entrenched in many European countries, offers a powerful challenge to governments attempting to entice viewers to adopt another delivery system and to pay for nationally produced programs rather than popular imports. Restrictions on content to protect national broadcasters may cause viewers to drop their subscriptions in favor of renting videotapes or eventually buying satellite antennas to receive American programs and films. Many European countries have recently encouraged decentralization of broadcasting, as well as local production on cable systems. Ironically, while localism is just catching on in Europe, DBS may undercut localism by reducing stations to mere outlets for national programming.

THE INSTITUTIONAL ENVIRONMENT

Satellites do not operate in isolation, but as part of a national or regional communication system. In Europe, the major carriers in these systems long predate the satellite era and have their own vested interests to protect. In their view, satellites are at best superfluous, at worst a threat. The PTTs have built their own terrestrial networks (primarily microwave, now being upgraded with optical fiber); they see no need for satellites. As major communication institutions, they have been dominant in formulating DBS policies. The PTTs control the distribution network and are the major market for telecommunications equipment, as well as a primary source of funding for research and development.

The broadcasters have a mandate to produce programs that reflect national cultures and provide jobs for national talent. They view satellites as competitors whose flashy commercial programming will lure away viewers. The French characterization of the Luxembourg-based Astra satellite as the "Coca Cola satellite" epitomizes this fear.

However, the institutional environment is changing. In domestic telecommunications, the United Kingdom authorized Mercury to compete with British Telecom (BT), and then privatized BT. It is also looking for ways to privatize more of the British broadcasting industry. France under a Socialist government introduced several new commercial channels and permitted foreign ownership by Italian media magnate Silvio Berlusconi. Having constructed Europe's most modern telecommunications network, France has now also embarked on a major national cable initiative, as has West Germany. The Low Countries and Scandinavia have allowed cable systems to proliferate, with the result that viewers in those countries can choose among several channels, including foreign programs delivered by satellite.

In many cases, these activities are viewed as necessary investments in the infrastructure of the information age, providing electronic pathways to every home and workplace. Yet, the new technologies must also generate revenues. Cable systems are attractive only if they offer appealing programs that are not available over the air (or now on videocassette). New telecommunications networks will stimulate new uses if tariffs are not prohibitive and innovation is encouraged rather than stymied by regulations or bureaucracies. Viewers will install satellite antennas only if the programming they can receive with them is more attractive than what is already available. Thus technological innovation implemented as part of an industrial strategy can result in changes in the structure, content, and even form of ownership of communication industries.

EUROPEAN EXPERIMENTAL ACTIVITIES

In 1967, France and Germany agreed to cooperate on the construction, operation, and utilization of an experimental satellite system. The Symphonie 1 and 2 satellites were launched in 1974–75, with a minimum life span of five years. The time frame in which the Symphonie satellites were planned and implemented paralleled that of NASA's ATS program and the joint U.S.-Canadian CTS satellite. (See chapter 5.) The Symphonie satellites used C-band (5/4 GHz) frequencies and had two coverage zones, "Euroafrican" and American, and could reach from France's territory of Réunion in the Indian Ocean to Quebec and the French territories in the Caribbean.[2] France conducted technical experiments and delivered programs to francophone populations in Africa, the Caribbean, and North America. Experiments using Symphonie were also carried out in India and China.

The European Launcher Development Organization (ELDO) was established in 1961 to coordinate the development of the Western European aerospace and telecommunications industry. In 1973, ELDO was replaced by the European Space Agency (ESA), which carries out space research and application activities, including the Ariane launching program. ESA members include Austria, Belgium, Denmark, France, Ireland, Italy, the Netherlands, Spain, Sweden, the United Kingdom, and West Germany, with Canada and Norway having observer status.[3] ESA developed the Orbital Test Satellites (OTS), which were used for technical experiments and for the delivery of television, including Sky Channel, Europe's first pay-television service.

EUTELSAT

Eutelsat was provisionally formed in 1977 as the coordinator for satellite development of CEPT (the European Conference of Posts and Telecommunications Administrations), the consortium of Western European PTTs. In 1982, twenty-six European nations adopted a convention establishing the definitive organization, which entered into force in 1985. Eutelsat was set up to ensure the establishment, operation, and maintenance of the space segment of the European satellite system. Eutelsat initially directed the communication satellite activities of ELDO, and has helped to design and implement a series of communication satellites in cooperation with ESA.

Eutelsat's objective is to provide its members with the space segment capacity necessary for meeting their telecommunications services requirements. Modeled on Intelsat, the organization consists of an Assembly of Parties and a European Communications Satellite Council (like the Intelsat Board of Governors). The council, composed of all members, is concerned with the development of the space segment, traffic forecasts, access conditions, charges, and earth station standards. The General Secretariat under the secretary general is responsible for the management of the organization, particularly its space segment. Financial participation is based on usage, following the Intelsat model.[4]

Eutelsat provides services that are not available via Intelsat in Europe, including the following:

- transmission of twelve television networks to eighteen countries for cable distribution, and of Eurovision programs;
- intra-European telephony and telegraphy;
- multiservice data communications for computer networking, facsimile, remote printing of newspapers, teleconferencing, and so on.

Eutelsat wholesales its capacity to national administrations, which then retail it to users. The system of payments for users is based on PTT practices rather than market forces. Thus, users such as television programmers may pay varying rates for access to a Eutelsat satellite, depending on the practices of their PTT, which leases the capacity from Eutelsat. The basic space segment charge is 1.8 million ECUs (equivalent to dollars) per year, plus 200,000 ECUs per country receiving the signal (excluding the transmitting country).[5] Eighteen standard transmit-and-receive stations are located in eight member countries. Approximately 180 television receive-only earth stations are in operation.

Eutelsat's space segment is coordinated by the European Space Agency (ESA), which procures spacecraft from European manufacturers. All satellites are launched by the European launcher, Ariane. Eutelsat administered a series of experiments which ended in December 1983 on the Orbital Test Satellite (OTS) developed by ESA and launched in 1978. The Ku-band OTS carried Sky Channel, a U.K.-based pay-TV cable channel, and France's TDF network. The experimental OTS was followed by another Ku-band satellite, ECS-F1, in 1983. Sky Channel switched to ECS for its pay-TV network; another customer was TV-5, a French-language channel jointly produced by the broadcasting organizations of France, Belgium, and Switzerland. Eutelsat's ECS-F2 was launched in 1984, with one transponder reserved for television and five for business applications.[6] Eutelsat also leases capacity on France's Telecom 1. The launch of ECS-F3 failed in 1985, and ECS-F4 has been delayed by problems with the Ariane and shuttle launchers. Eutelsat plans the launch of the first of its second-generation satellite in 1989.[7]

Secretary General Andrea Caruso points out that, unlike many other satellite systems, Eutelsat was not conceived to fill telecommunications gaps. "In view of the extensive European terrestrial network already in place, the objectives of the system are to satisfy specific European telecommunications requirements and to enable the European aerospace industry to develop a full range of technologies so that it may compete in the world market."[8] Eutelsat sees itself as a catalyst for the development of new technologies and services, and is currently studying a European DBS system and mobile communications via satellite.[9]

PAY TELEVISION

Sky Channel, which carries American and British general entertainment programming, has been operating since 1982, using Eutelsat's ECS-F1. Owned by Satellite Television Limited, a 90 percent subsidiary of Rupert Murdoch's News International multimedia group, Sky Channel is supported by advertising revenue. Murdoch's acquisitions of Twentieth Century Fox and U.S. television stations, as well as his new Fox Network, provide programming for Sky Channel.[10] Other new satellite-distributed cable channels are Music Box (similar to MTV), started by Thorn EMI and sold to the Virgin Group, the Children's Channel, and Premiere, also started by Thorn EMI (which later sold its share to Robert Maxwell) in collaboration with several Hollywood studios. These networks use leased capacity on Intelsat V satellites to reach cable systems in Europe. To compete with Sky Channel, the ITV stations, led by Granada and Thames, plan to offer European audiences an advertising-supported SuperChannel consisting of the best of their members' programming.[11]

FRANCE

A report entitled *The Computerization of Society,* presented by Simon Nora and Alain Minc to Giscard d'Estaing's government in 1976, signaled the importance of information technology for France's economic future and alerted policymakers to the convergence of computers and telecommunications.[12] The government had already invested billions of francs in modernizing France's antiquated telephone system, and followed this project with a *Programme Télématique* to develop new information technologies and services. The most visible result has been the Minitel, a simple computer terminal now found in more than four million households. (France Telecom computerized French telephone directories and gave away Minitels to subscribers as a means of diffusing the technology, which is now used for a wide range of interactive consumer and business services.)

The *Programme Télématique* was followed by a *Plan Cable,* also sponsored by the Direction Générale des Télécommunications (DGT), for a state-led national fiber-optic project, to be implemented in cooperation with local cable authorities. Furthermore, the Mitterand government has made major changes in French broadcasting policy. In 1984, it authorized a fourth channel, Canal Plus, to be operated as a commercial venture. A fifth channel, in addition to being licensed as a commercial operation, introduced foreign ownership: its concession was awarded to a joint venture headed by the Italian media magnate Silvio Berlusconi.

Meanwhile, France had made major advances in the satellite field. The French PTT initiated its own satellite venture, Telecom I, in 1979; the satellites were launched in 1984 and 1985. Telecom is the first national satellite system in Europe. The satellites cover France and the Atlantic region, including France's overseas territories of St. Pierre and Miquelon (in the Gulf of St. Lawrence) and Guadeloupe, Martinique, French Guiana, Mayotte, and Réunion, as well as Corsica. Telecom I and II are equipped with four C-band and six Ku-band transponders, and are used for occasional television transmission, business communications as part of Eutelsat's Satellite Multi-Service, and French military communications.[13]

France was also the major partner in the consortium set up by the European Space Agency to develop the Ariane rocket. French interests own the major share in Arianespace, the launch system operator.[14] In 1979, France and West Germany abandoned their support of ESA's proposed H-SAT project and announced a joint project for launching DBS satellites to cement their industrial alliance, which dates back to the Symphonie cooperation within ESA. The first step was to contract for two satellites, TDF-1 (France) and TV-SAT (West Germany) to be launched by Ariane and managed by the national authorities, Télédiffusion de France and the German Bundespost.

The apparent aim of this venture was to secure long-term cooperation in the hope of capturing a large share of the world market for satellites. The principal industrial beneficiaries were the German and French "national champions" AEG-Telefunken and Thomson-CSF in electronics, and aerospace companies Messerschmidt Boelkow Blohm (MBB) and SNIAS (Aerospatiale).[15] Governments in both countries took an active role in initiating and financing the project. It appears that the French-German project was undertaken purely as a matter of technological and industrial policy. The anticipated market was for hardware, and it was foreign, not European.

WEST GERMANY

In West Germany, the states, or Länder, are responsible for broadcasting under the constitution, while the federal government, or Bund, is responsible for telecommunications. The Bundespost is undertaking state-financed construction of cable television networks. Cable is progressing slowly at the state level, but the Bundespost is looking toward the future by funding projects to develop and test videotext (known as Bildschirmtext) and fiber optics (the BIGFON project). There have also been direct attempts to deregulate media in order to stimulate private entrepreneurial activity.[16] The goal of Christian Democrat policies has been to break the traditional public-services monopoly of broadcasting, to introduce commercial broadcasting, and to encourage small and medium-sized enterprises.

In 1984, the west beam of the ECS F1 satellite was allocated to a private consortium, SAT 1, formed by the major German publishing companies and some small private concerns. The news service was supplied by Aktell Presse Fernsehen (APF), a joint venture in which the German publisher Otto Springer had a major share. German public broadcasters also decided to join the satellite fray. The German public-service television services that produced the first TV channel (ARD) launched their own satellite channel (Eins Plus); the Second German TV network (Zweites Deutsches Fernsehen) joined with Austrian and Swiss networks to produce a German-language satellite channel (TV 3); and the Bavarian government sought satellite capacity so that its network, Bayerischer Rundfunk, could reach a national audience.[17]

West Germany's TV-SAT, a high-powered DBS-type satellite, will provide four channels of television to small rooftop antennas; it is to transmit three national television channels (ARD, ADF, and the Third Program). The satellite will also have a footprint for West Berlin. West Germany also plans to construct two domestic satellites known as Deutsche Fernmelde Satelliten (DFS) or Kopernikus. To be launched by Ariane, they will provide television, telephone, and data transmission, operating in Ku-band (11–14 GHz) and Ka-band (20–30 GHz). Germany's space and electronics companies have manufactured components for Eutelsat and Intelsat systems, and for the Ariane launching system.

THE UNITED KINGDOM

Under the Thatcher government, the United Kingdom has pursued a policy of privatization and introduced some competition in telecommunications. In 1982, the government authorized limited competition with British Telecom (BT) in the form of Mercury Communications; British Telecom was privatized through the offering of public shares in 1985. Both British Telecom International (BTI) and Mercury operate earth stations for international telecommunications services using Intelsat and Eutelsat.

Also in 1982, the Information Technology Advisory Panel (ITAP), representing the computer, electronics, and cable industries, produced a report urging the rapid development of high-capacity interactive cable networks. It stated that there were "powerful economic and industrial arguments for encouraging the growth of cable systems in the UK" and that "for British industry a late decision [was] the same as a negative decision."[18] The government established the Hunt Inquiry to consider the impact of the expansion of cable on the existing broadcasting system. It then passed the Cable and Broadcasting Act of 1984 which set up a Cable Authority empowered to issue franchises and to provide minimal regulation.

Thus the Thatcher government seized on an entertainment-led cable revolution as a means of obtaining the infrastructure for an information economy. Plans for a British satellite also resulted from industrial policy considerations, reinforced by the recommendations of the ITAP Report. In 1982, the government awarded DBS service to the BBC (instead of rival ITV).

Unisat was to have been built by United Satellites Limited (USL), a joint venture of Britain's "national champions" in space, electronics, and telecommunications: British Aerospace, Marconi Electronics, and British Telecom. In January 1984, the BBC announced that it would not lease a whole satellite system from the Unisat consortium because the estimated cost of DBS receivers was too great to attract a large enough audience. The BBC blamed the high projected costs for DBS receivers on the government's decision to use the Independent Broadcasting Authority's (IBA) MAC-C encryption standard. As it became clear that the cost of the system was beyond reach of the BBC, ITV was invited to participate. When the two networks could not agree on prices and programming, the government allowed private interests into the project. A consortium to program Unisat's three channels was established under joint ownership of the BBC (50 percent), ITV network companies (30 percent) and a group of twenty-one private companies (20 percent) known as the "21 Club," including Granada TV Rentals, Thorn EMI, Pearson Ltd. (publisher of the *Financial Times* and owner of Virgin Records), and Consolidated Satellite Broadcasting (whose principal owner was Radio-TV-Luxembourg).[19] A new authority, the Satellite Broadcasting Board, drawn from the BBC and IBA boards of governors, was proposed to set the standards, content, and transmission policies of Unisat's programming. However, by 1985, the BBC had estimated that it would incur additional costs of 75 million pounds annually to provide programming for Unisat, and that it might have to resort to advertising rather than increasing license fees to fund its DBS service. The outcry from ITV and the public led the government to withdraw its support.[20]

Following the demise of Unisat, the IBA licensed a private company, British Satellite Broadcasting (BSB) to provide three channels of direct broadcast television. BSB plans to use a high-powered Ku-band satellite built by Hughes, to be launched in 1989. In the interim, BTI has leased several transponders on Intelsat and Eutelsat, and also plans to use Astra (see below).[21]

LUXEMBOURG

A satellite for Luxembourg? Not exactly. Luxembourg's tiny size and population make it among the least likely candidates for satellite use.

However, three factors make it an attractive base for a regional DBS system: (1) it shares borders with Belgium and the major markets of West Germany and France, and lies near the Netherlands; (2) its inhabitants speak both French and German; and (3) Radio-TV-Luxembourg (RTL), the operating arm of the Compagnie Luxembourgeoise de Télédiffusion (CLT), plays a major role in the national economy as a program exporter and contributor to government revenues.

Coronet, a project to operate a DBS-type satellite for commercial television distribution throughout Europe, was initiated by the Luxembourg government in 1983, with the participation of Clay T. Whitehead, director of the Office of Telecommunications Policy in the Nixon White House and later president of Hughes Communications. Its promoters underestimated the power of vested interests in European television and telecommunications, but it received support from programmers, electronics companies, advertising companies, and some leading European venture capitalists.[22] After intense pressure from France and other sources, the Coronet system was canceled and replaced by a consortium called Société Européenne des Satellites. Late in 1985, SES procured a medium-powered satellite called Astra from RCA (now a subsidiary of General Electric), to be launched in 1989.

The French have dubbed Astra the "Coca Cola satellite," fearing that Luxembourg will become a beachhead for the penetration of the continent by U.S. commercial programs purveying American culture.[23] Similar concerns, particularly for the vulnerability of French broadcasting, spurred France to launch repeated attacks on Astra's predecessor, Coronet. At first, the French tried to block Coronet by offering CLT channel capacity on TDF-1 in exchange for CLT's promise to abandon the development of its own satellite. This compromise solution would have given CLT privileged access to the French market, as well as enhancing the commercial viability of TDF-1. However, French President Mitterand was also negotiating to allocate a new fifth national channel in France to a Franco-Italian group involving Silvio Berlusconi, an Italian entrepreneur known for his role in the commercialization and Americanization of Italian television. This channel and another associated with British publisher Robert Maxwell were later to operate on TDF-1.

Mitterand may have opted for political expediency by initiating the apparently inevitable expansion and commercialization of French television through popular decisions and excluding rival factions such as Rupert Murdoch and right-wing publisher Robert Hersant. However, the result, as one French observer put it, was a situation resembling "autocannibalisme": "anarchy was resulting from the pursuit of too many mutually contradictory options, without any respect for what the market or regulatory policy could bear."[24] In 1986, the new center-right government of Jacques Chirac further complicated matters by canceling the TDF-1 agreements and putting the TDF-1 channels out to tender, inviting bids from Murdoch, CLT, and Hersant.[25]

Coronet acted as a catalyst for change in West German television as well. In 1982, the West German publishing multinational Bertelsmann announced that it would take a 40 percent share in CLT, the holding company for RTL, in a new commercial German-language channel called RTL-Plus, to be broadcast eventually by satellite from Luxembourg. RTL-Plus began service in 1984. This development forced other West German interests to accelerate their plans for a new commercial TV channel (SAT 1), to be transmitted to cable systems and eventually to individual receivers. The states, or Länder, which are responsible for broadcasting, eventually moved toward a considerable measure of deregulation in the face of these new developments.[26]

Eutelsat has also viewed Coronet and its successor Astra as threats to its regional systems. When Coronet announced its plan for a broadcasting satellite in 1983, Eutelsat challenged the proposal, stating that the establishment of a private television-carrying satellite would cause "significant economic harm" to the Eutelsat organization of twenty-six European telecommunications authorities. (Eutelsat's Convention has a clause on economic harm similar to Intelsat's Article XIV(d); see chapter 3.)

The issue, according to Astra, is the applicability of the coordinating procedure concerning economic harm. The Luxembourg government's legal opinion is that the services to be provided by the proposed satellite system do not constitute public telecommunications services as defined in the Eutelsat Convention. Article XVI(a) of the treaty requires coordination with Eutelsat only by a party which intends to establish, acquire, or utilize space segment in order to meet the requirements of international public telecommunication services within the Eutelsat space segment service area.[27] Under the Convention, the only coordination required for "specialized telecommunications services," including broadcasting satellite services, is to ensure technical and operational compatibility; economic harm is not mentioned in this context.

The Astra system is designed to transmit TV programming to cable headends, master antenna systems, hotels and apartment blocks, and so on. However, Astra has coordinated with the ITU's International Frequency Registration Board under the fixed satellite service, rather than under the broadcasting satellite service, which is intended for direct-reception systems. Thus Eutelsat has claimed that Astra must coordinate as a public telecommunications service rather than as a broadcasting service; this coordination would require an examination of economic harm. Eutelsat would be able to argue that its monopoly should be protected to prevent such harm from a competitor.

A legal opinion prepared for Astra states: "Any assumption that Eutelsat enjoys a monopoly in everything it does or plans to do is absolutely unwarranted. Any such claim would be reminiscent of the . . . pretension of some of its founders that Intelsat should be a global and single world telecommunications system, a pretension strenuously resisted especially by its European members. It would be very ironical if Eutelsat were now to seek to assume that mantle in Europe."[28] Eutelsat's legal opinion is that Astra is providing an international public telecommunications service and is therefore bound to carry out economic coordination with Eutelsat. Secretary General Caruso says he would coordinate only under a lease/lease-back arrangement such as Eutelsat has enjoyed with France's Telecom 1.[29]

Eutelsat appears to be concerned with the threat not only of competition, but also of privately run satellite systems. Secretary General Caruso has compared Eutelsat to a PTT; if it did not have a monopoly, rural communities would be priced out of services in favor of higher-profit urban areas. He adds:

> Eutelsat has made reliable, varied and competitive telecommunications service available to its member signatories while operating on a sound economic and financial basis. This success . . . is that of an international organization backed by governments, where the risks are shared between dozens of partners who, as both shareholders and users in the same venture, have a vested interest in leading that venture to success. . . . The success of this organization serves as a clear example of international cooperation which would now be placed at risk by the financial interests of private investors.[30]

However, if Caruso were concerned solely with the risk involved in new satellite ventures, one wonders why he would want to prevent the private sector from bearing the risk rather than his members and their taxpayers.

Astra has proceeded without economic coordination with Eutelsat, but states that it has had difficulty in concluding deals with potential users because they want guarantees of uplink and downlink agreements with their PTTs without excessive negotiations. The PTTs in many cases are resisting such agreements because they want to preserve a monopoly over satellite links, and are supporters of Eutelsat.

THE NORDIC COUNTRIES

The Nordic broadcasting systems share a strong commitment to public-service broadcasting. Despite some confrontation during the past twenty years between proponents of commercial versus cultural approaches to broadcasting, the cultural approach has continued to dominate. Norway, Denmark, and Sweden have each introduced some local broadcasting within the public-service framework.[31] In 1958, Nordvision was established for the exchange of television programs among the Nordic countries. Although the exchange of programs has grown steadily, it still accounts for less than 5 percent of Swedish television content.[32]

The Nordic countries, fearing that satellite broadcasting would mean cultural domination of the small countries on the periphery of Europe, proposed their own satellite for regional program exchanges. In the 1970s, a Nordic commission recommended increased program exchanges, and a subsequent commission explored the possibility of a Nordic satellite system, or Nordsat. In 1979, the Nordsat report concluded that a Nordic television exchange via a DBS satellite was realistic. Five main motives for a full-scale Nordic television exchange were given:

- to promote increased cultural cooperation among the Nordic countries;
- to preserve the viability of Nordic cooperative broadcasting efforts in a situation where satellite broadcasting from non-Nordic countries becomes a common phenomenon;
- to provide greater freedom of choice of TV programs for citizens of Nordic countries;
- to contribute to better understanding of the Nordic languages;

- to improve the cultural situation for linguistic and ethnic minorities within the Nordic region.[33]

When the Nordsat report was distributed to the member countries, cultural organizations and public-service radio and television companies tended to be most critical, whereas Pan-Nordic organizations and industrial groups showed the greatest interest.[34] The critics were concerned about threats to national culture and the costs of the project. Supporters saw Nordsat as a means of introducing more television channels or as a source of jobs. In 1982, the members decided to continue the planning, but at the same time to consider using other satellites to get the program exchange started. Thus Nordsat was relegated to the status of a cultural initiative, without grounding in economic reality.

Meanwhile, Sweden's National Telecommunications Administration (Televerket) had begun work on an experimental satellite called Tele-X in conjunction with the Swedish Space Corporation, the space industry, and other entities. The project formed part of a national program of space research designed to give the Swedish space and electronics industry an opportunity to develop its expertise in satellites. The program's first satellite, Viking, was launched in February 1986 to conduct research on the ionosphere. The second satellite, Tele-X, is to be a DBS type. The Swedish Board for Space Activities has a controlling share in Tele-X, in partnership with Norway and Finland.[35]

Tele-X began primarily as a hardware project to boost the Swedish space and electronics industries. The project received little publicity in its early phases and as a result did not stimulate the controversy engendered by the Nordsat proposal. Content received scant attention in the development of Tele-X. There was little attempt made to ascertain the market for DBS services or to accommodate the Nordic program exchanges envisioned in the Nordsat proposal. The telecommunications administrations focused on developing a Nordic cable network and their participation in Intelsat and Eutelsat, which could be used for program exchanges without the expense of building and operating a dedicated satellite. In November 1985, the Nordic Council of Ministers decided that there should be two channels on Tele-X for program exchanges, but proposals requested from the broadcasters were rejected on economic grounds.

In the meantime, satellite broadcasting has already penetrated Scandinavia through delivery of commercial channels to cable systems. For example, Swedish Telecom, the largest cable operator, offers a basic cable package including Sky Channel, SuperChannel (incorporating Music Box), the French TV-5, Soviet Gorizont, CNN, and mandatory national and local channels.[36] It is therefore unclear what role Tele-X will play in Nordic broadcasting.

ITALY

In 1976, a judgment of the Italian Constitutional Court declared the public-service monopoly on broadcasting to be unconstitutional, except at the national level. By 1982, there were 1,500 television stations, of which 450 were broadcasting regularly. About 150 stations generated advertising revenues that exceeded those of the government-operated broadcaster RAI; 100 of these were soon controlled by three commercial networks. Imported television programming sky-rocketed; by 1982, Italy was the world's leading importer of both Japanese and American programming. One of the networks, Canale Cinque, bought the Italian option for the complete output of CBS; in an attempt to remain competitive, the public national network, RAI, signed an agreement with NBC.[37] Two side effects of these trends were the weakening of the Italian television production industry and the near collapse of the film industry.

Italy's first satellite, Sirio, was launched in 1977 to carry out experiments in cooperation with several Italian organizations, including RAI and the *Corriere della Sera* newspaper, which used it for remote printing. In 1983, Sirio was moved from its initial position at 15° W to a new position at 65° E, where it was used for joint Italian-Chinese experiments. Telespazio plans an operational national satellite system (Italsat) for the 1990s; meanwhile Italy will use one of the two transponders on ESA's experimental Olympus satellite for broadcast television. A new organization, SARIT (Satellite di Radiodiffusione Italiano), has been established to administer the Olympus transponder.[38]

BELGIUM AND THE NETHERLANDS

By the early 1980s, nearly 70 percent of the Netherlands and 90 percent of Belgium were cabled, as a result of the dual incentives of improving reception and importing programming from neighboring countries. The hardware was licensed by the PTTs, while content remained the responsibility of the Ministry of Culture. The promise of commercial satellite services led to pressure to deregulate content. In the Netherlands, the Media Policy Note of 1983 resulted in the government's effectively relinquishing much of its traditional control over programming, whereas the Belgian government continued to regulate domestic programming. However, publishing companies in both countries showed interest in commercial satellite broadcasting. For example, Groupe Bruxelles Lambert established Media International in partnership with Rupert Murdoch's News International and developed close ties with U.S. media interests.[39]

EUROPEAN BROADCASTING

Broadcasting satellite developments in Europe must be viewed within the context of changes in European broadcasting policy as well as changes in national policies. In June 1984, the European Economic Community (EEC) published a Green Paper entitled *Television without Frontiers,* which discussed "the establishment of the common market for broadcasting, especially by satellite and cable."[40] The report demonstrates that the provisions of the Treaty of Rome apply to at least certain types of broadcasting, and that the European Community can reasonably claim to have the power and duty to act in relation to certain aspects of broadcasting. However, other policy issues remain to be addressed.

Broadcasting services have traditionally been regarded as domestic activities governed by national legislation. However, with satellites coverage can extend to entire continents. The Treaty of Rome addresses free movement of goods and of "persons, services, and capital" across national boundaries. The Green Paper concludes that broadcasting is a service under the treaty definition of "services normally provided for remuneration," because television programs are provided, either directly or indirectly, in return for payment made by citizens or in return for payments from the advertisers, or in return for both types of remuneration. The transfrontier character of broadcasting makes it subject to the provision that "restrictions on freedom to provide services shall be progressively abolished . . . with no restrictions except on grounds of public policy, public security, or public health."[41]

The EEC's overall strategy is to create an integrated European television network, with programs coproduced by European Broadcasting Union members in various languages. The EEC has stated that Europe's broadcasters must work together to remove the legal and economic barriers hindering the free flow of programming if they are to be competitive producers and distributors in the international market as satellite and cable technologies develop.[42] The commission's proposed directive to permit free movement of services between member states, including broadcast programming, remains problematic at present since each country has its own copyright laws. The main barrier to the liberalization of broadcasting exchange is the European Agreement on the Protection of Television Broadcasts, the signatories to which are Belgium, Denmark, France, the United Kingdom, and West Germany.[43]

The Green Paper proposes that the European Community should work toward a directive which would establish minimum standards for advertising for use throughout the Community, that is, an agreement under which an advertisement, once produced in one member country in conformity with EEC standards, would satisfy the standards of all member countries and thus be acceptable for transmission in all. However, there is far from a common attitude toward advertising among EEC members. Belgium and Denmark prohibit advertising entirely, while the variations in advertising permitted in other European countries reported in the Green Paper ranged from 9 minutes per day in Finland to 90 minutes in the United Kingdom on ITV.[44]

Thus, in principle, the directives proposed in the Green Paper would appear to support Europe-wide broadcasting via satellite. However, as is evident from the above discussion, each country has its own policies and perspectives not only on its national broadcasting system but on strategies for introducing new technologies and services. As George Wedell states about the Green Paper, "the feeling remains that the authors have a good grasp of the trees but little idea of the nature of the wood."[45] Rupert Murdoch echoed similar sentiments in somewhat stronger language when describing the difficulties of introducing an advertising-supported pay-television channel to be delivered via satellite across Western Europe.[46]

A COLLISION OF INDUSTRIAL, TECHNOLOGICAL, AND COMMUNICATION POLICIES

In the past decade, Western European nations have introduced a myriad of initiatives that could be classified as industrial and technological policies. These policies stand in contrast to the marketplace approach that has dominated the U.S. satellite field since the introduction of "Open Skies." By apparently ignoring the market forces of consumer demand and the effects of the introduction of other technologies such as cable television and VCRs, European strategists may have limited the gains they hoped to achieve. A longer-term effect, however, may be that these new policies, implemented throughout the communication sector, will weaken or in some cases undermine the cultural policies which have been carefully nurtured since the early days of European broadcasting.

Since the inception of Intelsat, Western European powers have feared that the satellite industry would be dominated by the United States. European satellite development seems to have been stimulated originally by industrial considerations, e.g., the desire to promote national aerospace industries, electronics enterprises, and telecommunication carriers. In their 1976 report, *The Computerization of Society*, Nora and Minc stated: "[S]atellites are at the heart of telematics. Eliminated from the satellite race, the European nations would lose an element of sovereignty with regard to NASA, which handles the launching, and with regard to the firms that specialize in managing them, especially IBM. By contrast, if they were capable of building them, launching them, and managing them, the same nations would be in a position of power."[47]

The establishment of ESA, its experimental satellites, and the Ariane launch program were intended to develop European satellite technology and expertise. Viewed from this limited perspective, they were apparently successful. In particular, Ariane has become a major commercial success, with most of its business now stemming from non-European satellite systems, including Intelsat, several U.S. domestic satellites, and PanAmSat.

The satellites themselves have not fared as well as Ariane. Having developed the technology, the Europeans now must find a use for it. The term "use" is more apt here than "market," as many European applications are apparently not market-driven. Rather they appear to be part of a second phase, or industrial policy, designed to take the technology from the experimental stage to operational systems that will be built by European industry. However, an operational (as opposed to experimental) satellite system must generate revenues by providing telecommunications or broadcasting services.

In tandem with building satellites for their own use, the Europeans have been trying to develop global markets for their satellite systems,

particularly in developing countries. For example, they have conducted feasibility studies for an African regional satellite, an Andean
regional satellite, and a Chinese broadcasting satellite.

While satellite policies are being developed, national telecommunications and broadcasting policies are also being changed, again
often for what might be considered industrial policy reasons. As
Denis McQuail points out, "industrial policy—development for the
sake of employment and future markets for hardware and software—
may collide with cultural policy, concerned with protecting or promoting the national language and cultural products or ensuring that
the new electronic media continue to fulfil social functions belonging
to broadcasting, especially wide distribution of information, education and culture." In such an environment it becomes "more difficult
to operate a broadcasting cultural policy in the face of uncontrolled
access from abroad and, at the same time, it becomes increasingly
difficult to justify restrictions on such access."[48]

Satellites introduced into this policy cauldron may either be ignored or used in ways that undermine long-cherished principles of
cultural sovereignty and public-sector control over communications.
The West German TV-SAT and Scandinavian Tele-X may be orphans
with no significant market for their services, as was the stillborn
Unisat. The French TDF-1 will apparently have customers, but not
solely for French television. Eutelsat has provided an interim means
to distribute pay channels that carry mainly U.S. programming, and
seems destined to face continuing challenges from competing systems. Astra may prove to be a commercial success, using a U.S.-built
satellite to deliver primarily U.S.-produced and advertiser-supported
programs to a European audience. Similar ventures by the IBA and
Rupert Murdoch, for example, may also prove to be commercial
successes.

In some countries there is little coordination between satellite policy and other communication initiatives. The United Kingdom's DBS
policy has been called "more of a farce than a tragedy."[49] It may be
seen as part of an uncoordinated deregulation: "deregulation was
pursued, but with few signs of sustained central direction and control."[50] In France, satellites were mired in a battle of the technocrats
between Telecom 1 and TDF-1. However, in the face of the Luxembourg Coronet initiative, the French felt they had to enter the DBS
game.[51] The Nordic Tele-X was developed to further Scandinavian
industrial goals without taking into consideration parallel planning
for a regional Nordsat system.

It is difficult to predict what impact European satellites will have on Western European cultures, industries, and institutions. Perhaps satellites will soon be discarded as inappropriate and unnecessary for the enhancement of European telecommunications. On the other hand, for telecommunications services they may act as institutional Trojan horses, bypassing the PTTs to bring new or lower-cost interactive services, such as data transmission and teleconferencing, directly to end users. Satellites may also act as cultural Trojan horses, transmitting foreign programs across borders and eluding the grasp of the policymakers. No longer will even the major powers be able to keep foreign programming from crossing their borders. As two British researchers observed, the spread of the new media means that in Western Europe "we are all becoming small states now."[52]

Other
Industrialized Countries
The Soviet Union,
Australia, and Japan

The Soviet Union was the first nation to establish its own domestic satellite network, using a series of polar-orbit satellites. It also spearheaded the formation of Intersputnik, an international satellite system linking the U.S.S.R., Eastern bloc nations, and several developing countries. Like Canada, Australia has a large land mass and a relatively small population concentrated on its periphery. Australia recognized that satellite technology was an appropriate means of covering its vast territory. Japan has been experimenting with satellites since the mid-1970s and is leading the world in introducing high-powered DBS and satellite transmission of HDTV.

This chapter outlines the major developments in the introduction of satellites by these countries. It also attempts to identify the major issues and institutions that have shaped their decisions on implementation and applications.

THE SOVIET UNION:
DOMESTIC SERVICES AND A GLOBAL NETWORK

Experimental Activities

Like the United States, the Soviet Union began experimenting with satellites and space flight immediately after World War II. The Soviets first decided to pursue research on manned space flight in 1946.[1] This research led to the launching of Sputnik in 1957, which shocked the Western world into recognition of Soviet advances in space. However, the Soviets devoted a major part of their space program to establishing space stations operated by cosmonauts, building on knowledge gained from early space flights carrying animals. The space station Mir bears witness to Soviet progress in placing humans in space. This chapter, however, examines only the major satellite communication developments in the Soviet Union.

In 1977, an organization called Interkosmos composed of Socialist states was established for the purpose of collaborating on space research. Interkosmos now includes Bulgaria, Cuba, Czechoslovakia, East Germany, Hungary, Mongolia, Poland, Romania, the U.S.S.R., and Vietnam, that is, seven Eastern bloc countries and three developing countries.[2] In addition to Soviet satellites, the program has launched a Czech Magion satellite and a Bulgarian 1300 satellite. Cuba has used the Intersputnik system to access scientific data bases of the International Center of Scientific and Technical Information of the Comecon countries (CIIST), and was involved in gathering oceanographic data with East Germany and Mongolia via the remote-sensing satellite Interkosmos-21.[3]

In keeping with its commitment to assist developing countries in space research, the Soviet Union has launched four experimental satellites for India, for upper atmosphere research, gamma astronomy, satellite monitoring, and remote sensing. During the failure of Insat 1A in 1982–83, the U.S.S.R. gave India free access to one of its Intersputnik satellites for nearly a year.[4]

Soviet Domestic Communications

The Soviet Union was the first nation to use satellites for domestic communications, launching Molniya 1 shortly after Early Bird on April 23, 1965. A further sixteen Molniya 1–type satellites were launched into elliptical polar orbit before an improved version, Molniya 2, was introduced in 1971. These satellites form the space component of the Orbita domestic communications system. The elliptical polar orbit allows the signal to reach the extreme northern latitudes of the Soviet Union, with a perigee of 500 kilometers and apogee of 40,000 kilometers. (Nearly one-quarter of the Soviet Union's territory is above the 60th parallel.)[5] Each satellite is visible for approximately 6 hours, at which time the signal is transferred to another satellite entering its polar apogee. Two antennas are needed at each site to execute a synchronized handover as one satellite passes over the horizon and another emerges.

In accordance with directives of the Twenty-third Congress of the Communist Party of the Soviet Union, a system of television distribution from Molniya 1 satellites to twenty Orbita 1 earth stations was completed in 1967. The Orbita system was officially inaugurated at the fiftieth anniversary of the October Revolution in 1967. The televised ceremonies at Red Square were transmitted to some twenty locations in the Soviet Union, including Vladivostok.[6]

Molniya means "lightning" in Russian; a colloquial meaning is "news flash."[7] The Molniya system transmits television from two primary stations in Moscow and Vladivostok. In addition to one television channel, the system has some capacity for telephony, telegraphy, facsimile, and other services. The first Molniya 2 was launched in November 1971, and the first Orbita 2 earth station was inaugurated in September 1972. The Molniya system now operates with more than 100 12-meter tracking earth stations.

In March 1974, the Soviet Union launched its first Raduga satellite, designated as Statsionar-1, followed by a second geostationary satellite, Molniya A-1S in July 1974, the first in the Intersputnik system.[8] Unlike the Molniya system, the Raduga satellites are geostationary. In 1978, a second Raduga series, known as Statsionar-2, was launched. The Raduga satellites are used for telephone and telegraph services, television and radio distribution, and remote printing of newspapers. The Molniya and Raduga systems together provide complete coverage of the Soviet Union.

In 1979, the Soviet Union launched its first broadcasting satellite, called Ekran or Statsionar-T, which now transmits to more than 1,500 television receive stations. However, because the frequencies on Ekran are also used by terrestrial systems, the possibilities for expansion were limited. Therefore, another system was set up using transponders already available on the Gorizont satellites used for Intersputnik. (See below, pp. 131–133.) This additional system, called Moskva, uses a 40-watt transmitter to serve small antennas (2.5 meters in diameter).[9]

The Statsionar system consists of eleven geostationary satellites (the Gorizont, Raduga, and Ekran spacecraft) and several Molniya satellites in polar orbit. The Gorizont spacecraft are used for domestic and Intersputnik television distribution, international television exchanges, radio transmission, telephony, and data services. The Raduga satellites have much lower power, and are believed to be used primarily for domestic telephony. The Ekran satellite transmits domestic radio and television to Siberia, while the Molniya satellites are used for broadcasting and telecommunications to the high Arctic.[10]

Intersputnik

Intersputnik is the international satellite system established by socialist and communist countries. These countries did not join Intelsat initially because they felt that U.S. influence would be too strong, as Comsat then controlled more than 53 percent of the shares (see chapter 3). However, the origins of Intersputnik lie in the Khrushchev era, predating Intelsat. In 1959, some basic proposals for a cosmic retransmitter of television programs were written into the Soviet seven-year plan. In 1961, the president of the Soviet Academy of Sciences noted that high priority was being given to space communications in Soviet policy, apparently referring to the current emphasis on television over point-to-point communications. In April 1965, Premier Aleksey Kosygin proposed that socialist states collaborate on "long-distance radio communications and television."[11]

The first draft of Intersputnik's constitution emerged in 1968; the Soviets formally announced their intent to set up Intersputnik at the United Nations Conference on Outer Space in Vienna in August 1969. (By this time, Intelsat already had sixty-three members.) The agreement was signed in Moscow in 1971 and went into force in July 1972.

Intersputnik currently operates eighteen earth stations in seventeen countries. It has fourteen members, with nine other countries using the system. The current members are Afghanistan, Bulgaria, Cuba, Czechoslovakia, East Germany, Hungary, North Korea, Laos, Poland, Romania, Vietnam, the People's Democratic Republic of Yemen, and the U.S.S.R. Other countries served by Intersputnik include Algeria, Angola, Ethiopia, Iraq, Kampuchea (Cambodia), Libya, Mozambique, Nicaragua, and Sri Lanka.[12]

The main organ of Intersputnik is its board, which consists of one representative from each member state. Each representative has one vote. The executive and administrative body is the Directorate headed by the Director General, who is appointed by the Board for a four-year term. The Board also appoints the Deputy Director General and a three-member auditing committee, and must approve structural, operational, and financial activities and set tariffs. Unanimity is preferred, but a two-thirds vote is binding. A member stating objections in writing is not bound by a decision taken. Member countries are free to establish their own domestic systems or to participate in regional or other international satellites (no coordination is required as under Intelsat's Article XIV(d); see chapter 10). Afghanistan, for example, is a member of both Intelsat and Intersputnik. Most of the nonmember users of Intersputnik are members of Intelsat.

In principle, Intersputnik is financed from a statutory fund made up of members' contributions on a pro rata basis. The size of each state's contribution is based on its utilization of the space segment, with profits distributed in the same proportion. However, the U.S.S.R. has so far paid the total costs of the space segment and has borne part of the costs of the earth segment for several countries (including Cuba, Laos, Mongolia, and Vietnam).[13] The only guidelines on procurement state: "Communication satellites owned by the organization shall be launched, put into orbit, and operated by members which possess appropriate facilities for this purpose on the basis of agreement between the organization and such members."[14] In practice, the Soviet Union is the only member which possesses such "appropriate facilities."

According to the Intergovernmental Agreement on the Establishment of Intersputnik, Intersputnik was to be implemented in three stages. First, the earth segment was designed and tested, and the U.S.S.R. donated satellite capacity on Molniya 1 satellites. Then Intersputnik leased capacity on Soviet Molniya 2 satellites. Finally, in 1975, Intersputnik acquired its own space segment. The organization now operates four geostationary Statsionar satellites, also known as Gorizont (Horizon). The only major inhabited parts of the Earth's surface not covered by Intersputnik systems are central and western North America.[15]

Intersputnik is used for program distribution from the U.S.S.R. and for exchange of programming among members (e.g., the Eastern bloc and Cuba). Intersputnik is now responsible for about 40 percent of the television transmissions by Intervision, the Eastern European television exchange system managed by the Organization of International Radio and Television (OIRT) in Prague. The system is also used to broadcast sports and games such as soccer, hockey, and even chess. The 1980 Moscow Olympics catalyzed the expansion of television facilities overseas, for example in Cuba, Afghanistan, and Vietnam.[16]

The Role of Intersputnik

Intersputnik was founded as an alternative to Intelsat but appears to serve a more limited function. First, its membership consists only of

Eastern bloc and a handful of developing countries; a few developing countries (such as Algeria and Nicaragua) are users of Intersputnik but members of Intelsat. Second, the system's capacity appears to be devoted primarily to television transmission, as is the Molniya domestic system. The emphasis on television may reflect importance the Soviets attach to disseminating official information in communist countries rather than facilitating the exchange of information among individuals and organizations, a function more prevalent in democratic societies and market-oriented economies.

For developing countries, Soviet television as distributed through Intersputnik may serve other purposes besides providing access to information age technology. The Soviet Union's offer of technology and access to Intersputnik has both practical and symbolic value. Its transmissions of Soviet space flights not only showcase Soviet technological advances but also demonstrate Soviet commitment to Third World participation, in the form of Soviet cosmonaut teams that have included the first Latin American and black in space, as well as the first Mongolian, Vietnamese, and Indian cosmonauts.[17]

However, Soviet and Eastern bloc television has proved less interesting to Westerners than has U.S. and Western European television to the Soviet bloc. In one recent year Intervision took 5,440 of 6,410 items offered by the West's Eurovision; Eurovision took only 425 of 5,395 offered by Intervision.[18]

A Window on the Soviet Union

An unforeseen benefit of Soviet satellites has been the opportunity for Westerners to view Soviet domestic television. The highly inclined polar orbits of the Molniya satellites provide an acceptable signal in Europe and parts of North America. U.S. hobbyists first developed tracking antennas and signal converters to receive and process the Soviet domestic signals; Molniya receiving stations have now been installed by U.S. government agencies and several universities.

The reception of Soviet television has provided a window on the Soviet Union for outsiders. Students view the programs to study the Russian language and learn about Russian and other Soviet cultures. Government analysts and the Western news media follow Soviet coverage of major news stories, such as the Chernobyl nuclear disaster and the Armenian earthquake, and political events, such as visits by Western heads of state to Moscow. The advent of "glasnost" has widened the view from the window dramatically. However, the unspoken message of the medium may have even greater impact: "The view through this window goes right to the spine. The medium's most vivid 'message' bypasses reason and cognition: it is that people are people."[19]

Other International Activities

Satellites also play a role in superpower "hot line" communications. In 1971, Soviet and U.S. officials signed an agreement to replace the transatlantic cable and high-frequency "hot line" established after the Cuban missile crisis with a redundant satellite network. Two systems were used: an Intersputnik link between Fort Detrick, Maryland, and Vladimir, U.S.S.R., and an Intelsat link between Etam, West Virginia, and a station near Moscow.[20]

The Soviet Union is an active participant in several other international satellite organizations. It has a 14 percent share in Inmarsat, the forty-member maritime navigation satellite agency established in 1979, in which the United States has a 23 percent stake. Through Morflot (the Soviet Merchant Marine Ministry), the U.S.S.R. is a member of Cospas-Sarsat, a satellite system designed for maritime and other emergencies and rescue operations. Other participants are NASA, France's Centre Nationale des Etudes Spatiales (CNES) and Canada's Department of Communications.

AUSTRALIA: THE OUTBACK, MEDIA BARONS, AND TURF BATTLES

The Need for a Satellite

In terms of size and population distribution, Australia is similar to Canada. About 80 percent of Australia's 14.5 million inhabitants live along its eastern and southeastern coast. The rest live in a few cities and large towns, or are scattered over isolated farms, sheep stations, and aboriginal settlements. About 300,000 live in rural regions outside the coverage areas of the national broadcasting stations and conventional telecommunications. A further one million were unable to receive satisfactory signals from the Australian Broadcasting Corporation's (ABC) radio and television services before the introduction of the Australian domestic satellite, Aussat.[21]

Some Australian communication experts recognized in the mid-1970s that satellites offered major advantages over terrestrial technologies for reaching the isolated towns, homesteads, and aboriginal settlements of Australia's Outback. However, the decisions not only about whether to procure a satellite but also about who should own it and what services it should provide were widely debated, and influenced not only by government policies but by the telecommunications and broadcasting establishment.

Aussat Proprietary Ltd. was established in 1981 to procure, own, and operate a domestic satellite system. Aussat is now owned 75 percent by the Australian government and 25 percent by Telecom Australia, the operator of the national telecommunications system. The first generation of Aussat satellites was built by Hughes Aircraft, and closely resembles the SBS satellites and Canada's Anik C. Aussat 1 and 2 were launched in 1985, followed by Aussat 3 (the original on-ground spare) in August 1987. Each satellite has eleven 12-watt transponders and four 30-watt transponders, all using Ku-band frequencies.[22]

Aussat services include

- program feeds for the commercial television networks (seven 12-watt transponders)
- program feeds for the ABC (five 12-watt transponders)
- Homestead and Community Broadcasting Satellite Service (HACBSS), which provides direct reception of ABC radio and television to people beyond the reach of terrestrial transmitters or in areas of difficult or partial reception. HACBSS uses four 30-watt transponders operating four contiguous spot beams to provide high-power coverage for reception by small 1.2–1.5-meter antennas. HACBSS services are transmitted from the state capital of each region. Communities may also form cooperatives to purchase larger antennas, and use coaxial cable or low-power transmitters for rebroadcasting.
- remote commercial television service (RCTS), a commercial version of HACBSS. One commercial license has been granted to each region.
- distance education by the Special Broadcasting Service (two transponders)
- long-distance telephony
- business services such as teleconferencing and data communications.
- telecommunications and broadcasting services for Papua New Guinea.[23]

Background

By the early 1970s, the government department which had originally operated Australia's telecommunications had made substantial investments in the public switched network, which boasts the world's longest continuous microwave link (from Adelaide to Perth), and was firmly committed to terrestrial technology.[24] Telecom Australia, the statutory authority that was established to replace the government department in 1975, continued to maintain that a domestic satellite system was not economically justified.

In 1977, media owner Kerry Packer approached Prime Minister Malcolm Fraser with a proposal to launch a domestic satellite for television distribution. A report prepared by a Canadian consultant recommended a domestic C-band system. The government then established a task force headed by the general manager of Overseas Telecom Australia (OTC), the operator of international telecommunications services and Australia's Intelsat signatory. OTC considered itself a rival of its sister agency Telecom Australia and had guarded its autonomy when Telecom was established.

The task force proposed a higher-powered, multifrequency satellite. Finally, an interdepartmental committee established by the minister of post and telecommunications recommended a third option, an all-Ku-band system. Ku-band had the disadvantage of significant rain attenuation, a problem in rainy tropical areas, but would not require coordination with Telecom's existing terrestrial microwave systems. This last proposal was adopted, ensuring autonomy from Telecom. Because Aussat's senior management and much of its technical staff come from OTC, the rivalry with Telecom has continued. One of its consequences is that Aussat is not allowed to provide public telecommunications services, that is, interconnections with Telecom's public switched network. It can provide only private voice and data networks, as well as television.

Meanwhile the ABC was using Intelsat capacity leased by OTC to transmit television programs to rural and remote areas. As a side effect of this service, backyard antennas over a wide area of Southeast Asia and the South Pacific were able to pick up Australian television. This free access ended when the ABC switched to Aussat, which uses different frequencies, has a higher-powered and much more limited footprint, and adopted the encrypted B-MAC transmission system rather than the easily received PAL system.[25]

The Australian Labour Party, brought into power under Robert Hawke in 1983, considered cancelling Aussat but decided that such a decision would further alienate rural voters who typically supported the conservative opposition. The Hawke government chose not to allow Aussat to compete with Telecom, as the Fraser government had recommended, and to change the ownership mix from 49 percent government and 51 percent private sector, to 75 percent government and 25 percent Telecom.

Meanwhile, the networks realized that they could use the satellite to reach not only the small number of isolated rural Australians, but also at least 1.75 million viewers who lived just outside the range of the major metropolitan stations. The regional commercial broadcasters considered the satellite as a major threat to their government-sanctioned monopolies, which ensured substantial advertising revenue.[26] Rural broadcasters felt vulnerable to competition from metropolitan networks: 70 percent of their revenues, which came from national advertisers, might be lost to the networks if network coverage of their territory via satellite was permitted.

It took more than three years to find a formula allowing the networks access to the country while protecting the existence of the rural broadcasters. The Department of Communications concluded that rural television markets were too small to sustain three commercial competitors and decided to consolidate them into six larger markets of about one million subscribers each. Meanwhile, the Hawke government introduced media cross-ownership restrictions and limited any single proprietor's access to no more than 60 percent of Australia's viewers, precipitating a massive restructuring of commercial media in Australia in 1987.[27]

Services for the Outback

Faced with demands from rural Australians for access to more channels than those provided by the ABC, the Australian Broadcasting Tribunal decided to award a commercial franchise in each of the four regions where the ABC was to be distributed via a high-powered transponder direct to viewers. The most interesting case involved the Northern Territory. An aboriginal communication organization had started a radio station in Alice Springs to broadcast programming in aboriginal languages and to assist aboriginal people scattered in small settlements and on the land throughout the vast territory in obtaining improved communication services.

The organization applied for the Northern Territory television license, with support from Australian public broadcasters, in competition with a private consortium from Darwin. The aboriginal group's proposal for a television system called Imparja was accepted, and the decision to award Imparja the license was upheld on appeal from the Darwin applicant. Imparja, however, has limited resources for production and operation of the network. While it has received funding from various government sources, there is no ongoing government program for support of aboriginal communications as has been established for native communications in Canada.

Despite being publicized as the solution to the Outback's communication deficiencies, Aussat's role has been rather limited. The television redistribution services and HACBSS service will bring television to the most remote areas and an increased number of channels to less isolated rural viewers. However, Aussat has not been used to bring reliable two-way communications to unserved areas, particularly to aborigines. In many cases, the only access many aborigines have had to two-way communications was high-frequency radios operated by government agencies. Some time slots on these radios were donated for transmitting messages among aboriginal people, on what became called "chatter channels." Small earth stations, such as those used in Alaska and Northern Canada, or even less expensive VSATs now available with one or two channels of digital voice, appear to be ideally suited to the Outback's needs. However, as noted above, Aussat is not allowed to provide services that interconnect with the public switched network. Telecom Australia is committed to serving Outback settlements with terrestrial digital radio systems that are not yet fully deployed and are much more costly for remote areas than thin-route satellite installations.

Aussat, nonetheless, is the apparent successor to the high-frequency radios that brought the pioneering "School of the Air" to children on isolated homesteads for decades. Small earth stations can provide much higher-quality voice, as well as graphics and freeze-frame video. However, unlike the high-frequency radio network, which was a dedicated network that did not have to pay for its time, Aussat channels must be leased, and educators have complained about the increased costs of the transition to satellite service. Other educational institutions, including universities, have used the satellite for teleconferences and ongoing distance education.

A New Telecommunications Framework

The Australian government has recently completed a policy review in telecommunications, which has resulted in a new framework that will continue to authorize the existing carriers as the sole providers of basic network facilities and services, but will allow for competition in the provision and operation of value-added services and increase competition in terminal equipment. Telecom, OTC, and Aussat will each be free to participate in the value-added-services market and to compete with each other in this market. The opportunity now exists for Aussat to become a regional carrier, since the government has allowed it to extend its provision of private network facilities internationally to the limit of its present satellite footprint, that is, to Papua New Guinea and the Southwest Pacific.[28] Aussat and the other carriers have also been freed by new accountability procedures from some government constraints. The Australian government has further decided that Telecom's traditional PTT role as the primary regulator of telecommunications services is no longer appropriate, and has established a new regulator, the Australian Telecommunications Authority (Austel).[29]

It remains to be seen what impact these changes will have on Aussat's services and pricing. It is interesting to note that while competition was introduced in value-added services, no domestic competition in public voice and data services is yet allowed. Like Canada, Australia has decided that its national market is not large enough to tolerate competition without undermining cross-subsidies that help to keep rates affordable for rural and remote customers. It does appear that Aussat will be able to compete with Intelsat (and OTC) in the South Pacific as a provider of data and video services.

REGIONAL SERVICES

Aussat officials state that "although Aussat was conceived as a national satellite it has always had a regional orientation."[30] They point to the Memorandum of Understanding with Papua New Guinea (PNG) in 1982, authorizing PNG to access the system directly and to lease capacity from Aussat. They also note that the Aussat Board agreed in 1985 to modify Aussat 3 to provide better coverage of the Southwest Pacific, including New Zealand.[31] However, these facts ignore other evidence about the role of Aussat in the region. First, Aussat designers chose to use Ku-band frequencies rather than C-band, although Ku band is subject to severe rain attenuation in tropical regions such as the northern Australian coast, Papua New Guinea, and the South Pacific. (Problems of C-band interference with terrestrial microwave were cited, although the United States and

Canada, with much more extensive microwave networks, have several C-band satellites, and much of Australia has no terrestrial microwave. As noted above, the apparent reason for the choice was to avoid having to coordinate with Telecom Australia, which operates the terrestrial microwave.)

Australia has a strong political and economic (almost neocolonial) interest in Papua New Guinea,[32] and apparently wanted to include coverage of PNG on Aussat. The Memorandum of Understanding was signed before PNG even had television or had adopted any national policy concerning the introduction of television. Aussat has been used to deliver commercial Australian television to Papua New Guinea, but there appears to have been little use of the satellite for rural telephony, despite the limited availability of telephone service and the impenetrability of the jungles and mountains in many parts of PNG.

Although PNG was not clamoring for satellite service, there was considerable interest in the South Pacific in Aussat as a means of linking isolated islands. While Aussat 1 was in the early stages of construction by Hughes, the University of the South Pacific (USP) approached Aussat to provide an audio teleconferencing network to link its extension centers in ten island nations and territories. Based in Fiji, USP had been using NASA's experimental ATS-1 satellite for a decade and was looking for a permanent solution to its needs for voice and data links with its extension centers. However, Aussat management refused to reconfigure the satellite or move its unused Papua New Guinea beam to cover the South Pacific. USP has since negotiated with the carriers in its region to use Intelsat through their existing Intelsat earth stations (see chapter 10).

Lessons from Australia

It is too early to assess the impact of Aussat in improving Australian telecommunications and influencing the structure and priorities of Australian communications entities. While Aussat has made possible the delivery of voice, data, and video services virtually anywhere in the country and the region, Australians have not so far benefited fully from its potential: "In telecommunications, the existence of a satellite system has not fulfilled the promise of telephone services in remote areas, although it has accelerated pressure for deregulating the national carrier. And in television broadcasting, a tortuous policy-making process has still not succeeded in delivering the programmes rural dwellers were told would end their isolation."[33] The reasons for these shortcomings lie not in the technology but in the conflicting mandates and power struggles among the influential players in Australia: Telecom and OTC, rural and metropolitan broadcasters, labour and conservative governments.

As in Canada, the satellite was promoted as a means of serving isolated regions, but they have not been major beneficiaries. However, the successful coalition of aborigines and public broadcasters in the Northern Territory shows that public pressure can succeed in changing priorities. The future of satellite services to the Outback will depend on the commitment of the national and state governments to fund aboriginal broadcasting and distance education, and of the newly formed Austel to require Aussat and Telecom to provide reliable and affordable telecommunications to all Australians.

JAPAN: THE TECHNOLOGICAL IMPERATIVE

The Japanese Communications Environment

Japanese broadcasting includes both publicly supported and privately owned networks. The public network, NHK, is funded through a license fee system and is required to provide high-quality diversified programming and to contribute to the national culture. Its two television networks, the General Channel and Educational Channel, are available to almost all of Japan's thirty-eight million households. There are five commercial networks, which were originally licensed to cover specific prefectures but are now based in the Tokyo area.[34] New media are thus not likely to be introduced on the grounds of offering new content, as several content choices are already available, and the pool of additional indigenous talent capable of producing new programming is limited. Perhaps for this reason, cable television penetration is low, reaching only 13 percent of Japanese households.[35]

The Japanese telecommunications sector was opened to competition in 1985. Several competitors for domestic communications have proposed satellite systems. One of these is the Japanese Satellite Communications Corporation (JSC), a joint venture of C. Itoh, Mitsui, and Hughes Aircraft. Another is the Space Communications Company (SCC), owned by Mitsubishi. Both groups are advancing multipurpose satellites that can carry telecommunications and television traffic. The satellite operators predict that their main source of revenues in the early years will be from video services, that is, distribution of television to cable systems or to TVROs of 1 to 1.5 meters in diameter, and from satellite news gathering and video feeds. It should be noted that satellites are already being used to feed television programs to cable systems in Japan by Satellite Video Services, a commercial satellite venture started in 1985.[36]

Japanese Experimental Satellites

Despite recent investments in commercial satellites, most of Japan's satellite activities have been sponsored by the government. Japan's first satellite, a vehicle for meteorological research, was launched by NASA in 1977. Later that year, its first communication satellite, CS-1A, or Sakura (cherry blossom), was launched; Sakura was built by a consortium of Mitsubishi and Ford Aerospace, with transponders provided by Ford and Nippon Electric Company (NEC). CS-1A and CS-1B were experimental satellites with six Ka-band and two C-band transponders and a design life of three years. The Experimental Communication Satellites (ECS) were launched from 1979 to 1982. ECS-1 and ECS-2 were lost due to failure of the apogee kick motor and rocket, respectively. ECS-3 and ECS-4 were used to conduct technical experiments. ETS-5, launched in 1987, is an experimental mobile system using L band (1.5/1.6 GHz).[37] A 2-ton ETS-6 satellite is scheduled to be launched in 1992 on the H-2 launcher, Japan's first domestically built launcher, which is to be used for launching satellites for other countries.

Japan began experimenting with direct-broadcasting technology with the launch of an experimental satellite, BSE, in 1978. The Ministry of Posts and Telecommunications (MPT) took the initiative for the project and guided its development. Japan's National Space Development Agency (NASDA) built the satellite, while MPT built the operational control center and main earth station. NHK was responsible for the construction of the transportable transmitting and receiving stations and the receive-only stations. BSE was launched by a NASA Delta rocket in 1978 and was used for a variety of technical experiments.

The Transition to Operational Satellites

In 1983, the second generation of communication satellites, CS-2A and CS-2B, was launched by NASDA. These satellites, which are designed to provide basic communications to Japan's remote islands, are to be followed by a third generation (CS-3A and CS-3B). The first commercial satellites to use Ka-Band, they have the capacity for 4,000 two-way telephone circuits. Their applications include basic communication links between main and remote islands, emergency communications links for Nippon Telephone and Telegraph (NTT), and digital services, such as facsimile, data transmission, and teleconferencing.[38]

In 1984, NASDA launched the world's first operational direct-broadcasting satellite, BS-2A, or Yuri (lily), from its Tanegashima Space Center. Two of Yuri's three transponders failed shortly after launch. A replacement satellite, BS-2B, was launched in 1986.[39] Its signals can be received using small (.75–1 meter) antennas. BS-2A was used primarily to relay NHK signals to inaccessible mountainous areas and outer islands, and occasionally for news feeds from transportable uplinks, such as following the earthquake in Nagano prefecture in August 1984 and the crash of the Japan Airlines jumbo jet in August 1985.[40] On one transponder BS-2B now carries a mixture of programs from the General and Educational Channel and on the second one, a 24-hour international channel, carrying CNN news fed by Intelsat from the United States, news from SuperChannel and the BBC, business information, sports, entertainment, and music.[41]

NHK has also carried out several experiments on BS-2B that may indicate future directions for broadcasting satellites in Japan. HDTV has been demonstrated using the MUSE signal-reduction system, and has been promoted to the public through fairs and demonstrations. Multichannel pulse code modulation (PCM) sound-broadcasting experiments will provide data to facilitate the establishment of technical standards permitting twelve to sixteen channels of stereo sound broadcasting to be carried on one television channel. Encryption systems are being tested for eventual introduction on pay-television services, as are data-broadcasting techniques for multiplexing onto the data channel of the sound PCM signal.[42]

Two satellites in the BS-3 series, the second generation of operational satellites, are planned for launch in 1990 and 1991. NEC is the prime contractor, with General Electric's RCA Astro Electronics a subcontractor. BS-3 will have only three channels, two for NHK simultaneous broadcasts and the third for Japan Satellite Broadcasting (JSB), a commercial venture. JSB, a consortium of fourteen companies that initially applied individually for the license to run the private satellite service, appears to be particularly interested in subscription or pay TV.[43]

Satellites: Part of a Global Japanese Industrial Strategy?

While the new competition in domestic telecommunications is attract-ing private-sector investment in satellites, the government continues to play a major role. The satellites that Japan calls "operational" are still largely used for experimental rather than commercial operations. For example, both the Ministry of Posts and Telecommunications and NHK are committed to DBS; they jointly funded the current DBS-service BS-2 and will support BS-3. However, their goals cannot be simply to extend existing service or to distribute new content. NHK will use the satellite to reach only 400,000 homes on outlying islands without television service.

One major reason for their interest may be high definition televi-sion (HDTV). "The key to the future success of satellite broadcast-ing—and an important means by which to increase its popularity—is the development of HDTV."[44] At present it would be technically and economically difficult to introduce HDTV because of the limited capacity of terrestrial networks. But an important feature of satellites is that they have sufficient bandwidth for delivery of HDTV. However, lower-cost receivers and attractive program offerings will be neces-sary to develop a market for satellite-delivered HDTV.

Given the potential global market for HDTV, the statement above might be reversed: the key to the future of HDTV may be satellite broadcasting. As noted, satellites have the bandwidth that is needed for distribution of HDTV, either directly to households or to coaxial cable and optical-fiber local networks. By investing in DBS, the Japa-nese will have the means of delivering HDTV programming to their domestic market. But Japanese companies see a global market for HDTV, and are rushing to get their technology to U.S. consumers in order to preempt systems developed by U.S. and European manufac-turers. Thus DBS will enable the Japanese to be the first with HDTV delivery and to build on their domestic experience in their attempt to dominate the world market.

Another element in Japan's global strategy appears to be the devel-opment of satellite-construction and -launching capabilities. By the early 1990s Japan will be able to both build and launch a wide range of communication satellites, and will probably become a formidable competitor of the United States and Europe. Japanese companies are already major suppliers of earth stations, ranging from Intelsat Stan-dard A terminals to the smallest VSATs. With the strength of the

Japanese electronics and telecommunications industries, Japanese companies will soon be able to offer a complete range of satellite communications products and services from the satellite itself to earth stations, teleconferencing facilities, and television and telephone equipment.

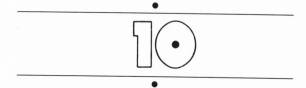

Intelsat Today

THE EVOLUTION OF INTELSAT

From the original twenty-three signatories, Intelsat's membership has grown to 114 nations, more than 80 percent of which are developing countries. Its thirteen operational satellites are used by 172 countries, territories, and dependencies.[1] Intelsat's traffic growth has far outpaced its increase in membership. In 1987, full-time international traffic carried by Intelsat reached a level of more than 100,000 derived channels, double the number carried in 1981, and almost 700 times the 150 channels carried in 1965, Intelsat's first year of operation.[2] Capacity has also increased: Early Bird (Intelsat I) had 240 telephone circuits; Intelsat VI has the capacity for 40,000 voice circuits, or more than 200 television channels (the equivalent of three billion bits of information per second).[3]

The Intelsat 1988 Annual Report states: "The goal today and in the future is the same as when Intelsat was established in 1964: to provide reliable, expanded, and cost-effective communications services to all nations, on a non-discriminatory basis, which will contribute to world peace and understanding."[4] Faced with the growth in its developing country membership and the United States' policy shift toward advocating international competition, Intelsat has had to reaffirm in recent years its commitment to goals that were established largely by the United States when it took the lead in founding Intelsat in the 1960s (see chapter 3).*

---

*It is ironic that the words in the annual report are attributed to Dean Burch, a former FCC chairman in the Nixon era and a conservative who has been a strong supporter of the role of the private sector and the marketplace in telecommunications.

This chapter examines Intelsat and its legacy a quarter century after it was founded. Intelsat has grown dramatically, but faces competition both from new satellite systems that are after a share of the international market and from new technologies, particularly optical fiber. In response, it has introduced a variety of technological innovations and new services. But what effects might be attributed to the global network that Intelsat has created? The globalization of television may be its most notable contribution to the international telecommunications environment. However, Intelsat will also contribute to the globalization of information work.

INTELSAT'S ORGANIZATIONAL STRUCTURE

As established in the Definitive Agreements, Intelsat has a four-tier structure consisting of the Assembly of Parties, the Meeting of Signatories, the Board of Governors, and the Executive Organ. The Assembly of Parties is composed of representatives of governments of Intelsat member countries (parties to the agreement) and normally meets every two years to consider resolutions and recommendations on general policy and long-term objectives. The Meeting of Signatories consists of representatives of signatories to the Operating Agreement (member governments or their designated telecommunications authorities) and generally meets once a year to consider issues related to the financial, technical, and operational aspects of the system.

The real power of the organization is vested in the Board of Governors, composed of representatives of signatories whose investment shares either individually or as a group meet or exceed the minimum share for membership on the board (currently set at 1.330618 percent). Two or more members may combine investment shares to meet the minimum for membership and be represented by one governor on the board. In addition, groups of five or more signatories within an ITU region may be represented by one governor provided that there are not more than two of the groups from any one region or more than five governors for all of the ITU regions. In 1988, there were twenty-eight governors representing 105 of the 114 signatories.[5] The board normally meets four times per year.

The Executive Organ, which is responsible for management and operations, is headed by the director general, who is the chief executive and reports directly to the Board of Governors. The current director general is Dean Burch of the United States. Intelsat staff are drawn from fifty-eight countries.

Intelsat operates as a financial cooperative, with ownership shared among the members in proportion to their use of the system (adjusted on an annual basis). The investment share determines each signatory's percentage of the total contribution required to finance capital expenditures and the portion of net revenues it receives. After deduction of operating costs, revenues are distributed to the signatories in proportion to their investment share as repayment of capital and compensation for use of capital (at a rate of 13.5 percent in 1987).[6] This rate of return is somewhat higher than that generally allowed by U.S. regulatory commissions for U.S. common carriers.

It should be noted that Intelsat is not regulated or overseen by any external authority. There is no mechanism for external analysis of costs, tariffs, internal cross-subsidies, and the like. Critics have argued that Intelsat's costs are higher than necessary because of overcapacity and unrealistically high projections of traffic growth. Competitors such as PanAmSat have contended that Intelsat is cross-subsidizing such new offerings as domestic transponder sales with revenues from other services. Intelsat denies these allegations, but is not required to make public any documentation of its costs and rate-setting procedures.

THE ROLE OF DEVELOPING COUNTRIES IN INTELSAT

At first glance, Intelsat's developing country members would appear to be in a position to dictate the organization's goals and priorities if they chose to do so, since they represent more than 80 percent of the membership. Indeed, Intelsat has emphasized the concerns of its Third World members in its recent efforts to stave off competition: "it is Intelsat's special duty and obligation to promote the cause of communication development that distinguishes Intelsat in a substantive and important way from U.S. entrepreneurs who are promising private transoceanic satellite systems."[7]

However, several other factors must be taken into consideration. First, the real power of Intelsat lies in the Board of Governors, where voting is weighted by usage. The OECD countries together control 70.27 percent of the shares, with the four largest users (the United States, the United Kingdom, Japan, France, and Germany) together controlling 53.16 percent (see table 10–1). Thus any change in policy

Table 10–1 Investment Shares of Intelsat Membership (1988)

OECD countries' investment share (70.27%)					
Australia	2.95	Greece	0.69	Norway	0.33
Austria	0.33	Iceland	0.18	Portugal	0.50
Belgium	0.69	Ireland	0.13	Spain	1.84
Canada	2.75	Italy	2.24	Sweden	0.64
Denmark	0.49	Japan	4.71	Switzerland	1.09
Finland	0.16	Luxembourg	0.05	Turkey	0.23
France	4.21	Netherlands	1.11	United Kingdom	14.21
West Germany	3.61	New Zealand	0.72	United States	26.42

Non-OECD countries' investment share (29.73%)					
Afghanistan	0.05	Haiti	0.16	Paraguay	0.11
Algeria	0.25	Honduras	0.05	Peru	0.56
Angola	0.11	India	1.22	Philippines	0.64
Argentina	1.01	Indonesia	0.38	Qatar	0.25
Bahamas	0.05	Iran	0.72	Rwanda	0.05
Bangladesh	0.17	Iraq	0.30	Saudi Arabia	1.54
Barbados	0.05	Israel	0.66	Senegal	0.05
Benin	0.05	Jamaica	0.38	Singapore	1.21
Bolivia	0.12	Jordan	0.30	Somalia	0.05
Brazil	1.29	Kenya	0.40	South Africa	1.15
Burkina Faso	0.05	Korea (Rep. of)	1.32	Sri Lanka	0.05
Cameroon	0.24	Kuwait	0.77	Sudan	0.19
Central African		Lebanon	0.13	Syria	0.12
Rep.	0.05	Libya	0.15	Tanzania	0.08
Chad	0.05	Liechtenstein	0.05	Thailand	0.58
Chile	0.58	Madagascar	0.05	Togo	0.05
China	1.54	Malaysia	0.70	Trinidad and	
Colombia	1.18	Mali	0.09	Tobago	0.05
Congo	0.05	Malawi	0.14	Tunisia	0.05
Costa Rica	0.05	Mauritania	0.05	Uganda	0.06
Côte d'Ivoire	0.26	Mexico	0.60	United Arab	
Cyprus	0.19	Monaco	0.05	Emirates	1.36
Dominican Rep.	0.10	Morocco	0.18	Uruguay	0.05
Ecuador	0.35	Nicaragua	0.05	Vatican	0.05
Egypt	0.70	Niger	0.05	Venezuela	1.00
El Salvador	0.05	Nigeria	0.97	Vietnam	0.05
Ethiopia	0.07	Oman	0.24	Yemen Arab Rep.	0.11
Fiji	0.05	Pakistan	0.39	Yugoslavia	0.20
Gabon	0.05	Panama	0.05	Zaire	0.24
Ghana	0.05	Papua		Zambia	0.13
Guatemala	0.05	New Guinea	0.05		
Guinea	0.05				

SOURCE: Intelsat Annual Report, 1987–88.

requires the endorsement of several of these countries. Developing country members' shares range from 1.54 percent for China and Saudi Arabia to .05 percent (the smallest unit allocated) for the users such as Gabon, Niger, Sri Lanka, and Papua New Guinea.[8] The developing countries themselves should not necessarily be considered a unified bloc. Some, including Indonesia, Brazil, India, Mexico, and the Arab states, now have their own satellites and may therefore not share the concerns of those who rely on Intelsat for domestic as well as international communication.

In addition, Third World countries are at widely varying stages of development, so that the needs of Thailand, for example, may differ greatly from those of Tanzania, and Singapore from the Sudan. Of course, industrialized countries may also not all share the same views; issues such as competition have placed the United States and, to a lesser extent, the United Kingdom at odds with France and West Germany, whose public telecommunications sectors operate as monopolies. Since most developing countries have adopted the European government-run PTT model for their telecommunications authorities, they tend to support policies that preserve the public sector monopoly.

One program designed specifically for developing countries was Project SHARE (Satellites for Health and Rural Education), which was announced in August 1964 as part of Intelsat's twentieth anniversary celebration ceremonies. Intelsat offered to provide free satellite time for health and education purposes; users had to provide their own earth-station facilities and support for the projects. The project's activities involved sixty-five countries on five continents. An analysis of Project SHARE is included in the case studies of developing countries' use of satellites in chapter 13.

CHANGES IN SATELLITE TECHNOLOGY

The Intelsat V series were built by Ford Aerospace, which also won the contract for the Intelsat VII series. The Intelsat VI series is being built by Hughes Aircraft, which built the previous generations all the way back to Early Bird (Intelsat I). While the early satellites were virtually exclusively U.S. products, the more recent projects include subcontractors from several Intelsat signatories (primarily European, with some Japanese participation), in response to pressures from these industrialized countries. From the founding of Intelsat, the

Western European members have expressed concern that the U.S. technological lead in satellites could make it difficult for other countries ever to compete successfully on procurements.

Recent satellites have been modified to provide higher power or more flexibility, to allow the use of smaller earth stations, and to make more domestic services available for developing countries. The Intelsat V-A is a modified version of the Intelsat V, with three more cross-polarized spot beams at 6/4 gigahertz for domestic leased services. Extended spot-beam coverage allows provision of business service over North America and a 4-gigahertz spot beam that can be reoriented to South America. All five Intelsat VI spacecraft are being modified for higher power in the 14/11-gigahertz band to promote the use of small earth stations.[9]

Users access Intelsat satellites through 660 sites containing 676 earth stations antennas.[10] Intelsat has in recent years introduced several new earth-station standards to facilitate provision of new services. They include the D series for Intelnet services, the E and F series for Intelsat Business Services (Ku and C band), G series for international lease services, and the Z series for domestic lease services.[11] In the early years, only the Standard A series (then 30 meters in diameter and costing several millions of dollars) could be used with Intelsat. The B series (10 to 13 meters in diameter) was introduced in the 1970s for smaller developing countries and others with more modest traffic requirements. The C series was introduced for international services using Ku band.

INTELSAT SERVICES

International telephony remains the backbone of Intelsat's operations, with 69 percent of Intelsat's revenues derived from full-time analog service in 1987. However, 25.9 percent of Intelsat revenues are now from digital, broadcast, and domestic services, compared to 15.5 percent five years ago. These services grew 26 percent in 1987 compared to only 0.3 percent for analog international telephony.[12]

Television Distribution

Intelsat's television transmission facilities are used for program distribution, news coverage, sporting events, entertainment programs, video conferencing, and direct broadcast services. International television services are provided through full-time leased transponders and occasional-use leases. Examples of occasional-use applications are coverage of special sporting events, such as the Olympics, Wimbledon tennis, and World's Cup soccer, and transmission of major news events, such as the ouster of Ferdinand Marcos in the Philippines, the funeral of Indira Gandhi, and the Reagan-Gorbachev summit. International teleconferences, or "space bridges," link groups in several countries to promote international understanding. Multisatellite hookups have been used to raise funds to fight famine and disease, as in the Live Aid concerts and other globally shared events.

Several television networks lease transponders for daily transmissions. CNN now transmits its news channel to Europe and Japan; U.S. networks feed programming to Australia; Japanese television is available on cable systems in New York; and U.S. networks use regular feeds from Europe. The U.S. Armed Forces distribute their Armed Forces TV Network package to U.S. bases around the world via Intelsat.

Television distribution is the fastest growing Intelsat service. Among the new television services offered are:

- digital television, which has compatibility with evolving improvements in TV quality and studio equipment;
- integrated quality digital TV, which combines video, audio, radio, and printed information transmissions on one transponder at Ku band; and
- cross-strapped international TV, which allows cable TV reception with small Ku-band antennas using existing C-band uplinks.[13]

International Business Service

Intelsat Business Service (IBS) is an integrated digital system designed to carry a full range of services including voice, data, and video. IBS enables antennas to be located on or near end-user premises and in major cities, providing direct satellite access and minimizing dependence on terrestrial switched networks. Use of IBS has increased more than ten times, growing from 323 to 4,382 channels since 1985.[14] IBS users are generally large multinational corporations. For example, Ford communicates directly between its headquarters near Detroit and its installations in the United Kingdom. Hewlett Packard uses IBS to communicate between Palo Alto, California, and operations in Europe and Asia. India's first IBS station was installed for Texas Instruments in Bangalore, where it transmits software developed by Indian engineers directly to TI headquarters in Texas.

Intelnet

The Intelnet service was designed for low-volume data transmission to VSATs, or "microterminals," operating through a central hub terminal. The system uses spread-spectrum techniques that eliminate interference even in urban areas with severe microwave congestion. Applications include dissemination of wire service copy, stock market data, and weather reports to receivers scattered over an area as large as one-third of the Earth's surface. The Intelnet I data-broadcasting service is used by Reuters to transmit its news service to Latin America and by China's Xinhua News Agency. The Intelnet II service uses slightly larger terminals and can send as well as receive data. India's National Informatics Centre has set up an Intelnet network known as Nicnet to transmit data from regional offices to its headquarters.

Vista

Vista provides telecommunications services such as voice and low-speed data transmission to rural and remote communities, and can be used for both domestic and international links. Small earth stations with antennas measuring 5 meters in diameter or less are designed to provide thin-route voice and telegraph-telex service in developing regions.[15] Super Vista is available to Vista networks under the control of a Demand Assigned Multiple Access (DAMA) system, and is tariffed at lower per channel unit rates than basic Vista to reflect the more efficient utilization of the Intelsat space segment provided by the DAMA equipment.[16]

Vista networks were introduced in 1987 in Mauritius, Vietnam, and Equatorial Guinea, with a total of 144 channels in service in 1988. Intelsat has tried to "prime the pump" for production of low-cost Vista terminals (similar to those used in Alaska and northern Canada with domestic satellites) by contracting with a manufacturer to produce a number of units to be available at a low-volume discount. These units are being manufactured by Scientific Atlanta. During 1987, three countries ordered up to twenty-two Vista terminals under the volume discount plan.

Vista service has been very slow to take off, despite the evidence of enormous demand for communications in developing countries, most of which still need to provide basic telephony in rural areas and have very little terrestrial infrastructure. The reasons reflect the many problems of increasing investment in telecommunications in developing countries which are discussed in chapter 11. One problem is to convince manufacturers that there is sufficient demand for the technology to justify building units in sufficient numbers to drive the price down to an acceptable level. A second problem is that many developing country officials give higher priority to improving the more profitable interurban services and to meeting a backlog of urban demand than to extending basic services to rural areas. Rural telecommunications investments often receive lower government priority than other rural infrastructure programs such as roads, electrification, and water supplies.

Finally, Intelsat cannot market directly to potential users in developing countries, but must work through its signatories, which may have other priorities. Thus rural customers may not be aware that affordable telecommunications facilities could be made available and may not request service from their administrations. Intelsat in recent years has attempted to publicize Vista and other low-cost services through a Small Earth Station Symposium and Exhibition, held in 1987, which was attended by representatives from more than seventy-five countries, and through demonstrations, including Project SHARE and Project Access (discussed below). However, demand for these services has remained low.

Domestic Services

Intelsat was formed to provide international satellite communication, that is, links between nations. However, it has also been used to provide domestic communications in countries where terrestrial facilities are unavailable or prohibitively expensive to construct. Intelsat began offering domestic service at the instigation of Algeria in 1976. Algeria negotiated a reduced rate for a preemptible transponder on a backup satellite, which theoretically could have been taken over by Intelsat to maintain service for full-rate customers if satellite problems caused any interruption in their service. However, none of the reduced-rate domestic transponders has ever preempted. At present, nineteen countries, of which fifteen are developing countries, lease transponders from Intelsat for domestic service.[17] (See table 10–2.) Other countries with domestic leases include Denmark (for Greenland), New Zealand, South Africa, and Spain.

Planned Domestic Service (PDS) was introduced in 1985 to enable member and user countries to lease or purchase transponders on a nonpreemptible basis for domestic communications. By the end of

Table 10–2 Developing Countries with Intelsat Domestic Leases

	GNP Per Capita (1986) (Dollars)	Telephone Density (1986) (Per 100 people)
Algeria	2,590	*
Argentina	2,350	8.6
Brazil	1,810	5.3
Chile	1,320	4.4
China	300	0.3
Colombia	1,230	6.3
Côte d'Ivoire	730	*
India	290	0.5
Indonesia	490	0.4
Libya	7,170[†]	0.5
Malaysia	1,830	6.1
Mexico	1,860	4.6
Morocco	590	1.1
Mozambique	210	*
Nigeria	640	*
Sudan	320	0.3
Thailand	810	1.2
Venezuela	2,920	9.1
Zaire	160	*

SOURCES: AT&T, *The World's Telephones* (1986); World Bank, *World Development Report* (1988).
*Nonreporting country.
[†]1985 data.

1987, forty-seven transponders had been sold to fifteen different signatories for more than $108 million. The Board of Governors decided in 1987 to continue the PDS program on Intelsat VI and follow-on spacecraft. PDS, coupled with the design of Intelsat VI spacecraft to include higher-power beams for domestic use, appears to be part of Intelsat's strategy to corner the market for supplying domestic services to countries that could benefit from satellite services but cannot afford or do not need dedicated satellites. PDS's timing coincides with the announcement of plans by PanAmSat to offer domestic services for Latin American countries. PanAmSat has charged that Intelsat tariffs for transponder purchase are set below cost. Although Intelsat documentation states that transponders may be purchased for $3 million to $5 million,[18] the average price per transponder of sales to date as derived from Intelsat's annual report is just $2.3 million.

Intelsat has also introduced Transborder Video Service for PDS customers to enable them to provide television coverage to neighboring countries. Intelsat states: "The service was designed to accommodate the inevitable spillover and desired international reception of domestic TV broadcast transmissions."[19]

Intelsat has more than 170 transponders available for lease or sale. Many of these are on the backup satellites required to provide full service redundancy for Intelsat customers. However, the amount of excess capacity is evidence that Intelsat's traffic growth forecasts have been overly optimistic, as the organization itself admits.

OTHER INTELSAT SERVICES

Temporary Communications

Intelsat has developed a 1.8-meter "flyaway" C-band earth station which can provide single voice channel service in remote areas.[20] In 1987, Intelsat introduced special temporary communications using transportable facilities for short-term or emergency requirements. The service is designed to provide voice and data links for emergency and disaster relief operations, diplomatic and state missions, and so on.[21] (Similar transportable facilities for video, such as satellite news gathering, are already in use.) However, aside from communications immediately following a natural disaster, it appears that Intelsat's facilities are generally not requested for ongoing disaster support efforts, such as coordinating relief aid to refugee camps and famine relief operations. Again, the problem appears to stem from institutional barriers posed by the PTTs between Intelsat and the relief organizations, many of which still rely on high-frequency radio in the field.

Caribnet

The Caribnet service was introduced in 1986 to meet the digital telecommunications needs of Caribbean countries through private networks. It offers a 50 percent reduction from Intelsat's IBS and Intelnet tariffs.[22] The cost justification for this price reduction is not specified. It appears that Intelsat has created a new service offering in order to justify pricing service for the Caribbean differently from other similar services. Without regulatory oversight, Intelsat is free to make such adjustments. In this case, the reason may be to preempt the loss of Caribbean traffic to U.S. domestic satellites that cover the region.

Broadband Digital Services

Intelsat also leases temporary satellite capacity for cable restoration after undersea cable failures, and will implement a special "cable in the sky" service, initially for the restoration of optical-fiber systems, that will transmit 40 megabits of data per second through a wideband transponder. At that rate, eight such transponders would be able to duplicate the capacity of the optical-fiber transatlantic TAT-8 cable. However, fiber may still take a sizable share of Intelsat's transatlantic and transpacific business. To compete with optical fiber, Intelsat revised its tariff structure in 1987 to encourage growth in its digital services and facilitate the transition from analog to digital technology. It plans to introduce ISDN (Integrated Services Digital Network) services that are globally interconnected.

New digital services include digital circuit-multiplication equipment (DCME) that will allow effective multiplication of Intelsat channels by four to six times, by concentrating telephone channels into a smaller number of transmission channels. Intelsat chose an open network approach to permit different manufacturers designing in accordance with the specifications to produce compatible equipment.[23] Intelsat also initiated the formation of the Satellite Coalition for ISDN—a working group composed of representatives including signatories, spacecraft manufacturers, and other satellite organizations—to generate cooperation in helping to make ISDN standards and satellite services fully compatible, and to ensure the recognition of the role of satellites in the implementation of global ISDN.[24]

THE INTELSAT LEGACY

The Globalization of Television

In 1964, the transmission of television coverage of the Tokyo Olympics across the Pacific via Syncom III was considered a technological marvel: "Live television coverage of this morning's opening of the Olympic Games in Tokyo was of superlative quality, a triumph of technology that was almost breathtaking in its implications for global communications. . . . The clarity and definition of the images from Japan were . . . nothing short of extraordinary."[25] Barely eight months later, the launch of Intelsat I, or Early Bird, heralded the age of television "live via satellite." Today, audiences for the Olympics and World's Cup exceed one billion people. The result of this growth in Intelsat television transmissions has been nothing less than the globalization of television.

In 1987, Intelsat satellites carried an average of 108 occasional video transmissions per day, and twenty-seven international video leases were in service.[26] Now there are at least twelve full-time international video networks, whereas there were none in 1982.[27] A number of transponder leases are for network feeds of news stories, special events, or programs for insertion in network broadcasts. Television networks now routinely carry on-the-spot coverage of breaking stories around the world, and daily coverage from their U.S. or European bureaus. The U.S. networks and Visnews lease transponders between the United States and the United Kingdom; Australian, French, and Japanese networks also lease transponders between the United States and their countries. Occasional transponder leases enable broadcasters to arrange coverage of special events. For example, for program feeds during the Gorbachev-Reagan summit in Washington, D.C., Intelsat carried 577 transmission hours of television on six satellites.

Intelsat is also used for satellite news gathering. The networks have begun to change their formats, and are originating more from outside the studio. For example, in February 1986, one American network's evening newscast originated in Moscow, a second originated in Washington, D.C., and a third in the Midwest. At the same time all three switched continually to their correspondents in Manila, where the Marcos regime continued to unravel.[28]

The greatest technical advance in live international coverage has been the emergence of very small, easily transportable earth terminals that range from 1.8 to 3 meters in diameter and fit in luggage-sized shipping crates. These terminals can access Intelsat directly. Two of the three U.S. networks used these transportable terminals to cover the Philippine elections and the fall of the Marcos regime from Manila (the third used a larger truck-mounted unit).[29] The networks fed their signal directly via an Intelsat Pacific Ocean satellite to Comsat's Santa Paula, California, earth station, and then via domestic satellite from a truck-mounted station hard-wired to the

Comsat station, to network headquarters in New York. Network officials said that the resulting picture was of higher quality than would have been achieved with terrestrial links, and that the direct satellite links gave them more flexibility for coverage than terrestrial systems or pooling with other networks on shared uplinks and transponders.[30]

Intelsat transponders are also used to distribute network programming, such as the U.S. Armed Forces Radio and TV Service, which is relayed to U.S. military bases around the world, including those in West Germany, Italy, Portugal, Iceland, South Korea, the Philippines, and Diego Garcia. CNN is now carried on some community and hotel cable systems in Western Europe and Japan. Australian networks carry U.S. television live late at night, as well as using U.S. programs and news stories in their regular schedules. The exchange flows east to west as well, as Japanese TV is now carried on a Manhattan cable system.

International radio broadcasters no longer have to cover the world via shortwave from their home country or via unreliable high-frequency relays. Broadcasters such as the Voice of America and the BBC also use Intelsat to distribute their radio programs to shortwave and medium-wave transmitters around the world.

One outcome of U.S. networks' use of Intelsat has been increased global dissemination of American programs. Australians watch American news and features. People living near U.S. bases watch American television carried by the Armed Forces Network. Even in areas far from U.S. bases, residents who want to watch U.S. television have installed their own earth stations to receive the Armed Forces Network. They are globalizing the backyard-antenna movement that began in Canada and spread to the Caribbean and Central America, as people installed their own earth stations to receive American channels from U.S. domestic satellites. This use of satellites appears to complement the phenomenal diffusion of VCRs, which have brought U.S. films and television programs to homes and hamlets all over the world. As discussed in the sections on Europe and developing countries, the demand for U.S. programming seems virtually insatiable. How increased access to this fare through satellites and VCRs will influence other nations' viewers and their broadcasting systems is still open to question. It appears that viewers remain loyal to their own media for coverage of news and public affairs, but find it hard to resist the lure of American entertainment.

GLOBAL TELEVISION FLOWS

A study on the international flow of television programs and news in 1972–73 found two clear trends. First, there was a one-way traffic flow from the big exporting countries to the rest of the world, and, second, entertainment dominates the flow.[31] A study of 1983 traffic flows found no clear changes in the worldwide proportion of imported programming. At a global level, the bulk of imported programs originate in the United States and, to a lesser extent, in Western Europe and Japan. These are primarily recreational programs featuring entertainment, movies, and sports. There is considerable intraregional exchange in some regions, notably Western and Eastern Europe and, to some extent, the Arab countries and Latin America.[32]

The 1983 study was done by sampling terrestrial broadcast transmissions. Much of the global traffic flow would have taken place through tape and film rather than live satellite transmissions. However, a study of Intelsat television transmissions during the same period came to similar conclusions. It found that in 1982 European point-to-point transmissions to other regions predominated, accounting for 62 percent of all transmission time, and that nearly 75 percent of all point-to-multipoint transmissions originated in Europe. It also found considerable intraregional exchange in Europe, the Arab states, and Latin America. Some 43 percent of all Intelsat transmissions originating in Latin America in 1982 were beamed to other Latin American countries; the corresponding figures were 57 percent in the Arab states, 49 percent in Asia, and 27 percent in Europe.

Not only had the total volume of television transmission hours increased by more than 25 times since 1973; the growth had been primarily in point-to-multipoint transmissions (49 percent in 1982 compared to 19 percent in 1969). The multipoint growth signaled an increase in syndicated programming, with syndicated news accounting for approximately one-quarter of the news programming in 1982.[33] This type of content did not exist in 1969. As noted above, since 1982, syndicated news programming has grown dramatically, with all three U.S. networks and several other networks now leasing Intelsat transponders for daily news feeds, and live reporting from global news spots has become commonplace.

New International Services: Worldnet

The U.S. Information Agency introduced Worldnet in 1983 to transmit television programs via Intelsat to U.S. embassies, consulates,

and cultural centers worldwide that are equipped with TVRO antennas. In 1988, there were 134 such sites in ninety-five countries.[34]
Worldnet produces "Dialogue," linking foreign journalists, aca-
demics, and other experts with senior U.S. policymakers for interactive teleconferences. Worldnet officials emphasize the opportunity
for foreign journalists to pose direct, uncensored questions to very
highly placed U.S. officials, stating that this access results in "an
extraordinary number of television, radio and newspaper stories."[35]
"America Today" is a live hour-long news and information program
giving global audiences a look at events in the United States through
interviews with members of Congress, civic leaders, artists, scientists, journalists, and entertainers. "Hour USA" offers 60 minutes of
American music, sports, entertainment, business, science, and travel
programs, and English-language instruction. "NewsFile" transmits
the day's top news stories directly to foreign broadcasters around the
globe, and is designed for delivery in multiple language versions.

Worldnet is one of several innovative USIA programs introduced
during the Reagan administration. It may serve as a public relations
prototype for other countries that want to provide a "window" on
their cultures. However, it is not inexpensive. USIA spends $10 mil-
lion to $12 million per year on the service, which includes the full-time
lease of Intelsat transponders on the Atlantic, Indian, and Pacific
ocean satellites and distribution via Eutelsat.[36]

Worldnet is designed to reach audiences much larger than those
who come to U.S. embassies and cultural centers to view the programs. It encourages cable networks and broadcast stations to retransmit the programs, and states that many of the stories are used in
foreign news programs. Ironically, another window has been opened
by the U.S. Armed Forces Network, which now transmits its radio
and television services to U.S. bases worldwide via Intelsat. People
living near the bases, of course, have long been able to pick up the
rebroadcasts of AFN programs, whether live or on tape. However, as
noted above, individuals, communities, and clubs in many countries
have installed TVROs to receive AFN television directly. AFN probably exposes a much larger number of people overseas to American
programming than Worldnet, and at no additional cost.

Satellite Television for Global Understanding

One of the most innovative uses of Intelsat has been for international
teleconferences, or "spacebridges," which foster greater global understanding. These "spacebridges" have been described as "a two-

way window in which people can look at each other while asking simple questions about one another's lives."[37] Examples of "space-bridges" include a reunion of World War II veterans in San Diego and Moscow; the transmission of a ceremony honoring Costa Rican President Arias, sponsored by the Beyond War organization; and the "US" Festival in 1983 and 1984, supported by Steve Wozniak, cofounder of Apple Computer, which connected 200,000 young Americans with their counterparts in Moscow. Ken Schaffer, who pioneered the reception of Soviet television from Molniya satellites in the U.S., proposes that off-peak transponder time be made available to encourage a few merely personal people-to-people events and exchanges as a social "return on investment" of satellite technology.[38] His proposal evokes the spirit of the Ford Foundation proposal in the 1960s that U.S. satellites be used for educational and other developmental purposes to repay U.S. citizens for their investment in the space program.

Another innovative humanitarian use of Intelsat has been the distribution of the many "Aid" events and concerts, beginning with Live Aid, that have increased global awareness of hunger and disease, as well as generating millions of dollars for such causes as famine relief and AIDS research. For example, Sport Aid, a fund-raising footrace run simultaneously in thirteen countries in May 1986, raised more than $100 million for famine relief in Africa. These global events involve mind-boggling technological logistics. Sport Aid used more satellites (fourteen) and more transponders (twenty-four) than any other television program. It involved eight Intelsat satellites, three Westar satellites, Satcom 1R, Anik C, and Europe's ECS-1. During the 3-hour telecast, which originated from sites in thirteen countries, eight feeds went to a satellite control facility in New York before being mixed and retransmitted for world broadcast. The subcontrol facility in London received seven international feeds, but had only three transatlantic circuits to New York. A digital effects unit was used to create two four-way split-screen signals carrying images of the feeds to New York for preview, with a third channel left open for programs to be selected for air from the "quad feeds."[39]

The real marvel of such satellite events, however, is not the technical wizardry, but the transparency of the technology to the viewer. We have now come to take for granted the ability to visually "be anywhere." The challenge is to harness the power to the medium for greater global understanding.

Beaming Jobs Overseas

Modern telecommunications and computer technology such as modem-equipped personal computers, cellular phones, and facsimile machines now make it possible to do information work virtually anywhere in the industrialized world. The Intelsat system extends the range of the telecommunications network globally. IBS and Intelnet services, for example, are designed to provide direct links to user premises. We are just beginning to see hints of the future effects of these services. Information work, of course, ranges from low-skilled jobs requiring basic literacy and typing skills such as data entry to research and development. At both ends of the scale, information industries are able to tap the most cost-effective resources globally.

American Airlines has hired keypunch operators in Barbados to enter data from its flight coupons, which is then fed by satellite and telephone lines back to American's central computers in Tulsa, Oklahoma. For American, this is a vital service, because it tells the airline whom and how much to bill for the ticket. "You don't know how much money you have made until the information is keyed and back in the computer in Tulsa," according to American's head of Caribbean Data Services. American reportedly saved $3.5 million on data processing in its first year of Caribbean data operations.[40] Mead Data Central, a provider of data base services, is one of the United States' largest users of overseas data processing to enter documents into its data bases that are not already computerized. More than 65 percent of its work is done overseas, primarily in Ireland, the Philippines, and South Korea. It is estimated that there are now at least seventy U.S. data-processing firms with overseas facilities.[41]

In the short run, these clerical jobs offer attractive employment opportunities for developing countries, particularly those, such as the Commonwealth Caribbean countries and the Philippines, with relatively high literacy rates and an English-speaking work force. However, not only do the workers in these jobs suffer the same disadvantages as their counterparts in industrialized countries (low pay, boredom, little chance of advancement, stress resulting from the pressure to achieve productivity targets or from computerized monitoring), but they also may be made obsolete by such newer technologies as optical scanning, which would enable typed (and eventually hand-printed) materials to be read directly into a computer.

Some countries and companies may be able to join forces using telecommunications to create a competitive advantage at the highly skilled end of the information work continuum. India has a huge pool of talented and well-educated engineers available at salary levels far below those in industrialized countries. As noted above, Texas Instruments' (TI) in Bangalore was the first site in India to install an IBS terminal. TI can use satellite communications to get access to talented engineers at a fraction of the cost of expanding its professional work force in the United States, and India can retain professionals who might otherwise join its massive brain drain. Since information work can be carried out virtually anywhere, we are likely to see major growth in international telecommuting, which will contribute to the further globalization of information work.

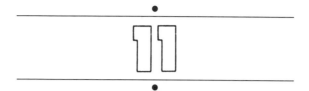

Satellites and Development

The Distant Promise

The past quarter-century has been marked by dramatic technological developments in computers and telecommunications, and the growing importance of information in all aspects of human life. Access to information, and to the facilities to produce, store, and transmit information, is now considered vital to development, so that the classifications "information-rich" and "information-poor" may mean more than distinctions based on GNP or other traditional development indicators.

While we tend to think of new communication and information technologies as the tools and toys of the industrialized world, they offer major benefits—and pose major policy dilemmas—for the developing world. Satellites are a classic example of a technology that holds dramatic promise for developing countries, but whose promise has remained largely unfulfilled. Satellite technology offers the opportunity to provide reliable communications—both interactive telecommunications and broadcasting—to virtually every human community. Yet access to the technology for domestic use has been generally limited to middle-income countries, and few of these are actually using this technology to help achieve development goals.

The following chapters examine the use of satellites by developing countries and the institutional, financial, and organizational obstacles that must be overcome for these countries to obtain the maximum developmental benefits from this technology. Several case studies are included to show both how developing countries are using communication satellites and what problems they face in harnessing the technology.

THE POTENTIAL BENEFITS OF SATELLITES

With satellites, the costs of providing a range of telecommunications services to small and scattered communities has been dramatically reduced. Satellites now make it possible to extend basic two-way communications and broadcasting services throughout a country or region, including the most remote islands and villages. Satellites can be used to provide basic telephony as well as specialized networks for transmission of banking and financial data, weather information, commodities prices, wire services, and so on. In addition, satellites can transmit national radio and television networks with multiple sound tracks for local languages or inserts of local programming. They can also be used to transmit educational programming, such as rural development information, and school curricula from primary to university level to outlying areas. Teachers, nurses, and other development personnel can further their education as well via satellite. Such services need not be one-way: teleconferencing via satellite can range from a simple audio network that serves as an improved version of the multiparty high-frequency radio services found in many developing regions, to enhanced systems that include features such as computer conferencing, audiographics (graphic communication over narrowband channels), freeze-frame video, or motion video using new bandwidth-compression techniques.

The benefits of telecommunications seem intuitively obvious: the ability to maintain personal contacts, to get help in emergencies, to manage projects, to find sources or markets for products and services, and to obtain and exchange information of all kinds. Users recognize that the value of the information they receive exceeds the price they pay to transmit or receive it. Yet in the telecommunications sector, planners tend to justify the provision of services on a cost-recovery basis, ignoring the indirect benefits to users and to the economy as a whole. Further, they also tend to assume that in rural and sparsely populated areas the costs of providing and maintaining service will substantially exceed the revenues.

However, advances in satellite technology and the results of recent research now make it both economically feasible and justifiable to provide the benefits of telecommunications to all segments of a society—whether they be farms, in villages, at mines or drilling sites, or in businesses where rapid access to current information is needed. What are the implications of these new services for national and regional development? Until recently, telecommunications has been viewed as a consequence rather than a cause of economic growth. However, recent studies shed considerable light on the ways in which and extent to which telecommunications contributes to development. The following section summarizes the major hypotheses and findings of this research.*

TELECOMMUNICATIONS AND DEVELOPMENT

Telecommunications is a tool for the conveyance of information and thus can be of critical importance to the development process. By providing information links between urban and rural areas and among rural residents, telecommunications can overcome distance barriers that hamper rural development. Access to information is key to many development activities, including agriculture, industry, shipping, education, health, and social services. The ability to communicate instantaneously can facilitate the development process in three major ways: by improving efficiency, or the ratio of output to cost; effectiveness, or the quality of products and services such as education and health care; and equity, or the distribution of benefits throughout the society.

The importance of information in social, cultural, and economic development was recognized by UNESCO's MacBride Commission, which stated: "There can be no genuine, effective independence without the communication resources needed to safeguard it."[1] While characterized initially in terms of news flow, the imbalance in access to information includes access to the tools of telecommunications and information, and the necessary expertise to utilize them effectively.

For many years telecommunications was virtually ignored by development scholars and planners. However, research conducted during the past decade offers evidence to support the following conclusions:

*For an in-depth treatment of telecommunications and development, see Heather E. Hudson, *When Telephones Reach the Village: The Role of Telecommunications in Rural Development* (Norwood, NJ: Ablex, 1984).

1. Investment in telecommunications contributes to economic growth.

2. The indirect benefits of telecommunications generally greatly exceed the revenues generated by the telecommunications network.

3. The availability of telecommunications can contribute significantly to rural economic activities.

4. The use of telecommunications can improve the quality and accessibility of education, health care, and other social services.

5. The benefits of investment in telecommunications may be greatest in rural and remote areas where distances are greater and telephone penetration is lower.

6. The intangible benefits of telecommunications, such as the fostering of the sense of community and the strengthening of cultural identity, while difficult to measure, contribute to the development process.

7. Telecommunications can be considered a complement in the rural development process; that is, other conditions must exist for the maximum developmental benefits of telecommunications to be achieved.

Telecommunications and Economic Growth

Numerous studies have demonstrated a strong positive correlation between telephone density and economic development measured in terms of GNP per capita or a similar statistic.[2] However, this simple correlation does not explain what appears to be a chicken-and-egg relationship: Does investment in telecommunications contribute to economic growth, or does economic growth lead to investment in telecommunications?

A methodology developed by Andrew Hardy has shown that investment in telecommunications can make a statistically significant contribution to economic growth as measured by gross domestic product (GDP).[3] Hardy's methodology is significant in providing for the first time a means of disentangling the relationship between telecommunication investment and economic growth. His analysis shows that the causality runs in both directions: While economic development leads to more investment in telecommunications, telecommunications also contributes to economic development. And the economic impact is comparatively greater in regions with low telephone density—those which are likely to be rural and remote areas.

This model has been used to predict the impact of investment in satellite earth stations for thin-route telephony on national GDP. A logarithmic relationship was found to exist between telephone density and the impact on GDP per earth station, such that the impact per earth station increases with lower telephone densities. Some threshold level of economic activity must probably be attained in order for economic benefits to be generated. However, delivery and administration of government-delivered services, such as health and education, would likely improve regardless of the regional economy.[4]

Indirect Benefits of Telecommunications

Why would investment in telecommunications contribute to economic growth? The answer lies in the indirect benefits of telecommunications that are related to the function of conveying information. Information is critical for development activities, but also has unusual economic properties in that it can be shared without being transferred and that its benefits may extend to others besides those directly involved in the information transaction. The benefits of a telephone call, for example, may accrue to both the caller and the person called, as well as to others who are not involved in the information transaction. For example, a farmer would benefit if an agricultural extension agent could contact an agronomist to find out how to eliminate a crop fungus, and a patient would benefit if the health worker at a rural clinic could get advice from a doctor at a regional hospital.

But even more important in terms of development is the fact that the society as a whole will benefit from these uses of telecommunications, both in economic terms and in improved quality of life. Access to a physician can reduce mortality rates and allow more people to be treated locally without having to be transferred to a hospital. Consultation with agronomists and veterinarians can improve crop yields and livestock production. Use of telecommunications to order supplies can reduce downtime of plants and machinery. Coordination of logistics using telecommunications can eliminate wasted trips and missed deliveries.

Yet planners do not generally take these indirect benefits into consideration in determining how much to invest in telecommunications and where and when to upgrade facilities. These decisions are more likely to be based exclusively on the anticipated revenue to be derived from the telecommunications network. Instead, telecommunications networks should be considered part of the basic infrastructure, like roads, water mains, and electrical power grids, which

are justified on the basis of their importance to economic development and quality of life.

Several studies sponsored by the ITU in collaboration with the
OECD,[5] by the World Bank,[6] and by other development agencies[7]
have documented the indirect benefits of telecommunications for
rural economic activities and social services. These studies show
ratios of benefits to costs of telecommunications usage from 5:1 to
more than 100:1 from improved efficiency in managing of rural enterprises, time savings in ordering spare parts, savings in travel costs
and time, and so on.

Among the benefits of telecommunications for improving efficiency and productivity are the following:

> *Price information:* Producers such as farmers and fishermen can
> compare prices in various markets, allowing them to get the highest
> prices for their produce, to eliminate dependency on local middle-
> men, and/or to modify their products (types of crops raised or fish
> caught, etc.) in response to market demand.

> *Reduction of downtime:* Timely ordering of spare parts and immedi-
> ate contact with technicians can reduce time lost because of broken
> machinery such as pumps, tractors, generators, and the like.

> *Reduction of inventory:* Businesses can reduce the inventories they
> need to keep on hand if replacements can be ordered and delivered
> as needed.

> *Timely delivery of products to market:* Contact between producers
> and shippers to arrange schedules for delivering products to mar-
> ket can result in reduced spoilage (for example of fish or fresh fruit),
> more efficient processing, and higher prices for produce.

> *Reduction of travel costs:* In some circumstances, telecommunica-
> tions may be substituted for travel, resulting in significant savings
> in personnel time and travel costs.

> *Energy savings:* Telecommunications can be used to maximize the
> efficiency of shipping so that trips are not wasted and consumption
> of fuel is minimized.

> *Decentralization:* The availability of telecommunications can help
> to attract industries to rural areas, thereby encouraging decentral-
> ization of economic activities away from major urban areas.

Three important conclusions can be derived from this analysis of
the indirect benefits of telecommunications:

- A telecommunications system is likely to yield a surplus of benefits over costs to its users.

- These benefits may accrue to both parties in the transaction, and to the society at large as well.

- Telecommunications revenues generally do not reflect the indirect benefits derived, which are likely to be much greater; or, from a requirements perspective, demand as measured by expected traffic and revenues may not adequately reflect the need for telecommunications.

GREATER INFORMATION GAPS?

The "information gap" between industrialized and developing countries is reflected in their access to telecommunications resources. There has been very little progress made in extending the access to telecommunications services within developing countries. Although there are now more than 600 million telephones in the world, it is estimated that two-thirds of the world's population have no access to telephone services. New York City alone has more telephones than the entire African continent. Nearly three-quarters of the world's population live in countries with ten telephones or fewer for every 100 people; over half the world's population live in countries with less than one telephone per 100 people, and most of these telephones are located in urban areas.[8] As a result, telephone density is likely to be much lower in rural areas, where the need for telecommunications is more critical because of the difficulty in communicating over longer distances. Lower-income countries show dramatically limited access to telecommunications. The highest telephone density among these countries is seven telephones per 1,000 people, while in many cases there is no more than one telephone per 1,000 inhabitants.[9]

Middle-income countries have benefited most from increased access to satellites for domestic and regional communications. About twenty-six middle-income countries are participants in domestic or regional satellite systems, or are leasing domestic capacity from Intelsat. Only seven of the thirty-four countries classified as low-income by the World Bank are participants in such systems. At present, there are nineteen developing countries leasing capacity from Intelsat for domestic use, primarily to provide communications to provincial or state capitals and major regional centers. Of these, seven are oil exporters and only three are among the least developed countries.

Even in most middle-income countries, including those with access to satellites for domestic communications, the infrastructure is still extremely limited. Brazil and Mexico, which now both have their own domestic satellites, have an average of seven telephones per 100 people; rural densities are much lower. Many other middle-income countries have even lower densities, including members of Arabsat and users of Indonesia's Palapa system.

Despite the rapid advances in technology in the past five years, it appears that most developing countries are not catching up with the industrialized world in access to these information tools. Only fourteen of the satellites launched between 1979 and 1986 were for the exclusive use of developing countries, and this number includes replacements for previously launched satellites and in-orbit spares. Even taking into consideration the fact that Intelsat satellites are used by both industrialized and developing nations, satellites for the exclusive use of industrialized nations make up 72 percent of the total.

The growth in industrialized countries' demand for specialized communication services such as data communications, broadcasting, and teleconferencing; the deregulation of long-distance telecommunications in the United States; and the growth of the satellite industry in Europe and Japan have resulted in a proliferation of satellites serving industrialized countries. In addition, innovations in satellite and earth-station design have reduced the costs, increased the capacity, or increased the efficiency of satellite technology.

The statistics cited above indicate the extent of underinvestment in Third World telecommunications, considering not only the much greater availability of facilities in the industrialized world, but also the major direct and indirect benefits of telecommunications in the development process. It is estimated that at least an additional $4 billion per year must be invested in Third World telecommunications if at least minimal worldwide access is to be achieved by the year 2000.[10]

Underinvestment in telecommunications affects satellite communications in two ways. First, the lack of funds has resulted in a lack of satellite facilities in developing regions where small earth stations are the most appropriate way of delivering two-way communications and broadcasting services, such as in much of Africa, the Amazon and Andean regions of South America, and the islands of the South Pacific. Second, even where earth stations have been or could be installed, the lack of funds for basic infrastructure leave the "last mile" unconnected; that is, there may be no local telephones or telephone exchange, and no transmitters to rebroadcast radio and television signals received via satellite.

There appear to be many reasons why the funding for telecommunications has not met even minimal needs:

- The revenue-producing nature of telecommunications has led planners and investors to concentrate on improving services that will generate profits, such as interurban and international links.

- The indirect benefits of telecommunications for socioeconomic development have not been widely understood or appreciated, so that telecommunications often receives a low priority in development plans.

- Telecommunications has been seen as an urban luxury rather than as an essential component of infrastructure that should be included in integrated development plans.

- The increased demand and competition in the industrialized world has resulted in product innovation, but suppliers have concentrated on the markets in industrialized countries.

- Inadequately trained technical and managerial personnel have often contributed to service problems which result in limit service and thereby limited benefits.

- Most developing countries do not have indigenous telecommunications-manufacturing industries, so they must buy their systems abroad. Spare parts must often compete with necessities such as food, medicine, and fossil fuels for scarce hard-currency reserves.

- The telecommunication sector's profits may be used to subsidize the postal service or to contribute to general government revenues, rather than being available for expansion and improvement of the network.

- Financial institutions and equipment suppliers may be reluctant to extend credit for telecommunications purchases if they perceive excessive risk due to the above factors.

The major sources of financing for telecommunications projects in developing countries are supplier credits, multilateral development banks, and bilateral aid agencies. Commercial bank involvement is generally limited to supplier credit agreements. Supplier credits are probably the most common funding source, and have several attractions. Credit is relatively simple to arrange; it involves no elaborate documentation and review process, once the creditworthiness of the telecommunications authority is verified. Procurement and installation can therefore proceed more quickly than when bilateral or multilateral agencies are involved, an advantage to both telecommunications administrations and suppliers. However, potential drawbacks of supplier credits for the developing country compared to longer-term multilateral loans are higher interest rates, the higher total cost of short-term loans, and the tendency to select suppliers based on their financing packages rather than on other criteria such as technical design, price, training offered, and so on.

Many industrialized countries have foreign assistance programs that provide support for telecommunications. Some countries such as the United States tend not to fund telecommunications projects per se, but to fund the telecommunications components of projects in other sectors such as rural education, health care delivery, railroads and airports, and the like. Other countries do provide direct support for telecommunications, although telecommunications loans are likely to be a very small part of their portfolio. The dominant philosophy among many aid agencies still appears to be that telecommunications is not a "basic need" and that, as a revenue generator, it does not require bilateral support. Countries that do provide funding for telecommunications often consider their aid programs as part of their industrial strategies, and tie the grants or loans to purchases of equipment from companies based in their home countries. Japan has recently announced a $50 million aid program in telecommunications, making it the world's largest bilateral donor.[11]

Of the multilateral development banks, the major lender for telecommunications is the World Bank, although telecommunications loans account for less than 2 percent of its portfolio. World Bank loans are usually based on an amortization period of twenty years, with a grace period of three to five years, and carry below-commercial interest rates. The poorest countries (GDP per capita less than $400 per year) receive concessionary financing through the International Development Association (IDA), which provides loans at no interest (subject only to an annual service charge) with a repayment term of fifty years. The World Bank considers itself a lender of last resort, since other sources of funding are available for telecommunications projects. The bank also encourages cofinancing of telecommunications projects with other development agencies and the private sector.[12] Other development banks for specific regions include the African Development Bank, the Asian Development Bank, the Arab Bank for Economic Development in Africa (BADEA), the Inter-American Development Bank, and the OPEC Fund.

The European Community also provides funding on behalf of its members to developing nations, specifically to countries in Africa, the Caribbean and the Pacific (known as ACP states). The third Lomé Convention (Lomé III) was signed in 1984 by sixty-five ACP states, of which forty-four are African, thirteen are Caribbean, and eight are Pacific, with a total population of 368 million.[13] Special privileges are accorded to the least developed, land-locked, and island ACP states (now comprising fifty-three of the ACP signatories). European Community funding under Lomé is provided through the European Development Fund and European Investment Bank (EIB). The EIB participates in cofinancing with other European bilateral aid organizations, multilateral organizations, and development banks. The Lomé Convention has been used to finance telecommunications projects, such as Intelsat earth stations in the South Pacific. As in many bilateral programs, funding under Lomé is generally tied; that is, recipients are expected to procure equipment and services from European Community members.

Few satellite projects have been financed by bilateral and multilateral agencies for several reasons. First, international satellite terminals are generally considered to be highly profitable, so that funding from commercial sources can be obtained. Domestic and particularly rural satellite networks may not attract aid because they may not be profitable enough; like commercial lenders, most development agencies evaluate telecommunications projects on their potential profitability or internal rate of return. Finally, recent developments in earth-station technology, particularly for rural areas and small users, are often greeted with skepticism by engineers in these agencies, who tend to be drawn from conservative telecommunications administrations and to have been educated before these technologies were developed.

SATELLITES AND DEPENDENCY

Satellite technology has an almost seductive appeal. The capability of satellites to reach virtually any location from a single point is a powerful attraction for television broadcasters and for governments concerned with building or preserving national unity. The satellite system is an alluring status symbol for governments anxious to demonstrate their commitment to space age technologies. During the 1980s, the satellite has become the telecommunications equivalent of the national airline: countries may invest in a satellite for prestige as well as for the technological advantages it offers.

Yet the very power of the satellite that makes it attractive also makes it one of the most difficult technologies to use successfully. The procurement of a satellite involves an investment of at least $200 million for the satellite and a spare, the launch, insurance, and master control station. Total investment including the earth stations needed to transmit and receive signals from the satellite will of course be much higher, depending on the number and size of the stations (which may be provided by the government, the carrier, and/or the end user depending on national policy). For most countries, this investment requires reliance on a foreign supplier, as there are still only a handful of industrialized countries with industries capable of manufacturing satellites. Fewer still (notably at present the United States, the Soviet Union, France and China) have the capacity to launch a satellite to geosynchronous orbit. China and India are the only developing countries now capable of building their own communication satellites, although they have relied on foreign-built satellites (Intelsat and Insat) for their first national systems. Both countries plan to build their own domestic communication satellites in the 1990s.

Technological dependency is only one of the problems facing developing countries that invest in satellites. Making effective use of the satellite is an even greater challenge. One reason is the limited life span of the satellite. Today's satellites are built to last ten years. For many countries, ten years is too short a time to build the facilities needed to take advantage of the satellite's capacity. Transmitters must be installed to rebroadcast television programs carried by satellite. In many cases, local power systems must be installed to power the transmitters and possibly the television sets. Local telephone facilities must be installed or upgraded if the satellite is to be used to provide telephone services. Typically, "last mile" problems of providing reliable links from the earth stations to the users result in underutilization of the satellite for interactive services such as telephony and teleconferencing.

If the country intends to develop special programming to be distributed by satellite, the time constraints may prove even more difficult. The countdown clock to the launch date starts ticking from the date the contract for the satellite is signed. This period may last only two to three years, a very short time to plan, fund, and start producing special programming. Typically, this planning and allocation of funds is not completed, and may not even have begun, when the government makes the commitment to procure a satellite. Planning for the production of developmental programming may involve consultations with numerous government and other agencies, such as the ministries of education, health, and agriculture. Coordination among several agencies may take from many months to several years.

Thus the launch date may arrive with very little infrastructure in place to deliver services to users and very little programming ready to be transmitted. Such a loss of time may be very serious for a developing country, because the resources for the satellite have already been committed, and wasted time becomes a wasted investment.

ACCESS AND CONTROL

Many countries have expressed concern about the transmission of unwanted video programs across their borders by satellite. The experience in North America shows that this phenomenon is already occurring. Yet there is evidence that the power of this medium can also be harnessed to serve development goals. Even where the television delivery system is already in place, television can be turned into a developmental tool if it can be made relevant and participatory, and if interactive media and conferencing networks are also included.

In North America, the advent of communication satellites has brought television to the most remote regions. Canada's Anik satellites transmit the Canadian Broadcasting Corporation's network to Indian and Inuit communities in the far north. Alaska natives receive U.S. network television from the Aurora satellite. For $2,000 or less, a satellite earth station can be installed. An inexpensive mini-TV transmitter can rebroadcast the signal, allowing access to all the families in a given village. Other satellite signals are also available, because the footprints of U.S. domestic satellites cover most of Canada, as well as the Caribbean and Central America. Thus, in the Caribbean and in Latin America as far south as Venezuela and Colombia, satellite earth stations have popped up behind wealthy homes and in poor villages to receive American television.

In other parts of the developing world, VCRs appear in the poorest neighborhoods and most remote villages. At this point, we know little about the impact of the foreign programming delivered by satellite and VCR. The term "foreign" should not be thought of only in terms of programs imported from another country, although this definition is applied in much of the developing world. It also applies to programming produced by a foreign culture within the same national boundaries.

There have been several indigenous responses to the perceived negative impact of television. One strategy is to put the medium of television to work for indigenous people. The state of Alaska pioneered in using satellite technology to bring educational programming to isolated villages through its innovative Learn/Alaska network. In northern Canada, the Inuit decided to establish the Inuit Broadcasting Corporation (IBC) to produce native-language programs that are distributed via Anik. Similarly, the Australian aborigines have established a television network to distribute aboriginal programming via Aussat.

But some indigenous groups have chosen to respond to the threat of television by turning to other media. Where television is distributed by satellite, other capabilities of the satellite—for interactive communications and for radio broadcasting—have also been put to use for development purposes. The Learn/Alaska network used audioconferencing for tutorials and educational administration. In Canada, several native groups consider radio the most important medium for development. For example, the Wawatay Native Communications Society, which serves the Indian people of northern Ontario, has established a native radio network that links the region by satellite. The University of the South Pacific based in Fiji operates an audioconferencing network connecting ten regional centers.

Broadcasters recognize that the popularity of imported entertainment and the cost of local production are formidable obstacles to increasing indigenous programming. Some countries have reacted by setting quotas on imported programming. Others have attempted to ban imports, but the combination of transborder reception in some countries and the proliferation of VCRs virtually everywhere has breached the dike regardless of legislation. A more creative approach may be to use revenues from imports to finance local production. For example, taxes on videocassettes and VCRs and on the revenues of cable television systems could be used for local production. Similarly, in countries that allow advertising on television, a percentage of these revenues (often associated with popular imported programs) could also be set aside for local production.

While audio and video cassettes are often seen as a threat to indigenous music and video, they may offer a lesson in how to encourage local talent. In many countries, musicians have reached a national audience through cassettes, which are much simpler to reproduce than vinyl records (or compact disks). Portable video equipment has reduced the cost of video production as well. However, instead of forcing video artists to distribute their content solely on cassettes, broadcasters could buy programs from independent producers. This approach would increase the amount of available indigenous content and foster the growth of indigenous production.

While the control issue is often portrayed in terms of the incursion of foreign programming, it may also involve centralized control of media content within a country. The easiest way to use a satellite is to transmit programs from a single location for reception throughout the country. However, cultural, linguistic, and geographical diversity often indicates that a decentralized approach would better serve development goals. Some countries such as India are setting up regional production centers to produce programs in several languages tailored to regional needs. A less expensive approach is to provide access to local transmitters that rebroadcast national programs. In Canada, a policy of local access to CBC transmitters in remote areas has worked successfully for nearly twenty years. Local groups incorporate a broadcasting society and negotiate with the CBC for periods of access to the transmitter. The local society receives a license that requires it to operate responsibly, with some flexibility when local custom differs from national norms. (For example, local societies must avoid libel and slander, but in some regions a chief may turn off the transmitter when there is a death in the community and may preempt national programs during a local emergency.)

Community groups in numerous developing countries have been using video as a tool for community development and cultural preservation: to communicate ideas from one village to another; to teach new techniques of farming, infant care, and sanitation; and to preserve endangered cultures. In many cases, the process of using video is considered to be just as important as the video product, a philosophy that can be traced back to the pioneering work of the National Film Board of Canada's Challenge for Change program in the 1960s. Challenge for Change used film and later videotape not only to document community problems, but to involve the community—and the decision makers whom the community was seeking to influence. The content of the film was developed and reviewed by the community. Once the community approved the production, it was shown to the officials who could remedy the problem, whether it was substandard housing or the closing of a factory. The officials' response was then videotaped and shown to the community. Often the presence of the tape recorder and the knowledge that the taped response would be shown in the community was enough to motivate an official to act.

The portability and simplicity of today's video equipment makes it possible for virtually anyone anywhere to use video in this kind of interactive process. For example, Australian aborigines have used video to document their culture and to disseminate information about issues that affect their future. Videocassettes are being used to share traditional songs, dances, and stories, as well as to create visual archives. Tapes in aboriginal languages about land claims, alcoholism, and education allow village groups to discuss these issues and reach consensus on the appropriate response. A tape on the capabilities of Australia's domestic satellite, Aussat, helped people to think about their communication priorities.[14]

THE IMPORTANCE OF TWO-WAY COMMUNICATION

Another approach to limiting the centralization of satellite transmissions is to ensure that two-way communication is installed in conjunction with any broadcasting facilities. Despite the popularity of television or video, it should be noted that this is generally not the greatest communication need in rural and remote areas. Around the world, isolated people agree that reliable two-way communication is their top priority, so that they can get help in emergencies, stay in touch with families and friends, and get the information they need for economic survival. For these isolated groups two-way communication provides vital links between leaders and to sources of information necessary for their social and economic development. In many regions, broadcast radio may take second priority because transistor radios are widely available and because radio programs are relatively simple and cheap to produce. Television may rank third, because it is more expensive and because the programming is likely to be less relevant.

In other words, broadcasting should be provided only where there is telephone service. A policy that brings in television without telephones not only deprives people of the means of getting help in emergencies, but of the means of influencing their own development.

Often, the same earth station can be used to provide both telephony and broadcasting. Such coordinated planning of telecommunications happens all too rarely, often because the telecommunications and broadcasting functions are under the control of separate agencies. Yet the need for integrated planning is particularly important with satellite systems, because the technology can be used to deliver a wide variety of communication services.

WILL THE POTENTIAL BE REALIZED?

Satellite technology combined with advances in low-cost earth station design, solar power supplies for remote communications installations, bandwidth compression techniques to facilitate transmission of motion video, and new techniques for low-cost data communications—all promise a wealth of new services, the extension of services to new users, and, most important, social and economic benefits for society as a whole. But will this promise be fulfilled? The answer depends not on the technology, but on a variety of other factors.

Pricing policy: Will new services be offered at prices which attract widespread use? Will tariffs reflect the advantages of the new technologies—for example, cost-independence of distance, point-to-multipoint distribution, economical uses of satellite power and/or bandwidth? Or will existing tariffs be extended to these new services? Will new tariffs be instated to maximize revenues from large users or subsidize the costs of other services?

Ownership of facilities: Will users such as broadcasters be able to own their own satellite-receive terminals (downlinks) and transmit stations (uplinks)? Or will they be required to lease them from a telecommunications carrier that will recover several times their cost in lease charges?

Terrestrial facilities: Will resources be allocated to solve the "last mile" problem, that is, to install local loops or radio links, rebroadcast transmitters, power supplies, and so on?

Competition or exclusion: Will the established communication networks take advantage of the technology to lower their costs and reach new customers? Will they pass on these savings to their customers or absorb them as additional profit? Will they attempt to block the entry of new networks designed to reach unserved customers or to reach existing users at lower cost?

Role of government: Will government policies be flexible enough to facilitate maximum use of the technology—through licensing of new or expanded broadcasting networks, support for pilot projects, and the adoption of policies to minimize users' costs and to encourage new entrants to supply both equipment and services?

Integration with development plans: Will satellite applications and site locations be coordinated with development plans as part of a national development strategy?

Time and resources for software development: Will governments and other users devote sufficient time and funds to applications so that valuable transponder capacity is not left idle?

Participatory planning: Will potential users such as broadcasters, educators, health care providers, and extension workers be involved in determining needs and planning and implementation of satellite services?

Flexibility and innovativeness: Will organizations that could apply satellite technology to better serve their constituencies be flexible and innovative enough to adopt it? Will they be able to integrate telecommunications-based services into their organizations? Or will they see them as unaffordable luxuries or threats to their established hierarchy?

The answers to these questions are still open. The experience in other countries has been that technological innovation is not necessarily accompanied by institutional innovation. In Canada, users were not allowed to own downlinks for many years after Telesat began offering its services in 1973; only recently have broadcasters been allowed to own uplinks. Special native-oriented programming for Canada's indigenous peoples, especially those living in the remote north, was slow to be implemented.

In the United States, satellites ushered in an era of competition in the skies, but the large telecommunications carriers did not welcome new competitors. Government policies of deregulation and the threat of antitrust suits were necessary to force widespread competition in the telecommunications industry. In Western Europe, the commitment to design and build satellites and other advanced telecommunications systems seems to have preceded the commitment to make the institutional changes required if the new and expanded services made possible by the technology are to materialize.

Developing nations now have the opportunity to harness telecommunications and information technology to overcome the barriers of distance and the diseconomies of reaching scattered users. Whether these societies will reap the full benefits of satellites and other new technologies will depend less on the technologies themselves than on the commitment of policymakers to allow them to flourish.

12

Satellite Use
by Developing Countries

An Overview

CURRENT STATUS OF SATELLITE
USE BY DEVELOPING COUNTRIES

For domestic communications of voice, data, and/or broadcasting services by satellite, developing countries at present have three alternatives: leased capacity from Intelsat, use of a regional satellite system; or procurement of a domestic satellite system.

Nineteen developing countries currently lease capacity from Intelsat for domestic use, primarily to provide communications to provincial or state capitals and major regional centers.[1] Regional satellite services are now available in the Middle East and Southeast Asia. The Arabsat system, launched in February 1985, was designed to provide domestic and regional services for its twenty-two members in the Middle East and North Africa. Palapa B, the second generation of Indonesia's domestic satellite system, provides domestic and regional services throughout Southeast Asia.

Developing countries with their own domestic satellites include India, which has been operating the Insat system since 1983; Brazil, which initiated the Brasilsat system in 1985; and Mexico, which launched the Morelos system in 1985. China has launched its own experimental satellites and is planning a domestic satellite for telecommunications and broadcasting. Other developing countries considering domestic systems include Argentina, Colombia, Nigeria, Pakistan, and Thailand. Regional systems have been proposed for the Andean nations and for sub-Saharan Africa.

The sections below give an overview of satellite systems and their applications in Indonesia, Mexico, and the Arab world. Regional systems proposed for Asia and the Pacific, sub-Saharan Africa, the Andean region, and the Caribbean are then briefly described. The following chapter includes four case studies on Insat, Brasilsat, the AID Rural Satellite Program, and Project SHARE.

Indonesia: Palapa

Indonesia is the fifth most populous country in the world, with 163 million people, and possibly the most dispersed, with more than 13,600 islands. Because of its limited infrastructure and widely scattered population, a satellite seemed an ideal technology to deliver telecommunications and broadcasting throughout the country. Indonesia was the first developing country to procure a domestic satellite system. Palapa A was built by Hughes Aircraft and launched by NASA in 1976, in time for president Suharto's birthday. Hughes was commissioned to design and construct the spacecraft and two base stations on the island of Java. Another four earth stations were built by Ford Aerospace and ITT.

The system was used solely for domestic television and telephone traffic until June 1978 when a contract was signed with Domsatphil, the Philippine Satellite Telecommunications Company, to use Palapa for Philippine domestic communications. Later Thailand and Malaysia signed similar agreements. In 1979, the Intelsat Assembly of Parties agreed to coordinate the second generation, Palapa B, under Article XIV, so that it could be used as a regional system (the second such system coordinated, following Eutelsat). The first generation was replaced in 1983 with the second-generation Palapa B-1, which is designed to provide service to other Southeast Asian countries. (Palapa B-2 was launched in 1984 from the space shuttle, but failed to reach geosynchronous orbit and was later recovered by another shuttle crew. Hughes has refurbished the satellite and resold it.) The second generation is nearly twice as powerful as the first, and the satellite's capacity has doubled to twenty-four transponders. Four members of the Association of Southeast Asian Nations (ASEAN) have entered into agreements with the Indonesian telecommunications agency, Perumtel, to lease capacity on Palapa B, namely, Malaysia, the Philippines, Thailand, and Singapore.[2]

When Palapa A was put into service, there were only forty earth stations. More than a decade later, less than 100 additional earth stations have been installed, despite the existence of a domestic earth-station manufacturing industry. The "last mile" problem also limits the utility of the earth stations for telephone service. Indonesia's telephone density is only 0.4, and much lower in rural areas. Since the government has allocated few resources to rural telecommunications, where local telephone networks do exist they are often limited and of poor quality. In addition, Indonesians are not allowed to buy or install their own satellite earth stations. However, many have illicitly assembled their own backyard TVRO antennas, using components from Singapore, in order to watch Malaysian television, which is carried on a Palapa transponder for Sarawak and Brunei. (Malaysian television reflects its government's Moslem conservatism, but does allow some imported commercial programs.)

Indonesian television is constrained by several factors. Limited budgets and a requirement that production be done by the government television network (TVRI) rather than purchased from independent Indonesian producers stifle indigenous production. The government banned television advertising in 1981, apparently because it was creating demand for products that many people did not need or could not afford (ranging from soft drinks to motorcycles). Thus there is no advertising revenue to support production.

The pricing of Palapa transponders discourages other users. For example, Indonesia's new Open University would like to use the satellite to transmit educational programs. The TVRI transponder could be used in the daytime, as TVRI does not begin transmission until late afternoon. However, TVRI wants $10,000 per hour for this time, a rate the Open University cannot afford.

Perhaps the most restrictive factor is the Indonesian government's attempt to control content. The government maintains tight control on Indonesian media and discourages Indonesians from obtaining information from the outside world. New technologies are seen as a threat rather than an opportunity to forge new links and share information. Indeed, after a lecture in Jakarta by the author on the potential developmental impact of new technologies, Indonesia's chief censor asked: "How can these new technologies help me do my job better?"[3] What apparently concerned the censor was the influx of foreign programming, primarily via pirated videocassettes, but also via TVROs picking up Malaysian TV from Palapa. Although many would argue that simply easing travel restrictions has increased the flow of foreign information and products into Indonesia, the government still seems determined to plug the crumbling dike.

Arabsat

Satellites appear to be an ideal means to deliver telecommunications and broadcasting services to the villages and oases scattered across the deserts of the Arab peninsula and North Africa. Algeria was the first nation to lease an Intelsat transponder for domestic use (see chapter 10). Since then, Saudi Arabia, Morocco, Sudan, Libya, and Oman have all leased Intelsat capacity. However, the Arab nations now also have their own satellite for regional and domestic communications.

Arabsat evolved from a 1953 Arab League Agreement to develop regional telephone, telex, and telegraph telecommunications. Following the Yom Kippur war between Egypt and Israel, the Arab states under the leadership of the Arab League planned for their own regional satellite. The Arab Space Communication Organization was established in 1976 and has twenty-two members (see list which follows). Arabsat's organization is similar to that of Intelsat, with a General Assembly composed of the ministers of communications of all the Arab member states, a board of directors composed of representatives of nine member states (the five biggest shareholders are permanent members and the other four are elected every two years), and an executive body headed by a director general who is elected for a three-year term.[4] The organization's original capital was $100 million divided into 1,000 shares, although it has since been increased several times. Shares are tied to usage after two years' operation. In 1985, more than 50 percent of the shares were owned by Saudi Arabia, with 35 percent, and Kuwait, with 18 percent. The third largest shareholder is Libya, with 8 percent.[5]

Members of Arabsat

Algeria	Palestine Liberation
Bahrain	Organization
Djibouti	Qatar
Egypt	Saudi Arabia
Iraq	Somalia
Jordan	Sudan
Kuwait	Syria
Libya	Tunisia
Mauritania	Yemen Arab Republic
Morocco	Yemen People's Democratic
Oman	Republic
	United Arab Emirates

Comsat acted as a consultant in the design of the system. After lengthy disputes concerning a boycott of companies doing business with Israel, the contract for construction of the spacecraft was awarded to the French firm Aerospatiale, with Ford Aerospace acting as a subcontractor. Two satellites were launched in 1985, with the third an on-ground spare. Each spacecraft has twenty-five C-band transponders that can handle 9,000 telephone circuits and seven television channels, and one transponder that uplinks in C band and downlinks in S band (2.5 GHz). The latter is for community television reception via inexpensive S-band terminals similar to those used first with ATS-6 and now with Insat in Indian villages (see below). Arabsat documentation states: "These stations can be operated by batteries and also by solar energy converters. The cost of each station including the monitor will not be more than $3,000. This will allow educational TV programs to be set up in all the Arabsat member states and is one of the unique features of the Arabsat system."[6] However, the S-band transponder has not been used to date.

In fact, the Arabsat system is extremely underutilized. In 1986, only 1,300 of the 9,000 available circuits were being used.[7] One problem is the lack of earth stations. The construction and operation of the earth stations is the responsibility of the individual administrations. Initially, only six countries had earth stations: Saudi Arabia, Bahrain, Jordan, Oman, Tunisia, and Kuwait. The others were slow not only to construct earth stations but also to make the contributions they had pledged to Arabsat, which was financed primarily by Saudi Arabia. Several countries have held on to their Intelsat leases rather than switch to Arabsat.

A more substantive issue is the difficulty in developing cooperation among the members. Initially, the members talked about television exchanges across the Arab world, but there are many political and cultural differences in the region. Strictly traditional Moslem states such as Saudi Arabia prohibit imported programming considered immoral or decadent. Members such as Kuwait, Syria, Jordan, and Libya espouse extremely diverse political ideologies.

Despite the investment in a regional satellite, the Middle East paradoxically shows the highest VCR penetration and lowest satellite use. VCRs are owned by over 80 percent of television households in Kuwait and Saudi Arabia, and by over 70 percent in Oman and the United Arab Emirates, for example. A Saudi official has referred to his country as the first videotape society. VCRs enable Arabs to see foreign programs that their governments will not permit to be shown on television because of their perceived harmful cultural influence. Arab television, however, is less dependent on U.S. and European content than that of other regions because of the availability of popular regional content, for example from Egypt, Kuwait, the United Arab Emirates, and Saudi Arabia. About 42 percent of programs in the Arab world are imported, with about one-third of the content from other Arab states, one-third from the United States, and the remainder from various sources.

By the time Arabsat was launched in 1985, Egypt, a leader in the system's planning and the most advanced producer of television in the Arab world, had been expelled from the Arab League following the peace accord between Egypt and Israel. The headquarters of the satellite organization was moved to Riyadh. Some telecommunications experts believe that until Egypt becomes reinstated as a member, television exchanges will continue to be minimal.

Mexico: Morelos

Mexico has a population of more than 77 million, of whom 20 million live in villages without telephone, telegraph, or television services. This rural population is spread throughout the country in more than 100,000 villages, of which 14,000 have populations ranging from 500 to 2,500 inhabitants.[8] The 1949 General Law of Telecommunications Rights placed all forms of Mexican telecommunications under the control of the Ministry of Communications and Transportation (SCT). Under SCT, telecommunications is divided into telephone service, which is primarily provided by Telefonos de Mexico (Telmex); all other forms of communications are provided by the General Directorate of Telecommunications (DGT). Telmex provides telephone service to towns of 1,500 or more, while DGT serves smaller communities.[9] SCT is responsible for Mexico's domestic satellite program.

Televisa, the nation's largest television network, proposed a Mexican satellite for television distribution and communications for rural areas in the late 1970s. A contract between the Mexican government and Hughes Aircraft was eventually signed, with Televisa still playing a major role. In 1982, the Mexican constitution was modified to designate satellite communications as a strategic area under the exclusive charge of the state. This change was apparently a response of the newly elected president Miguel de la Madrid to controversy surrounding his predecessors' contract with Hughes Aircraft for a domestic satellite system, and pressure from the television conglomerate Televisa for more influence in the system.[10] Mexico first introduced satellite services for telecommunications and television by leasing capacity on both Intelsat and Westar.

Mexico's domestic satellite system was launched in November 1985 and became operational in 1986. The Morelos system (named after a hero of Mexican independence) consists of an operational satellite and an in-orbit spare. Morelos has twenty-two transponders: twelve narrowband 36-megahertz transponders and six wideband 72-megahertz transponders in C band, and four 108-megahertz Ku-band transponders.[11] The satellite is used for long-distance communications between major Mexican cities, national television transmission, and radio and data communications via two master earth stations and 272 local earth stations.[12] Three transponders are used for transmitting television channels from Mexico City and one for a television station uplinked from Tijuana.[13]

The satellite system operates at less than 50 percent of capacity, with estimated losses of more than $20,000 per day, as a result of SCT's poor planning and mismanagement of the system.[14] Primary users of Morelos continue to be previous users of transponders leased from Intelsat, who have practical experience and technical know-how. SCT plans to add up to 250 new earth stations and to increase the number of Morelos users. Private networks include Bancomer and Banamex, two of Mexico's most important banks.

After several years of lobbying, a Mexican entrepreneur now based in the United States has been successful in setting up private networks, apparently because of Telmex's inability to keep up with the rapidly growing demand for telecommunications and the inefficient management of the Morelos system.[15] These networks include cross-border communications with sites in the southwestern United States within the Morelos footprint, which are much less expensive to establish and operate than networks using leased Intelsat capacity. A major customer is Telenales, the Mexican telegraph company, which is building the first satellite-based electronic mail network in Mexico to link three major Mexican cities and four remote sites in southeastern Mexico. Honeywell will link an assembly plant in Tijuana with a California office for voice and data. The private network operator, Intelconsult, is establishing a teleport in San Diego to accommodate much of the transborder communications for the assembly plants known as *maquiladoras* on the Mexican-U.S. border. These plants were constructed on the border because the U.S. government allows them to import components from the U.S., assemble them, and reexport them into the United States without paying duty. Thus

U.S. and foreign firms can assemble products for the American market at much lower cost than in the United States because of Mexico's low wage rates.

Despite these innovations in services, much of rural Mexico remains without basic telephone service, even where earth stations have now been installed for television reception. The "last mile" problem is critical in Mexico; there are only 4.6 telephone lines per 100 people nationwide, and far fewer in the countryside. SCT and Telmex have failed to make basic telephone services for rural communities a major priority.

PanAmSat

Pan American Satellite is the first U.S. satellite system to operate international services in competition with Intelsat. (See chapter 14 for more on the introduction of international competition.) Its RCA Astra series 3000 satellite was launched on an Ariane rocket in June 1988. PanAmSat offers high-powered C-band satellite services to all of Latin America, the Caribbean, and the southern United States, and Ku-band services to the United States and Europe. PanAmSat has a Latin American beam that provides relatively high-powered coverage to all of Latin America and three spot beams for Latin America and the Caribbean, primarily for domestic telecommunications and also for regional video and data services. A European beam allows communication between North and South America and Western Europe. PanAmSat officials originally planned to market the system as a satellite "condominium," by selling customers space segment that they could then use for their own purposes. However, they found that international carriers preferred the traditional half-circuit lease format, and few customers had the expertise or interest in purchasing raw bandwidth, preferring instead end-to-end services.[16]

One proposed service is video networking for television distribution to broadcasters and cable systems. In Latin America, the cost of video networking has been very high where terrestrial microwave exists; using Intelsat is also expensive, because its relatively low power requires larger and more costly earth stations. PanAmSat also plans to offer data services, which have been slow in reaching Latin America because of the poor quality of existing telecommunications facilities, unmet demand for basic telephone service, and high markups charged by PTTs. PanAmSat proposes bypass systems using spread-spectrum technology (similar to the Intelnet service).

VSATs could be owned directly by the customers or leased to them by the PTT or a specialized common carrier, if approved by the country.

Many PTTs are hostile to PanAmSat because, as Intelsat signatories, they see competition as a threat to the Intelsat system, and because PanAmSat raises the specters of privatization and competition, trends which are greatly feared throughout much of Latin America. PanAmSat's strategy has been to develop a service structure that requires only minimal cooperation from the PTT to operate. Where operation through or with a PTT is not feasible, PanAmSat will work with local entrepreneurs to establish satellite service companies that will be closely affiliated with the PanAmSat operating company. These companies will offer a range of data services, including data broadcasting and two-way data with bandwidth, end-to-end services and software packages tailored to the needs of particular customers.[17] By avoiding telephone service and concentrating on data and video requirements, PanAmSat hopes to succeed in a market that has traditionally been peripheral to the PTTs' business interests. PanAmSat's success will depend on its ability to find business users who can lobby their governments or their PTTs for the appropriate licensing. As Douglas Goldschmidt notes, the problem in Latin America is not demand, which is substantial for all types of specialized services, but access to customers to meet that demand.[18]

China

China launched its first experimental satellite in 1970 and has since launched at least seventeen satellites, of which five were for remote sensing. Its first geosynchronous communications satellite (STW-1) was launched in 1984, followed by its second telecommunications and broadcasting satellite in 1986. The Chinese plan to use their own satellites for television reception, but have also leased capacity on Intelsat for television distribution to remote areas such as Tibet and Xinjiang.

The Chinese are using satellite distribution to carry the TV University as well as CCTV, the national television network. CCTV used to be transmitted via microwave to major cities, but apparently satellite reception is of higher quality. To reach remote areas, CCTV previously had to record its programs and send videotapes by plane to local television stations in regions such as Xinjiang in northwest China, where audiences watched the programs three days late. In southern Xinjiang, with no civilian airports, programs were as much as fifteen days late.[19]

"China needs 10,000 earth stations to cover its vast territory. In the next five years, the total number of earth stations for both television and telecommunications will reach 5,000," according to Li Xianglin, director of the Electronics Vitalization Leading Group, the policy-making body designed to coordinate the Chinese electronics industry.[20] China has decided to opt for community reception rather than DBS-type systems because of the higher cost of DBS receivers compared to over-the-air redistribution and the increase in number of channels with a lower-powered satellite. "China's present economic strength does not allow such an expensive project, because one DBS receiver costs as much as four color TV sets," according to the chief engineer of the same group.[21]

China appears to have had more immediate success with remote sensing, which has been used for agriculture, forestry, geological prospecting, environmental protection, and urban planning since 1974. Satellites were used to complete the measurement of each province and to ascertain the distribution and area of arable land in 1983. In one instance, satellites helped locate seven prospective locations for iron mines near Beijing, while in another, a construction project for a coal mine was found to be lying on a fault and was therefore halted.[22]

China plans to build and launch its own satellites in the 1990s, as well as to provide launch services for the rest of the world. It is also aiming to launch its own space station and space shuttle by the year 2000.[23] Australia intends to launch its next generation of Aussat satellite (being built by Hughes Aircraft) on the Chinese "Long March" rocket. The launch requires a waiver from the U.S. government because of U.S. concern about allowing the Chinese access to U.S. space technology.

PLANS FOR REGIONAL SATELLITE SYSTEMS

Several other satellite systems for developing regions are being planned. Although these systems are all intended for regions with limited infrastructure and a huge unmet demand for basic telecommunications, they have been slow to develop past the early planning stage. The reasons cited for the slow progress are usually financial; the countries cannot afford the investment because of other economic problems and development priorities. However, political and institutional factors are likely to be equally important. For regional systems the major questions are which country will control the satellite, how much each member will contribute to capital and operating costs, and how the revenues are to be apportioned. In each region, certain factions oppose satellite systems not only because of their cost, but also because they fear that the technology will drain funds needed for other priorities or will increase their dependence on industrialized countries.

Recently there have been proposals by business consortia for regional satellites that are more market-oriented than politically driven. PanAmSat, now offering commercial services in the United States, Latin America, and Europe, was the first to be launched. Satellites designed for the Asian and Pacific markets will also be launched in the next two years.

The Andean Nations: Condor

The feasibility of a regional satellite for the Andean pact countries has been under consideration since the mid-1970s. The Andean regional telecommunications organization, ASETA (Asociacion de Empresas Estatales des Telecommunicaciones del Acuerdo Subregional Andino) is composed of the public international telecommunications authorities of Bolivia, Colombia, Ecuador, Peru, and Venezuela. By the early 1970s, these countries had all installed Intelsat earth stations which had dramatically improved their international telecommunications and demonstrated the promise of satellite technology. In 1974, the newly established ASETA began a feasibility study for a regional satellite system. However, Project Condor, as it became known, is still not off the drawing boards despite numerous subsequent feasibility studies by ASETA members as well as U.S., Canadian, and European entities.[24]

Since ASETA is composed of international carriers, it could not operate a combined national and regional satellite, and therefore established in 1988 a new organization to manage Condor, the Organizacion Andina de Telecommunicaciones por Satellite (OATS).[25] However, much more than an organization stands between ASETA and a regional satellite. The major problems is financing. The capital cost of the space segment, estimated at $210 million, is to be prorated among the members in the same proportion as their participation in ASETA. Members' revenues from existing services are not sufficient to cover these capital costs, so that external financing will be required. Revenues generated by Condor will be in regional currencies rather than in the hard currencies needed to pay foreign suppliers.

A much larger investment will be required for earth stations, estimated at more than twice the cost of the space segment, or nearly $500 million.[26] These estimates seem rather high. At $100,000 for a basic earth station for voice, telex, and television reception, this amount would buy 5,000 earth stations. VSATs are much cheaper, under $3,000 for data reception and under $10,000 for two-way data (although a hub or master station costing approximately $200,000 must be built into the system). Even if each country had several large earth stations at up to $1 million each, $500 million would still buy several thousand earth stations.

Other factors that need to be addressed include the mix of traffic: voice, data, and video; interurban versus rural; domestic versus regional. The mechanism for participation of radio and television broadcasters has not been decided. Many of these broadcasters are private commercial entities that could represent an important source of revenues for Condor if they were to lease transponders. However, any attempt to offer regional programming would require the kind of cooperation on goals and ideology that has eluded Arabsat members. Putting the satellite to use for development purposes would require the sort of collaboration among telecommunications and development agencies that has proved troublesome for planners at the national level, without the additional problems of regional coordination. Of course, each country could use the satellite solely for its own domestic needs, but would still face the challenge of coordination among telecommunications planners and development planners. Nonetheless, Peru has demonstrated how telecommunications planners and health and rural development agencies can join forces in its Rural Communication Services Project (described under the AID Rural Satellite Program in chapter 13).

Another option available to Andean countries is to lease or buy Intelsat transponders under Intelsat's PDS (Planned Domestic Service) program. Three of the five Andean countries (Colombia, Peru, and Venezuela) lease Intelsat capacity for domestic services. Additional Intelsat transponders could provide one solution to the region's needs. However, a study by Intelsat that recommended additional transponder leases was rejected since the transponders at this point would not have been on the same satellite. ASETA members were also concerned that they would be dependent on Intelsat for domestic, regional, and international communications.[27] Furthermore, since Intelsat satellites are intended for high-volume international use, they are relatively low-powered and therefore not ideally suited for thin route and other domestic services. The next generation of Intelsat satellites will have capacity specifically designed for developing countries' domestic and regional services.

Transponders for domestic or regional services could also be leased or bought from PanAmSat. (In fact, Peru was the first country to sign a connecting agreement with PanAmSat.) Or, as Sylvia Ospina points out, ASETA or other countries could take advantage of Article III(e) of the Intelsat Agreement, which states that "Intelsat may, on request and under appropriate terms and conditions, provide satellites or associated facilities separate from the Intelsat space segment for: (i) domestic public telecommunications services in territories under the jurisdiction of one or more Parties, (ii) international public telecommunications services between or among territories under the jurisdiction of two or more Parties."[28] Ospina proposes that OATS could for its first generation lease or buy transponders under the Intelsat PDS program, and then, if appropriate, acquire its second-generation system from Intelsat, although it is not clear that there would be an advantage in using Intelsat as a broker as opposed to directly procuring a regional system.

Given these options, availability of satellite capacity does not seem to be the problem. ASETA could acquire transponders from Intelsat or from PanAmSat, or even from Brasilsat, which has a footprint covering much of the region and has announced that transponders are available for lease to neighboring countries. If ASETA or the individual members do not pursue one of these options, the reasons will likely be more political than technical or even economic.

The Caribbean

The Caribbean nations have also taken preliminary steps toward building a regional satellite system. The Caribbean region contains fourteen island nations and continental countries, speaking five major languages and varying widely in size, resources, forms of government, and culture. Basic telecommunications infrastructure varies within the region, but is often quite limited. Telephone density ranges from 29.0 per 100 people in the Bahamas and 25.0 in Barbados to 3.4 in Guyana and lower in the Dominican Republic and Haiti.[29] Domestic telecommunications services are generally government-run. An exception is Belize, which has transformed the Brazilian Telecommunications Authority into an autonomous entity that provides both domestic and international telecommunications.

The major international carrier in the Caribbean is Cable and Wireless, which operates international systems for several countries and participates in joint ventures in, for example, Jamaica and Trinidad and Tobago. Nine Caribbean countries have their own Intelsat stations. As of late 1986, only 10 percent of Intelsat circuits in the region linked Caribbean countries; the rest carried traffic between the Caribbean and other nations in the Western Hemisphere and Europe. The new Intelsat Caribnet service is intended to respond to this need.[30]

The Caribbean region is within the footprint of U.S. satellites, so that these countries can receive television channels intended for distribution to U.S. cable television operators. Many individuals in the region have installed their own TVROs to watch American television, while in some countries cable companies and even broadcast stations pick up U.S. channels and retransmit them to viewers. The FCC has authorized several American domestic satellites to provide services between the United States and the Caribbean, so that U.S. satellites may be used for some types of communication to the U.S. from countries that authorize this access rather than using Intelsat.

The Caribbean nations, with assistance from the ITU have examined their needs for regional communications and considered several options, including a regional satellite system. Several Caribbean nations stated at the ITU's Regional Administrative Radio Conference (RARC) on broadcasting satellites in 1983 and at the 1985 Space WARC (World Administrative Radio Conference) that they planned eventually to operate a regional broadcasting satellite. As in the Andean region, however, the constraints on regional communication seem more political than technical. Transponders on Intelsat or PanAmSat could be leased for a broadcasting service. The number of countries involved poses economic problems, because the international carriers set tariffs that may be prohibitively expensive for regional broadcasting and teleconferencing. However, the countries of the region will first have to develop a prototype of a regional network and then determine how best to deliver it throughout the region.

Sub-Saharan Africa

For more than a decade, one or more regional African satellite systems have been under discussion. Africa's huge land mass; hostile terrain of deserts, jungles, and mountains; and limited infrastructure pose formidable problems for improving communications. Satellites that can provide communications to any location without extending the terrestrial network appear to be the best solution for many African telecommunications needs. Terrestrial networks such as the Panaftel microwave system have proved to be extremely vulnerable to outages. For example, in some regions the shortage of fuel and trucks make it difficult to deliver diesel oil to the generators that power the microwave repeaters. If the generator fails, the transmitter ceases to operate, and the network goes down. Solar power offers a promising alternative, but many repeaters are located on mountaintops or other inaccessible sites, so that it is difficult and expensive to reach equipment for maintenance and repair. Stories abound of people helping themselves to the diesel fuel or to copper wire, probably because they themselves receive no benefit from a telecommunications network carrying interurban traffic right past their villages. In contrast, small solar-powered satellite earth stations could be located in villages to provide basic telephone and broadcasting services.

Several studies of African telecommunications needs have been made. The United Nations Economic Commission for Africa (UNECA) examined the feasibility of a satellite system for development. The ITU proposed a system called GLODOM, whose specifications were ideally suited to use by developing countries; that is, they called for relatively high-powered C-band transponders for communication with small solar-powered earth stations. The ITU coordinated an African satellite planning project called RASCOM. Other studies have been conducted by French, British, and German consultants, who appear to be primarily interested in finding a market for European satellites. The political fragmentation of African telecommunications creates many obstacles in the search for a viable system. Not only do the various countries differ in their perspectives, they also belong to several telecommunications organizations, including the Pan African Telecommunications Union (PATU), which is composed primarily of anglophone countries; Union Pan-Africaine des Telecommunications (UPAT), with a francophone membership; the regional broadcasting organization (URTNA); and so on.

Several sub-Saharan African countries now lease Intelsat transponders for domestic communications, among them Ivory Coast, Mozambique, Nigeria, Sudan, and Zaire. However, these countries use Intelsat to reach major cities and provincial or state capitals, leaving most of the population unserved. At one time, Nigeria was considering its own domestic system, but that proposal seems to have been shelved because of lack of funds, although Nigeria does lease capacity from Intelsat for domestic services and purchased a tethered-balloon system to cover part of the country, which ended up an expensive failure.

One option for African rural communications would be to lease or purchase transponders on Intelsat's next generation (Intelsat VII), which will have capacity optimized for thin-route rural services. A regional satellite for sub-Saharan Africa faces the same political, organizational, and economic problems that confront Arabsat and the ASETA countries. Leasing capacity from Intelsat or possibly some other satellite entity may prove the most viable solution.

Asia and the Pacific

In geographical terms, the Asia-Pacific region can be divided into countries with large land masses and relatively densely populated rural areas, and island nations with small and widely scattered populations. Satellites offer considerable promise for both types of countries. Indonesia and India have their own domestic satellite systems, and China plans to operate its own satellite in the 1990s. However, for many countries, sharing satellite capacity may be the most cost-effective solution. Two satellites for the region are now planned that offer innovative organizational approaches. Asiasat 1, which is to be launched in 1989, will offer coverage of China and Southeast Asia. The investors in the system are the Chinese government, Cable and Wireless, and Hutchison Telecommunications (a Hong Kong company).[31]

Asiasat 1 is actually a refurbished Hughes satellite that was launched from the space shuttle in 1984 as Westar VI. The satellite failed to achieve geostationary orbit and was retrieved by another NASA shuttle crew. This C-band satellite, with higher power than Intelsat, can be used for voice, data, and video transmissions. China will use the satellite for domestic communications; Thailand may be another domestic customer. The satellite will also be available for regional communications.

Another Asia-Pacific satellite venture to watch is Pacstar, a company whose investors include the government of Papua New Guinea and TRT, a U.S. carrier now owned by Pacific Telecom (headquartered in Vancouver, Washington). Pacific Telecom, whose Alascom subsidiary provides telecommunications services in Alaska, including satellite service to Alaskan villages, is also a partner in a new fiber-optic cable between Asia and the United States. Details on Pacstar have not been released, but it apparently will provide C-band transponders with beams covering the island nations of the South Pacific, and is designed for low-cost, thin-route, and regional communication as well as coverage of the major cities of Southeast Asia.

Several developing countries are in various stages of planning their own domestic satellite systems, including Thailand, Pakistan, Iran, Nigeria, Colombia, and Argentina. Some of these nations see leases from Intelsat or a regional system as transitional steps toward their own domestic systems. Others may find that shared capacity is adequate for their needs and that the costs of purchasing and operating their own domestic systems outweigh the political benefits of investing in this highly visible technology.

Satellites and Developing Countries

Case Studies

INTRODUCTION

This chapter includes four case studies that examine in greater detail satellite applications for development, problems in implementation, and strategies needed to integrate satellite planning and applications with development goals. The cases identify the difficulties developing countries have faced in reaping the full benefits of the technology in their political, cultural, and institutional contexts. The experiences of India and Brazil with domestic satellites form the subject of the first two sections. The sections that follow examine two projects designed to help developing countries gain experience in applying satellite technology for development: the U.S. Agency for International Development's (AID) Rural Satellite Program and Intelsat's Project SHARE.

CASE STUDIES ON DOMESTIC SYSTEMS: INDIA AND BRAZIL

Both India and Brazil have made major commitments to satellite technology by procuring domestic satellite systems. Both nations also have the technological expertise to design and build their own earth stations, and may eventually build their own commercial satellites. Both nations contend with a lack of basic communications to rural and remote areas, low literacy rates, and limited health care and other social services—problems that could be addressed through use of their satellite technology. India, however, has made much more progress to date than Brazil in harnessing the developmental potential of its satellite, despite its own political and bureaucratic obstacles.

India: Insat

Space research in India began in 1962. In 1965, India approached the United Nations Development Programme (UNDP) to fund the establishment of a Centre for Training and Research in Satellite Communications for Developing Countries in Ahmedabad. The visionary Dr. Vikram A. Sarabhai, founder of the Indian space program, recognized the potential of satellite communication for India, particularly for mass communication and education. Sarabhai, the first chairman of the Indian Space Research Organization (ISRO), disagreed with the approach of extending television gradually from New Delhi, and thought that satellite technology could be used to bring educational television directly to the rural areas which had 80 percent of the population but the least access to information and education.

Indian engineers visited NASA in 1967 to study its plans for ATS-6, which was to include capacity designed for low-cost rural reception. Based on comparative studies of four alternatives, the engineers recommended that India invest in a satellite system to provide networking of signals, with terrestrial retransmission in urban areas and direct community reception in rural areas.[1] These requirements were incorporated into the design adopted for Insat more than a decade later. Meanwhile, ISRO negotiated with NASA for access to the ATS-6 satellite for a one-year pilot project to study the delivery of educational television. The memorandum to undertake the project using ATS-6 was signed by Indian and U.S. officials in 1969, following a year of interagency committee meetings chaired by the dedicated and persuasive Dr. Sarabhai.[2] This SITE (for Satellite Instructional Television Experiment) project took place in 1975–76, after the ATS-6 satellite was moved to an orbital location over the Indian Ocean (it was later moved back to cover the United States).

The goal of the SITE project was to learn how to use satellite technology to bring education and information to Indian villagers, as Sarabhai had advocated. SITE delivered educational and general television programming to more than 2,400 villages equipped with

Indian-built television sets and chicken-wire antennas. The televised programs addressed such development topics as agriculture, family planning, health, and nutrition. The evaluators found that despite their efforts to adapt these programs for different regions by translating them into several languages, the variations in climate and culture across the country limited their relevance.

Perhaps the most important effects of SITE were related to the planning and implementation process itself. SITE provided important experience for engineers, program producers, and the social scientists who served as planners and evaluators. The high technical standards achieved and the project managers' demonstrated ability to cope without excessive reliance on foreign technical assistance strengthened India's confidence. SITE served as a stimulus to the Indian electronics industry, which manufactured Indian-designed antennas and earth-station components. Finally, it set India's national television on what development analysts considered an unprecedented course, toward a program service aimed to serve rural citizens.[3]

Yet SITE had less impact on the content of programming distributed by Insat than might have been expected. Bella Mody points out the importance of examining "the context of power within which the stages of innovation diffusion take place."[4] Institutional frictions plagued India's satellite plans from the start. The SITE project—from hardware and software to planning, implementation, and evaluation—was managed by ISRO rather than the telecommunications and broadcasting authorities. Officials at Doordarshan, the government television network, perceived that ISRO was invading their turf; the extension of broadcasting services was their responsibility. Thus, Doordarshan initially rejected the conclusion that satellite transmission was superior to its terrestrial plan. Similarly, the Ministry of Posts and Telecommunications (now the Ministry of Communications), which was responsible for extending telephone service, also favored terrestrial networks. The ministries of agriculture, education, health, and family planning considered the SITE project a drain on their resources with little potential benefit for their bureaucracies.

These institutional concerns seems to have been reflected in the planning for Insat as well. Operational services were taken from the mandate of ISRO and placed with the Ministry of Posts and Telecommunications and Doordarshan. By 1978, the MPT seemed to have seen "the writing on the wall" and realized that a satellite was destined for India's future, but viewed the technology solely as a means of filling the gaps in areas that were not to be served terrestrially, rather than as part of a national plan that would use the most appropriate mix of technologies to meet the country's needs.[5]

The decision to produce a domestic satellite was announced by the Indian Cabinet in December 1975, five months into the SITE project. In addition to the technical and developmental arguments that had been made in favor of the satellite, evidence of the political benefits of satellite-delivered television proved persuasive. Prime Minister Indira Gandhi had apparently learned about the power of television to reach the public directly during the era when she had suspended the constitution and imposed censorship on all the media. During this period she frequently spoke to the populace in television broadcasts, and Doordarshan programming showed only the government's version of events.[6]

Between SITE and the beginning of Insat, India gained additional technical experience with several experimental satellites. The first Indian satellite, Aryabhata (named after a fourth-century astronomer), was built by India for technical experiments and launched by the U.S.S.R. in 1975.[7] In 1977–79, under an agreement with the Franco-German Symphonie satellite administration, Indian researchers conducted the STEP Project (Symphonie Telecommunications Experimental Project) to experiment with fixed, mobile, and emergency earth stations and satellite transmission techniques. Project APPLE (Ariane Passenger Payload Experiment) in 1981–83 launched a satellite designed and fabricated in India on an Ariane development flight. Technical experiments were carried out on the satellite over the two-year period.

India's own domestic satellite, Insat 1A, was built by Ford Aerospace and launched by NASA in April 1982. However, it was deactivated following the depletion of on-board propellants for station keeping in September 1982, and replaced with Insat 1B in 1983. Insat combines features of a fixed satellite, broadcasting satellite, and meteorological satellite into a single space platform. Each satellite is equipped with twelve national-coverage transponders operating in C band, each capable of handling two television channels or 1,332 one-way telephone channels; two high-powered S-band broadcast transponders, each capable of handling one direct-reception television channel with five audio carriers; a very-high-resolution radiometer for scanning; and a data channel to relay meteorological, hydrological, and oceanographic data from collection platforms.[8]

The first two years of Insat's operation witnessed a phenomenal expansion in television broadcasting. For more than twenty years after the introduction of television in 1959, the growth in the number of transmitters took place largely around major cities and towns; by 1982, there were only twenty-five television transmitters in India, covering just 25 percent of the population. By 1986, 180 transmitters fed by satellite covered 70 percent of the population. Insat 1 provides two television rebroadcast channels for nationwide coverage: one for networking of terrestrial transmitters and the other for direct transmission from the satellite to augmented community television receivers for rural areas. In addition, 2,000 Indian-built community receivers with 3.6-meter, chicken-wire antennas receive programs from the S-band transponder.[9]

Insat customers include Doordarshan, which uses the satellite for networking and for direct broadcasting of television to community receivers; All India Radio, for networking radio programs; the Post and Telegraph Department, for telecommunications traffic; and the Indian Meteorological Department, for meteorological warning systems. Insat now transmits educational programs produced by the Ministry of Education to primary schools in the morning and university-level enrichment programs in the afternoon. Rural education programs in health and agriculture are transmitted in the evening to reach adults after work, in conjunction with network news, sports, and entertainment programs. All India Radio (AIR) has replaced its shortwave and microwave communications with satellite links for regional networking and program distribution, using some of the subcarriers on the S-band transponder. These can also be used for multiple language sound tracks.

Unlike most other developing countries, India has a well-developed domestic film industry that can provide content for television. However, to date there has been little independent television production, as Doordarshan prefers to keep its production in house. Limited production facilities and training opportunities have restricted Doordarshan production. In 1983, imported content accounted for a maximum of 10 percent of programming on Doordarshan. Content is changing, as India imports more programs to satisfy viewer demand. Also, Doordarshan has introduced advertising, generating $52 million in revenues in 1985. It projects an audience of 80 percent of India's population, which could generate advertising revenues of $170 million in 1990.[10] Doordarshan now has more incentive to offer the most popular programs, such as imported entertainment and Indian soap operas, rather than educational programs.

VCRs have also had a major impact in India. In 1982, the government eased restrictions on imports of color television sets and VCRs to enable Indians to watch the 1984 Asian Games (which India was televising in color to the rest of the world). Indians working in the Gulf states also brought home VCRs. Today imported as well as locally made VCRs can be bought in India, and it is estimated that there are more than one million VCRs in the country. VCRs are used not only for family viewing of foreign programs, but also for makeshift community video theaters where entrepreneurs make money showing foreign films or even pirated tapes of Indian films at lower prices than those charged by movie theaters.

Regarding voice and data services on Insat, by 1990 the public telecommunication segment is to comprise about 120 earth stations with 6,500 circuits, plus dedicated earth stations for business subscribers. Insat's five-year plan includes the following objectives in satellite communications:

- provision of reliable long-distance trunk circuits to distant rural areas
- coverage of district centers currently not served by terrestrial media
- substantial increases in the number of transportable emergency earth stations
- provision of links for business users
- plans for data-broadcasting and rural telegraph networks
- investigation of unconventional sources of energy, such as solar and wind power, for low-capacity earth stations.[11]

However, India still has one of the lowest telephone densities in the world (0.5 per 100 people), despite ambitious plans to extend the telephone network. Without a major commitment of resources to install thousands of public telephones and village exchanges, the satellite system will be able to serve only a tiny fraction of the rural population.

The domestic Insat-1B is being used to capacity, and there are plans to offer new services on Insat-1C. The Ministry of Communications now allows users to own their own customer premises and terminal equipment. To date, domestic bypass is not permitted. Earth stations for direct access to Insat can apparently be installed where there is no reliable communication, for instance, at factories in remote and backward areas. However, customers must use the switched network even if it is highly congested. There appears to be a strong and growing demand for data processing and computer networking, as industries and the service sector, especially banking and reservation services, expand. Indonet, a data network established by CMC (a government-owned corporation), began with 5 sites with access to IBM and DEC computers via leased lines. It intends to replace inter-city terrestrial links with Insat-1C circuits and plans to grow to 35 sites within a year and to 100 sites by the end of the decade. India also leases Intelsat capacity for service to remote areas and for the Nicnet service, which provides low-speed interactive data services using VSATs and spread-spectrum technology for the National Informatics Centre (see chapter 10).

In assessing India's experience in applying satellite technology to development goals, we must note several points. With regard to technology transfer, India was concerned from the beginning about indigenization of hardware. Indian engineers arranged training sessions during the construction of ATS-6, and engineers from ISRO and MIT's Lincoln Laboratories undertook a joint study on the spacecraft to plan Insat. India built its own satellite terminals and television sets for ATS-6, and currently builds its own terminals for television reception from Insat. India has negotiated an agreement for domestic manufacture of the Intelnet-type terminals now being installed for the Nicnet network, which currently runs on Intelsat, but similar technology could be used with Insat. India was also responsible for the design of its own domestic satellite, and a team of Indian engineers worked closely with Ford Aerospace during the construction of the Insat satellites.

While the government's commitment to Indian technological development has remained strong, political and economic conditions have in many ways changed dramatically since the days of SITE. These changes include the growth of the middle class, a new commercial orientation in public television, the liberalization of regulations, and increased support for entrepreneurship and joint ventures under Prime Minister Rajiv Gandhi. All these factors influence India's current satellite use and prospects for the future. We may see less emphasis on televised education and more on low-cost data services for business and government agencies, for example. Despite formidable governmental and commercial barriers, India has done more with its domestic satellite system than any other developing country, and has at least tried to use its technology for developmental purposes.

Brazil: BRASILSAT

Brazil is the largest country in South America, with 8.5 million square kilometers. Its 128 million inhabitants make it the sixth most populous country in the world. Its telephone density is 5.3 lines per 100 people.[12] The cities are relatively well served, although there are long waiting lists in many areas, and underinvestment in capacity, coupled with traffic growth, have resulted in high blockage rates. Some of the agricultural communities in southeastern Brazil have basic telephone service, but most rural areas have no telephone service.

As in India, a space agency and a visionary scientist introduced satellites to Brazil. Fernando Mendonça, founder of INPE, the national space agency, saw in satellites a way to deliver education and other social services to the impoverished people of rural Brazil. In 1968, INPE sponsored a pioneering study called SACI/EXERN, to demonstrate how satellite distribution of televised classes could improve primary-level instruction in rural Brazil.[13] It soon became clear that the success of the project would depend on the development of educational software and the availability of an appropriate telecommunications infrastructure. Despite the encouraging results of the study, INPE did not have the political influence or funding necessary to secure the commitment of the Brazilian government to a national satellite system.

The agencies involved with the Brazilian satellite system (SBTS) were the National Space Research Institute (INPE), in the early experimental phases, and Embratel, the national long-distance telecommunications company, for implementation and operation. Brazilian telecommunications is under the jurisdiction of the Ministry of Communications (Minicom), founded in 1967. Minicom controls the state-owned holding company Telebras, of which Embratel and approximately thirty state and local companies are subsidiaries. Embratel was established in 1965 to operate Brazil's telecommunications networks.

Brazil installed an Intelsat earth station in 1969 to improve international communications and generate revenue for the domestic network. This station has been immensely profitable, having generated more than enough revenue to pay for its $6 million capital cost in the first year. In the first half of 1975 alone, it earned $60 million.[14] In 1974, Brazil began leasing capacity from Intelsat for domestic services to regional centers, including major towns in isolated areas. The Amazon region has a population of 8.5 million in an area of 5 million square kilometers, much of which is covered by dense jungle and accessible only by boat or plane. It is almost impossible to provide service to the region by terrestrial means. Until 1974, communication with the state capitals and some other cities in the Amazon Basin was achieved by troposcatter radio relay systems, a very expensive system with limited capacity.

Planning for a domestic satellite was assigned to Embratel in 1976, although there was strong opposition in Embratel from senior management and engineers who favored terrestrial technologies. This opposition was finally overcome by an alliance of satellite supporters within Embratel, the armed forces, and government research institutions.[15] Embratel was authorized in 1982 to contract for, implement, and operate Brasilsat. The prime contractor for the satellite was Spar Aerospace of Canada, with Hughes Aircraft serving as a subcontractor. Brazilian satellite engineers (most of whom had been educated at U.S. universities) favored U.S. satellite technology because of its proven reliability, but a Western European consortium made a tantalizing offer including more advanced technology and attractive financing. According to Hughes officials, they approached Spar (which had been a subcontractor to Hughes for Canada's Anik satellites) when they realized that they could not get U.S. government or private bank support to offer a financing package as attractive as the offer of the Western European consortium. The Canadian government put together a package of incentives, including attractive financing from a group of Canadian banks, training and technology transfer commitments, and some barter provisions.

Thus Spar Aerospace of Canada was the prime contractor for the supply of two Hughes Aircraft satellites launched in 1985 and 1986 on Ariane rockets. Brasilsat 1A took over seven transponders of video and telephone traffic from Intelsat transponder leases, as well as transmissions of private Brazilian television networks. Together these networks form one of the world's leading television industries. Brazil's four commercial television networks now use Brasilsat to feed their signals to regional stations and transmitters. Several Brazilian companies manufacture backyard-type TVROs, which individuals are able to purchase. More than 2,000 TVROs have been installed by viewers in remote areas.

However, Brasilsat remains underutilized and provides few innovative services. Intelsat had been used for interurban links for telephone and television transmission only, whereas market surveys by Embratel showed that the more promising markets in the future would be for television reception, rural telephony, and private data communication networks.[16] Brasilsat today has been slow to offer these services and basically provides an additional telecommunications link in an extensive terrestrial system.

It appears that the greatest barriers to both social service and commercial applications have been political or institutional, rather than technical. By concentrating on short-term issues such as satellite design and financing, the planners failed to take into consideration the potential for a national market for satellite services or the complexity of organizing and funding large-scale social applications. Despite the fact that the satellite is underutilized and therefore not generating the revenue it could, there does not seem to be a strong incentive to increase its use. The problem appears to be primarily institutional. Brasilsat is a subsidiary of Embratel with virtually no autonomy, unlike, for example, Telesat in Canada. Strong opposition to Brasilsat still exists in Embratel, although enough political momentum is gathered behind the second-generation satellite for implementation to proceed regardless of the commercial success of the first.

One of the problems in diffusion of the technology is that earth stations must be provided by Embratel. Neither the state telephone companies nor users can purchase or install their own earth stations. Thus, in Amazonas, where Brasilsat could provide communications to isolated settlements in the jungle, the state telephone company, Telamazon, has chosen to install terrestrial radio links in more accessible locations and is waiting for Embratel to install earth stations for service to more isolated areas. Banks and brokers could not set up data networks using VSATs for several years because Embratel had not introduced VSAT service. But Embratel is not willing to allow telecommunication services to be provided by any other entity that might have the capital to provide earth stations or sell them to users and establish new networks. In fact, when contracts were signed in 1987 between Embratel and two Brazilian companies that planned to provide VSAT-based data networks, Embratel's union employees called a nationwide strike because they feared that this network would set a precedent that could undermine Embratel's monopoly and thereby jeopardize their jobs. In 1989, Embratel signaled a change in this policy by proposing to authorize private VSAT networks that would operate through an Embratel-owned hub station. This compromise may provide an interesting model for other PTT-operated domestic satellites.

These problems are exacerbated by Brazil's continuing economic crisis. The telephone companies must contend with various inflation-fighting restrictions in their attempts to expand public-sector services. Their revenues are turned over to the state, which then allocates funds for future operations. Thus the telephone companies do not control their own budgets. They cannot reinvest their profits by upgrading and extending their own networks. But, as telephone company executives point out, they generate enough revenues to finance their own expansion, and better telecommunications would facilitate the growth of other economic activities. Several telephone company executives interviewed by the author expressed great frustration at not being able to use their revenues to implement their development plans. Of course, this policy affects more than satellite use, but it serves to hinder both the extension and upgrading of service. Brazilian telephone facilities are now inadequately maintained, and waiting lists have grown, so not only are more people unserved, but the quality of existing services has deteriorated.

In addition, Embratel suffers from what might be called "marketing myopia." Like other government-run monopolies, it has little experience in marketing and innovation in services. The result is that innovators within Brasilsat receive little support for proposals to introduce new services and attract new customers. As a result, Brasilsat has neither served any useful developmental purposes nor has it fulfilled its commercial potential. Underutilization of the system, combined with higher-than-expected satellite costs, means that Embratel must now allocate 10 percent of its revenues to cover losses incurred by the satellite system.[17]

Few attempts have been made to plan for applications of satellite technology to education and social services, despite the pledge by Brazilian president Sarney in November 1985 that "by the end of my administration, we are going to unite the resources provided by the satellite and the vast field of informatics to modernize education in Brazil."[18] Lack of support from Brasilsat, lack of information among health and education ministries about the satellite and its possible uses, and lack of coordination among the ministries are to blame. The ministries are chronically underfunded; their staffs include professionals who are suspicious of technology that they do not understand and that may increase their dependency on other countries. The network of educational television stations, FUNTEVE, receives only 0.9 percent of the Ministry of Education's budget and would face much higher tariffs if it switched from microwave to satellite. Like Indonesia's government-run Perumtel, Embratel has not been willing to make price concessions to encourage the use of satellites in meeting national goals.

As Joao Carlos Albernaz points out, the availability of forty-eight transponders, or the equivalent of 50,000 telephone channels, makes it possible to deliver new commercial services as well as providing new means of applying telecommunications for social programs.[19] However, political and institutional disincentives to innovation have so far limited the role of Brasilsat in Brazilian development.[20]

PILOT PROJECTS TO ENCOURAGE
DEVELOPMENTAL APPLICATIONS OF SATELLITES

During the 1980s, two ambitious initiatives were undertaken to encourage the use of satellite technology for developmental purposes. The Rural Satellite Program, sponsored by the U.S. Agency for International Development (AID), was designed to help countries with access to satellites use them to solve development problems. Pilot projects were carried out in Indonesia, the West Indies, and Peru. Intelsat's Project SHARE provided free access to Intelsat satellites for health and education demonstrations and projects.

AID Rural Satellite Program

By the late 1970s, the U.S. Agency for International Development had determined that there were major obstacles to the utilization of satellites for development, including a lack of visible, ongoing projects to serve as models, a lack of planning capacity and relevant experience in developing countries with access to satellites, and a lack of awareness among development agencies and telecommunications lenders of the role satellites could play in rural development.[21] Thus in 1979, AID undertook an exploratory program to aid the developing world in testing the use of satellite communications for development. The program was experimental not in its technology, although certain hardware innovations were introduced, but rather in its applications of satellite technology for development.

The goal of the program was to assist developing countries that already had access to a satellite to use it for developmental purposes, rather than planning new satellite capacity more appropriately designed for development use. AID officials decided to concentrate on interactive narrowband telecommunications rather than on broadcast community television because of the successful applications of audioconferencing in Alaska and the South Pacific, the low cost of narrow-band equipment, and the simple production techniques required.

In Indonesia, AID supported a project that used Palapa to enhance higher education by linking thirteen new universities in the Indonesian archipelago. These eastern islands universities suffered from a severe shortage of specialized faculty, particularly in basic sciences and agriculture. The satellite audioconferencing system enabled a professor at one institution to teach students at several locations. The network was also used for faculty training and for administration, enabling administrators to meet electronically between infrequent face-to-face meetings. Sites were also equipped with facsimile machines and electronic blackboards for transmission of material written or drawn on graphic tablets. At most locations, the sites accessed existing Perumtel earth stations through telephone lines.

The Indonesian project had mixed success. Numerous technical problems had to be overcome in order to make the multiple site conferencing links perform adequately, to modify equipment that was not designed for tropical conditions, and, most importantly, to solve the "last mile" problem of poor-quality telephone links between the site and the earth station. Once these problems were overcome, the network did function adequately for university-level distance education and regional administration. Institutional problems that had slowed implementation were almost fatal at the post-project stage. No agency had clear responsibility for the project, although it appeared that the recently established Open University, which offered university credit via correspondence courses, was the logical choice to take over the network. However, the Open University did not have the resources for even minimal staffing and support. Perumtel also often seemed a reluctant participant, but did agree to continue to provide technical support.

The Peru Rural Communications Services Project (RCSP) was developed and administered by Entel Peru (Empresa Nacional de Telecomunicaciones del Peru) with support from AID. The goal of the project was to use satellite communications via Intelsat to provide basic telephone service and teleconferencing to support development activities in an isolated region of Peru. The RCSP provided public telephone service and audioconferencing facilities to seven communities in the Department of San Martin, a high jungle area east of the Andes. Satellite earth stations were installed in three communities, and four smaller towns were linked via VHF radio to one of the earth stations.

Despite numerous setbacks relating to technical problems with both the earth stations and the VHF radio system, the project did implement telecommunications services for rural residents and government agencies. There was an immediate demand for the project's telephone services. During the first two and a half years of operation, 207,441 calls were completed, generating about $272,000 in revenue. The heaviest callers used the system for business purposes to a significant extent.[22]

The teleconferencing activities were developed in cooperation with Peruvian agriculture, health, and education ministries, and incorporated a wide variety of administrative, training, diffusion, and promotion strategies. A total of 658 audioteleconferences were sponsored by the ministries and Entel during 1984 and 1985, involving almost 12,000 participant hours.[23] The health sector was the most active and most successful user, perhaps because it had a stable organizational structure and a pressing need for communication to support its operations. Entel itself became a major user of teleconferencing for training purposes. At the end of the two-year period, Entel transferred responsibility for teleconferencing development to its commercial sector, with plans to promote teleconferencing among government agencies and private business.

While rural telephone traffic exceeded expectations, revenues did not cover operating costs, let alone contribute to capital recovery, during the first two years of operation. The development agencies themselves did not have sufficient discretionary budgets to sustain ambitious telecommunications activities without additional government support.[24] However, the benefits to the users were substantial. Individual users stated that they would have been willing to spend approximately $4.75 on alternatives to the telephone system such as telegrams, letters, travel, and so on. This amount was higher than the charge for an average call. For institutional users, face-to-face instruction would have cost about twice as much as the typical teleconferencing seminar.

The third satellite project supported by the AID Rural Satellite Program was the University of the West Indies Distance Teaching Experiment (UWIDITE). UWIDITE built on the experience gained in a previous experiment called Project Satellite, which used NASA's ATS-3 and ATS-6 satellites to link the Jamaica and Barbados campuses of UWI with its St. Lucia extension center in 1978. UWIDITE began with five dedicated teleconferencing rooms, one at each of the main campuses (Jamaica, Barbados, and Trinidad) and one at each of two extension centers (St. Lucia and Dominica). Each room was equipped with audioconferencing equipment and slow-scan television; telewriters and microcomputers were added.[25]

The main applications of the network were for extension studies, or courses for credit toward a university degree; extramural studies, or special nondegree courses; and extension services to support agricultural development and information distribution. A typical weekly schedule included inservice classes for teachers, UWIDITE coordinators' meetings, class sessions for Challenge Examinations (which allow students to take their first year of university in their home countries), continuing medical education classes, and medical case consultations.[26]

UWIDITE has continued past the pilot-project phase, with support from various agencies. Teleconferencing facilities at other UWI extension centers have been added. Ironically, the project turned out not to be completely satellite-based. Each center is connected to the appropriate international gateway via leased four-wire telephone lines. Jamaica is linked to Trinidad via Intelsat, and the eastern Caribbean islands are interconnected via terrestrial troposcatter and microwave systems operated by Cable and Wireless. More than one-third of UWIDITE's annual costs were for leased lines. One of the problems in implementing a regional telecommunications network is that several different carriers are involved. Negotiating a reasonable tariff and maintenance agreements can be therefore much more complex than dealing with a single carrier. Both UWI and the University of the South Pacific (described under Project SHARE below) had to negotiate at length with the carriers in their regions to establish simple audioconferencing systems, and must continually look for funding to pay for their leased lines.

One of the most valuable functions of the AID Rural Satellite Program was to compile a set of guidelines based on informal assessments and formal evaluations of its projects. Some of the most important lessons learned were summarized by the evaluators of the Peru project:

The transfer of sophisticated telecommunications technology is not, and probably will not be for the foreseeable future, a straightforward exercise. Even the most thorough plans require revision, endless patience and dedication if they are to be implemented successfully. New and innovative communication strategies require extensive promotion as well as innovative management structures, especially when changes in standard operating procedures are involved.[27]

Among the specific lessons identified by the Rural Satellite Program staff were the following:[28]

Planning

- Include the telecommunications authorities in all technical planning steps and in all technical training efforts.
- Accurately assess the stages of growth and maturity of the user institutions before creating an implementation plan.
- Do not assume that an existing institution or association of institutions implies common needs among its members.
- Do not assume standard administration practices or structure are present at all participating institutions.

Implementation

- Although telecommunications can provide a reliable link between members of a group, it does not solve any existing problems in the coordination and organization of that group.
- A strong management structure is essential to a successful teleconferencing project.
- The introduction of an innovative system does not automatically mean that the users will adopt innovative ways of utilizing such a system.
- Preparation of support materials is one of the most important elements in distance instruction.
- Preparation and distribution of support materials are two of the biggest problems for management staff.
- The presence of a local tutor greatly enhances student acceptance, attendance, interaction, participation, and, by extension, learning.
- A picture is not always worth a thousand words!

Technical

- In planning rural telephone systems, do not underestimate the tremendous pent-up demand for service.
- Audioconferencing is the true "workhorse" of a teleconferencing network.
- Make every effort to field-test electronic classroom equipment before committing to a bulk purchase.

- In choosing equipment, start simple and make it more complex only if the staff, time, money, and skills are available to support it.
- Everything takes more time than expected!

To summarize:

> The basic tenets of any development project about the need for strong institutional support, sound management, and dynamic leadership are equally important for a telecommunications-based project. . . . Communications support projects that are truly effective . . . must be based on thorough analysis, sound design, and realistic expectations. Technical networks must be integrated into institutional operations and supported with user and operator training. A state-of-the-art technical network alone does not ensure that desired benefits will accrue. It is the usefulness of programming and the suitability of applications which will determine the communications support project's impact on development. A network that fully satisfies important communications needs will prove to be well worth the investment.[29]

These micro-level lessons apply to many development projects. Satellite projects are particularly difficult because of the scale of the technical investment and the limited availability of satellite time (either because of the limited life of the satellite or because of constraints in access to transponders). Such projects necessarily involve telecommunications and technical officials who are not likely to have experience with users—whether they be businesses or social services. The users, in turn, are not likely to be familiar with the technology or technical agencies.

Project SHARE

Intelsat announced Project SHARE (Satellites for Health and Rural Education) in August 1984 as part of its twentieth-anniversary celebration ceremonies. Intelsat offered to provide free satellite time for health and education purposes; users had to provide their own earth-station facilities and support for the projects. Project SHARE was initially limited to sixteen months, and was extended twice, through the end of 1987. Its activities involved sixty-five countries on five continents.

Intelsat's final evaluation states that Project SHARE served as a stimulant and a catalyst: "It is, at least in part, because of Project SHARE that we have seen parallel progress on other Intelsat services designed for distant and rural users. Vista, volume purchase of Vista terminals, Super Vista . . . and the expanded rural applications of Intelnet all were to some degree spurred by Project SHARE."[30] But to what degree? Growth of these services, as noted in chapter 10, has been very slow. But perhaps more telling, very few of the Project SHARE activities have actually been continued.

The initial sixteen-month period was in fact a very short time for the initiation of a project, which would normally involve developing the idea, obtaining commitments from social service organizations and from the Intelsat signatory, and finding support for hardware and operating costs. In addition, many projects would require development of curricula, training, program production, and soon, all of which could take much longer than the time available, once a decision was made to proceed. It is not surprising, then, that the initial proposals were mostly for one-shot teleconferences, which take much less effort to plan and produce than other types of activities such as distance education, consultation, training, and the like. In addition, most initiators of projects came from international organizations or industrialized countries rather than developing countries.

Intelsat states that Project SHARE applications were divided almost equally between one-time or short-term video events or videoconferences and longer-term or recurring programs. Of the twenty completed projects summarized in the final evaluation report, eleven involved videoconferences, and four used audioconferencing. Most of the videoconferences were one-time events, whereas the audioconferences were generally conducted over an extended period. Three projects involved computer communications: a computer conferencing network between Indonesia and Canada, a link for the Pan African News Agency, and a demonstration of Intelnet in Senegal. One project, China's TV university, used television for distance education; another took the form of a television show called "The Day of Five Billion," sponsored by the United Nations Foundation for Population Studies and Turner Broadcasting System, which was designed to increase global awareness of the plight of an increasingly crowded world.

It is impossible to assess from the limited information available the impact of the teleconferences, although most appear to have been highly valued by the participants. Nevertheless, commercial video teleconferences are expensive, and apparently most were not considered to be cost-effective enough to be continued after the project. In some cases, such as one-time conferences in conjunction with a specific event (e.g., International Women's Year), follow-on activity might not be expected. But then it is hard to see how Intelsat could justify the donation of satellite time as market development leading to future use.

Comments from the brief project summaries reveal some of the difficulties participants faced in continuing their activities:

- Of a truncated series of teleconferences between the United States and South America (two were held, but a longer series was planned) it was reported: "The evaluation form rated the experience as very positive. Nevertheless, no further videoconference exchanges are contemplated."[31]

- Of a series of sixteen video teleconferences between Ireland and Jordan a participant wrote: "The lecture presentations were largely prerehearsed, and thus in theory prerecorded lectures on videocassettes might have been sent to Jordan to be played on VCRs. This would have allowed satellite time to be reserved for question and answer. Such a system was proposed for a follow-on project, but this was not undertaken."[32]

- Of a medical link between Newfoundland, Canada, and East Africa it was stated: "Nearly $200,000 in electronic terminal equipment was donated and some $100,000 in terrestrial communications links in Canada and East Africa were also made available for the test and demonstrations. The direct and indirect equipment, services and staff costs of this project combined with the University of the West Indies project [another project involving Memorial University of Newfoundland] are estimated to be close to $1 million."[33] While obtaining such donations for a finite-term project may be possible, coming up with the resources to pay for them on an ongoing basis is much more difficult, regardless of the perceived value to the participants.

On the other hand, several projects, including those undertaken by the University of the South Pacific, China's TV University, the World Health Organization, and the Pan African News Agency, all found satellite technology to be a cost-effective means of meeting their goals in projects designed to fit in with their long-term plans. The University of the South Pacific based in Suva, Fiji, is a regional institution serving ten island nations and territories. In 1974, it received permission from NASA to use the experimental ATS-1 satellite (see Chapter 5) for a simple audioconferencing link to its extension centers. Since 1980, USP has been exploring options for continuing the audioconferencing network on an operational satellite. After nearly twenty years, ATS-1 finally drifted out of its geostationary orbit. USP was able to use Project SHARE as a transitional step to operational service, using Intelsat's Pacific Ocean satellite and existing Intelsat earth stations in eight countries. The network is used for tutorials and administration, and now provides facsimile, data, and slow-scan video in addition to audio teleconferencing.[34]

China used Project SHARE as the first step in implementing a national TV University. The goal is to deliver university instruction to students at their workplace because of a critical shortage of places for qualified students in China's universities. Courses were initially transmitted over the terrestrial network used for broadcast television, but much of the country was not covered by this system. Using Intelsat, educational programs were transmitted to fifty-three locations. Following the pilot-project phase, China purchased two transponders and leased a third from Intelsat. By mid-1988, some 5,000 TVRO terminals built in China had been installed, and the TV University had an estimated student body of more than one million.

A third promising project was undertaken by the Pan African News Agency (PANA) to link researchers, journalists, and news agencies in five countries, as a step toward setting up a national African news and information-exchange network. The only investment at most sites was for modems and printers for personal computers to be connected to the network. Like the USP network, the African one could be continued using existing Intelsat facilities, although dedicated Intelnet terminals could also be used. Also, like USP and the Chinese TV university, this project was built on an existing organizational foundation and designed to be an incremental step toward accomplishing a priority goal. However, unlike these other projects, it apparently did not start with a commitment for follow-on support if the pilot project proved successful.

Intelsat officials state that essentially only about 10 percent of Project SHARE's activities constituted serious prospects for conversion to commercial service. They point out that the larger and more extensive users, such as China's TV University project, did convert. However, the role of the project in the goals and plans of the user organization may be a better criterion for assessing follow-on potential. Both China's TV University and the University of the South

Pacific planned to use satellite facilities as part of their distance education strategy and saw Project SHARE as a step toward that goal. The failure of most projects to be continued past the experimental period is reminiscent of the ATS and CTS experiments in the United States and Canada during the 1970s. In each case, most projects were not continued because the management of the participating organization did not give them high enough priority to warrant the ongoing allocation of the necessary resources, including funding, staff, and facilities.

Thus Project SHARE served to demonstrate what can be accomplished by satellite, and what difficulties and obstacles must be overcome to actually achieve the technology's potential. Intelsat's Board of Governors has authorized a follow-on to Project SHARE known as Project Access, which is to be more market-driven. Project Access is designed to stimulate service to rural and remote areas while emphasizing the potential for commercial applications. It also will provide free use of spare space-segment capacity for educational, health, or closely related social services. Project Access is intended for areas where current communications are limited or where new communications access can be developed.[35]

14.

Innovation in Satellite Communications

Monopoly and Competition

It is necessary to analyze institutional structures in order to understand how innovation occurs in applications of satellite communications, and who is likely to benefit from new services. As we saw in the chapters on U.S. satellite policy, the decade-long debate over public versus private ownership of satellites, and monopoly versus competition was resolved in favor of an "open skies" policy within the United States that allowed for several privately owned satellite systems. From the 1960s to the 1980s, the United States also moved toward a more competitive general telecommunications environment, introducing competition first in private line services, then in customer premises equipment, and eventually in public long-distance services. Other countries began with a public-sector monopoly model for telecommunications, usually operating their telecommunications services through a government agency, the ministry of posts, telegraph, and telephones (PTT). Some countries have granted the PTT more autonomy, splitting off telecommunications as a separate operation with the authority to retain and reinvest its revenues. A few are now moving toward privatization and competition. Satellite systems are generally also structured as a publicly owned monopoly.

Developing countries have generally emulated the European PTT model, in many cases retaining the structure established by colonial administrations. There is little incentive for innovation in such an

222

environment. The telecommunications revenues are frequently used to subsidize the postal service; in other cases, these revenues go directly to the national treasury. Telecommunications officials cannot count on using their revenues to upgrade or expand their networks. Demand from unserved customers is often enormous, so that there is constant pressure to meet urban needs, and few resources are committed to extend services to rural areas. Under these conditions, innovative strategies to reduce the capital burden on the PTT might be attractive: for example, allowing customers to buy their own satellite earth stations, or licensing private networks that would provide a package of services to customers, including satellite facilities (such as VSATs and other on-premises equipment) and access to the network. This approach would have the further advantage of generating more revenues in lease and toll charges. However, most PTTs have rejected such approaches because they fear loss of monopoly control.

This chapter examines the institutional structures that may hinder or facilitate innovation in satellite communications, particularly for developing countries. It first analyzes the role of the PTT as gatekeeper in developing country telecommunications. It then examines the policy issues associated with the introduction of competition with Intelsat. Finally, it traces the steps leading to the United States' authorization of competitive international satellite systems.

THE PTT AS GATEKEEPER

The convergence of computers and telecommunications provides many new opportunities for accessing, analyzing, and disseminating information in both developing and industrialized countries. The reduction in cost and increase in computing power of microcomputers have been accompanied by reductions in size and cost of satellite equipment such as "micro earth stations," or VSATs. These advances should make affordable voice and data communications available virtually anywhere. Yet the diffusion of microcomputers in developing countries has been much more rapid, whereas only a few hundred VSATs are currently being used in developing countries. In order to understand how institutional structures and policies act as gatekeepers in the diffusion process, it is helpful to compare the institutional environments of microcomputers and VSATs.

Applications of Computer Communications via Satellite

VSATs offer a low-cost means to provide one-way and interactive data communications. Among the applications of computer communications for development are the following:

News Services: The flow of information within the developing world has been hampered by the cost of distribution and by lack of access to telecommunications facilities in rural areas. VSAT technology now makes it possible for wire-service information to be disseminated to virtually any location. Wire-service copy is transmitted by satellite from a hub earth station, which may be shared with other data, voice, and video customers. The information is received on terminals costing approximately $2,500 and measuring less than 0.8 meters in diameter. These micro earth stations may be powered using photovoltaics or portable generators. For example, the World Broadcast Service (WBS) based in Hong Kong uplinks wire-service feeds to Intelsat's Indian Ocean satellite, which covers 80 percent of the world's population. The first customer for the WBS is China's Xinhua News Agency.

Information Acquisition and Management: Microcomputers or terminals linked to mainframes via interactive VSAT technology can be used to collect and update information from the field. A VSAT network called Nicnet operated by the Indian government's National Informatics Centre (NIC) now links 160 locations, and will be expanded in the next stage to more than 500. The 1.8-meter VSAT terminals transmit data at speeds ranging from 1,200 to 9,600 kbps (kilobits per second). Similar systems may be used for electronic banking, to link teller machines to computers or remote bank branches to headquarters, and for other interactive applications, such as reservation systems, weather and pipeline monitoring, and other field data collection.

Electronic Mail: Microcomputer users worldwide can now interact using various packet-switched electronic mail networks. These services are cheaper than voice communications and overcome the time zone differences that hinder real-time communications. Specialized electronic mail networks have been established for developing-country users.

Access to Data Bases: Computer terminals or microcomputers with modems linked to the telecommunications network can provide access to data bases anywhere in the world. Agricultural researchers, for example, can access the U.N.'s Food and Agriculture Organization (FAO) data bases in Rome. Medical researchers can search the data base of the National Library of Medicine in Bethesda, Maryland. Others may search domestic data bases, such as those for agriculture and energy in India and for development project management in Malaysia.

Again, packet switching can reduce the cost of these searches through local node access to networks such as Telenet and Tymnet in many countries. However, costs could be further reduced if these searches were localized. Data bases could be downloaded onto computers within developing countries on tape, floppy disks, or laser disks, with updates transmitted at regular intervals using telecommunications. For example, the same VSAT technology used for the news services described above could also be used for downloading these updates. The search then becomes local, without the cost of connect time.

Information Exchange via Facsimile: Another technology with widespread development applications is the facsimile machine, which enables any type of hard copy, including print, graphics, and handwritten messages, to be transmitted over a telephone line or narrowband satellite channel. As the Japanese have demonstrated, facsimile is ideal for handwritten information such as characters or other writing systems that are not easily typed. Thus any written language can be transmitted without transliteration for a typewriter keyboard. In addition, facsimile may be combined with VSATs for collecting and disseminating information. For example, development workers and reporters in the field could send in reports by fax, which would then be edited and published in newsletters or other publications in the city. Posters and newssheets could be faxed to the rural communities, and newsletters could be faxed either directly to the communities or to regional centers for duplication and dispatch to the villages in their territory. Information obtained from news services, data bases, and teleconferences could also be disseminated to development workers throughout the country via facsimile.

As these examples show, that microcomputers and small satellite earth stations together can together provide low-cost access to information virtually anywhere in the world. Yet microcomputers have diffused much more rapidly, albeit to a more specialized user population. The number of VSATs for low-volume data communications in developing countries is only a few hundred. Of course, data can be transmitted over telephone lines and reliable radio circuits. Yet today about 80 percent of the world's population has no access to reliable telecommunications, despite the availability of VSATs and other low-cost radio systems (VHF, UHF, microwave, cellular radio, etc.)

Of course, a VSAT can also be used to benefit an entire community or organization. Therefore, the relevant indicator of diffusion is not likely to be simply absolute numbers of microcomputers or VSATs, but access to them. The typical indicator for telecommunications is the number of telephone lines per 100 people. For VSATs, it might be the number of VSATs per permanent settlement and development site (mining camp, relief center, tourist lodge, etc.)

The User and the Network

In order to understand the diffusion of these technologies, it is necessary to understand the various participants and gatekeepers in the diffusion process. While a microcomputer is a stand-alone technology (despite the fact that it can be linked to other computers through a network), a telecommunications system by definition requires both multiple users and a network to connect them. A telephone set and a VSAT are useless by themselves; they require a network. Thus, no matter how great the need, customers cannot meet the need for telecommunications alone by buying a telephone set or a VSAT. They must be able to connect to a network.

Public networks are generally operated by the PTT, a government agency. Frustrated customers may set up their own private networks in some instances (using anything from high-frequency radio to satellite links), but the rule holds nonetheless: Individuals cannot meet their communication needs alone; they must join a network. Private networks must also be sanctioned by a government authority, usually also the PTT or ministry of communications.

The PTT is the gatekeeper in the diffusion of VSAT technology. The satellite carrier generally cannot market directly to the end user, but only to the PTT. The equipment supplier can try to reach end users as well as the PTT, but the power to make decisions on adoption of the technology rests with the PTT. Evidence of user demand can take the form of waiting lists, alternative "pirate" networks, and results of pilot projects or demonstrations, but if the PTT does not respond to this demand, the user has nowhere else to turn.

In contrast, diffusion of microcomputers does not rely on a single gatekeeper. There may be multiple wholesalers and retailers. The government may intervene to control supply, however, by limiting imports and/or encouraging local production of technology as a development strategy. The government may also encourage local production by ignoring international patent and/or copyright laws, thus encouraging proliferation of locally copied hardware and/or software. Users may influence supply and price through their activities in the marketplace. If government controls or other factors limit supply, they may acquire equipment through other channels, such as the black market or relatives traveling or working abroad.

The Diffusion of VSATs and Microcomputers

The following tables and figures present the participants and process in the diffusion of VSATs and microcomputers. Table 14–1 compares the attributes of VSATs and microcomputers. Both are relatively low-cost technologies. Microcomputers can be used either as a stand-alone tool or as part of a network, but VSATs are useful only for communication. Computers are generally sold by private retailers in a competitive marketplace; VSATs in most countries can be obtained only through the PTT, which may lease them to customers.

Table 14–2 outlines the roles of the developing country's government in the diffusion process. For both VSATs and computers, governments may impose controls to protect national industries, generate revenues from duties, and/or control what they perceive to be "subversive" technologies. They may enforce international patent agreements or sanction the copying (or "cloning") of technologies by local manufacturers. They may also apply broader policies for technology transfer to satellite equipment and microcomputers, to encourage joint ventures or require local assembly, for example. Through the PTT, the governments in countries where telecommunications operates as a public monopoly exert influence in many other areas, as discussed below.

The participants in the diffusion of VSATS and computers in developing countries are shown in Figures 14–1 and 14–2. Tables 14–3 and

Table 14–1. Comparison of Microcomputers and VSATs

	Computers	*VSATs*
Connectivity	Stand-alone	Network
Cost/unit	$1,000 and up	$2,500 and up
Distribution	Retailer	Government
	Competitive	Monopoly

Table 14–2. The Role of Government in the Diffusion Process

Role of Government for Microcomputers:

Import restrictions and duties	Protect national industries Control "subversive" technology Generate revenue
Industrial oversight	Enforce patent and copyright (or ignore P&A to protect local industry or placate consumers)

Role of Government for VSATs:

Provision of service	Installation } Maintenance } of network
Pricing	Of network use; often of equipment

14–4 outline the roles of these participants. Here we see the role of the PTT as gatekeeper. From the equipment and service suppliers' point of view, the PTT blocks their access to the customer. As a representative of PanAmSat stated, the problem in Latin America has not been demand, but access to that demand. From the customers' point of

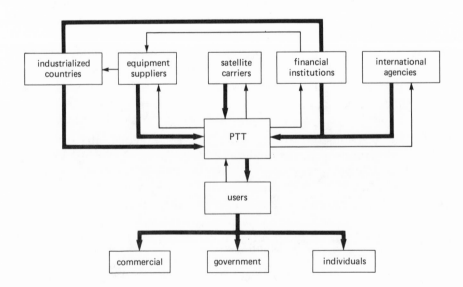

Figure 14–1: Diffusion Model for VSATs

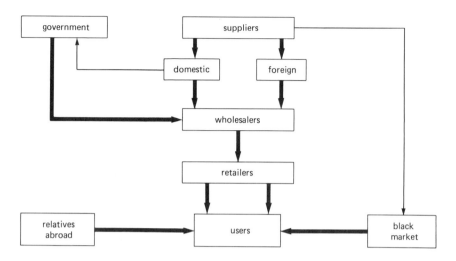

Figure 14–2:   Diffusion Model for Microcomputers

view, the PTT blocks their access to the equipment and services they need and may be ready to pay for. Banks and brokers in Brazil, for example, have waited several years to establish dedicated financial networks. Businesses in India can neither set up their own systems to bypass the unreliable urban telephone systems nor obtain higher-quality services from the telecommunications authorities. Villagers around the world wait for basic telephone service.

The PTTs set technical standards for equipment. These standards may discourage technical innovations that are designed to reduce the cost of equipment or transmission. The PTTs control the pricing of both equipment and services. They are generally the sole suppliers, and frequently prefer to lease rather than sell equipment. They also set the tariffs for use of the network, including charges for bandwidth and time. In some cases, the rate structure may actually hinder national development. In Brazil, for example, the fee to obtain a telephone line now exceeds $1,500, but long-distance charges are very low. Thus the threshold for access to the network is very high, but the revenues from actual use are too low to support even routine maintenance and upgrading. In the Cook Islands, there are no off-peak rates for international calls; Cook Islanders living in New Zealand tend to accept expensive collect calls from their relatives in the islands as a familial obligation until they can no longer pay their telephone bills, and their phones are disconnected. In Indonesia, TVRI (the government television network) charge $10,000 per hour to

Table 14–3. The Participants in the Diffusion of VSATs:

PTT:
Acts as major gatekeeper
Controls provision of networks
Issues tenders for equipment
Sets equipment specifications
Sets import controls and duties*
Sets priorities for extension and improvement of service
Makes forecasts, plans for service
Obtains loans for new, improved services*

Satellite Carriers:
Provide satellite capacity
Market to PTT
Set tariffs for services
Set technical standards for services

Equipment Suppliers:
Provide VSAT equipment
Market to PTT
May market to end user, but network provision and access is controlled
   by PTT

Financial Institutions:
Provide loans for equipment
Set conditions for loans
May participate in barter, counter trade

Industrialized Country Governments:
Provide financial aid and technical assistance
May provide attractive financing for their suppliers

International Agencies:
Set international technical standards
Provide technical assistance, training
Sponsor pilot projects and demonstrations

Users:
Cannot establish or utilize networks without PTT approval
May establish alternative "pirate" networks

*May be done in conjunction with other government ministries (e.g., planning,
finance).

Table 14–4. Participants in Diffusion of Microcomputers

Suppliers:
May be domestic or foreign, or combination

Government:
Sets import controls and duties
May encourage local production through incentives or import barriers
May uphold or ignore patent and copyright laws

Wholesalers

Retailers

Users:
May obtain products from multiple suppliers (retailers)
May use alternative sources of supply such as black market or friends/
relatives abroad

---

the government's Open University for transmissions during the day, when it is not on the air; the Open University cannot afford these rates and therefore rarely uses the PALAPA system.

There are many participants in the diffusion of VSAT technology other than those shown in figure 14–1 and table 14–3, including the equipment suppliers, satellite carriers (for international or regional networks), financial institutions that provide loans for equipment purchases or network expansion, and other sources of financial aid and technical assistance, among them multilateral and bilateral aid agencies. However, the PTT is the most important, in that it controls access to the customer. In contrast, there are few institutional barriers between the customer and stand-alone technologies such as computers and VCRs.

STRATEGIES TO INCREASE ACCESS
TO COMPUTER COMMUNICATIONS

The diffusion of satellite technologies and services responds to institutional barriers and incentives as well as to consumer demand. Based on the analysis above, the implementation of one or more of the following strategies could help to reduce the information gaps in the developing world:

- private ownership of VSATs and other terminal equipment to satisfy demand and reduce the cost to the PTT

- authorization of private networks where the public network cannot meet demand. License fees and other charges could be levied to ensure that some private network revenues are used to upgrade the public network
- pricing to encourage utilization without overburdening the network (such as lower off-peak rates to encourage evening and weekend use)
- use of techniques to minimize transmission costs, such as packet-switching, spread-spectrum, and digital-compression techniques
- storefront access: public telephones, telex, facsimile machines, and microcomputers made available in easily accessible locations, such as post offices and neighborhood shops
- pilot projects and demonstrations to field-test technologies and applications, and to make users aware of equipment and services
- adoption of these technologies by development agencies to manage projects and to provide access to their constituents (farmers, health workers, teachers and students, etc.)

INTELSAT AND THE DIFFUSION OF INNOVATIONS

Of the two threats to Intelsat, competing technologies and competing providers, the latter may be the more damaging. As Intelsat faces more competition, one of its principal strategies has been to introduce new services. As an unregulated monopoly, Intelsat has not needed to emphasize innovation and marketing. However, even if Intelsat's own corporate culture can be changed, Intelsat cannot succeed without the cooperation of the PTTs because it can only market to its signatories, the PTTs, which in turn are responsible for making their customers aware of these new services. As we have seen, the PTTs themselves are generally structured as public monopolies with few incentives to innovate.

Former Intelsat director general Richard Colino realized that Intelsat had to adopt a new approach: "What we need to ask ourselves is whether we will be the ones to meet these consumer demands for new technology, new and cheaper communication services!"[1] But the PTTs are slow to switch from what Colino calls a "service orientation" to a "market orientation." For example, Intelsat polled its more than 100 members in 1985 concerning the new services it had introduced. Only forty signatories responded, and of those only a dozen were offering Intelsat Business Service, and only two were offering new video services or Intelnet low-speed data services. Colino considered the PTTs' intransigence a threat to their own and Intelsat's survival: "By so failing, they invite 'competition' and prospects that their 'basic charters' will be challenged."[2]

Intelsat has tried to turn a liability into an asset by using the excess capacity it needs to ensure 99.99 percent reliability and continuity of service into a resource for many new services. However, excess capacity exists also because of Intelsat's members' overly optimistic traffic projections; its rate of growth actually declined from 24 percent in 1981 to 10 percent in 1985.[3] Overcapacity is particularly acute in the Atlantic region: in 1984, there was a 31 percent shortfall in anticipated demand.

There is at the moment a tremendous product-awareness gap in many countries. Untold numbers of potential customers do not know that small earth stations—for example, for data communications or thin-route telephony—even exist. If they do know of their existence, they must then pressure the telecommunications authorities to provide the service. A clear case of market pressure occurred with the transportable "flyaway" earth stations used by broadcasters to cover news stories. These terminals were first introduced in the United States, where broadcasters could use their own equipment and arrange directly with the many competitive satellite providers to lease capacity. Manufacturers then developed equipment that would work with Intelsat satellites; the broadcasters took the new technology to other countries, where they had to negotiate with the PTTs to gain access to Intelsat. On a domestic level, this process is likely to be too slow and time-consuming to be of interest to more than the most determined and well financed customers.

One marketing strategy that did avoid the PTT's resistance to innovation was devised by the developers of Intelnet data terminals for India's Nicnet service. The marketers of the technology realized that although there was substantial demand for low-speed data communications in India, working through the Ministry of Telecommunications would be an extremely slow process. However, they did find innovators in the National Informatics Centre (NIC) to endorse the VSAT project, which they saw as the only solution to their data-acquisition and -distribution problems. NIC was also well connected to Prime Minister Rajiv Gandhi, who favors modernization and technical innovation. In 1987, NIC, the department of the government which was in charge of collecting and distributing statistics throughout the nation, installed an interactive data network using spread-spectrum technology and VSATs working into a hub earth station. Department officials plan to link all state capitals and more than 400 political subdivisions, or districts. Information is to be transferred from the districts to the state capitals, and then to the national data base in New Delhi. Eventually the network is planned to reach into 5,000 smaller political subdivisions, or blocks.[4] Prime Minister Rajiv Gandhi has taken a personal interest in the project.

The Nicnet network is an example of low-cost, low-volume data communications that holds promise for other developing regions where infrastructure is lacking or inadequate. It is also an interesting example of an innovative strategy to circumvent the bureaucratic inertia of a PTT. Without waiting for Intelsat to market Intelnet or for the telecommunications authorities to approve its introduction, the manufacturer of the technology found an innovative potential user, itself a government department able to secure high-level approval for the network. Once the system was installed, the Department of Telecommunications decided to adopt the technology, and is now planning a similar system to extend telegram and telex to remote areas and to provide digital voice for emergency and low-volume use. Other services to be offered are facsimile; electronic mail; computer networks for banks, manufacturers, and airlines; and so on.

As the Nicnet example shows, bypassing the PTT is one strategy for introducing innovation in telecommunications. Sometimes the effect of this strategy may be to encourage the PTT itself to introduce new services or more flexible pricing. Innovation can also be stimulated by the introduction of competition, as shown in the next section.

INTELSAT AND COMPETITION

From the beginning of Intelsat the issue of the diversion of traffic has been a subject of controversy. Although Intelsat's goal was to be a "single, global system," the negotiators of the Definitive Agreements recognized that other systems would be developed. The United States was the leading advocate of system exclusivity: "A U.S.-led attempt to foreclose establishment by Intelsat members of other space segments for international services was resoundingly rejected. It was clear that many nations saw the potential development of other satellite systems as a critical element of their own communications—

and industrial—policy."[5] U.S. policymakers argued that a single global system would:

1. avoid wasteful duplication of expensive satellite and earth-station facilities;

2. facilitate communication between all countries, without regard to political blocs; and

3. ensure technical compatibility between satellites and earth stations, conserve frequency spectrum, and promote operational efficiency and flexibility in routing.[6]

The compromise that evolved is embodied in Article XIV of the Definitive Agreements, which seeks to ensure technical compatibility with Intelsat and to prevent "significant economic harm" to the Intelsat system:

To the extent that any Party or Signatory . . . intends individually or jointly to establish, acquire or utilize space segment facilities separate from the Intelsat space segment facilities to meet its international public telecommunications service requirements, such Party or Signatory, prior to the establishment, acquisition or utilization of such facilities, shall furnish all relevant information to and shall consult with the Assembly of Parties, through the Board of Governors, to ensure technical compatibility of such facilities and their operation with the use of the radio frequency spectrum and orbital space by the existing or planned Intelsat space segment and to avoid significant economic harm to the global system of Intelsat.[7]

The term "significant economic harm" has never been legally defined. In fact, U.S. negotiators of the Definitive Agreements have stated that there never was any clear definition of the term, and that it was intentionally left vague.[8] The measure of economic impact might be derived from a comparison of projected Intelsat costs and utilization charges had the system not been constructed, with the projected Intelsat costs and utilization charges given the competitive system. A corollary measure would be the extent to which signatories not participating in the separate system would have to increase their investment share to cover Intelsat's costs as a result of losing revenues from international services that would have been provided by the Intelsat system. In practice, the measure of economic harm has evolved into the following formulation:

With respect to full-time international traffic proposed to be carried on any non-Intelsat system, the Director General considers that . . . it is of the utmost importance to Intelsat that Signatories seeking Article XIV(d) coordination be able to demonstrate that such traffic would not, in the absence of the proposed system, have been carried on Intelsat.[9]

From the early days of Intelsat, U.S. officials, while continuing to support the economic efficiency and technical coordination criteria of Article XIV, began to pave the way for flexibility. For example, in the 1973 Policy Governing the Provision of Launch Assistance, U.S. policy on launching satellites intended for international public telecommunications services is described:

First, the United States will provide launch assistance for those "satellite systems on which Intelsat makes a favorable recommendation in accordance with Article XIV."

Second, in the absence of a favorable recommendation, the United States will provide assistance "for those systems which the U.S. supported within Intelsat so long as the country or international entity requesting the assistance considers in good faith that it has met its relevant obligations under Article XIV."

Third, in the absence of a favorable recommendation and where the U.S. has not supported the system, "the United States will reach a decision on such request after taking into account the degree to which the proposed system would be modified in light of the factors which were the basis for the lack of support within Intelsat."[10]

Thus while recognizing its commitment to Intelsat as the single global communications satellite system, U.S. officials acknowledged the possibility that other nations might want to use non-Intelsat space segment. (Although the launch assistance policy was cast in terms of other nations' requests, its principles apply to U.S. satellites as well. The United States did not have to consider this possibility until more than a decade later, when competitive international satellites were proposed.)

The Communications Satellite Act of 1962 states in section 102(d): "It is not the intent of Congress by this Act to preclude the use of the communications satellite system for domestic services where consistent with the provision of the Act nor to preclude the creation of additional communications satellite systems, if required to meet unique government needs or if otherwise required in the national interest."[11]

In a case which concerned the provision of services via U.S. domestic satellites to Canada, Central America, and the Caribbean, the FCC interpreted the phrase "required in the national interest" to be subsumed by the traditional public convenience and necessity standard applied by the FCC in reviewing requests for authorization to provide new communications services. The FCC rejected Comsat's claim that under section 102(d) only Comsat and the Intelsat system could transmit international commercial satellite traffic, finding that the provision of international services in areas within the spillover of the beam of U.S. domestic satellites was both legally permissible and in the public interest.[12]

INTELSAT AND COMSAT:
THE THREATENED MONOPOLIES

International transmission between the United States and other countries is now a transmission duopoly, with traffic split between carrier-operated cable systems and Intelsat. (The FCC has in the past enforced a split of traffic between the two technologies. This split is being phased out.) The difference is not only in the technology but in the ownership structure. Under the Indefeasible Rights of Usage (IRU) structure of cable systems, each carrier's ownership extends to mid-ocean. Cable systems have high fixed costs and low variable costs. User-owners have an incentive to use the cables as intensively as possible. However, under the Intelsat cooperative structure, carriers do not enjoy proprietary rights to circuits. They cannot depreciate their investment; and since their financial obligations, including capital subscriptions, are based on usage, a reduction in use means a reduction in required financial contribution. Since there is no penalty for procuring capacity but not using it, members may overestimate demand without penalty, because the costs of excess capacity are shared by all users.[13]

Intelsat is an unregulated monopoly, subject to the same cost-control problems that have afflicted monopoly telephone companies. Costs are passed through to end users who have no other options, and because the system offers a means for telecommunications administrations to increase their revenues, there are no incentives for cost minimization.[14] Douglas Goldschmidt points out that Intelsat is a monopolist supplier of capacity and its owners are monopsonists (the only buyers) for its services. Intelsat is vulnerable because it cannot market services to anyone but its owners. Intelsat is at the mercy of owners who may have objectives other than continued use or growth of Intelsat. Thus Intelsat had the incentive to attempt to forestall competitive entry.[15]

As an international organization, Intelsat is not regulated by any public body and is not publicly accountable to anyone but its owner-members. Unlike Intelsat, Comsat is subject to U.S. regulation and antitrust laws. The major vehicle for U.S. government control of Comsat is the instructional process. Before a meeting of Intelsat's Board of Governors, Comsat notifies the government and interested private parties of the issues that are likely to be raised. Parties can submit recommendations to the government on the position Comsat should take. The government, through a collaboration of the FCC, State Department, and National Telecommunications and Information Administration (NTIA), decides how Comsat should vote. The State Department then issues a letter to Comsat with these instructions. This process has limitations. Issues may come up that were not addressed in the instructional letter. Comsat may take actions outside the formal meetings that are not subject to oversight. Much of the information furnished to Intelsat is considered proprietary and not available, making it difficult for other parties to comment knowledgeably.[16]

These problems have been inherent since the early days, but were not really visible to more than a few entities, such as the international carriers, until the upheavals of the 1980s when other companies proposed to compete with Intelsat and the U.S. administration came out in favor of competition. Then Comsat had to endorse and promote policies against its own and Intelsat's interest.

In its Authorized User decision, the FCC had ruled that Comsat should be a carriers' carrier; that is, it would limit access to Comsat to international service carriers (AT&T plus the international record carriers). The role of Comsat as middleman is typical of the role played by Intelsat signatories that buy satellite capacity from Intelsat and then mark it up for resale to their customers, which themselves may be carriers rather than end users. Intelsat's charges represent only 10 percent of the total cost of international communications to the end user; operating costs for the earth stations, charges for the terrestrial telephone services, and administrative costs and profits for each of the middlemen between Intelsat and the end users account for 90 percent of the end users' bill.[17]

The Authorized User policy began to erode in the late 1970s, when the Spanish International Network (SIN) argued that it should be able to deal directly with Comsat to arrange imports of television programming from Latin American countries, rather than with the intervening international carriers that charged fees but added nothing to the service. After requests from other users, the FCC modified its Authorized User policy to enable Comsat to deal directly with end users and to get into other types of business, such as satellite-system planning, consultation services, and the production of high-technology equipment and components. To facilitate Comsat's entry into these new markets, the FCC chose to restructure Comsat and separate its monopoly operations from its competitive activities.

An authorized user is now any U.S. organization that wishes to purchase half-circuits from Comsat. All customers are to be charged rates equal to those charged the carriers; the new policy thus redefines who may act as a wholesaler and breaks the international service carriers' oligopoly. Now users can purchase half-circuits at the same rates as common carriers, and it is then up to them to purchase the other half-circuit from appropriate foreign operating entities.[18] Customers can now own their own earth stations. However, they may not go directly to Intelsat; they must still go through Comsat.

Comsat's entry into non-Intelsat-related businesses has been less than totally successful. As a participant in Satellite Business Systems, the first satellite system designed for data communications, it suffered large losses. In 1984, Comsat sold its interest in SBS to its partners, IBM and Aetna. (SBS was later acquired by MCI.) Comsat made another major effort at diversification in the field of direct-broadcast satellites with the formation of Satellite Television Corporation (STC), but suspended STC in November 1984 after failing to find partners to share the risk.[19]

TACKLING THE "SEPARATE SYSTEMS" ISSUE

Arabsat and Palapa-B (designed to provide domestic services for Malaysia, Thailand, and the Philippines as well as Indonesia) were coordinated on the basis of the very low volume of international traffic anticipated. The European Communications System (ECS) was coordinated because it planned to carry traffic that was would usually be carried by terrestrial networks. But separate international systems that planned to compete directly with Intelsat were vehemently opposed by many Intelsat signatories.

By 1984, the number of coordinations of separate international satellite networks had been growing, and no request for coordination had been rejected by the Board of Governors. Faced with the likelihood of more requests, the director general of Intelsat proposed revised criteria that would have made future coordination of alternative international satellite systems more difficult, but these were rejected by the Board of Governors. Ironically, he argued that the new services, apparently introduced to make Intelsat more competitive, should be protected from competition; if Intelsat offered new digital communication services or domestic services, others should not be allowed to do so.[20]

In April 1983, a U.S. firm called Orion filed an application with the FCC for authorization of a separate international system, touching off extensive controversy within the federal government. The FCC's position on international competition was clear:

> Experience in the international communications market, as well as our observation of the economy as a whole, has convinced us that competition can play an important role in protecting the interests of international telecommunications users. . . . Indeed we believe that the domestic experience clearly demonstrates that service innovation and rate competition flourish best in a freely competitive market and that the development of such a market in the international sphere will be the best way to protect international telecommunications users.[21]

On April 6, 1983, the Department of State and the Department of Commerce sent a joint letter to the FCC requesting that the commission refrain from taking any final action on the application until an executive branch group could review and study the application's impact on the national interest and foreign policy of the United States. The Commerce Department supported the administration's view that international competition was in the national interest, in accordance with the general competitive and deregulatory policies of the Reagan administration. The State Department was concerned that the U.S. had taken the leading role in establishing Intelsat commitment to a single global system. U.S. embassies in many countries received requests from other governments (primarily developing countries) not to approve the applications, citing the founding role of the United States and the potential for "significant economic harm" to Intelsat.

By 1984, five organizations had filed applications with the FCC to construct, launch, and operate international satellite systems. A Senior Interagency Group (SIG) was established to review U.S. policies. Finally, on November 28, 1984, President Reagan signed a presidential determination that alternative satellite systems were "required in the national interest" within the meaning of the Communications Satellite Act.[22]

In February, 1985, the Department of State and Department of Commerce jointly submitted a white paper on new international satellite systems to the FCC, in which they reviewed current U.S. telecommunications policies and international obligations to determine whether and under what conditions authorizing satellite systems and services in addition to the Intelsat system would be (1) consistent with prevailing U.S. law, practice, and international treaty obligations; (2) compatible with sound foreign policy and telecommunications policy goals; and (3) in the U.S. national interest. Taking into consideration the United States' role as the primary force behind the development of Intelsat, the white paper stated that the limited competition proposed would not adversely affect Intelsat and, in particular, its ability to provide affordable services to developing countries: "Since the new satellite systems would not be able to provide public-switched services, Intelsat would retain its commercial core" of revenues and would not be harmed.

The authors of the white paper further concluded that there would be little possibility of economic harm to developing nations, which were concerned that the entrance of competing satellite systems would divert substantial amounts of traffic from profitable routes and result in increases in communications costs. They reached this conclusion because "1) the entrants would be unable to compete with a majority of Intelsat's service offerings; 2) even with significant cross-elasticities between the conventional and customized markets, both markets are growing rapidly and revenue siphoning would not occur; 3) Intelsat is in a good position to compete for the customized services market."[23]

In September 1985, the FCC echoed these views in its Separate Systems decision, finding that "separate systems will provide substantial benefits to the users of international satellite communications services without causing significant economic harm to Intelsat."[24] The conditions it imposed included no interconnection with the public switched network (i.e., message telephone service could not be offered over the alternative systems), restrictions on separate systems operators from operating as common carriers, and no minimum unit of capacity.[25] Its opinion summarized the views not only of the FCC but of the Reagan administration:

> We have concluded that the proposed separate systems will offer substantial benefits to international communications users. Separate systems will provide users with special communications needs with currently unavailable means of packaging and transmitting information over satellite networks. Separate systems will also stimulate technological innovation and service development, improve network efficiencies, reduce user costs, create new business and trade opportunities through improved international communications. Further, we have concluded that authorization of the proposed separate systems subject to the Executive branch service restrictions will provide reasonable assurance that Intelsat will not incur significant economic harm. These service restrictions will protect Intelsat's revenues obtained from supplying space segment capacity for international switched message services by prohibiting separate systems from interconnecting with public switched networks. Public-switched services by far compose Intelsat's largest source of revenue. Only peripheral or "customized" services would be subject to competition between Intelsat and separate systems. We believe that entry will stimulate the overall international satellite communications market beyond the levels anticipated by Intelsat and that Intelsat stands to benefit from such expansion. Entry of competing suppliers will also put pressures on Intelsat to improve the efficiencies of its operations and provide services at minimum costs, consistent with reasonable service standards.[26]

The FCC's Separate Satellite Systems order gave provisional authorization to enter the international satellite market to five companies: Cygnus, ISI, Orion, RCA, and PanAmSat. The competitors intend to provide specialized services, primarily data and video transmission that may be both superior and less expensive than Intelsat's. These companies have a competitive edge in their design for specific services and in their limited focus. Intelsat's design was optimized to provide global interconnectivity, but has not in the past been optimized power levels for particular services. The entrants can provide higher power, which permits customers to use smaller and less expensive earth stations and to achieve higher transponder capacity with these earth stations than would be the case with Intelsat. The entrants' space segment should be less expensive than Intelsat's because single-purpose satellites will be less costly than Intelsat's hybrid satellites with many special features (e.g., cross-strapping, multiple frequency reuse), which are not required in satellite systems for specific groups of users in fixed areas.

However, the new competitors face formidable entry barriers. First and foremost, the competitor must secure a foreign partner or correspondent. To do this, it must convince a foreign administration, which is virtually certain to be the Intelsat signatory, to allow the new carrier to provide international services to and from its country. All of the applicants plan to offer service between the United States and Europe; PanAmSat was the only one of the original applicants that also planned to provide service to the developing world. (PanAmSat has since purchased Cygnus, and RCA has withdrawn from the market.) ENTEL Peru was the first entity to become a PanAmSat correspondent. PanAmsat was the first of the competing systems to initiate Article XIV(d) coordination, with the governments of the United States and Peru requesting that consultations be initiated. PanAmSat has three high-powered spot beams for domestic and regional service for Latin America, and a regional beam for coverage of all of Latin America.[27] Its "Simon Bolivar" satellite was launched in June 1988.

INTELSAT RESPONDS

Since there is no regulatory body for international communications, Intelsat alone may decide whether competitors' proposed systems pose "significant economic harm" to Intelsat under its Article XIV(d): "What we see is a monopolist with the right to determine whether a new entrant to its markets will cause it significant economic harm. The monopolist gets to define what this harm is. The possibilities for abuse here are clear."[28] Estimates of the impact of competition ranged widely from virtually no impact, because competitors would be offering new services or only those carried terrestrially, to projections for Intelsat of a loss of 96.9 percent of Intelsat traffic and an increase in Intelsat circuit prices of 1,100 percent due to competition by the year 2003.[29] However, as former director general Colino himself pointed out, poor traffic forecasting and excess capacity had already made Intelsat inefficient.

Intelsat launched an aggressive lobbying campaign to discourage its members from approving PanAmSat's application for coordination and to attempt to prevent any nation from becoming a correspondent with a new entrant. Intelsat also attempted to warehouse orbital slots requested by the new entrants, and introduced a series of price cuts for those domestic services most immediately affected by the entry of competition. For example, it reduced the cost of domestic transponder leases, and introduced nonpreemptible leases at prices lower than those of preemptible leases, and the sale of transponders.

While the strategies of introducing new services and reducing prices for existing services were predictable responses to competition, the competitors and some economists argued that Intelsat was engaging in predatory pricing, or setting its prices below costs. However, without a regulatory forum that could compel Intelsat to file information on costs and pricing formulas, analysts could base their judgments only on what limited documentation was publicly available. As the U.S. signatory to Intelsat, Comsat had access to internal Intelsat documents but refused to make them available. Comsat is now required by the FCC to provide informational access to Intelsat's documents and technical proposals to other companies equal to that which it provides its subsidiaries.

Comsat still operates in a conflict of interest in relation to Intelsat. As a founder of Intelsat and the original operator of the system, it is a strong supporter of the Intelsat monopoly. As the U.S. signatory, it must adopt and support U.S. international satellite policy. The U.S. government by 1985 had publicly endorsed international competition. Rather than advising the U.S. government on international satellite policy, as it had for more than twenty years, Comsat was now told to sell the United States' new pro-competition position to Intelsat signatories. However, Comsat has been a less-than-willing supporter of the pro-competition stance of the Reagan administration, and competitors feel it has not provided full access to Intelsat documents as now required. U.S. firms offering IBS and Intelnet services are still concerned that Comsat's markups are excessive and are depressing U.S. demand for these new services.

THE PTTs: THE REAL TARGET?

"It is the PTTs, and their terrestrial monopoly on communications services, which are the true targets of most of the changes in U.S. policy."[30] As noted in the first part of this chapter, the PTTs are generally the gatekeepers in the diffusion of satellite services. Private international systems could bypass these administrations. In Latin America, the first customers of PanAmSat were domestic television networks frustrated with the limited capacity and high rates of the PTTs. Banks and other businesses with pent-up demand for private data communications may also be early customers.

Ironically, Intelsat itself could be used to provide such specialized services. Indeed, the Nicnet system in India is operating on an Intelsat satellite, and demonstrates that it is possible to develop a strategy to bypass the PTT using Intelsat. However, since Intelsat's signatories are the telecommunications administrations, Intelsat itself is likely to find it difficult to initiate such strategies. It must rely on equipment vendors and potential customers to open these doors, and hope that the same threat of competition that spurred its own reluctant innovations will motivate the PTTs as well. Thus, Intelsat's innovations in service offerings are a necessary but far from sufficient strategy for ensuring future viability.

15

Space Policy

Access to the Geostationary Orbit

This chapter first outlines the international policy framework that applies to satellite communications and then summarizes recent international activities concerning access to and utilization of the geostationary satellite orbit. The implications of conferences on allocation of frequencies and orbital locations and of other international telecommunications negotiations are in fact much greater than the technical issues on the formal agenda. They concern equitable access to the tools of the information age—the means of accessing, transmitting, and sharing information that is the key to social and economic development. The latter part of the chapter discusses the issues of equitable access, resource sharing, and technology transfer, and their relationship to international satellite policy.

As noted in chapter 1, geostationary satellites are positioned in an orbit 22,300 miles (36,000 km) above the Earth. At this location, as Arthur C. Clarke theorized in 1945, an object will revolve around the Earth once every 24 hours, thus appearing stationary from the earth. The significance of this phenomenon is that satellite earth stations do not need to be able to track the satellite across the sky, and can thus be much simpler and cheaper to build than the antennas required for nongeostationary satellites.

Satellites have particular advantages for developing countries that have not made major investments in terrestrial infrastructure. Services can be provided to any location simply by installing a satellite earth station in the community, without having to use terrestrial lines or microwave repeaters. Thus, rural and remote regions can be served according to development priorities, without waiting for the extension of services from major cities. Satellite systems are likely to be highly reliable because each earth station is easily accessible for maintenance, since it can be located in or near a settlement, and an outage of one station affects only that location. In contrast, breakdowns in terrestrial systems will affect all locations "down the line," and the problem may be difficult to locate and repair (e.g., inaccessible mountaintop repeaters, remote poles downed in a storm, breaks in undersea cables, etc.) Thus satellites are particularly appropriate for serving countries with large land masses, such as many African and Latin American countries; difficult terrain, such as mountains, jungle, or desert; or scattered islands such as the South Pacific and the Caribbean.

The geostationary orbit was recognized early on as an important resource for developing as well as industrialized countries. Although space may be considered infinite, the "Clarke belt", as it has been called,[1] is a finite resource, because only at 22,300 miles above the equator can satellites be placed in geosynchronous orbit. The limitation in practical terms is not so much physical as electronic. It is not likely that satellites would be in danger of colliding, but their signals could interfere with each other. Thus the "orbit spectrum"—that is, those frequencies available for communicating between Earth and geostationary satellites—is a vital resource to all users of satellite technology.

INTERNATIONAL POLICY FRAMEWORK FOR SATELLITE COMMUNICATIONS

The International Telecommunication Union

The major institution concerned with space communications is the International Telecommunication Union (ITU), although various other U.N. agencies have also played a role in some space policy issues. Now a U.N. agency, the ITU predates both the United Nations and the League of Nations. It was established as the International Telegraph Union by European nations in 1869 to develop a regulatory framework for transborder telegraph services. The ITU now consists of 165 members, more than two-thirds of which are developing countries. The ITU divides the world into three major regions: Region 1 consists of Europe, Africa, and the Middle East; Region 2 includes the Americas; Region 3 covers Asia and the Pacific.

The ITU activities involving satellite communications are conducted through its entities concerned with radio frequency regulation, the International Frequency Registration Board (IFRB), which compiles a master list of all frequencies in use by member nations for various services, and the International Radio Consultative Committee (CCIR), which has numerous working groups dealing with satellites, with major participation by members and telecommunications carriers. (Other entities within the ITU oversee "telecommunications" by wire or cable.) Policies concerning satellites are formulated by Administrative Radio Conferences, which may be regional (RARCs) or worldwide (WARCs). The principles concerning common heritage and equitable access to the geostationary orbit developed by these conferences will be discussed below.

The United Nations General Assembly

Through its resolutions, the United Nations General Assembly (UNGA) has formulated general principles concerning the utilization of space by communication satellites. The UNGA

> has asserted its own competence to provide a focal point for international cooperation in the peaceful exploration and use of outer space in general, and to contribute to the further progressive development of the law of outer space, in particular. Accordingly, the General Assembly has undertaken the legislative function of elaborating on behalf of the international community certain principles and rules concerning space activities, including those applicable to communications satellites.[2]

The General Assembly's involvement in the regulation of outer space activities began a decade before Sputnik. Resolution 110 (II) of November 3, 1947, condemned "propaganda designed or likely to provide or encourage any threat to the peace, breach of the peace, or act of aggression,"[3] and was made applicable to outer space by the Outer Space Treaty of 1967. Before the 1967 treaty, the UNGA passed resolutions in 1961 relating to satellites. Resolution 1721 of 1961 recommended that the U.N. Charter and other principles of general international law apply to outer space and expressed hope that "communication by satellite should be available to the nations of the world as soon as practicable on a global and non-discriminatory basis."

In 1963, the UNGA responded to the formation of Intelsat, founded as an international cooperative and managed initially by Comsat, a U.S. corporation established by Congress. Resolution 1962 in 1963 declared that "states bear international responsibility for national activities in outer space, whether carried on by governmental agencies or by non-governmental entities."[4]

The United Nations Committee on the Peaceful Uses of Outer Space

The UNGA created in 1958 an ad hoc Committee on the Peaceful Uses of Outer Space (COPUOS), which was replaced by a permanent committee the following year. Its purposes were "to review, as appropriate, the area of international cooperation and to study practical and feasible means of giving effect to programs in the peaceful uses of outer space which could appropriately be undertaken under United Nations auspices"; and "to study the nature of legal problems which may arise from the exploration of outer space."[5]

The U.N. Outer Space Affairs Division

In response to requests by COPUOS, the U.N. established a small Outer Space Affairs Division to act as a source of expertise and assistance to the committee. The division sponsored conferences on the exploration and peaceful uses of outer space in 1968 and 1982. UNISPACE 82 is discussed below.

UNESCO

Under its mandate of "promoting collaboration among the nations through education, science, and culture," the United Nations Educational, Scientific, and Cultural Organization (UNESCO) established a Space Communications Program within its Division of Communication Research and Policies. The program's purposes are to promote the free flow of information, to expand the use of television broadcasting for education, and to promote cultural exchanges.[6] UNESCO's involvement in satellite policy stems from its interests in using mass communications, as stated in its charter: "[It] shall . . . collaborate in the work of advancing the mutual knowledge and understanding of peoples through all means of mass communication."[7]

International Satellite Organizations

At present, there are three international satellite organizations which share the resources of the geostationary orbit with domestic satellites. Intelsat provides international communications through three satellite systems located in geostationary orbit above the Atlantic, Indian, and Pacific oceans. For many developing countries, Intelsat brought reliable telecommunications links with the rest of the world for the first time. Approximately twenty developing countries also use Intelsat for domestic communications by leasing transponders for their own internal use.[8] Intelsat is not a member of the ITU, although it is a major user of the geostationary orbit spectrum. Only nation states may be members of the ITU, so that Intelsat's interests must be represented by member nations, some of which may also own and operate their own satellites.

The Intersputnik system was established by the Soviet Union, and has twelve members, most of them Comecon states. Intersputnik also serves several developing countries, including Algeria, Cuba, and Nicaragua. The Inmarsat system provides communications for ships. Its membership is comprised of both industrialized and developing countries.

Domestic and Regional Satellite Systems

The major domestic users of satellite communications are the United States, with approximately thirty satellite systems, followed by the Soviet Union with two domestic systems. Other industrialized countries with their own satellite systems are Canada, Australia, and Japan, soon to be joined by France and West Germany. Developing countries with their own domestic satellites include Indonesia, India, Brazil, and Mexico. The Arabsat system serves twenty-two Middle Eastern and North African nations. Eutelsat provides regional services in Western Europe.[9]

THE COMMON HERITAGE
AND SHARED RESOURCE PRINCIPLES

The Outer Space Treaty

One of the first resolutions of the UNGA relating to outer space included the principle of sovereign equality and the exploitation of outer space for the benefit of all mankind.[10] These principles were enshrined in the Outer Space Treaty of 1967 which states:

> Article I: The exploration and use of outer space . . . shall be carried out for the benefit and in the interests of all countries, irrespective of their degree of economic or scientific development, and shall be the province of all mankind.
>
> Outer space . . . shall be free for exploration and use by all States without discrimination of any kind, on a basis of equality and in accordance with international law, and there shall be free access to all areas of celestial bodies.
>
> Article II: Outer space . . . is not subject to national appropriation by claim of sovereignty, by means of use or occupation, or by any other means.
>
> Article III: States Parties to the Treaty shall carry on activities in the exploration and use of outer space . . . in accordance with international law, including the Charter of the United Nations, in the interest of maintaining international peace and security and promoting international cooperation and understanding.[11]

The common heritage of mankind principle was also incorporated in the 1967 Moon Treaty, which attempted to set guidelines for the utilization of the resources to be found on the moon. These resources are to serve the best interests of all people, with special consideration to the technologically advanced states that explored the resources and the needs of developing countries.[12]

ACCESS TO THE GEOSTATIONARY ORBIT: THE ROLE OF THE ITU

The 1959 WARC

As the specialized agency of the U.N. responsible for telecommunications, the ITU took an early interest in the potential applications of communication satellites. The ITU first expressed an interest in satellite communications at its 1959 Administrative Radio Conference, which had been convened to review and revise the ITU's Radio Regulations. The fact that the U.S.S.R. had successfully launched Sputnik 1 in 1957 impressed upon the delegates the potential significance of space for communications. (Sputnik was not a geostationary satellite; the first commercial geostationary satellite was Intelsat I, also known as Early Bird, built by Hughes and launched by NASA in 1965. See chapter 2.) Realizing that it was too early to know for certain how the new satellite service would evolve, the conference limited itself to extending the frequency table and allocating a few frequencies for space research purposes.[13] In addition, the 1959 conference recommended that the ITU convene a special conference to examine "the allocation of frequency bands for the various categories of space radio communication."[14]

The 1963 EARC

The ITU subsequently decided to consider the needs of all space communications services at the 1963 Extraordinary Administrative Radio Conference (EARC). This conference had to deal with the many developments in satellite communications since 1959. It recognized new services (such as the Meteorological Satellite Service) and allocated 2,800 megahertz of frequencies for satellite communications. Of particular importance, the conference also decided that radio frequencies for satellite services should be allocated on a "first come, first served" basis, in a manner similar to that used for allocating frequencies to most terrestrial services in the past. Under the "first come, first served" approach, a national administration notifies the ITU's IFRB of the frequencies that it desires to use for a specified radio service. The board then examines the frequencies for conformity with the International Telecommunication Convention and pertinent provisions of the Radio Regulations. If the board gives a favorable finding, the frequencies are recorded in the Master Frequency Register and protected from that time on from harmful interference by the radio stations of other administrations.

A lengthy discussion also took place at the 1963 conference over a U.N. resolution suggesting that satellite communication be organized on a global basis, to allow all nations access to its benefits. During the debate, a number of developing countries expressed their concern that if something along these lines was not done, satellite communications would soon be monopolized by the richer members of the ITU.[15] The final result was a recommendation stating that: "[All] members and associate members of the Union have an interest in and right to an equitable and rational use of frequency bands allocated for space communications" and that the "utilization and exploitation of the frequency spectrum for space communication be subject to international agreements based on principles of justice and equity permitting the use and sharing of allocated frequency bands in the mutual interest of all nations."[16]

The 1971 WARC

The third ITU conference devoted to satellite communication issues was the 1971 World Administrative Radio Conference for Space Tele-communications. The most controversial issues confronting the 1971 conference concerned the acquisition of rights to geostationary orbital positions and the frequencies necessary for their use. Several developing-country delegations expressed concern that under the system adopted in 1963, all of the available space resources would have been utilized by the more developed countries by the time that the developing countries were able to engage in satellite communication.[17]

Despite these concerns, the conference decided to extend the rights-vesting mechanism established earlier for allocating satellite frequencies to the geostationary orbit as well. This was accomplished by the introduction of a notification and coordination procedure for planned satellite systems. According to this procedure, an administration planning to introduce a satellite system is obliged to notify the IFRB well in advance of putting it into operation, to supply the IFRB with the necessary technical details, including the orbit location, and, if necessary, to coordinate its system with agencies in other countries that may be affected. If the administrations concerned are unable to agree on a means of coordination, they are permitted to seek the help of the IFRB. A system already registered by the IFRB, however, is under no obligation to make changes to accommodate a new system.

Many developing-country delegates felt that this procedure gave early users of satellite systems an undue advantage over latecomers; some of the delegates advocated dividing up both the frequencies allocated to space communications and the geostationary orbit among all countries intending to use satellite communications. Interestingly, the United Kingdom and France were the chief advocates of a satellite planning conference. Apparently, they were already interested in the potential of domestic and regional direct-broadcast services (DBS) for Europe. After almost twenty years, France and West Germany are about to launch broadcasting satellites, and the United Kingdom plans to introduce broadcast satellite services (see chapter 8).

To address the concerns of developing countries, Recommendation Spa 2–1 and Resolution Spa 2–2 were adopted, stating that "all countries have equal rights in the use of both the radio frequencies allocated to various radio communication services and the geostationary satellite orbit for these services" and that "registration with the ITU of frequency assignments for space radiocommunication services and their use should not provide a permanent priority for any individual country or groups of countries and should not create an obstacle to the establishment of space systems by other countries."[18] In addition, the authors' of recommendation requested that the next appropriate administrative radio conference examine the whole process of rights vesting if countries began to encounter "undue difficulty" in gaining access to these resources.

The 1971 conference also defined several new services, including the Broadcasting Satellite Service (BSS), or service for direct home reception. It adopted a resolution requesting that the new BSS be made the focus of a comprehensive plan to be negotiated at a special conference called for that purpose. Apparently, most delegations were thinking in terms of a treaty that would allot portions of the geostationary orbit and associated frequencies to any country that planned to use satellites for broadcasting, and would protect them from unwanted broadcast signals from other countries.

The 1973 Plenipotentiary

The delegates to the 1973 ITU Plenipotentiary Conference continued the debate over satellite communication resources. They eventually sided with those countries that wanted to get away from vesting permanent rights on a "first come, first served" basis, adding the following wording to the ITU Convention: "In using frequency bands for space radio services, Members shall bear in mind that radio frequencies and the geostationary satellite orbit are limited natural resources, that they must be used efficiently and economically so that countries or groups of countries may have equitable access to both in conformity with the provisions of the Radio Regulations, according to their needs and the technical facilities at their disposal."[19]

The 1977 WARC

The delegates to the 1977 Broadcasting Satellite Conference decided that the preferred method of achieving the goal of equitable access to the Broadcasting Satellite Service was to formulate a long-term *a priori* plan that would allot to each member of the ITU a portion of the geostationary orbit and the frequencies necessary for its use. The conference thus abandoned the "first come, first served" approach to access in favor of a predetermined allocation of orbital slots and frequencies. A minimum of five television channels per country was allocated in Region 1 (Europe, Africa, and the Middle East) and three to four channels in Region 3 (Asia and the Pacific). Largely at the insistence of the United States, it was decided to postpone the formulation of a plan for Region 2 (the Americas) until 1983.[20]

The 1983 RARC

The 1983 Regional Administrative Radio Conference which met to plan the Broadcasting Satellite Service for Region 2 was successful in drafting a more flexible plan for the Americas. The largest share of the resources in the plan was allocated to the United States, which received eight of the forty-eight available geostationary orbital slots and 256 frequency channels. The 1983 plan also included two allotments for satellite broadcasting services to be shared by groups of nations.[21]

The actions of these two conferences resulted in a completely new approach to the appropriation of space resources: "Instead of requiring the newcomer to seek such accommodation as the [first-comers] are willing to provide, the superior bargaining position now rests with the state whose service conforms to the plan—whenever it plans to orbit its system and regardless of how long a nonconforming service has been in operation."[22]

CURRENT STATUS OF ACCESS
TO THE GEOSTATIONARY ORBIT

Calls for a Space WARC

At the 1979 WARC, a long debate took place over the relative merits of *a priori* planning versus the "first come, first served" approach. Many developing countries' delegations stated their preference for the *a priori* approach. India pointed out that it had already encountered significant difficulty, under the coordination procedures mandated by the 1971 WARC, in obtaining the orbital position and frequencies it desired for its domestic satellite system, which was then under construction. Indonesia had also experienced difficulties in coordinating its PALAPA satellite system, launched in 1976. Many industrialized countries argued in favor of the older system of rights vesting.[23] Without resolving the dispute, the 1979 WARC passed a resolution calling for a conference to "guarantee in practice for all countries equitable access to the geostationary satellite orbit and the frequency bands allocated to space services." In the same resolution, the conference recognized that the geostationary orbit and the associated radio frequency spectrum are "limited natural resources."[24]

The 1982 Plenipotentiary Conference authorized the calling of the proposed conference and reinforced the emphasis on equitable access to space resources when it added the following slightly amended paragraph to Article 33 of the ITU Convention:

> In using frequency bands for space radio services Members shall bear in mind that radio frequencies and the geostationary satellite orbit are limited natural resources and that they must be used efficiently and economically, in conformity with the provisions of the Radio Regulations, so that countries or groups of countries may have equitable access to both, taking into account the special needs of the developing countries and the geographical situation of particular countries.[25]

The 1985 Space WARC (WARC ORB-85)

The result was the World Administrative Radio Conference on the Use of the Geostationary Satellite Orbit and the Planning of the Space Services Utilizing it (the Space WARC), held in two sessions in 1985 and 1988. The purpose of the first session (WARC ORB-85) was to "decide which space services and frequency bands should be planned; establish the principles, technical parameters and the criteria for planning . . . , establish guidelines for regulatory procedures in respect of services and frequency bands not covered [by a plan]," and "consider other possible approaches that could meet the objective [of guaranteeing equitable access]."[26]

Seven planning methods were proposed at the CCIR Preparatory Meeting held in July 1984:

1. A worldwide or regional detailed long-term (ten to twenty years) *a priori* plan

2. A periodically revised (three to five years) worldwide or regional detailed plan

3. A worldwide, regional, or subregional plan with guaranteed access

4. Guaranteed access by means of multilateral coordination

5. Coordination procedures and technical factors to be revised periodically

6. An *a priori* plan for a period of about ten years using generalized parameters

7. A worldwide plan covering about one satellite generation lifetime (about ten years).[27]

This was by no means a definitive set of planning options. Administrations could reject all of these methods, modify them, and/or introduce other methods during the conference. The question of how—or, indeed, whether—to plan the geostationary orbit occupied the conference delegates for several weeks. First, the conference members agreed that only the fixed satellite service (FSS) would be subject to planning. Finally, a mixed approach was adopted as a compromise. The final agreements called for planning of 300 megahertz of uplink and 300 megahertz of downlink in C band (4–6 GHz) and 500 megahertz in Ku band (12–14 GHz) in new frequencies, or "expansion bands," allocated to the FSS at the 1979 WARC. The approach adopted for these new frequencies is a regional allotment plan, under which each country would be guaranteed at least one unspecified slot in a regional orbital arc. Improved coordinating procedures, which might include conferences of affected parties and burden sharing among all parties, are to be developed for the rest of the C-band and Ku-band frequencies. The old "first come, first served" system of frequency allocations, with notification and coordination through the IFRB, would continue, with simplications, for the remaining frequencies assigned for satellite services.[28] Thus the agreements included *a priori* allotment planning for new frequencies, improved coordination for currently used C-band and Ku-band frequencies, and an unchanged "first come, first served" approach for other satellite frequencies.

The conference agreed to take into consideration "the requirements of multi-administration systems created by governments and used collectively, without affecting the rights of administration with respect to national systems."[29] In other words, common-user organizations such as Intelsat, Inmarsat, Eutelsat, and Arabsat would be included in an allotment plan, but would not be given priority over national systems. The wording specifically excluded private international systems (such as PanAmSat), which the ITU does not distinguish from national systems. Thus, the interests of the common-user organization were protected, but not given priority. Members were to develop specific proposals for implementation of the decisions for consideration at the second session in 1988.

1988 Space WARC (WARC ORB-88)

For five weeks in 1988, delegates from 119 countries met in Geneva for the second session of the Space WARC, known as WARC ORB-88. The purpose of the conference was to finish the business begun in 1985, by converting the general guidelines adopted at ORB-85 into specific policies. The 1985 session determined that the 1988 session would:

- develop an allotment plan in 800 megahertz of specified "expansion bands" for the fixed satellite service (FSS);
- improve coordination in the currently used FSS bands through an ill-defined mechanism dubbed multilateral planning meetings (MPMs), to be used along with existing procedures to assure access by all administrations;
- complete work on a feeder-link plan for the Broadcast Satellite Service (BSS) in Regions 1 and 3.

By the time the conference began, the United States, which had proposed the MPM in 1985 as a means of increasing communication during coordination of new satellite systems in the currently used FSS frequencies, had decided that its proposal was unworkable. Despite ongoing concerns about the need for more formal consultation, the conference agreed that the present radio regulations (Articles 11 and 13) governing coordination of satellites would continue to be the normal means of consultation, and that MPMs, still to be defined, would be convened only when the usual procedures did not prove satisfactory. The MPM process could be invoked by an administration dissatisfied with the usual coordination procedures, and would involve only affected administrations. Costs of participating in the MPMs would be borne by participants, reducing the risk that parties would participate solely for political reasons. The conference limited the applicability of the MPM process to the currently used FSS bands, and did not extend it to additional frequencies.[30]

The most difficult item on the agenda was to implement a plan that would guarantee every nation an orbital slot in the 800 megahertz of "expansion bands" in the Fixed Satellite Service (FSS) that had been set aside for planning in 1985. The allotment plan was to provide for at least one nominal orbital position for each administration, a national coverage area, and a predetermined orbital arc within which the operational orbit location would be chosen. Computerized planning models developed by the IFRB with the assistance of Japan during the intersessional period had difficulty accommodating existing systems and possible regional systems along with an orbital slot for each country. However, mechanisms were finally approved that preserved the goal of flexibility in the form of a dynamic plan that used the predetermined arc approach to so that countries could be assured of an orbital location within the arc, depending on their future requirements. Requests for specific locations and arcs and special parameters, such as high elevation angles, tasked the model and its developers to their limits. The plan that was finally approved will be administered by the IFRB. How well it will function in practice remains to be seen.

A problem arose in including existing systems that had begun coordination before the first Space WARC session in 1985. The plan could not accommodate both existing and planned systems, so the eventual solution was to divide these into allotments (Part A) and existing systems (Part B). Existing systems will be granted a guaranteed operational period until 2010, after which renewals will have to be addressed through the additional-use provisions. These additional-use provisions were seen by developing countries as a mechanism for ensuring inclusion of subregional systems. Since many smaller developing countries may find shared systems the most cost-effective solution to their telecommunications needs, they argued that they had no guarantee of access unless these subregional networks were included in the plan. Some developing countries wanted to limit the additional-use provisions to subregional systems alone. However, the United States and other industrialized countries wanted the flexibility to implement systems not in accordance with the plan if necessary. A final compromise stressed the political goal of reserving spectrum for the allotment plan, while providing for additional uses outside the plan in limited cases.[31]

The conference also agreed on a plan to allocate uplink frequencies for the Broadcast Satellite Service. In addition, it adopted a resolution that the introduction of satellite-delivered HDTV be made pursuant to a worldwide frequency allocation and that the frequency range of 12.7 to 23 gigahertz be considered at a future conference.[32]

ACCESS TO THE GEOSTATIONARY ORBIT: UNRESOLVED ISSUES

Although the ITU conferences in this decade have developed many plans and procedures for access to the geostationary orbit, many fundamental issues that will affect whether and how these orbital locations will be used remain unresolved.

Equitable Access

U.N. and ITU documents on the geostationary orbit mention the concept of equity but do not define it. Equity may be described as "the traditional label given to the set of normative questions about how benefits should be distributed."[33] Equity in this context refers to the principle that all countries should benefit from the shared resources of outer space. Equity should not be interpreted as equality or equal sharing among all nations. The principles of access and sharing were further refined at the ITU's 1982 Plenipotentiary, in the Nairobi Convention, which states that radio frequencies and the geostationary orbit are limited resources "that must be used efficiently and economically . . . so that countries or groups of countries may have equitable access to both, taking into account the special needs of the developing countries and the geographical situation of particular countries."[34]

However, while developing countries may have special needs that differ from those of industrialized countries—for example, in relying on satellite communications exclusively to reach much of their population—they may also differ in their criteria for determining efficient and economic use. For example, closer satellite spacing makes more efficient use of the geostationary orbit, but requires more complex and therefore expensive earth station design. Similarly, shifting to higher frequencies to find more available spectrum may not be economical for developing countries because these frequencies are subject to interference from particles in the atmosphere such as rain, sand, and dust.

A priori planning, burden sharing, and improved coordination have all been proposed under the rubric of achieving "equitable access." Much of the early debate focused on two very different approaches to accommodating the needs of ITU members for spectrum and orbital positions: the "first come, first served," or a posteriori, approach commonly used for other services; and an a priori approach, which would assign the use of the orbit and frequencies in advance. Burden sharing refers to requirements that would reduce the "latecomer penalty." Under "first come, first served," the latest entrants must adjust to the systems already coordinated, and may therefore have to use less than optimal orbital locations or make technical modifications to avoid interference with existing systems. Burden sharing would require existing systems to accommodate newcomers by making some technical or orbital adjustments, or providing some compensation to newcomers who had to modify their specifications. Improved coordination was seen as a means of increasing participation by administrations in the coordination process, rather than simply relying on filings with the IFRB.

Difficulties with Planning

Although *a priori* planning has great appeal as the simplest means of guaranteeing access to the limited natural resource of the geostationary orbit, it also has disadvantages that have already become evident from the 1977 broadcasting satellite plan. First, it is very difficult to predict future use of telecommunications services. Thus, countries tend to inflate their "requirements" in order to be sure to get all they need. For example, the U.S. requirement for 256 channels for broadcasting satellites was simply the sum of all the channels requested in applications for DBS systems to the FCC. To date, no DBS systems have been built in the United States, and the current thinking is that there probably is not enough demand for direct-to-home reception because more than 40 percent of television households subscribe to cable television systems, 80 percent have access to cable, and more than two million backyard antennas for use with existing low-powered satellites have already been installed.

Second, it is difficult to build flexibility into plans to accommodate future changes in requirements. For example, the plan for Europe allocated several channels for each country but did not contemplate shared systems. Now that there are plans for DBS systems to serve all of Western Europe, it has been extremely difficult to accommodate them given the rigidity of the 1977 plan. The predetermined-orbital-arc approach developed at the 1988 Space WARC is an attempt to build flexibility into *a priori* planning, but has yet to be tested.

Third, the technical assumptions used for planning are based on current technology. They risk obsolescence in the face of new developments. Technological innovation may make it possible to place satellites closer together or to reuse frequencies, for example. However, it may be difficult to modify the plan to take these improvements into account.

Industrialized countries point out that to date it has been possible to accommodate new satellite systems, and that technological innovations should make it possible to find room for all future satellite systems. However, developing countries are unwilling to accept technological dependency on engineering solutions from industrialized countries implied in this argument. They are also aware that, even if accommodated, latecomers may be forced to modify their systems to meet constraints imposed by those already in orbit. (Indonesia and India have already faced difficult negotiations with Intelsat and the U.S.S.R. in seeking optimal locations for their domestic satellites.)

Thus, developing countries appear at present unwilling to abandon some form of *a priori* planning. However, there are many possible variations on the theme of *a priori* planning, and developing countries now tend to recognize the value of building flexibility into planning approaches to accommodate changing national and regional requirements as well as changes in technology, while at the same time guaranteeing equitable accommodation of all satellite systems.

Resource Allocation: Monetary Provisions

No commercial provisions currently exist concerning access to the geostationary orbit. Several economists have proposed various pricing mechanisms to collect rents from users of geostationary orbit locations. The assumption is that since this is a limited resource, it has monetary value to those entities that want to use it. Generally, these proposals take the form of an *a priori* plan that allocates locations and frequencies to each country. Countries that are not yet ready to use their allocation could rent it to their neighbors.[35]

However, these proposals have not received serious consideration at ITU conferences so far. Clearly, industrialized countries do not want to see a precedent established for rents or other spectrum-usage fees. While some developing countries, such as Costa Rica, have floated the idea informally, it has not received widespread support among developing countries. It may be that most ITU members fear that introducing monetary compensation would be excessively divisive or unworkable in the ITU context.

ACCESS TO INFORMATION RESOURCES: THE BIGGER PICTURE

By the first session of the Space WARC in 1985, there were more than 150 commercial satellites in orbit, 80 percent of which had been launched in the previous five years. Despite rapid advances in technology, there is evidence that most developing countries are not catching up to the industrialized world in access to satellites. Much of the growth in the use of satellites was due to demand in industrialized countries for broadcasting, data communications, telephony, and specialized communications services. The deregulation of long-distance telecommunications in the United States and the growth of the satellite industry in Europe and Japan had also contributed to the proliferation of satellites.

Only fourteen satellites serving developing countries were launched between 1980 and 1985. Even taking into consideration that Intelsat satellites are used by both industrialized and developing nations, satellites for the exclusive use of industrialized countries made up 72 percent of the total. Middle-income countries have benefited most from increased access to satellites for domestic and regional communications. By 1985, forty-five middle income countries had participated in domestic or regional satellite systems through lease or membership, while only nine low-income countries had used satellites for domestic services.[36]

Access to basic telecommunications in the developing world has not improved significantly in recent years. Nearly three-quarters of the world's population live in countries with ten telephones or fewer for every 100 people, and most of these are in urban areas. Thus increased funding for telecommunications, transfer of technology, and training will all be necessary to give rural populations actual access to the benefits of satellite technology. The ITU's 1982 Plenipotentiary established an Independent Commission for Worldwide Telecommunications Development (the Maitland Commission) to investigate these needs. The commission's report, *The Missing Link*, recommended more resources for training and transfer of technology, and more investment in telecommunications infrastructure in developing countries. The commission estimated that $8 billion from all sources was invested in telecommunications in developing countries in 1983, and that at least an additional $4 billion per year would be necessary if minimal worldwide access to telecommunications was to be achieved by early in the next century.[37]

U.N. and ITU documents on the geostationary orbit stress the goal of transferring technology and expertise to developing countries. For example, the recommendations of the UNISPACE 82 Conference[38] included:

- establishing a substantial program for human resource development involving a number of fellowships to provide personnel in developing countries with in-depth exposure to space science, technology, and applications;

- stimulating greater cooperation among developing countries through exchange of information and by encouraging use of equipment developed in these countries;
- setting up an international space-information service.[39]

Efforts to improve utilization of telecommunications through support for training and developmental applications have also been disappointingly limited. The International Programme for Development Communication (IPDC) was established by UNESCO in 1979. So far, it has generated a long list of proposed projects, but very little funding. Recent bilateral initiatives include the U.S. Telecommunications Training Institute, established in 1982 in time to be announced at the Nairobi Plenipotentiary. USTTI provides short-term technical training through U.S. companies. However, longer-term technical training in country is also required, along with experience in planning and implementing multi-agency development projects using satellite communications.

In 1985, the ITU established the Centre for Telecommunications Development, as recommended by the Maitland Commission's report. The purpose of the Centre is to complement and extend the training activities of the United Nations Development Program in telecommunications, which are carried out by ITU staff and consultants. However, the center is to be supported by voluntary contributions and through staff seconded from private companies and telecommunications authorities. It may be difficult to find a compelling incentive for the private sector to participate in such activities in an era of increasing competition within the industrialized world. Equipment suppliers and operating entities are increasingly concerned with short-term profitability and the threat of competition at home. To date, contributions have been very modest.

It may seem strange that these larger issues were not formally raised at the 1985 and 1988 Space WARCs. The reason usually given is that the agenda dealt only with technical matters related to the geostationary orbit. Yet sharing of limited resources is of necessity a political issue, and many developing countries advocated such policies as *a priori* planning and burden sharing in an attempt to guarantee access to the orbit. The question of how the developing countries would finance their guaranteed access to the orbit was not addressed. Perhaps it will surface at future ITU forums. Developing countries aligned in regional or political blocs (such as the nonaligned countries) could force the members of the ITU to confront these problems with more than words.

As noted in the introduction to this chapter, access to the geostationary orbit is a necessary but far from sufficient condition for developing-country utilization of satellite technology. Unless more progress is made on the underlying problems of financing for developing-country telecommunications, transfer of technology, and training in both management and applications, a guarantee of access to the geostationary orbit may be a hollow victory for the developing world.

THE FUTURE OF THE ITU

Generally, ITU members have confidence in the organization as a competent and effective vehicle with more than a century of experience in developing principles and mechanisms for sharing the radio frequency spectrum. The character of the ITU has certainly changed in the past twenty-five years, with the membership reflecting increasing numbers of newly independent developing countries and with the exponential growth in use of the frequency spectrum for telecommunications. Although these changes and new demands have burdened the ITU financially and technically, the organization has been able to adapt remarkably well. There appears to be general consensus among the members that, while streamlining and simplification of some policy-making mechanisms are overdue, the organization itself continues to be a viable means of regulating access to the shared resource of the frequency spectrum.

After the 1979 WARC, some U.S. delegates and conservative U.S. government officials suggested that the United States abandon the ITU because it was becoming "too political." This view was shared by some members of the Reagan administration after the 1982 ITU Plenipotentiary, during which a debate over whether or not to exclude Israel delayed the agenda debates for several days. At the first session of the Space WARC in 1985, there were some rumblings among U.S. government officials that withdrawal from the ITU would become an option if the conference delegates insisted on *a priori* planning of the geostationary orbit.

Interestingly, except among some ultraconservative officials in the government and the private sector who believe that U.S. participation in any U.N. activity is politically damaging and a waste of resources, the United States' withdrawal from UNESCO has heightened U.S. respect for the ITU. In contrast with UNESCO, the ITU is reasonably well managed and avoids the issues of content that almost totally paralyze UNESCO in the communications field. While the "pull-out option" does not now seem to be taken seriously, the United States has guarded its freedom to operate outside ITU regulations by taking reservations on some key resolutions and by successfully championing additional-use provisions in the 1988 expansion-bands allotment plan.

A more pressing issue may be the relevance of the ITU. An international organization is still very valuable as both policymaker and traffic cop in overseeing the myriad technical issues involved in international telecommunications. However, technological change may render many of the current regulations moot by the time they are put to use. As one developing country's delegate at WARC ORB-88 put it, just a few of the satellite systems discussed will ever be built and orbited, and many of those that do see the light of day will not be ready for as many as twenty years. By that time, he concluded, technology will have advanced so far that today's concerns regarding spacing, interference, and power will have been taken care of anyway.[40]

Increasingly, the crucial issues are not technical. Equitable access to information resources involves much more than orbital positions. Funding, equipment, and training are critical; the development of information services is as much a matter of trade as of technology. Whether any international forum can adequately address these issues may become a more urgent question in the 1990s than the complex but perhaps less significant problems of frequency and orbit allocation.

16

Other Satellite Services and Prospects for the Future

In addition to satellites designed for fixed (voice, data, and point-to-point video transmission) and broadcasting services, which are the focus of this book, satellites have also been designed for a variety of other purposes including land mobile, maritime, and aeronautical communications; navigation and global positioning; meteorological data collection; and remote sensing. The following sections provide a brief overview of these services.

MOBILE SATELLITE COMMUNICATIONS

As well as providing communications between fixed points on the Earth's surface, satellites may also be used for mobile communications. The first mobile system was designed for ships, but new mobile satellite systems are being planned for communication with airplanes, trucks, and other vehicles. In 1971, the ITU recognized the mobile satellite service (MSS) and allocated some relatively vacant spectrum in the maritime and aeronautical bands for this service. At the 1979 WARC, frequencies were allocated for the Aeronautical Mobile Satellite Service and the Radio Navigation Satellite Service, allowing for the development of the U.S. Global Positioning Service.

The 1987 Mobile WARC had the greatest impact on the future development of mobile satellite communications. Two mobile communication technologies reviewed were Land Mobile Satellite Service

(LMSS) and Radiodetermination Satellite Service (RDSS), both of which were given worldwide frequency allocations, in effect "legitimizing" these technologies in the international community. Developed in 1982, RDSS combines both mobile communications and positioning and location capabilities.[1] The first commercial RDSS system is being developed by Geostar, a U.S. company, which will offer satellite communications from mobile digital terminals for radiolocation, position determination, directional guidance, and terrain and collision avoidance warnings. Geostar also plans to offer interconnection to digital data bases and voice messaging.[2]

While the LMSS did receive some L-band frequencies at the 1987 Mobile WARC, it did not receive all of the bandwidth that it may require for global operational service. Another problem to be resolved is determining who will provide the service, since only one systems provider may exist in one large geographical area. In the United States, LMSS is considered by many to be an extension of cellular radio service. Twelve companies initially filed applications with the FCC in 1985 to construct mobile satellite systems. Because it felt that so many separate services would be impractical, the FCC decided that only one service provider should be authorized. However, it rejected lotteries, now used for some cellular radio licenses, and the usual lengthy hearings to decide who was best qualified, instead requiring joint ownership or the formation of a consortium to implement MSS. Eight companies signed a joint ownership agreement in 1988 to form the American Mobile Satellite Consortium (AMSC).[3] AMSC plans to cooperate with Telesat Canada in joint procurement and operation of satellites and ground stations for separate U.S. and Canadian mobile satellites, and will offer distinct but coordinated services throughout North America for aeronautical, land mobile, and maritime mobile communications.[4] AMSC hopes to launch its first satellite in the early 1990s; Telesat's Mobile Satellite (MSAT) is to be launched in late 1992.[5]

The European Space Agency (ESA) has developed a mobile data communications system called Prodat, being tested using the Marecs A satellite, which is owned by ESA and leased full-time by Inmarsat. The L-band system is being tested on trucks, ships, and planes.[6] Trucking applications appear the most attractive because at present no unified mobile communications system exists for all of Europe, and trucking companies need to be able to communicate with their fleets across national boundaries. The French national space agency (CNES) has also established a new commercial enterprise called Locstar to develop a European radiodetermination satellite system.[7]

The market for mobile communications is growing, with a U.S. cellular-radio subscriber base of two million predicted by the early 1990s.[8] However, what share of mobile services will be offered by satellite versus terrestrial technologies remains uncertain. One way to respond to consumer demand and increase market share is to develop hybrid systems, for example, combining mobile voice communications with positioning or data communications. Such hybrids are now planned using the new Global Positioning Service (GPS).[9]

Maritime Communications: INMARSAT

Inmarsat is an international cooperative organization, similar to Intelsat, which provides satellite communications for ships and offshore industries. Beginning in 1973, the International Maritime Organization, a specialized agency of the United Nations, convened a series of conferences to consider the establishment of an international maritime satellite system. Inmarsat was established in 1979, with the signing of the Inmarsat Convention and Operating Agreement, and became operational in February 1982.[10]

The structure of Inmarsat is similar to that of Intelsat. The organization is financed with contributions from its signatories, which are to be repaid at a rate of 14 percent.[11] The Assembly, similar to Intelsat's Assembly of Parties, meets every two years to review long-term policy and objectives. Each signatory has one vote. The Council, like the Intelsat Board of Governors, holds the real power in the organization. The Council consists of the eighteen signatories with the largest investment share, plus four representatives of the other signatories elected by the Assembly on the principle of geographical representation (taking into account the interests of developing countries). Members of the Council have voting power equivalent to their investment share and, like a board of directors, make the major policy decisions for the organization. Administrative functions are carried out by a London-based directorate under a director general appointed by the Council for a six-year term.[12]

Inmarsat has forty-four members and also provides services to nonmember countries. It now provides communications for approximately 5,000 ships and offshore drilling platforms using C-band and L-band frequencies. Inmarsat was the first to offer mobile satellite services with its Maritime Mobile Satellite Service. Inmarsat got into business by leasing satellite capacity from other providers. In 1982, it leased transponders on Comsat General's Marisat satellites, which were launched in 1976 to provide global maritime coverage. Inmarsat now leases transponders on the British-built Marecs satellites for coverage of the Atlantic and Pacific ocean regions, and on Intelsat V for Indian Ocean coverage. Capacity on other Intelsat and Marisat satellites is leased for backup. In 1989, Inmarsat plans to launch its own Inmarsat-2 satellites, built by British Aerospace. These satellites will triple the capacity available in the Atlantic region, where traffic is highest.[13]

Signatories operate the coast earth stations, which provide links between the satellites and the onshore networks. The ship earth stations are purchased or leased by ship owners and operators. These stations typically use 85-to-125-centimeter parabolic antennas housed in a fiberglass "radome" and mounted on a stabilized platform that enables the antennas to track the satellite despite movement of the ship. These antennas cost about $25,000. Inmarsat is developing a digital Standard B station and a Standard C station that will offer a much smaller terminal with an omnidirectional antenna and 5-kilohertz channel spacing to be used for low-speed data (600 bits per second) and telex. This antenna, expected to sell for $4,000 to $5,000, is aimed at the small-boat market, including fishing boats and yachts.[14]

Telex is the most popular service; Inmarsat also provides voice, facsimile, data communications at up to 1.5 megabits, and group calls (broadcast calls by shore-based users to selected ships).[15] Interactive data services include videotext, navigational and weather information, and search and rescue.[16] Inmarsat satellites can also be used for land mobile communications for emergency relief work (e.g., in cases of drought, famine, or earthquakes), to reestablish communications or to provide basic service where there is no alternative. Inmarsat can also be used with the Future Global Maritime Distress and Safety System (FGMDSS) to alert people on shore for coordination of rescue activities.[17]

Aeronautical Communications

Although radio technology has been adapted for telephone service from airplanes, it is limited to use over land because it relies on ground stations with a range of about 400 miles. There is no commercially available system for travelers who wish to make business or personal calls during international flights. Inmarsat intends to extend its services into international mobile communications, particularly aeronautical mobile services, and in 1985 amended its convention to include the provision of aeronautical communications. Inmarsat expects to provide aeronautical satellite services for passenger communications, company communications, and eventually for air traffic control.

However, U.S., Canadian, and European entities have also proposed aeronautical systems for domestic services. For example, Aeronautical Radio Inc. (Arinc), an airline-industry-owned company, has established Aviation Satellite Corp. to provide satellite communications to airlines. The recently incorporated American Mobile Satellite Consortium also hopes to offer aeronautical communications.[18]

OBSERVATION SATELLITES

From the early experimental satellites and the photographs taken by the first astronauts, two significant applications of satellite technology in addition to communications emerged: use of satellites for determining location on earth and thereby for navigation, and for observation of the Earth for civilian and military purposes.[19] The recognition of the potential of Earth observation from space has led to meteorological observation of the environment and natural resources on land and in the oceans, for both civilian and military reconnaissance use. Techniques such as false-color analysis have been used to identify different parameters of the image, such as vegetation, environmental pollution, geological formations, and so on.

In an orbit with a plane close to that of the North and South Pole, the Earth's rotation beneath the satellite as it orbits is slightly displaced longitudinally; thus total coverage of the world is repeated every so many days, depending on the orbit. Observation satellites are placed in both polar and equatorial orbits, at altitudes ranging from a few hundred miles to geosynchronous orbit. Multispectral scanners using frequencies in the visible and infrared spectrum allow daytime and nighttime scanning, but they cannot penetrate clouds. Radar sensors that can penetrate cloud cover are also being introduced.

Initially, relatively poor resolution of 90 meters was possible, but the technology has advanced in recent years, permitting resolution from 10 to 30 meters. Military reconnaissance satellites developed in the early 1970s have resolution to a fraction of a meter. At first, Soviet and American satellites jettisoned their film capsules periodically, using retrorockets and then parachutes to slow the descent of the capsules, which were then retrieved for processing. Now data is transmitted from the satellites electronically.[20]

Another important application of satellites is for earth and ocean observation, or "remote sensing." NASA pioneered in the development of remote-sensing satellites with its Landsat series of satellites (originally called the Earth Resources Technology Satellites). Their payload consists of a multispectral scanner and thematic mapper, with current spatial resolution of 30 meters. The Landsats are in a polar orbit of 705 kilometers with a sixteen-day repeat cycle. Data are transmitted either directly or via NASA's Tracking and Data Relay Satellite (TDRS). Landsat satellites have provided a wealth of information about the Earth's condition and resources. Humanitarian applications include information on conditions of ice flows, location of icebergs, levels of pollution, forest fires, and the like. Commercial uses include locating mineral deposits, monitoring the status and extent of agricultural crop growth, water management, and so on. NASA has made Landsat images available at very low cost and has trained developing-country technicians to analyze and interpret Landsat data through the U.S. Agency for International Development (AID).

The Landsat satellites were operated by NOAA until the U.S. government decided that the service should be privatized. Operation has been taken over by Eosat, a joint venture of Hughes Communications and GE Americom (which now owns RCA). The decision to privatize Landsat has been controversial because of the humanitarian as well as commercial value of remote-sensing data. Developing countries in particular have expressed reservations about the privatization of remote-sensing satellites. Their first concern is for low-cost access to the humanitarian data so that it can be used effectively. The second has to do with the data with commercial implications. Many developing countries feel that they should control access to data pertaining to their countries; others want to ensure that they can obtain at least the information about their countries that might prove commercially advantageous to multinational corporations and foreign investors. If remote sensing becomes a strictly commercial undertaking, data may become available only to customers who can afford to pay commercial rates.

The French have developed their own remote-sensing satellites. In 1986, the French launched their first commercial remote-sensing satellite, known as SPOT (Satellite Probatoire d'Observation de la Terre), owned by CNES of France. SPOT offers 20-meter-resolution color images and 10-meter panchromatic resolution. Its two high-resolution Vidacom cameras make possible stereoscopic imaging. Its steerable beams allow it to be programmed to acquire an image or a particular area on successive cycles.[21] The French government's SPOT Image marketing organization has been successful in establishing franchises in many countries.

The Japanese are developing a marine observation satellite (MOS) and earth resources satellite (JERS) to be launched in the early 1990s. The European Space Agency is developing an advanced earth resource satellite (ERS-1) to be launched in 1989 for provision of wind and wave information as well as land observation. Other countries planning land observation satellites are Canada (Radarsat), the United Kingdom, China, India, and the Netherlands with Indonesia (for TERS, Tropical Equatorial Resources Satellite.)[22]

Meteorological Applications

NOAA operates a series of satellites known as TIROS (Television/ Infrared Observation Satellites). These satellites are in a "near polar orbit" of 870 kilometers. They measure surface temperature, cloud cover, and vegetation; produce a vertical temperature profile; and track ozone distribution in the atmosphere. They also carry a Sarsat search-and-rescue transponder for locating and relaying ship and aircraft distress beacons.[23] NOAA also operates the GOES satellites (Geostationary Operational Environmental Satellites) positioned in geostationary orbit, but they have been plagued by sensor failures.

Western Europeans, through an international meteorological organization called Eumetsat, operate the Meteosat system of geostationary weather satellites built by the European Space Agency. The Japanese space agency (NASDA) also operates a series of geostationary meteorological satellites known as GMS, or Himawari.[24]

NAVIGATION SATELLITES

"In the last two decades, satellites have been used to replace the stars."[25] In the 1960s, the U.S. Navy developed the Transit satellite system to assist nuclear-powered submarines in establishing their position. The transit system consisted of a series of satellites in low polar orbits which continuously transmitted signals that could be picked up by antennas located on nuclear-powered submarines. By means of triangulation, the crews could establish the location of the ship.[26] The United States agreed to allow civilians to use the ground stations, and the Transit navigational system was extended for use by the merchant marine shipping industry and offshore oil platforms throughout the world. Transit is now being replaced by the Global Positioning System of the U.S. Navstar satellite system, which consists of eighteen satellites, allowing global positioning with extremely high accuracy.

FUTURE PROSPECTS

Many factors will influence the growth of the satellite industry and applications of the technology in the next quarter-century. Among them are the reliability and cost of satellite launches, competition from other technologies such as optical fiber, and changes in business and residential demand for communication services. For developing countries, the most important issues will be availability of funds for expanding and upgrading telecommunications facilities, and government commitment to providing access to basic communications for all.

Launching Facilities

The explosion of the U.S. Space Shuttle Challenger, the failure of a French Ariane launch, and the malfunction of a Delta rocket launched from Vandenberg Air Force Base in California—all in the first five months of 1986—temporarily halted the launching of geostationary satellites by Western space agencies. However, these catastrophes will eventually be considered only a temporary setback, although one which may have a permanent impact on the cost of satellite insurance and the mix of rocket versus reusable (shuttle) launchers. These failures also opened the door for other entrants into the launching business, the most prominent of which is the Chinese "Long March" rocket. Australia's selection of the Long March rocket for the launch of its next generation of Aussat satellites was viewed with consternation by the U.S. government, which was reluctant to allow U.S. satellite technology (the Aussat series is being built by Hughes) to be examined by Chinese scientists. However, the United States has now agreed to the Long March launch. The Soviet Union is also offering commercial launches, and Japan plans to enter the international launching business in the near future.

Satellites and Competing Technologies

Another factor of greater long-term significance is the installation of optical fiber on high-volume routes, both intercity and international. For example, the new transatlantic cable (TAT-8) consists of optical fiber, as do the new transpacific cables, and a private optical-fiber link (PTAT) is also planned. The deregulation of the U.S. telecommunications industry has encouraged several long-distance carriers—such as US Sprint and MCI, as well as Bell operating companies and regional carriers—to build their own long-distance, optical-fiber networks.

It is unclear at this point to what extent optical fiber will divert existing and projected traffic from satellites. Fiber optics have an advantage on fixed-route, point-to-point, high-density networks where the traffic volume justifies the enormous bandwidth. The low cost per circuit-mile of fiber is dependent on high-traffic volume to cover fixed costs. As Andrew Inglis points out, claiming low cost per circuit-mile is comparable to claiming that the Boeing 747 has the lowest cost per seat-mile of all commercial aircraft. This is true, but it is significant only if most of the seats are filled with revenue passengers.[27]

Fiber-optic costs per circuit-mile are high for low utilization but decline rapidly as the number of circuits in use increases; satellite costs per circuit-mile are lower at low utilization but decline more slowly. While fiber will take over the heavy-volume point-to-point traffic, it may be complementary to satellites for other applications such as local area networks that will feed data to office building rooftops, and short-haul links to connect users to teleports.

However, the point-to-multipoint distribution capability of satellites is unmatched by any terrestrial alternative. Thus satellites will probably continue to play a major role in point-to-multipoint services such as radio and television distribution, broadcasting, video programming feeds to cable television systems, broadcast data networks (weather, stock prices, etc.), and video teleconferencing. Satellites also appear to be the least expensive solution for a variety of new multipoint-to-point interactive services such as credit-card verification, communications between field office and home office, and remote data collection and monitoring.

The U.S. Fixed Services Market

In late 1988, the FCC authorized the construction of thirteen new domestic fixed service satellites and granted permits for the launching of ten replacement satellites. With these new grants, there will be a total of forty-two U.S. commercial satellites in orbit. Three U.S. satellites (Hughes' Galaxy 1, Contel's ASC-1, and GTE's Gstar 1) will have to be moved, as the FCC implements 2-degree spacing to accommodate increased demand on the orbital arc.[28] At present, an oversupply of transponder capacity has caused a drop in leasing charges and created a "buyers' market." However, the delays in new launches as a result of the 1986–87 launch failures may delay deployment of additional capacity.

U.S. satellites will continue to be used for distribution of video channels to cable television systems, radio and television network feeds to local affiliates, and point-to-multipoint data services such as news, weather, and stock market information services. It appears that the market for interactive VSAT networks will continue to grow, as vendors offer shared networks and hybrid systems in addition to dedicated networks, as well as higher-bandwidth data and video services.

Direct Broadcasting Satellites

The commercial viability of direct broadcasting satellites that would bring multiple channels of television to every household via very small rooftop antennas, as predicted a decade ago, is now highly questionable. While more than two million individuals have installed backyard antennas, and antennas to receive special signals are sprouting on many buildings, it appears unlikely that DBS will achieve the penetration of cable, since most of the country is already cabled. Current DBS satellite designs, which have increased the number of transponders compared to proposed systems a decade ago, cannot offer as many channels as are available on most cable systems.

Although originally DBS programmers planned to offer programming not available from other sources, the proliferation of specialized programming from cable television, pay television, and VCRs has made this marketing strategy obsolete. If DBS succeeds, it will be because the four parties of interest—the program producers, the program suppliers, the satellite operators, and the cable systems— are able to use DBS to increase their revenues and protect their interests. Cable companies, for example, may market DBS services for low-density areas surrounding their franchise area, where cabling costs are prohibitive. However, while it appears that DBS is attractive for noncabled rural areas, many of these viewers have already installed C-band antennas to pick up the channels being fed to cable systems. Rural electrical cooperatives have now negotiated with several cable channels to offer a package of satellite programming to rural subscribers who purchase earth stations. Waivers by the FCC that enable rural telephone companies to own cable television systems will also increase the number of cable subscribers in small towns.

Some analysts think the future of DBS is tied to HDTV, which requires enormous bandwidth to deliver the digital information necessary to display a film-quality television picture. At present, there is considerable debate about the future of this technology, generically known as advanced television technology (ATV). Proponents of this technology consider it vital for the United States to play a leading role in ATV in the next phase of the electronics revolution:

> There is no doubt that ATV will offer viewers pictures of exceptional, perhaps mesmerizing caliber. However, underlying the development of ATV is a technological revolution whose consequences for the entire electronics industry, and those industries dependent upon electronics, are of staggering proportions.
> . . . The market for the myriad interrelated industries—products, services, processes—could be worth tens of billions of dollars. Hundreds of thousands of jobs are at stake."[29]

Although other analysts question the strategic importance of HDTV, it appears that higher-resolution television will be offered in the industrialized world and that satellites may be the most cost-effective delivery medium, whether they bring the signal directly to households or to community headends for redistribution via optical fiber.

Applications for Remote Areas and Developing Countries

A disadvantage of satellites for voice communications is the delay resulting from the transmission of the signal more than 44,600 miles to and from the satellite, and twice that distance in double-hop systems. Therefore, in the industrialized world, voice telephone service will migrate to terrestrial technologies, except in remote areas where satellites remain the only viable solution. In developing countries, satellites will likely continue to play an important role in providing telephone and telex services to remote areas, as well as in television distribution. The advantages of satellite systems—reliability, flexibility of capacity, and, most importantly, the ability to install communication facilities wherever they are needed without the need for extension of terrestrial networks will continue to make them valuable for developing countries. More satellite terminals will be solar-powered as the cost per watt of photovoltaics drops. Improvements in radio technologies such as digital microwave, cellular radio, and rural radio systems (known as BETRS, Basic Exchange Telephone Radio Service in the United States) may enable rural satellite stations to function as hubs, whose spokes, or "last miles," to surrounding communities are covered by terrestrial radio systems.

To summarize . . .

- The launch failures of 1986–87 may eventually be seen as temporary setbacks. Of greater long-term import is the internationalization of manufacturing and launches, as Europe, Japan, China, and India catch up with the United States and the U.S.S.R.
- Optical fiber has advantages for heavy-volume point-to-point traffic, whereas satellites will continue to be cost-effective for multipoint and thin route services.
- VSATs and teleports will proliferate for interactive data services, teleconferencing, and business television.
- DBS may not emerge as a competitor to cable, but medium-power DBS may be used to serve rural areas and to provide business services.
- Satellites may be used to deliver HDTV, either directly to homes via high-powered DBS systems or to community headends for redistribution via optical fiber.
- Competition with Intelsat will result in new specialized satellites over the Atlantic and the Pacific, but Intelsat will likely remain a strong competitor.
- Industrial policy to promote satellites in Europe may dramatically influence the future of European broadcasting.
- As earth station technology becomes smaller and cheaper, its appropriateness for developing countries increases, but problems of financing, training, and integrating telecommunications with development strategies will likely remain.

Thus, it is safe to say that communication satellites will remain an important element in global telecommunications for the foreseeable future, although their role may differ from that predicted twenty years ago or even five years ago.

THE IMPACT OF COMMUNICATION SATELLITES

Communication satellites epitomize the reality of two phenomena that are already clichés but are not yet fully understood: the "global village" and the "information age." Satellites can bring the power of information to virtually everyone on the planet and can enable us to share experiences instantaneously. Yet we still have much to learn about the effects of this technology. For example, satellites have the potential to eliminate the barriers of distance that have hampered economic growth, social-service delivery, and public participation in rural and remote areas of both industrialized and developing countries. We need to learn how satellites can be used to increase rural residents' access to information, to raise agricultural productivity, and to promote other rural industries. Also, it will be important to examine the extent to which the availability of satellite communications for high-quality voice and data communications encourages other industries to decentralize their operations away from major cities.[30]

It will also be important to evaluate the impact of satellites on education, not only in the classroom, but in the home and workplace. Satellites can bring specialized courses to small schools to help upgrade and enrich their curricula. Engineers, nurses, and other employees can study where they work, with instruction delivered by satellite from universities around the country. Physicians, lawyers, and other professionals can keep up with advances in their fields by taping specialized programs delivered by satellite and cable for viewing at their convenience. And adult education courses delivered to homes offer lifelong learning opportunities to all. We need to learn from successful models such as the National Technological University, Lifetime, and the Learning Channel how to use satellites effectively to meet the specialized learning needs of diverse populations.

Internationally, satellites have the power to bring about a "global village." There is much still to be learned about the impact of global television on the knowledge and attitudes of viewers in the United States and other countries. We understand very little as yet about how people can be mobilized to act through common viewing of a global program and how the diverse cultural and educational backgrounds of viewers affect their interpretation of what may now be called "global television."

Perhaps the most significant contribution of satellites will be to bring basic communications to people in developing countries.

Smaller and cheaper earth stations, many of them solar-powered, coupled with new and improved radio technologies, should make it possible to reach virtually every human settlement. Yet developing countries will still face decisions about how to invest their limited resources to improve basic infrastructure, including communications, transportation, electricity, and water supplies. Planners in developing countries will therefore need guidance on what priority to assign to communications and how to gain the greatest benefits from telecommunications investments. Thus, research on how the extension of telephone and broadcasting services can contribute to social and economic development will continue to be needed to assist planners and policymakers in the next decade.

SATELLITES AS A NEW TECHNOLOGY

At a more general level, satellites can be viewed as an example of a new technology that needs to be studied within its economic, political, and cultural contexts. Through the case studies in this book I have tried to look at satellites through the various facets of this prism. At this point, the case studies perhaps raise more questions than we can answer. For example, in Western Europe, will the industrial and technological policies that are driving the investment in broadcasting satellites and cable systems result in the dismantling of broadcasting policies that for the past fifty years have sought to reinforce national cultures and foster indigenous talent? As part of their industrial strategy, will the Europeans export their satellite technology to the developing world, and if so, will it be appropriately designed for thin-route voice and data services and community broadcast reception?

In North America, will satellites fulfill the promise of programming diversity, or will the result be primarily specialized channels that offer "more of the same" sports, news, and movies? Will satellites, along with the VCR, fragment the viewing audience, thereby challenging both the dominance of the major networks and the strategies of advertisers? Will the market for bypass VSAT networks be eroded if a deregulated AT&T lowers its rates significantly? Will demand for HDTV be large enough to attract investors for DBS systems? Or will the telephone companies install optical fiber so that satellites will deliver HDTV and other video services to community headends for redistribution on their networks rather than via direct reception or cable television systems?

Will the result of the new phenomenon of global television be the homogenization of television content as U.S. entertainment programs appear on screens around the world, or greater diversity of content through the exchange of programs? In the developing world, will the PTTs facilitate rather than hinder the diffusion and use of satellite technology? And, most important, will the technology be effectively used to help meet development goals?

The answers to these questions will depend more on policy than on technology. Satellites and other new technologies create formidable challenges as well as opportunities. Countries that foster cultural diversity can use satellite technology to reach many different groups or to feed the same programs to all. The goal of fostering local production and talent can be achieved by exporting and exchanging programs, or undermined by importing the cheapest available programs. Developing countries can foster rural development by investing in their communication infrastructure and setting rates that ensure affordable access to basic communications, or stifle development by limiting diffusion of the technology or pricing its use beyond the means of most customers. Satellites can be used to educate children and adults at school or in the community, but only if educators as well as broadcasters are fully committed and have the resources to make and utilize effective programs.

REALIZING THE VISION

Perhaps the most fitting way to conclude is to return to Arthur Clarke, who proposed not only a new technology but a means of linking people that could have profound developmental impact. "I believe," said Clarke, "that communication satellites can unite mankind."[31] In some respects we have progressed faster than Clarke anticipated. He claims he never expected to witness commercial development of communication satellites in his lifetime. Yet, the first steps have perhaps been the easiest. As the examples in this book have shown, our record in utilizing this technology has been mixed, with some outstanding successes but many failures.

After the first twenty-five years of satellite use Clarke's vision still waits to be realized. Harnessing satellite technology to realize its full potential for the benefit of all will be a major challenge in the next quarter-century.

Notes

Chapter 1

Realizing the Dream

1. Arthur C. Clarke, "Extra-Terrestrial Relays: Can Rocket Stations Give World-Wide Radio Coverage?" *Wireless World*, October 1945, pp. 305–308.
2. Arthur C. Clarke, *Voices from the Sky: Previews of the Coming Space Age* (New York: Harper and Row, 1965), p. 19.
3. Joseph N. Pelton and John Howkins, *Satellites International* (New York: Stockton Press, 1988).
4. Delbert D. Smith, *Communication via Satellite: A Vision in Retrospect* (Leyden: A. W. Sijthoff, 1976), p. 16.
5. Pelton and Howkins, *Satellites International*, p. 5.
6. Smith, *Communication via Satellite*, p. 17.
7. G. B. Bleazard, *Introducing Satellite Communications* (Manchester: National Computing Centre, 1985), p. 71.
8. Pelton and Howkins, *Satellites International*, p. 3.
9. Bleazard, *Introducing Satellite Communications*, p. 38.
10. Ibid., p. 38.
11. Pelton and Howkins, *Satellites International*, p. 3.

Chapter 2

The Early Years

1. Smith, *Communication via Satellite*, p. 26.
2. Ibid., p. 18.
3. Ibid., p. 18.

4. Ibid., p. 26.

5. Ibid., p. 29.

6. Ibid., p. 31.

7. Ibid., p. 32.

8. Ibid., p. 35.

9. Apparently the Soviets were not particularly interested in the communication potential of satellites at that time. Sputnik 1 was followed by Sputnik 2, which carried the first passenger—a dog—into space.

10. Jonathan F. Galloway, *The Politics and Technology of Satellite Communications* (Lexington, MA: D.C. Heath, 1972), p. 12.

11. Quoted in Smith, *Communication via Satellite*, p. 38.

12. *National Aeronautics and Space Act of 1958.* Public Law 85–568, 85th Cong., 72 Stat. 426, 29 July 1958.

13. Smith, *Communication via Satellite*, p. 44.

14. Ibid., p. 44.

15. Ibid., p. 43.

16. Ibid., p. 56.

17. Quoted in Smith, *Communication via Satellite*, p. 50.

18. Quoted in Smith, *Communication via Satellite*, p. 63.

19. Smith, *Communication via Satellite*, p. 71.

20. Quoted in Smith, *Communication via Satellite*, p. 77.

21. Quoted in Smith, *Communication via Satellite*, pp. 77–78.

22. Smith, *Communication via Satellite*, p. 47.

23. Ibid., p. 68.

24. Ibid., p. 83.

25. Ibid., p. 54.

26. For more detailed accounts of the early days of satellites see Delbert Smith, *Communication via Satellite* (1976); Arthur C. Clarke, *Voices from the Sky: Previews of the Coming Space Age* (1965) and *The Coming of the Space Age* (1967); and Jonathan Galloway, *The Politics and Technology of Space Communications* (1972).

27. Galloway, *Politics and Technology*, p. 18.

28. Smith, *Communication via Satellite*, p. 58.

29. Galloway, *Politics and Technology*, p. 78.

Chapter 3

The Beginning of International Satellite Communications

1. Quoted in Galloway, *Politics and Technology*, p. 23.

2. Jack Oslund, "'Open Shores' to 'Open Skies': Sources and Directions of U.S. Satellite Policy," in *Economic and Policy Problems in Satellite Communi-*

cations, ed. Joseph Pelton and Marcellus Snow (New York: Praeger, 1977), p. 165.

3. Quoted in Galloway, *Politics and Technology,* p. 26.
4. Galloway, *Politics and Technology,* p. 26.
5. Ibid., p. 58.
6. Ibid., p. 59.
7. Quoted in Galloway, *Politics and Technology,* p. 38.
8. Quoted in Galloway, *Politics and Technology,* p. 40.
9. Quoted in Galloway, *Politics and Technology,* p. 42.
10. Oslund, "'Open Shores' to 'Open Skies,'" p. 167.
11. Ibid., p. 162.
12. Quoted in Robert S. Magnant, *Domestic Satellite: An FCC Giant Step* (Boulder, CO: Westview Press, 1977), p. 65.
13. Quoted in Oslund, "'Open Shores' to 'Open Skies,'" p. 163.
14. Quoted in Smith, *Communication via Satellite,* p. 95.
15. Galloway, *Politics and Technology,* p. 41.
16. Ibid., p. 55.
17. Ibid., p. 63.
18. Ibid., p. 37.
19. Magnant, *Domestic Satellite,* p. 58.
20. Quoted in Joseph Pelton, *Global Communications Satellite Policy: INTEL-SAT, Politics, and Functionalism* (Mt. Airy, MD: Lomond Books, 1974), p. 52.
21. *Communications Satellite Act* (47 USC, Section 701 et seq.) quoted in Oslund, "'Open Shores' to 'Open Skies,'" p. 145.
22. McGeorge Bundy, quoted in Pelton, *Global Communications Satellite Policy,* p. 50.
23. Pelton, *Global Communications Satellite Policy,* p. 52.
24. *Communications Satellite Act* (47 USC, Section 701 et seq.), Section 305.
25. Galloway, *Politics and Technology,* p. 90.
26. Quoted in Galloway, *Politics and Technology,* p. 85.
27. Pelton, *Global Communications Satellite Policy,* p. 46.
28. Ibid., p. 65.
29. Galloway, *Politics and Technology,* p. 83.
30. Smith, *Communication via Satellite,* p. 135.
31. Pelton, *Global Communications Satellite Policy,* p. 53.
32. Ibid., p. 55.
33. Smith, *Communication via Satellite,* pp. 138–39.
34. Pelton, *Global Communications Satellite Policy,* p. 58.

35. Quoted in Galloway, *Politics and Technology*, p. 96.
36. Galloway, *Politics and Technology*, pp. 91–92.
37. Smith, *Communication via Satellite*, p. 142.
38. Ibid., p. 143.
39. Ibid., p. 146.
40. Ibid., p. 73.
41. Pelton, *Global Communications Satellite Policy*, p. 141.
42. Intelsat Definitive Arrangements quoted in Smith, *Communication via Satellite*, pp. 150–51.
43. Pelton, *Global Communications Satellite Policy*, p. 111.
44. Oslund, "'Open Shores' to 'Open Skies,'" p. 169.
45. Quoted in Galloway, *Politics and Technology*, p. 76.
46. Smith, *Communication via Satellite*, p. 121.
47. Quoted in Galloway, *Politics and Technology*, p. 156.
48. Galloway, *Politics and Technology*, p. 103.
49. Magnant, *Domestic Satellite*, p. 73.
50. Quoted in Galloway, *Politics and Technology*, p. 123.
51. Galloway, *Politics and Technology*, p. 126.
52. Ibid., pp. 128–29.

Chapter 4

United States Domestic Policy: Toward Open Skies

1. *Communications Satellite Act*, quoted in Oslund, "'Open Shores' to 'Open Skies,'" p. 145.
2. Smith, *Communication via Satellite*, p. 158.
3. Ibid., p. 158.
4. Ibid., p. 157.
5. Quoted in Michael E. Kinsley, *Outer Space and Inner Sanctums: Government, Business, and Satellite Communication* (New York: John Wiley and Sons, 1976), p. 134.
6. Smith, *Communication via Satellites*, p. 159.
7. Ibid., p. 162.
8. Ibid., p. 160.
9. Ibid., p. 161.
10. Ibid., p. 161.
11. Harvey J. Levin, *The Invisible Resource: Use and Regulation of the Radio Spectrum* (Baltimore: Johns Hopkins University Press, 1971), p. 310.
12. Comsat internal memo, quoted in Kinsley, *Outer Space and Inner Sanctums*, p. 146.

13. Kinsley, *Outer Space and Inner Sanctums*, pp. 153–54.

14. Quoted in Kingsley, *Outer Space and Inner Sanctums*, p. 148.

15. Message from the President of the United States, House of Representatives, 90th Congress, 1st session, August 1967, quoted in Magnant, *Domestic Satellite*, p. 144.

16. Magnant, *Domestic Satellite*, p. 144.

17. Ibid., p. 151.

18. Quoted in Smith, *Communication via Satellite*, pp. 165–66.

19. Quoted in Smith, *Communication via Satellite*, p. 168.

20. White House Memorandum for Honorable Dean Burch, Chairman, FCC, of January 23, 1970, reprinted in FCC Docket 16495, First Report and Order, March 24, 1970, quoted in Kinsley, *Outer Space and Inner Sanctums*, pp. 157–58.

21. Smith, *Communication via Satellite*, pp. 169–71.

22. Quoted in Smith, *Communication via Satellite*, p. 173.

23. Kinsley, *Outer Space and Inner Sanctums*, p. 176.

24. Smith, *Communication via Satellite*, p. 175.

25. Ibid., p. 180.

26. Ibid., p. 180.

27. Magnant, *Domestic Satellite*, p. 42.

28. Kinsley, *Outer Space and Inner Sanctums*, p. 164.

29. Lawrence Roberts, "Data by the Packet," *IEEE Spectrum*, February 1974, quoted in Magnant, *Domestic Satellite*, p. 120.

30. U.S. Congress, Senate Subcommittee on Communications, *Overview of the FCC*, 93rd Congress, February 22, 1973, pp. 65–66.

31. Ibid., p. 62.

32. Kinsley, *Outer Space and Inner Sanctums*, p. xi.

33. Quoted in Kinsley, *Outer Space and Inner Sanctums*, p. vi.

34. Quoted in Kinsley, *Outer Space and Inner Sanctums*, p. 166.

35. Quoted in Kinsley, *Outer Space and Inner Sanctums*, p. 186.

36. Kinsley, *Outer Space and Inner Sanctums*, p. 168.

37. Ibid., p. 167.

38. Ibid., p. 191.

39. Ibid., p. xii.

Chapter 5

The Evolution of Domestic Satellite Services in the United States

1. Heather E. Hudson and Edwin B. Parker, "Medical Communication in Alaska by Satellite," *New England Journal of Medicine*, December 1973, p. 6

2. Walter B. Parker, "The Evolution of the Present Alaska Telecommunications System," in *Telecommunications in Alaska*, ed. Robert M. Walp (Honolulu: Pacific Telecommunications Council, 1982).

3. James M. Janky and James G. Potter, "The ATS-6 Health Education Telecommunication (HET) Experiment" in *Communication Satellite Systems: An Overview of the Technology*, ed. R. G. Gould and Y. F. Lum (New York: IEEE Press, 1976), p. 7.

4. Dennis R. Foote, Heather E. Hudson, and Edwin B. Parker, *Telemedicine in Alaska: The ATS-6 Biomedical Demonstration* (Palo Alto, CA: Stanford University Institute for Communication Research, 1976).

5. W. M. Evans, N. G. Davies, and W. H. Hawersaat, "The Communication Technology Satellite (CST) Program" in Gould and Lum, eds., *Communication Satellite Systems*, p. 13.

6. See, for example, Rashid Bashur, "Technology Serves the People: The Story of a Cooperative Medical Project by NASA, the Indian Health Service, and the Papago People," Proceedings of the Telecommunications Policy Research Conference (Norwood, NJ: Ablex, 1983).

7. Maxine Rockoff, "Telecommunications Technology: Can It Lead to Health Care Delivery Reform?" Hermes: (The Communications Technology Satellite): Its Performance and Applications (Ottawa: The Royal Society of Canada, 1977).

8. Heather E. Hudson, "How Close They Sound: Applications of Telecommunications for Education and Public Participation in Alaska," *Systems, Objectives, Solutions*, November 1982, p. 199.

9. Ibid.

10. Ibid.

11. Alascom is now owned by Pacific Power and Light of Vancouver, Washington.

12. Richard G. Gould, "US Domestic Communication Satellite Systems" in Gould and Lum, eds., *Communication Satellite Systems*, p. 38.

13. Kinsley, *Outer Space and Inner Sanctums*, p. 164.

14. Pelton and Howkins, *Satellites International*, p. 253.

15. Kinsley, *Outer Space and Inner Sanctums*, p. 163.

16. W. J. Howell, Jr., *World Broadcasting in the Age of the Satellite* (Norwood, NJ: Ablex, 1986), p. 262.

17. Ibid., p. 261.

18. Quoted in Scott Chase, "Radio and Satellites," *Via Satellite*, September 1988, p. 12.

19. Chase, "Radio and Satellites," p. 18.

20. John Garabedian, quoted in Chase, "Radio and Satellites," pp. 15–16.

21. Chase, "Radio and Satellites," p. 17.

22. Scott Chase, "Home Satellite Dishes: Up Against the Wall," *Channels '89 Field Guide to the Electronic Environment*, December 1988, p. 125.

23. Ibid., p. 125.

24. Kevin Pearce, "SMATV: Still Kicking," *Channels '89 Field Guide to the Electronic Media,* December 1988, p. 118.

Chapter 6

Satellites in the U.S. Today: The Growth of Specialized Services

1. *The 1988 Satellite Directory* (Potomac, MD: Phillips Publishing, 1988), pp. 7–100.

2. Howell, *World Broadcasting,* p. 273.

3. Donald LeDuc, quoted in Howell, *World Broadcasting,* p. 273.

4. Howell, *World Broadcasting,* p. 273.

5. Andrew F. Inglis, "The United States Satellite Industry: An Overview," *FIBRESAT 86 Conference Proceedings,* Vancouver, B.C., 1986.

6. *The 1988 Satellite Directory,* pp. 4, 77.

7. Bleazard, *Introducing Satellite Communications,* p. 292.

8. Ibid., p. 291.

9. For example, L. L. Bean uses this technique to update its catalogs. Scott Howard, L. L. Bean, personal communication, July 1988.

10. "Batched Data Main Business Application," *Communication News,* March 1989, p. 26.

11. Edwin B. Parker, quoted in Guy Stephens, "Equatorial's Focus on C Band," *Satellite Communications,* February 1986b, p. 22.

12. Alan Stewart, "VSAT Technology Provides a Price-Stable and Strategic Tool for Handling Corporate Growth," *Communication News,* May 1988, p. a14.

13. Eugene R. Cacciamani and Michael K. Sun, "Overview of VSAT Networks," *Telecommunications,* June 1986, p. 39.

14. "Farm Report Network Links VSATs, E-Mail," *Communications News,* March 1989, p. 25.

15. W. G. Quackenbush, "Nation's First Two-Way Private VSAT Network," *Telecommunications,* June 1986, p. 45.

16. Edward A. Terhar, quoted in W. G. Quackenbush, "Nation's First Two-Way Private VSAT Network," *Telecommunications,* June 1986, p. 45.

17. Stewart, "VSAT Technology Provides a Price-Stable and Strategic Tool," p. a17.

18. "Retail Chains Cut Customer Waiting Time," *Communications News,* March 1989, p. 26.

19. *Communications News,* March 1989, p. 7.

20. Tamara Bennett, "VSATs for Growth," *Satellite Communications,* November 1987, p. 24.

21. "Full Service Shared Hubs Offer Economy," *Communications News*, March 1989, p. 26.

22. Keith Dunford, "TSAT: A Low Cost Solution for Satellite Networking," *Via Satellite*, March 1989, p. 28.

23. Bleazard, *Introducing Satellite Communications*, p. 301.

24. Thomas B. Cross, "Teleconferencing, Teleports, and Intelligent Buildings," in *Teleports and the Intelligent City*, ed. Andrew D. Lipman, Alan D. Sugarman, and Robert F. Cushman (Homewood, IL: Dow Jones–Irwin, 1986), pp. 156–57.

25. R. Michael Feazel, "The Birds Fly Low," *Channels '89 Field Guide to the Electronic Environment*, December 1988, p. 123.

26. *Via Satellite*, August 1988, p. 26.

27. Bleazard, *Introducing Satellite Communications*, p. 295.

28. *National Technological University Bulletin: 1988–89 Academic Programs*, Fort Collins, CO, 1988.

29. Polly Rash, "The TI-IN Network," *Via Satellite*, September 1988, p. 22.

30. Lipman, Sugarman, and Cushman, eds., *Teleports and the Intelligent City*, p. 4.

31. Ibid., pp. 7–8.

32. World Teleport Association, *WTA Update*, Winter 1988, pp. 2–6.

33. Lipman, Sugarman, and Cushman, eds., *Teleports and the Intelligent City*, p. 17.

34. Ibid., p. 20.

35. *Via Satellite*, August 1988, p. 24.

36. ELRA Group, "Teleports: An Update," in The 1988 Satellite Directory (Potomac, MD: Phillips Publishing, 1988), p. 132.

37. *Via Satellite*, August 1988, p. 38.

38. *In the Matter of Regulation of Domestic Receive-Only Satellite Earth Stations*, 74 FCC 2d 205 (1979), in "Satellite Regulation—A Short History" in Lipman, Sugarman, and Cushman, eds., *Teleports and the Intelligent City*, p. 73.

39. *Reconsideration of Licensing of Space Stations in the Domestic Fixed Satellite Service*, FCC 84–487 (released January 9, 1985), cited in Cangelosi, "Satellite Regulation," p. 75.

40. Cangelosi, "Satellite Regulation," p. 74.

41. FCC Declaratory Order 3588 (April 9, 1986) and FCC Report DS-610 (March 27, 1987).

42. Kurt R. Oliver, "Is Your VSAT by the Book?" *Communications News*, March 1989, p. 27.

43. FCC, *In the Matter of Domestic Fixed-Satellite Transponder Sales*, 90 FCC 2d 1238 (1982).

44. *In the Matter of Policy and Rules Concerning Rates for Competitive Common Carrier Services and Facilities Authorizations Therefor (Fourth Report and Order)*, 95 FCC 2d 554 (1983).

45. Allan McArtor, quoted in Guy Stephens, "Big Business, Small Dishes," *Satellite Communications*, February 1986a, p. 20.

Chapter 7

Canada's "Magic from the Sky"

1. Robert R. Bruce, Jeffrey P. Cunard, and Mark D. Director. *From Telecommunications to Electronic Services*. London: Butterworth, 1986.

2. Canadian Radio-Television and Telecommunications Commission, CRTC Telecom Decision 77–10, Ottawa, 1977.

3. Gordon E. Kaiser, "Developments in Canadian Telecommunications Regulation," In *Marketplace for Telecommunications*, ed. Marcellus Snow (New York: Longman, 1986).

4. Government of Canada, Order in Council P.C. 1981–3456, Ottawa, December 8, 1981.

5. Quoted in Arthur Collin, "The Canadian Space Program," in *Canada, The United States, and Space*, ed. John Kirton (Toronto: Canadian Institute for International Affairs, 1986).

6. W. M. Evans, "Canada's Space Policy" in *Tracing New Orbits: Cooperation and Competition in Global Satellite Development*, ed. Donna Demac (New York: Columbia University Press, 1986).

7. Canada's Interim Space Plan, 1985–86, Ottawa, 1985.

8. Evans, "Canada's Space Policy" in Demac, ed., *Tracing New Orbits*, p. 133.

9. Alex Curran, "The State of Canada's Industry," in Kirton, ed., *Canada, The United States, and Space.*

10. Lyndsay Green, and David Simailak, "The Inukshuk Project: Use of TV and Satellite by Inuit Communities in the Northwest Territories" (Paper presented at the annual conference of the American Association for the Advancement of Science, Toronto, January 1981).

11. Heather E. Hudson, "The Role of Radio in the Canadian North," *Journal of Communication*, Autumn 1977.

12. Gerard I. Kenney, *Man in the North: Parts I and II* (Montreal: Arctic Institute of North America, 1971).

13. See Hudson, "The Role of Radio in the Canadian North."

14. N. G. Davies, "Canadian Space Applications: New Models for the Developing World," in *New Directions in Satellite Communications: Challenges for North and South*, ed. Heather E. Hudson (Dedham, MA: Artech, 1985).

15. Ibid.

16. Gail Valaskakis, R. Robbins, and T. Wilson, *The Inukshuk Project: An Assessment* (Ottawa: Inuit Tapirisat of Canada, 1981).

17. Andre H. Caron and James R. Taylor, "Cable at the Crossroads: An Analysis of the Canadian Cable Industry," in *Cable Television and the Future of Broadcasting*, ed. Ralph Negrine (London: Croom Helm, 1985).

18. Hal Glatzer, *The Birds of Babel* (Indianapolis: Howard A. Sams, 1983).

19. Canadian Department of Communications, DOC NR-84-5265E, April 10, 1984.

20. Canadian Department of Communications, *Towards a New National Broadcasting Policy*, Ottawa, February 1983.

21. Heather E. Hudson, "Viewing Patterns in Two Canadian Cities," unpublished paper, June 1969.

22. Gail Valaskakis, "Socio-Economic Implications in Canada of Satellite Communications," FIBRESAT 86 Conference Proceedings (Vancouver, September 1986).

23. Quoted in Timothy Hollins, *Beyond Broadcasting: Into the Cable Age* (London: British Film Institute, 1984).

Chapter 8

Satellites for Western Europe: Industrial, Technological, and Cultural Policies Collide

1. Kenneth Dyson and Peter Humphreys, eds., *Policies for New Media in Western Europe* (London: Frank Cass, 1986), p. 107.

2. Pelton and Howkins, *Satellites International*, p. 180.

3. Howell, *World Broadcasting*, p. 256.

4. Pelton and Howkins, *Satellites International*, p. 136.

5. Ibid.

6. Howell, *World Broadcasting*, p. 255.

7. Pelton and Howkins, *Satellites International*, p. 136.

8. Ibid., p. 31.

9. Ibid.

10. Dyson and Humphreys, *Policies for New Media*, p. 117.

11. Ibid., p. 118.

12. Simon Nora and Alain Minc, *The Computerization of Society* (Cambridge, MA: MIT Press, 1980).

13. Pelton and Howkins, *Satellites International*, p. 180.

14. Ibid., p. 181.

15. Dyson and Humphreys, *Policies for New Media*, p. 98.

16. Ibid., p. 105.

17. Ibid., p. 118.

18. Quoted in Dyson and Humphreys, *Policies for New Media*, p. 103.

19. Howell, *World Broadcasting*, p. 260.

20. Ibid.

21. Pelton and Howkins, *Satellites International*, p. 245.

22. Mario Hirsch, "The Doldrums of Europe's TV Landscape: Coronet as Catalyst," in Demac, ed., *Tracing New Orbits*, p. 115.

23. Dyson and Humphreys, *Policies for New Media*, p. 110.

24. Ibid., p. 112.

25. Ibid., p. 111.

26. Ibid., p. 109.

27. Hirsch, "The Doldrums," p. 48.

28. Bin Cheng, quoted in Mario Hirsch, "A Monopoly Challenged," *Cable and Satellite Europe*, no. 2, 1987, p. 50.

29. Glyndwr Matthias, "The Monopoly Strikes Back," *Cable and Satellite Europe*, no. 3, 1987, p. 40.

30. Andrea Caruso, "The European Telecommunications Satellite Organization," in Pelton and Howkins, *Satellites International*, p. 31.

31. Lennart Weibull and Ronny Severinsson, in "The Nordic Countries in the Age of Satellite Broadcasting," Negrine, ed., *Satellite Broadcasting*, p. 78.

32. Ibid., p. 79.

33. "Nordic Radio and Television via Satellite, Final Report, 1979," quoted in Weibull and Severinsson, "The Nordic Countries," p. 80.

34. Weibull and Severinsson, "The Nordic Countries," p. 81.

35. Pelton and Howkins, *Satellites International*, p. 237.

36. Weibull and Severinsson, *"The Nordic Countries,"* p. 89.

37. Dyson and Humphreys, *Policies for New Media*, p. 114.

38. Pelton and Howkins, *Satellites International*, p. 196.

39. Dyson and Humphreys, *Policies for New Media*, p. 113.

40. George Wedell, "Television without Frontiers?" EBU Review, vol. 36, no. 1, January 1985, p. 21.

41. Quoted in Wedell, "Television without Frontiers?" p. 22.

42. Howell, *World Broadcasting*, p. 275.

43. Wedell, "Television without Frontiers?" p. 24.

44. Quoted in Wedell, "Television without Frontiers?" p. 23.

45. Wedell, "Television without Frontiers?" p. 24.

46. Rupert Murdoch, speech to the International Institute of Communications annual conference, Washington, D.C., September 1988.

47. Quoted in Dyson and Humphreys, *Policies for New Media*, p. 108.

48. Denis McQuail, "Policy Perspectives for New Media in Europe," in *New Communications Technologies and Public Interest*, ed. Marjorie Ferguson (London: Sage, 1986), p. 126.

49. Brenda Maddox, quoted in Howell, *World Broadcasting*, p. 259.

50. Dyson and Humphreys, *Policies for New Media*, p. 103.

51. Ibid., p. 110.

52. Ibid., p. 122.

Chapter 9

Other Industrialized Countries: The Soviet Union, Australia, and Japan

1. *Krasnaya Zvezda*, Jan. 24, 1980, quoted in John D. H. Downing, "Cooperation and Competition in Satellite Communication: The Soviet Union," in Demac, ed., *Tracing New Orbits*, p. 283.

2. Downing, "Cooperation and Competition," p. 283.

3. Ibid., p. 284.

4. Ibid., p. 286.

5. Ken Schaffer, "A Television Window on the Soviet Union," in Demac, ed., *Tracing New Orbits*, p. 306.

6. Ploman, *Space, Earth, and Communication*, p. 83.

7. Martin P. Brown, Jr., "The USSR Domestic System (MOLNIYA/ORBITA)" in Gould and Lum, eds., *Communication Satellite Systems*, p. 29.

8. Ibid.

9. Pelton and Howkins, *Satellite International*, p. 256.

10. Ibid.

11. Downing, "Cooperation and Competition," p. 287.

12. Pelton and Howkins, *Satellites International*, p. 129.

13. Ibid., p. 128.

14. Ibid., p. 129.

15. Downing, "Cooperation and Competition," p. 288.

16. Ibid., p. 298.

17. Ibid., p. 298.

18. Ibid., p. 296.

19. Schaffer, "A Television Window," p. 309.

20. Brown, "The USSR Domestic System, (MOLNIYA/ORBITA)" in Gould and Lum, eds., *Communication Satellite Systems*, p. 27.

21. Pelton and Howkins, *Satellites International*, p. 151.

22. Ibid., p. 152.

23. Ibid., p. 151.

24. Ian Reinecke, "Satellite Broadcasting in Australia," in Negrine, ed., *Satellite Broadcasting*, p. 197.

25. Ibid., p. 201.

26. Ibid., p. 203.

27. Ibid., p. 207.

28. Neil Primrose, "Australian Telecommunications: A New Framework" (Paper presented to the annual conference of the International Institute of Communications, Washington, D.C., September 14, 1988), p. 8.

29. Ibid, p. 9.

30. Pelton and Howkins, *Satellites International*, p. 151.

31. Ibid., p. 152.

32. See Neil D. Karunaratne, "Telecommunication and Information in Development Planning Strategy," in *Communication Economics and Development*, ed. Meheroo Jussawalla and Donald Lamberton (Honolulu: East-West Center, 1982).

33. Reinecke, "Satellite Broadcasting in Australia," p. 198.

34. Negrine, ed., *Satellite Broadcasting*, p. 249.

35. Ibid., p. 250.

36. Ibid., p. 251.

37. Pelton and Howkins, *Satellites International*, p. 199.

38. Ibid.

39. Ibid.

40. Yuko Nakamura, "Direct Broadcasting in Japan: An Overview," in Negrine, ed., *Satellite Broadcasting*, p. 256.

41. Ibid., p. 257.

42. Ibid., p. 258.

43. Negrine, ed., *Satellite Broadcasting*, p. 251.

44. Nakamura, "Direct Broadcasting in Japan," p. 265.

Chapter 10

Intelsat Today

1. Intelsat. Intelsat Annual Report, 1987–88, Washington, D.C., 1988, p. i.

2. Ibid., p. 2.

3. Dean Burch, "Intelsat: The Tomorrow Organization" in Pelton and Howkins, *Satellites International*, p. 25.

4. Intelsat Annual Report, 1987–88, p. iii.

5. Ibid., p. 32.

6. Ibid., 1987–88, p. 38.

7. Burch, "Intelsat," in Pelton and Hawkins, p. 26.

8. Intelsat Annual Report, 1987–88, pp. 41–45.

9. Ibid., p. 7.

10. Ibid., p. 2.

11. Ibid., p. 11.

12. Ibid., p. 19.
13. Pelton and Howkins, *Satellites International*, p. 123.
14. Derived from Intelsat Annual Report, 1987–88, p. 21.
15. Pelton and Howkins, *Satellites International*, p. 123.
16. Intelsat Annual Report, 1987–88, p. 24.
17. Derived from Intelsat Annual Report, 1987–88.
18. Burch, "Intelsat," in Pelton and Hawkins, p. 25.
19. Intelsat Annual Report, 1987–88, p. 28.
20. Ibid., p. 16.
21. Ibid., p. 24.
22. Ibid., p. 22.
23. Ibid., p. 15.
24. Ibid., p. 16.
25. Quoted in Scott Chase "Live via Satellite," *Via Satellite*, April 1988, p. 50.
26. Intelsat Annual Report, 1987–88, p. 25.
27. Burch, "Intelsat," p. 25.
28. Jim Plante, "Reporting by Satellite: A Challenge for the Networks," *Intermedia*, May 1986.
29. Ibid.
30. Ibid.
31. Tapio Varis, "Global Traffic in Television," *Journal of Communication*, vol. 24, no. 1 (Winter 1974), pp. 102–9.
32. Tapio Varis, "The International Flow of Television Programs," *Journal of Communication*, Winter 1984, pp. 143–52.
33. Olof Hulten and Charly Hulten. "Intelsat: The Changing Pattern of TV Transmission," *Intermedia*, January 1985, p. 30.
34. Presentation by Worldnet staff, Washington, D.C., September 1988.
35. "Discover America," Worldnet brochure, USIA, Washington, D.C.
36. Presentation by Worldnet staff, Washington, D.C., September 1988.
37. Schaffer, "A Television Window," p. 310.
38. Ibid.
39. "Satellites: Flying Higher than Ever," *Broadcasting*, July 14, 1986, p. 53.
40. Bruce Stokes, "Beaming Jobs Overseas," *National Journal*, July 27, 1985, p. 1727.
41. Stokes, "Beaming Jobs Overseas," p. 1729.

Chapter 11

Satellites and Development: The Distant Promise

1. MacBride Commission, *Many Voices, One World* (Paris: Unesco, 1980).
2. See, for example, literature reviewed in Heather E. Hudson, *When Telephones Reach the Village* (Norwood, NJ: Ablex, 1984).

3. Andrew P. Hardy, "The Role of the Telephone in Economic Development," *Telecommunications Policy*, vol. 4, no. 4, December 1980.

4. Heather E. Hudson, Andrew P. Hardy, and Edwin B. Parker, "Impact of Telephones and Thin Route Satellite Earth Stations on GDP," *Telecommunications Policy*, December 1982.

5. See for example, William B. Pierce, Jr., and Nicolas Jequier, *Telecommunications for Development* (Geneva: International Telecommunications Union, 1983).

6. Robert J. Saunders, Jeremy Warford, and Bjorn Wellenius. *Telecommunications and Economic Development* (Baltimore: Johns Hopkins University Press, 1983).

7. For example, the U.S. Agency for International Development and UNESCO; see *A Bibliography of Telecommunications and Socio-Economic Development*, ed. Heather E. Hudson (Norwood, MA: Artech House, 1988).

8. Independent Commission for Worldwide Telecommunications Development, *The Missing Link* (Geneva: International Telecommunications Union, 1985).

9. AT&T, *The World's Telephones, 1985–86* (Morristown, NJ: AT&T, 1988).

10. Independent Commission for Worldwide Telecommunications Development, *The Missing Link*.

11. Keynote address, Pacific Telecommunications Conference, Honolulu, January 1989.

12. For additional information on the World Bank's role in telecommunications, see Saunders, Warford, and Wellenius, *Telecommunications and Economic Development*.

13. Kenneth Simmonds, "The Third Lomé Convention," *Common Market Law Review*, July 1985.

14. Eric Michaels, personal communication, 1984.

Chapter 12

Satellite Use by Developing Countries: An Overview

1. Derived from Intelsat Annual Report, 1987–88.

2. Pelton and Howkins, *Satellites International*, p. 192.

3. Lecture by the author for the Ministry of Information, Djakarta, Indonesia, June 1986.

4. Pelton and Howkins, *Satellites International*, p. 135.

5. Ibid.

6. Ibid.

7. Charles Griffith, "The Arab World: Elusive Accord," *Intermedia*, July–September 1986, p. 71.

8. Miguel E. Sanchez-Ruiz, "Key Issues in Satellite Communications: The Mexican Satellite Program," in *New Directions in Satellite Communications:*

Challenges for North and South, ed. Heather E. Hudson (Norwood, MA: Artech, 1985), p. 113.

9. Kathleen A. Griffith, "Mexican Teleconnectivity," *Proceedings of the Pacific Telecommunications Conference* (Honolulu, January 1989), p. 548.

10. Ibid.

11. Sanchez-Ruiz, "Key Issues in Satellite Communications," p. 113.

12. Kathleen A. Griffith, "Mexican Teleconnectivity," p. 549.

13. Pelton and Howkins, *Satellites International,* p. 213.

14. Kathleen A. Griffith, "Mexican Teleconnectivity," p. 550.

15. Ibid.

16. Douglas Goldschmidt, "Pan American Satellite and the Introduction of Specialized Communication Systems in Latin America" in *Proceedings of the Pacific Telecommunications Conference* (Honolulu, February 1988), pp. 343–346.

17. Ibid., p. 344.

18. Ibid., p. 345.

19. Zhou Yougao, "China: Leaping Forward," *Intermedia,* July–September 1986, p. 78.

20. Ibid.

21. Ibid.

22. Ibid., p. 79.

23. Ibid., p. 79.

24. Sylvia Ospina, "Project CONDOR: The Andean Regional Satellite System: When Will This Bird Fly?" *Proceedings of the Pacific Telecommunications Conference* (Honolulu, January 1989), p. 118.

25. Ibid., p. 119.

26. Ibid.

27. Ibid., p. 118.

28. Quoted in Ospina, "Project CONDOR," pp. 122–23.

29. Donna Demac and Aggrey Brown, "Future Regional Satellite Systems: The Case of the Caribbean," in Pelton and Howkins, *Satellites International,* p. 80.

30. Ibid., p. 81.

31. Angela Prenner, "The Ups and Downs of Third World Satcoms," *Developing World Communications* (London: Grosvenor Press International, 1989), p. 163.

Chapter 13

Satellites and Developing Countries: Case Studies

1. Bella Mody, "Contextual Analysis of the Adoption of a Communications Technology: The Case of Satellites in India," *Telematics and Informatics,* vol. 4, no. 2 (1987), p. 153.

2. Ibid., p. 155.

3. Clifford Block, Dennis R. Foote, and John K. Mayo, "SITE Unseen: Implications for Programming and Policy," *Journal of Communication*, August 1979, p. 116.

4. Mody, "Contextual Analysis," p. 151.

5. Personal interviews by the author, New Delhi, 1978.

6. Mody, "Contextual Analysis," p. 156.

7. Pelton and Howkins, *Satellites International*, p. 191.

8. G. K. Gupta and R. N. Khapre, "India: A Boost for Development," *Intermedia*, July-September 1986, p. 79.

9. Ibid., p. 80.

10. Mody, "Contextual Analysis," p. 157.

11. Gupta and Khapre, "India," p. 81.

12. AT&T, *The World's Telephones, 1985–86*.

13. For a detailed evaluation of the project, see Emile G. McAnany, G. and Joao Batista de Oliveira, *The SACI/EXERN Project in Brazil: An Analytical Case Study* (Paris: UNESCO, 1980).

14. Euclides Quandt de Oliveira, quoted in Greta Nettleton and Emile McAnany, "Brazil's Satellite System and the Politics of Applications Planning," *Telecommunications Policy*, June 1989.

15. Nettleton and McAnany, "Brazil's Satellite System."

16. Joao Carlos Fagundes Albernaz, "Brazil: Bird over the Amazon," *Intermedia*, July–September 1986, p. 72.

17. Nettleton and McAnany, "Brazil's Satellite System."

18. Quoted in Nettleton and McAnany, "Brazil's Satellite System."

19. Joao Carlos Fagundes Albernaz, "The Brazilian Satellite Communications Program," in Hudson, ed., *New Directions in Satellite Communications*.

20. Nettleton and McAnany, "Brazil's Satellite System."

21. Clifford Block, Douglas Goldschmidt, Anwar Hafid, et al., "Satellite Telecommunications for Rural Development: The A.I.D. Rural Satellite Program and Its Projects in Indonesia, Peru, and the Caribbean," *Proceedings of the Pacific Telecommunications Conference*, (Honolulu, January 1984).

22. John K. Mayo, Gary R. Heald, Steven J. Klees, et al., *Peru Rural Communication Services Project: Final Evaluation Report* (Tallahassee, FL: Center for International Studies, Learning Systems Institute, Florida State University, 1987), p. ii.

23. Ibid., p. iii.

24. Ibid., p. iv.

25. Block, Goldschmidt, Hafid, et al., "Satellite Telecommunications," p. 29.

26. Ibid.

27. Mayo, Heald, Klees, et al., *Peru Rural Communication Project*, p. iv.

28. Karen Tietjen, *AID Rural Satellite Program: An Overview* (Washington, D.C.: Academy for Educational Development, 1987), pp. 111–114.

29. Ibid., pp. 111, 114.

30. Intelsat, *Project SHARE: A Final Report and Evaluation* (Washington, D.C.: Intelsat, 1988), p. 1.

31. Ibid., p. 4.

32. Ibid., p. 6.

33. Ibid., p. 7.

34. Ibid., p. 11.

35. Intelsat Annual Report, 1987–88, p. 29.

Chapter 14

Innovation in Satellite Communications:
Monopoly and Competition

1. Richard R. Colino, "PTTs, INTELSAT, Monopoly and Competition," *Space Communication and Broadcasting*, vol. 4, 1986, p. 5.

2. Ibid., p. 7.

3. Ibid., p. 6.

4. Michael Blair, "VSATs in Developing Countries," *Satellite Communications*, July 1988, p. 28. Problems that the installation crew faced were variations in power supply 20 to 30 percent above or below the standard 220 volts, and temperatures ranging from 45 degrees Celsius to sub-freezing in the Himalayas, where deicers were required. In some remote areas equipment was moved on donkey carts.

5. Veronica M. Ahern, "Communication Satellites," in *Telecommunications in the U.S.: Trends and Policies*, ed. Leonard Lewin (Dedham, MA: Artech House, 1981), p. 88.

6. Lee McKnight, "The Deregulation of International Satellite Communications: U.S. Satellite Policy and the International Response," *Space Communication and Broadcasting*, vol. 3, 1985.

7. Quoted in Ahern, "Communication Satellites," p. 88.

8. Personal communications with the author.

9. Quoted in Ahern, "Communication Satellites," p. 89.

10. Ahern, "Communication Satellites," p. 92.

11. *Communications Satellite Act of 1962*, As Amended, Public Law No. 624, 87th Congress, 2d sess., August 31, 1972, 47 USC Section 701 et seq.

12. McKnight, "The Deregulation of International Satellite Communications," p. 50.

13. Goldschmidt, "Pan American Satellite," p. 123.

14. Ibid., p. 124.

15. Ibid.

16. Ibid., p. 125.

17. McKnight, "The Deregulation of International Satellite Communications," p. 46.

18. Ibid., p. 44.

19. Ibid., p. 42.

20. Ibid., p. 54.

21. FCC, *Authorized User Policy,* (Policy Revised, 1982), quoted in McKnight, "The Deregulation of International Satellite Communications, p. 39.

22. FCC, *In the Matter of Establishment of Satellites Systems providing International Communications* (CC Docket 84-1299), released September 3, 1985, p. 8.

23. Ibid., p. 10.

24. Ibid.

25. Ibid., p. 7.

26. Ibid., paragraph 265.

27. Douglas Goldschmidt, "Leveling the Playing Field in International Satellite Communications," *Telematics and Informatics,* vol. 4, no. 2 (1987), p. 122.

28. Ibid., p. 127.

29. Study by Future Systems Inc., quoted in McKnight, "The Deregulation of International Satellite Communications," p. 56.

30. McKnight, "The Deregulation of International Satellite Communications," p. 57.

Chapter 15

Space Policy: Access to the Geostationary Orbit

1. For Arthur C. Clarke, who first described the geostationary orbit and its potential in a 1945 article in *Wireless World* (see chapter 1).

2. UNESCO, Meeting of Governmental Experts on International Arrangements in the Space Communications Field, Paris, 1969, p. 10.

3. Quoted in Nicolas M. Matte, *Aerospace Law: Telecommunications Satellites* (Toronto: Butterworth, 1982), p. 29.

4. Quoted in Matte, *Aerospace Law,* p. 30.

5. UNGA Resolution no. 1472 (XIV), 1959, quoted in Matte, *Aerospace Law,* p. 32.

6. Matte, *Aerospace Law,* p. 44.

7. UNESCO Constitution, Article 1, Paragraph 2, quoted in Matte, *Aerospace Law*, p. 43.

8. Intelsat Annual Report, 1987–88.

9. Heather E. Hudson, "Access to Information Resources: The Developmental Context of the Space WARC," *Telecommunications Policy*, March 1985.

10. UNGA Resolution no. 1348 (XIII), Preamble, 1958, quoted in Matte, *Aerospace Law*, p. 76.

11. *Treaty on Principles Governing the Activities of States in the Exploration and Uses of Outer Space, Including the Moon and Other Celestial Bodies*, of Jan. 27, 1967, quoted in Matte, *Aerospace Law*, p. 77.

12. *Agreement Governing the Activities of States on the Moon and Other Celestial Bodies* (The Moon Treaty), 1979, quoted in Matte, *Aerospace Law*, p. 77.

13. International Telecommunication Union (ITU), *Radio Regulations, Edition of 1959* (Geneva: International Telecommunication Union, 1959).

14. Ibid.

15. E. D. Ducharme, R. R. Bowen, and M. J. R. Irwin, "The Genesis of the 1985–87 World Administrative Radio Conference on the Use of the Geostationary Satellite Orbit and the Planning of Space Services Utilizing It," *Annals of Air and Space Law*, vol. 7, 1982, p. 265.

16. International Telecommunications Union, Extraordinary Administrative Radio Conference to Allocate Frequency Bands for Space Radiocommunication Purposes, *Final Acts* (Geneva: International Telecommunication Union, 1963), Recommendation 10a (3).

17. Ibid.

18. ITU, World Administrative Radio Conference for Space Communications, *Final Acts* (Geneva: International Telecommunication Union, 1971).

19. International Telecommunication Union Convention, Malaga-Torremolinos, 1973, Article 33(2).

20. ITU, World Administrative Radio Conference for the Planning of the Broadcasting Satellite Service, *Final Acts* (Geneva: International Telecommunication Union, 1977).

21. ITU, Regional Administrative Radio Conference for the Planning of the Broadcasting Satellite Service, *Final Acts* (Geneva: International Telecommunication Union, 1983).

22. M. A. Rothblatt, "ITU Regulation of Satellite Communication," *Stanford Law Review*, vol. 18, no. 12 (1982).

23. Anthony M. Rutkowski, "Six-Ad Hoc Two: The Third World Speaks Its Mind," *Satellite Communications*, vol. 4, no. 23 (March 1981).

24. International Telecommunication Union, *Radio Regulations, Edition of 1982* (Geneva: International Telecommunication Union, 1982), Resolution no. 3.

25. International Telecommunication Union, International Telecommunication Convention, Nairobi, 1982, Article 33(2). Emphasis added.

26. ITU, World Administrative Radio Conference, Geneva, 1979, Resolution no. 3.

27. CCIR Preparatory Meeting report draft (Geneva: International Telecommunication Union, July 1984).

28. Heather E. Hudson, "Mixed Planning Approach at Geneva," *Telecommunications Policy*, December 1985.

29. Quoted in Hudson, "Mixed Planning Approach," p. 272.

30. Leslie A. Taylor, "Depoliticizing Space WARC," *Satellite Communications*, January 1989, p. 29.

31. Ibid, p. 31.

32. Ibid.

33. A. G. Vicas, "Efficiency, Equity, and the Optimum Utilization of Outer Space as a Common Resource," *Annals of Air and Space Law*, vol. 5, 1980, pp. 589–609.

34. Paragraph 154, *1982 Plenipotentiary Final Acts*, Nairobi, International Telecommunication Union, 1982.

35. See, for example, C. G. Wihlborg and P. M. Wijkman, "Outer Space Resources in Efficient and Equitable Use: New Frontiers for Old Principles," *Journal of Law and Economics*, vol. 24, April 1981, pp. 23–43. See also Harvey J. Levin, *The Invisible Resource: Use and Regulation of the Radio Spectrum* (Baltimore: Johns Hopkins University Press, 1971).

36. Heather E. Hudson, "Access to Information Resources: The Developmental Context of the Space WARC," *Telecommunications Policy*, March 1985.

37. Independent Commission for Worldwide Telecommunications Development, *The Missing Link*.

38. United Nations Conference on the Exploration and Peaceful Uses of Outer Space, Vienna, August 9–21, 1982.

39. Yash Pal, "UNISPACE 82 and Beyond," *Journal of Space Law*, vol. 10, no. 2 (1982), p. 183.

40. *Satellite News*, October 10, 1988, p. 6

Chapter 16

Other Satellite Services and Prospects for the Future

1. Laura A. Huff, "Developments in Satellite Communications," in *The 1988 Satellite Directory* (Potomac, MD: Phillips Publishing, 1988), p. 19.

2. *The 1988 Satellite Directory*, p. 102.

3. *Telecommunications Reports*, May 9, 1988, p. 29.

4. *Telecommunications Reports*, September 26, 1988, p. 20.

5. *Satellite News*, September 26, 1988, p. 8.

6. Tamara Bennett, "Prodat Enters Europe's Mobile Fray," *Satellite Communications*, March 1988, p. 23.

7. *Satellite News*, November 7, 1988, pp. 2–3.

8. Huff, "Developments in Satellite Communications," p. 20.

9. Ibid.

10. Pelton and Howkins, *Satellites International*, p. 130.

11. Ibid., p. 29.

12. Ibid., p. 130.

13. Ibid., p. 131.

14. Ibid., p. 132.

15. Ibid., p. 29.

16. Ibid., p. 133.

17. Ibid., p. 30.

18. Guy M. Stephens, "Antennas for the Air," *Satellite Communications*, July 1988, p. 21.

19. Geoffrey K. C. Pardoe, "The 'Other' Applications Satellites," in Pelton and Howkins, *Satellites International*, p. 99.

20. Ibid., p. 100.

21. Ibid., p. 102.

22. Ibid., p. 103.

23. Ibid., p. 101.

24. Ibid., p. 101.

25. Ibid., p. 101.

26. Ibid., p. 100.

27. Inglis, "The United States Satellite Industry," p. 79.

28. *Satellite News*, November 21, 1988, pp. 1–2.

29. Rhonda Crane, "Advanced Television: An American Challenge," Boston Globe, November 6, 1988, p. 46.

30. For an examination of these issues in the United States, see Edwin B. Parker, Heather E. Hudson, Don A. Dillman, and Andrew D. Roscoe, *Rural America in the Information Age: Telecommunications Policy for Rural Development* (Washington, D.C.: Aspen Institute and University Press of America, 1989).

31. Arthur C. Clarke, quoted in Scott Chase, "After Thirty Years, Satellite Communications Are 'All Systems Go,'" in *The 1988 Satellite Directory* (Potomac, MD: Phillips Publishing, 1988), p. 5.

Glossary

ABC: American Broadcasting Company; also Australian Broadcasting Corporation.

ACP states: The countries in Africa, the Caribbean, and the Pacific that are associate members of the European Economic Community (EEC) under the Lomé Convention.

ACSN: Appalachian Community Services Network.

ACTS: Advanced Communications Technology Satellite.

AESP: Appalachian Educational Satellite Project.

AID: U.S. Agency for International Development.

AIR: All India Radio.

AFN: U.S. Armed Forces Network.

AMCEE: Association for Media-Based Continuing Engineering Education.

Amplifier: A device used to increase the power of a signal.

AMS: Agricultural Marketing Service.

AMSC: American Mobile Satellite Consortium.

Analog transmission: A way of sending signals in which the transmitted signal is continuous, or "analogous," to the original signal.

APBC: Alaska Public Broadcasting Commission.

Aperture: The area of a parabolic antenna.

APPLE: India's Ariane Passenger Payload Experiment.

Arabsat: A regional satellite system owned by a consortium of twenty-two Arab countries.

ARPA: Advanced Research Projects Agency.

ASEAN: Association of Southeast Asian Nations.

ASETA: Asociacion de Empresas Estatales des Telecommunicaciones del Acuerdo Subregional Andino, Andean regional telecommunications organization.

AT&T: American Telephone and Telegraph Company.

ATS: NASA's Applied Technology Satellites (e.g., ATS-1, ATS-3, ATS-6).

ATV: Advanced Television. *See also* HDTV.

Audiographics: Graphic communication over narrowband channels.

Aussat: The Australian domestic satellite.

Austel: Australian Telecommunications Authority.

BADEA: Arab Bank for Economic Development in Africa.

Bandwidth: The difference in hertz between the highest and lowest frequencies in a signal, or the frequencies needed for transmission of a signal; a measure of the volume of communications traffic that the channel can carry. A voice channel typically has a bandwidth of 4 KHz; a TV channel requires about 6.5 MHz.

baud: bits per second.

Beam shaping: Configuring the antenna pattern of a satellite to cover a specific region with minimal spillover into adjacent areas.

BET: Black Entertainment Television.

BETRS: Basic Exchange Telephone Radio Service. A radio communications service for rural areas.

B-MAC: An encryption system used to prevent unauthorized reception of satellite video signals.

Broadband: A range of frequencies greater than that required for voice communications; a transmission system with capacity greater than voice bandwidth. Coaxial cable and optical fiber are examples of broadband transmission systems.

Broadcasting: Transmission of signals for reception by the general public; point-to-multipoint transmission (e.g., of data or video.)

BSS: Broadcasting Satellite Service, intended for direct individual or community reception.

BT: British Telecom. **BTI:** British Telecom International.

Bypass: A service that avoids use of some or all of the telephone network. A satellite network for data communications with on-premises earth stations is an example of a bypass system.

Cable television: A transmission system using a broadband cable (coaxial cable or optical fiber) to deliver video signals directly to television sets, in contrast to over-the-air transmissions.

Caribnet: A service introduced by Intelsat in 1986 to meet the digital telecommunications needs of the Caribbean through private networks.

Carrier's carrier: An organization that carries telecommunications traffic only for other carriers and not for the public.

C band: Portion of the electromagnetic spectrum in the 4-to-6-GHz range used for satellite communications.

CBC: Canadian Broadcasting Corporation.

CBS: Columbia Broadcasting System.

CCIR: International Radio Consultative Committee of the International Telecommunication Union. The CCIR is responsible for coordinating frequencies and orbital locations for communication satellites.

CCTV: China's national television network.

Cellular telephone: A mobile telephone system linking vehicles from a broadcast point located within the range of the moving vehicle. The broadcast point in turn can be connected to the public network so that calls can be completed to or from any stationary telephone.

CEPT: European Conference of Posts and Telecommunication Administrations.

Channel: A segment of bandwidth used for one communication link.

CIIST: International Center of Scientific and Technical Information of the Comecon countries.

CLT: Compagnie Luxembourgeoise de Télédiffusion, Luxembourg's television network.

C-MAC: An encryption system used to prevent unauthorized reception of satellite video signals.

CNES: The French national space agency.

CNN: Cable News Network.

Comecon countries: Nations belonging to the Council for Mutual Economic Assistance; Eastern bloc countries.

Common carrier: An organization licensed by the Federal Communications Commission (FCC) and/or by various state public utility commissions to supply communication services at established and stated prices.

Comsat: Communications Satellite Corporation. A corporation authorized by the Communications Satellite Act of 1962 to represent the United states in international satellite communications.

CONUS: Continental United States; also the name of a U.S. satellite network.

COPUOS: U.N. Committee on the Peaceful Uses of Outer Space.

CRTC: Canadian Radio-Television and Telecommunications Commission.

CTS: Joint U.S.-Canadian Communications Technology Satellite; also known as Hermes in Canada.

DAMA: Demand-assigned multiple access. A way of sharing a channel's capacity by assigning capacity on demand to an idle channel or an unused time lot.

DAT: Digital audio tape.

DBS: Direct broadcast satellite. A satellite system designed with sufficient power to enable small inexpensive earth stations to be used for direct residential or community reception.

DCME: Digital circuit multiplication equipment.

DGT: Direction Générale des Télécommunications (France).

Digital signal: A discontinuous signal consisting of discrete elements. To digitize is to convert an analog, or continuous, signal into a series of electrical "on-off," "high-low," or "1-0" pulses instead of continuously varying signals as in analog transmission.

Digital switching: A connection in which binary encoded information is routed between an input and an output port.

DOC: Department of Communications (Canada and Australia).

DOD: Department of Defense (United States).

Downlink: An earth station used to receive signals from a satellite; the signal transmitted from the satellite to earth.

DRL: Digital Radio Laboratories.

EARC: Extraordinary Administrative Radio Conference (ITU).

Earth station: The antenna and associated equipment used to receive and/or transmit telecommunications signals via satellite.

ECS: Experimental Communication Satellite; also European Communications System.

ECSC: European Conference on Satellite Communications.

EEC: European Economic Community.

EIB: European Investment Bank.

ELDO: European Space Vehicle Launcher Organization.

Entel Peru: Empresa Nacional de Telecommunicaciones del Peru, the Peruvian telephone administration.

ESA: European Space Agency.

ESRO: European Space Research Organization.

EUTELSAT: European Telecommunications Satellite Organization.

Facsimile: The transmission of documents by electronic means.

FAO: U.N. Food and Agriculture Organization.

FCC: Federal Communications Commission. A U.S. regulatory agency overseen by a board of five members (commissioners) appointed by the President and confirmed by the Senate under the provision of the Communications Act of 1934. The FCC has the power to regulate interstate communications.

FGMDSS: Future Global Maritime Distress and Safety Service. An Inmarsat service that alerts people onshore for coordination of rescue activities.

Fiber optics: A technology using glass strands for transmission of modulated light waves for communication. *See* Optical fiber.

Footprint: The geographical coverage area of a satellite signal.

Freeze-frame television: A technique for transmitting still video pictures over a narrowband channel such as a telephone line. *Cf.* slow-scan television.

Frequency: Cycles per second (expressed in hertz).

Frequency spectrum: The range of frequencies useful for radio communication, from about 10 KHz to 3,000 GHz.

FSS: Fixed satellite service, intended for transmission between fixed points, with terrestrial distribution to end users.

GDP: Gross domestic product.

Geostationary satellite: A satellite with an equatorial orbit 22,300 miles (36,000 km) above the Earth. The satellite revolves about the Earth in the same direction and with the same period as that of the Earth's rotation (i.e., 24 hours), and thus appears stationary when viewed from the Earth.

Geosynchronous orbit: Synchronous with the Earth. An orbit 22,300 miles above the Earth's equator where satellites circle the earth once in 24 hours, thereby appearing stationary to an observer on Earth.

GHz: Gigahertz (billions of cycles per second).

GLODOM: A global domestic satellite system for developing countries proposed by the ITU.

GNP: Gross national product.

GOES: Geostationary Operational Environmental Satellites.

GPS: Global Positioning Service.

Green Paper: The EEC's policy paper on telecommunications.

GSO: Geostationary or geosynchronous orbit.

HACBSS: Australia's Homestead and Community Broadcasting Satellite Service, which provides direct reception of ABC radio and television to people beyond the reach of terrestrial transmitters or in areas of difficult or partial reception.

HBO: Home Box Office. A U.S. movie channel delivered by satellite and cable television.

HDTV: High definition television. A system for transmitting a digitized television signal with far greater resolution than the standard television picture.

Hermes: Canadian name for the joint U.S.-Canadian Communications Technology Satellite (CTS).

Hertz: Cycles per second.

HET: Health Education and Telecommunications experiments on the ATS-6 satellite.

HF: High-frequency; the frequency band from 3 to 30 MHz. *Cf.* Shortwave.

Hub station: A satellite station through which all traffic is routed in a star-type satellite network.

IBC: Inuit Broadcasting Corporation (Canada).

IBS: Intelsat Business Service. An integrated digital service designed to carry a full range of services, including voice, data, and video.

ICSC: Interim Communications Satellite Committee.

ICBM: Intercontinental ballistic missile.

IDA: International Development Association (United Kingdom).

IFRB: International Frequency Registration Board of the ITU.

IGY: The International Geophysical Year, which lasted from July 1957 to December 1958.

Inmarsat: The International Maritime Satellite Organization, which provides satellites for maritime and aeronautical communications.

INPE: India's national space agency.

Intelnet: An Intelsat service using VSATs for one-way or interactive low-volume data communications.

Intelsat: The International Telecommunications Satellite Organization. A worldwide consortium of national telecommunications organizations that provides global satellite services.

Interkosmos: An organization composed of Socialist states that collaborate on space research.

Intersatellite links: Links that enable one satellite to communicate with another without retransmitting signals to earth.

Intersputnik: The international satellite system established by the U.S.S.R. and other Communist countries.

IPDC: International Programme for Development Communication (UNESCO).

IRU: Indefeasible Right of Usage.

ISDN: Integrated Services Digital Network. An electronic "superhighway" for transmitting digital signals using internationally accepted standards.

ISRO: Indian Space Research Organization.

ITAP: Information Technology Advisory Panel.

ITFS: Instructional Television Fixed Service.

ITT: International Telephone and Telegraph Corporation.

ITU: International Telecommunication Union, the U.N. agency responsible for telecommunications.

JSC: Japanese Satellite Communications Corporation.

Ka band: Portion of the electromagnetic spectrum in the 20-to-30-GHz range; used for satellite communication.

KHz: Kilohertz (thousands of cycles per second).

Kbps: Kilobits per second.

Ku band: Portion of the electromagnetic spectrum in the 12-to-14-GHz range; used for satellite communication.

LDC: Less developed country.

LMSS: Land mobile satellite service.

Low earth orbit: A satellite orbit closer to Earth than geosynchronous orbit, typically 500 kilometers or less above the Earth's surface.

LTN: Alaska's Legislative Teleconferencing Network.

Maser: Microwave amplifier.

Mercury: A company that provides domestic telecommunications services in the United Kingdom (owned by Cable and Wireless).

MHz: Megahertz (millions of cycles per second).

Microprocessor: A miniaturized electronic circuit that performs the logic functions of a digital computer.

Microwave: The short wavelengths from 1 GHz to 30 GHz used for point-to-point transmissions and satellite systems.

Minicom: Brazil's Ministry of Communications.

Modem: Acronym for MOdulator/DEModulator. Equipment which converts digital signals to analog signals and vice versa.

Molniya: A Soviet satellite system that uses several polar-orbit satellites to transmit television throughout the country.

MPM: Multilateral planning meetings (ITU).

MPT: Japan's Ministry of Posts and Telecommunications.

MSS: Mobile Satellite Service.

MTV: Music Television. A satellite-delivered channel of contemporary music.

Multiplex: To combine two or more signals on a single channel for transmission.

Narrowband: A channel carrying only voice or slow-speed data signals.

NASA: National Aeronautics and Space Administration (U.S.).

NASDA: Japan's National Space Development Agency.

NBC: National Broadcasting Company.

NHK: Japanese Broadcasting Corporation.

NIC: The Indian government's National Informatics Centre.

Nicnet: An interactive satellite data network operated by India's National Informatics Centre.

NJT: National Jewish Television.

NOAA: National Oceanic and Atmospheric Administration (U.S.).

Noise: An unwanted signal that interferes with the reception of the desired information.

Nonsynchronous transmission: A method of data transmission which allows characters to be sent at irregular intervals by preceding each character with a start bit. This method is used by most personal computers to communicate with other PCs and with mainframes today.

Nordsat: Proposed regional satellite for Nordic countries.

NTIA: National Telecommunications and Information Administration, under the U.S. Department of Commerce.

NTT: Nippon Telephone and Telegraph.

NTU: National Technological University.

OECD: Organization for Economic Cooperation and Development.

Oftel: Office of Telecommunications, the British telecommunications regulatory authority.

OIRT: The Eastern bloc Organization of International Radio and Television.

"Open Skies": A U.S. policy authorizing multiple domestic satellite systems.

Optical fiber: A thin, flexible glass fiber the size of a human hair which will transmit light waves capable of carrying large amounts of information.

OTC: Overseas Telecommunications Corporation (Australia).

OTS: Orbital Test Satellite.

Packet switching: A technique of switching digital signals by breaking the signal stream into packets and then reassembling the data in the correct sequence at the receiving end.

Palapa: Indonesia's domestic satellite.

PANA: Pan African News Agency.

PATU: Pan African Telecommunications Union.

PBX: Private branch exchange. A private telephone switching system usually located at the customer's premises.

PCM: Pulse code modulation. A technique by which a signal is sampled, and each sample is quantified with a binary number.

PDS: Planned Domestic Service. An Intelsat service introduced in 1985 for developing countries, enabling member and user countries to lease or purchase transponders on a nonpreemptible basis.

Photovoltaic: Material which develops voltage and electrical current when light shines on it, used for solar power systems.

PNG: Papua New Guinea.

Point-to-multipoint service: A circuit in which a single signal goes from one originating point to many destination points. An example is a television signal or news service feed transmitted by satellite.

Point-to-point service: A circuit in which a signal goes between two points.

Project SHARE: Intelsat's pilot project on Satellites for Health and Rural Education.

PTAT: Private transatlantic cable; a transatlantic optical-fiber link.

PTT: Ministry or department of posts, telephone, and telegraph; a government-operated administration that provides telecommunications services.

RARC: Regional Administrative Radio Conference (ITU).

RCA: Radio Corporation of America.

RCSP: The U.S. Agency for International Development's Rural Communications Services Project in Peru.

RCTS: Remote Commercial Television Service (Australia).

RDSS: Radiodetermination Satellite Service.

Repeater: A device inserted at intervals along a circuit to boost, amplify, and/or regenerate the signal being transmitted. A repeater is needed because the quality and strength of a signal decays over distance.

S band: Frequencies in the 2.5-GHz range, used for community reception from satellites.

SBS: Satellite Business Systems.

SBTS: Brazilian satellite system.

SCC: Space Communications Company (Japan).

SCORE: Signal Communication by Orbiting Relay Equipment. The world's first active satellite for space communication.

Scrambling: A method of altering a signal to prevent reception by persons without authorized decoders.

SCT: Mexico's Ministry of Communications and Transportation.

SES: Société Européenne des Satellites.

Shortwave: Frequencies in the 3-to-30-MHz range of the electromagnetic spectrum.

SIG: Senior Interagency Group, in the executive branch of the U.S. government.

SIN: Spanish International Network.

SITE: India's Satellite Instructional Television Experiment.

Slow-scan television: A technique for transmitting still video pictures over a narrowband channel such as a telephone line. *Cf.* freeze frame television.

SMATV: Satellite Master Antenna Television.

SNG: Satellite news gathering.

SNV: Satellite news-gathering vehicle.

Solar cells: Devices that convert solar energy into electrical energy, used, for example, to power telecommunications equipment.

Space station: A facility in space for relay of communications signals; may also be used as a base for other space activities.

Spillover: The signal from a satellite that can be received outside its intended service area.

Spread-spectrum technique: A means of spreading a transmitted signal over extra bandwidth to permit redundancy in transmission and reception without interference from other signals using similar frequencies.

Sputnik: The first communications satellite, launched by the Soviet Union in 1957.

STC: Satellite Television Corporation.

STD: Satellite Technology Demonstration on NASA's ATS-6 satellite.

STEP: Symphonie Telecommunications Experimental Project.

STS: Space Transporation System. The U.S. space shuttles.

Subcarrier: An additional signal imposed on the broadcaster's carrier to transmit additional information such as a second language track, subtitles, or financial data.

Syncom: The first satellite launched into geosynchronous orbit.

T-Carrier: A medium capable of transmitting 1.5444 megabits per second, or multiples thereof (T1, T2, T3, T4, etc.).

TCTS: Trans-Canada Telephone System; now Telecom Canada.

TDRS: NASA's Tracking and Data Relay Satellite.

Teleconference: An audio and/or visual interconnection that allows communications among three or more individuals in two or more locations.

Tele-education: Use of telecommunications for education and training; distance education.

Teleglobe: Canada's international telecommunications organization.

Telemarketing: A method of marketing that emphasizes the creative use of the telephone and other telecommunications systems.

Telematics: A term derived from the French "télématique" describing the study of the new technologies resulting from the convergence of telecommunications and computers.

Telemedicine: Use of telecommunications for medical consultation, supervision, and education.

Telenet: A U.S. value-added network.

Teleport: A communications facility or center that switches voice, data, and video communications, primarily using steerable and frequency-agile satellite antennas.

Telmex: Telefonos de Mexico, the telephone administration of Mexico.

Transistor: A semiconductor device performing the same functions as an electron tube, but smaller and using less power.

Transmitter: The device that sends the telecommunications signal through a wire or cable or through the air.

Transponder: A microwave receiver, amplifier, and transmitter in a satellite that amplifies and changes the frequency of a signal from an earth station and retransmits it to earth.

Troposcatter Radio Relay System: A telecommunications transmission system that bounces signals off the troposphere.

TSAT: T-Carrier small-aperture terminal.

TVRI: Indonesia's television and radio network.

TVRO: Television receive-only earth station.

TVSC: Television Videotape Satellite Communications.

Tymnet: A U.S. value-added network.

UHF: Ultra-high-frequency; the frequency band from 300 MHz to 3,000 MHz (3 GHz).

UNDP: United Nations Development Programme.

UNECA: United Nations Economic Commission for Africa.

UNESCO: United Nations Educational, Scientific, and Cultural Organization.

UNGA: United Nations General Assembly.

UPAT: Union Pan-Africaine des Télécommunications.

Uplink: An earth station used to transmit to a satellite; the transmission from the Earth to the satellite.

URTNA: Association of African radio and television networks.

USCI: United Satellite Communications Incorporated.

USDA: U.S. Department of Agriculture.

USIA: U.S. Information Agency.

USP: University of the South Pacific.

UWIDITE: University of the West Indies Distance Teaching Experiment.

Value-added service: The addition of special service features, usually computer-related, to services purchased from other carriers, and the package of service and features is then resold to end users.

VCR: Videocassette recorder.

VHF: Very-high-frequency; the frequency band from 30 MHz to 300 MHz.

Videotext: The generic name for a system that transmits alphanumeric and graphic information for display on a video monitor.

Vista: Intelsat thin-route service for developing countries.

VSAT: Very-small-aperture terminal.

WARC: World Administrative Radio Conference of the ITU.

WBS: World Broadcast Service.

Wideband: Usually refers to a channel of greater bandwidth than a voice-grade channel. *Cf.* Broadband.

Worldnet: A satellite network operated by USIA that transmits programming to U.S. embassies around the world.

Bibliography

Ahern, Veronica M. "Communication Satellites." In *Telecommunications in the U.S.: Trends and Policies*, ed. Leonard Lewin. Dedham, MA: Artech, 1981.

Albernaz, Joao Carlos Fagundes. "The Brazilian Satellite Communications Program." In *New Directions in Satellite Communications: Challenges for North and South*, ed. Heather E. Hudson. Dedham, MA: Artech House, 1985.

———. "Brazil: Bird over the Amazon." *Intermedia*, July-September 1986.

Alfian and Godwin C. Chu, eds. *Satellite Television in Indonesia*. Honolulu: East-West Center, 1981.

Antola, Livia, and Everett M. Rogers. "Television Flows in Latin America." *Communication Research*, April 1984.

Asian Mass Communication Research and Information Centre. *Satellite Technology: The Global Equalizer*. Singapore: AMIC, 1985.

AT&T. *The World's Telephones, 1985–86*. Morristown, NJ: AT&T, 1988.

Bashur, Rashid. "Technology Serves the People: The Story of a Cooperative Telemedicine Project by NASA, the Indian Health Service and the Papago People." *Proceedings of the Telecommunications Policy Research Conference*. Norwood, NJ: Ablex, 1983.

"Batched Data Main Business Application." *Communication News*, March 1989.

Baylin, Frank, and Brent Gale. *Satellites Today: The Guide to Satellite Television*. Columbus, OH: Howard W. Sams and Co., 1986.

Bell, Daniel. *The Coming of Post-Industrial Society*. New York: Basic Books, 1973.

Bennett, Tamara. "VSATs for Growth." *Satellite Communications*, November 1987.

———. "Prodat Enters Europe's Mobile Fray." *Satellite Communications*, March 1988.

Blair, Michael L. "VSAT Systems in Developing Countries." *Proceedings of the Pacific Telecommunications Conference*. Honolulu, February 1988.

————. "VSATs in Developing Countries." *Satellite Communications*, July 1988.

Blatherwick, David E. S. *The International Politics of Telecommunications.* Berkeley: University of California Institute of International Studies, 1987.

Bleazard, G. B. *Introducing Satellite Communications.* Manchester: National Computing Centre, 1985.

Block, Clifford H. "Satellite Linkages and Rural Development." In *New Directions in Satellite Communications: Challenges for North and South*, ed. Heather E. Hudson. Dedham, MA: Artech House, 1985.

Block, Clifford, Dennis R. Foote, and John K. Mayo. "SITE Unseen: Implications for Programming and Policy." *Journal of Communication*, August 1979.

Block, Clifford, Douglas Goldschmidt, Anwar Hafid, Gerald C. Lalor, and Angel Velasquez. "Satellite Telecommunications for Rural Development: The A.I.D. Rural Satellite Program and Its Projects in Indonesia, Peru, and the Caribbean." *Proceedings of the Pacific Telecommunications Conference.* Honolulu, 1984.

Boyd, Douglas A., and Joseph D. Straubhaar. "Developmental Impact of the Home Video Cassette Recorder on Third World Communities." *Journal of Broadcasting and Electronic Media*, Winter 1985.

Brotman, Stuart N. *The Telecommunications Deregulation Sourcebook.* Norwood, MA: Artech House, 1987.

Bruce, Robert R., Jeffrey P. Cunard, and Mark D. Director. *From Telecommunications to Electronic Services.* London: Butterworth, 1986.

Burch, Dean. "Intelsat: The Tomorrow Organization." In *Satellites International*, ed. Joseph N. Pelton and John Hawkins. New York: Stockton Press, 1988.

Cacciamani, Eugene R., and Michael K. Sun. "Overview of VSAT Networks." *Telecommunications*, June 1986.

Canadian Department of Communications. DOC NR-84-5265E. Ottawa, April 10, 1984.

Canadian Radio-Television and Telecommunications Commission. CRTC Telecom Decision 77-10. Ottawa: CRTC, 1977.

Cangelosi, Carl J. "Satellite Regulation—A Short History." In *Teleports and the Intelligent City*, ed. Andrew D. Lipman, Alan D. Sugarman, and Robert F. Cushman. Homewood, IL: Dow Jones–Irwin, 1986.

Caruso, Andrea. "The European Telecommunications Satellite Organization." In *Satellites International*, ed. Joseph N. Pelton and John Howkins. New York: Stockton Press, 1988.

Chase, Scott. "After Thirty Years, Communication Satellites Are 'All Systems Go.'" In *The 1988 Satellite Directory.* Potomac, MD: Phillips Publishing, 1988.

————. "Live Via Satellite." *Via Satellite*, April 1988.

————. "Radio and Satellites." *Via Satellite*, September 1988.

————. "Home Satellite Dishes: Up Against the Wall." *Channels '89 Field Guide to the Electronic Environment*, December 1988.

Chu, Godwin C., Alfian, and Wilbur Schramm. "Bringing Television to Rural Indonesia." *Intermedia*, July-September 1986.

Clarke, Arthur C. "Extra-Terrestrial Relays: Can Rocket Stations Give World-Wide Radio Coverage?" *Wireless World*, October 1945.

————. *Voices from the Sky: Previews of the Coming Space Age*. New York: Harper and Row, 1965.

————., ed. *The Coming of the Space Age*. New York: Meredith Press, 1967.

Codding, George A., Jr. "Confidence Building and the 1985 Space WARC." In *New Directions in Satellite Communications: Challenges for North and South*, ed. Heather E. Hudson. Dedham, MA: Artech House, 1985.

Codding, George A., Jr., and Anthony M. Rutkowski. *The International Telecommunication Union in a Changing World*. Dedham, MA: Artech, 1982.

Colino, Richard R. "PTTs, INTELSAT, Monopoly and Competition." *Space Communication and Broadcasting*, vol. 4, 1986.

Collin, Arthur. "The Canadian Space Program." In *Canada, The United States, and Space*, ed. John Kirton. Toronto: Canadian Institute for International Affairs, 1986.

Communications Satellite Act of 1962, As Amended, Public Law No. 624, 87th Congress, 2d sess., August 31, 1972. 47 USC, Section 701 et seq.

Comsat. *Annual Report*. Washington, D.C., 1984.

Cook, Rick. "Satellite Communications at Down-to-Earth Prices." *High Technology*, December 1986.

Crane, Rhonda. "Advanced Television: An American Challenge." *Boston Globe*, November 6, 1988.

Curran, Alex. "The State of Canada's Industry." In *Canada, The United States, and Space*, ed. John Kirton. Toronto: Canadian Institute for International Affairs, 1986.

Davies. N. G. "Canadian Space Applications: New Models for the Developing World." In *New Directions in Satellite Communications: Challenges for North and South*, ed. Heather E. Hudson. Dedham, MA: Artech House, 1985.

Demac, Donna, ed. *Tracing New Orbits: Cooperation and Competition in Global Satellite Development*. New York: Columbia University Press, 1986.

Demac, Donna, George R. Codding, Jr., Heather E. Hudson, and Ram Jakhu. *Equity in Orbit: The 1985 Space WARC*. London: International Institute of Communications, 1985.

Demmert, Jane P., and Jennifer L. Wilke. "The LEARN/ALASKA Networks: Instructional Telecommunications in Alaska." In *Telecommunication in Alaska*, ed. Robert M. Walp. Honolulu: Pacific Telecommunications Council, 1982.

de Tarle, Antoine. "Dream Factories Go International." *Intermedia*, July-September 1986.

Developing World Communications. London: Grosvenor Press International, 1989.

Dizard, Wilson. *The Coming Information Age*. 2d ed. New York: Longman, 1985.

Dordick, Herbert S. *Understanding Modern Telecommunications*. New York: McGraw-Hill, 1986.

Downing, John D. H. "Cooperation and Competition in Satellite Communication: The Soviet Union." In *Tracing New Orbits: Cooperation and Competition in Global Satellite Development*, ed. Donna Demac. New York: Columbia University Press, 1986.

Ducharme, E. D., R. R. Bowen, and M. J. R. Irwin. "The Genesis of the 1985–87 World Administrative Radio Conference on the Use of the Geostationary Orbit and the Planning of Space Services Utilizing It." *Annals of Air and Space Law*, vol. 7, 1982.

Dunford, Keith. "TSAT: A Low Cost Solution for Satellite Networking." *Via Satellite*, March 1989.

Dyson, Kenneth, and Peter Humphreys, eds. *The Politics of the Communications Revolution in Western Europe*. London: Frank Cass, 1986.

ELRA Group. "Teleports: An Update." In *The 1988 Satellite Directory*. Potomac, MD: Phillips Publishing, 1988.

Feazel, R. Michael. "The Birds Fly Low." In *Channels '89 Field Guide to the Electronic Environment*, December 1988.

Federal Communications Commission. *In the Matter of Regulation of Domestic Receive-Only Satellite Earth Stations*. 74 FCC 2d 205 (1979).

——. *In the Matter of Domestic Fixed-Satellite Transponder Sales*. 90 FCC 2d 1238 (1982).

——. *In the Matter of Policy and Rules Concerning Rates for Competitive Common Carrier Services and Facilities Authorizations Therefor (Fourth Report and Order)*. 95 FCC 2d 554 (1983).

——. *FCC Declaratory Order 3588* (April 9, 1986) and *FCC Report DS-610* (March 27, 1987).

Filep, Robert. "The World Communications Satellite Market Through 2000: Analysis and Forecast." *Satellite Communications: Developments, Applications, and Future Prospects*. London: Online Publications, 1984.

Firestone, Charles M., ed. *International Satellite and Cable Television*. Los Angeles: UCLA Communication Law Program, 1985.

Firestone, Charles M., and Daniel L. Brenner, eds. *Following the Footprints: Protecting Film and TV Rights in the World Satellite Marketplace*. Los Angeles: UCLA Communication Law Program, 1987.

Foote, Dennis R., Heather E. Hudson, and Edwin B. Parker. *Telemedicine in Alaska: The ATS-6 Biomedical Demonstration*. Palo Alto, CA: Stanford University Institute for Communication Research, 1976.

Forester, Tom, ed. *The Information Technology Revolution*. Cambridge, MA: MIT Press, 1985.

——., ed. *The Microelectronics Revolution*. Cambridge, MA: MIT Press, 1981.

"Full Service Shared Hubs Offer Economy." *Communications News*, March 1989.

Galloway, Jonathan F. *The Politics and Technology of Satellite Communications*. Lexington, MA: D. C. Heath, 1972.

Gavin, Joseph, Jr. "The United States Industry." In *Canada, The United States, and Space*, ed. John Kirton. Toronto: Canadian Institute for International Affairs, 1986.

Glatzer, Hal. *The Birds of Babel*. Indianapolis: Howard A. Sams and Co., 1983.

———. *The Telecommunications Revolution: Who Controls the Airwaves?* Indianapolis: Howard W. Sams, 1984.

Golden, David. "The Uncertain Future of Domestic Commercial Communications Satellites." In *Canada, The United States, and Space*, ed. John Kirton. Toronto: Canadian Institute for International Affairs, 1986.

Goldschmidt, Douglas. "Leveling the Playing Field in International Satellite Communications." *Telematics and Informatics*, vol. 4, no. 2 (1987).

———. "Pan American Satellite and the Introduction of Specialized Communication Systems in Latin America." *Proceedings of the Pacific Telecommunications Conference*. Honolulu, February 1988, pp. 343–346.

Gould, R. G., and Y. F. Lum, eds. *Communication Satellite Systems: An Overview of the Technology*. New York: IEEE Press, 1976.

Government of Canada. Order in Council P.C. 1981–3456. Ottawa: December 8, 1981.

Government of India, Planning Commission. "The Approach to the Seventh Five-Year Plan, 1985–90." New Delhi, July 1984.

Green, Lyndsay, and David Simailak. "The Inukshuk Project: Use of TV and Satellite by Inuit Communities in the Northwest Territories." Paper presented at the annual conference of the American Association for the Advancement of Science, Toronto, January 1981.

Griffith, Charles. "The Arab World: Elusive Accord." *Intermedia*, July-September 1986.

Griffith, Kathleen. "Mexican Teleconnectivity." *Proceedings of Pacific Telecommunications Conference*. Honolulu, January 1989.

Guo Liyu. "Information Network Spans Vast Area." *China Daily*, June 5, 1986.

Gupta, G. K., and R. N. Khapre. "India: A Boost for Development." *Intermedia*, July-September 1986.

Hanley, Peter. "Industry Sector Analysis: Telecommunications." Beijing: U.S. Embassy, August 1983.

Hardy, Andrew P. "The Role of the Telephone in Economic Development." *Telecommunications Policy*, vol. 4, no.4. (December 1980).

Hills, Alex. "Alaska's Rural Satellite System." *IEEE Spectrum*, July 1983.

Hirsch, Mario. "The Doldrums of Europe's TV Landscape: Coronet as Catalyst." In *Tracing New Orbits: Cooperation and Competition in Global Satellite Development*, ed. Donna Demac. New York: Columbia University Press, 1986.

———. "A Monopoly Challenged." *Cable and Satellite Europe*, no. 2, 1987.

Hollins, Timothy. *Beyond Broadcasting: Into the Cable Age*. London: British Film Institute, 1984.

Howell, W. J., Jr. *World Broadcasting in the Age of the Satellite*. Norwood, NJ: Ablex, 1986.

Hudson, Heather E. "The Role of Radio in the Canadian North." *Journal of Communication*, Autumn 1977.

———. "How Close They Sound: Applications of Telecommunications for Education and Public Participation in Alaska." *Systems, Objectives, Solutions*, November 1982.

———. "Medical Communications in Rural Alaska." *Telecommunications in Rural Alaska*. Honolulu: Pacific Telecommunications Council, 1982.

———. "Satellites and Socio-Economic Development: A Synthesis of Recent Research." *Proceedings of the Fourth World Telecommunications Forum*. Geneva: International Telecommunication Union, 1983.

———. *Three Case Studies on the Benefits of Telecommunications in Socio-Economic Development*. Geneva: International Telecommunication Union, 1983.

———. "Demand and Need: Problems of Planning Telecommunications Services for Rural and Sparsely Populated Areas." *Proceedings of the Pacific Telecommunications Conference*. Honolulu, January 1984.

———. *When Telephones Reach the Village: The Role of Telecommunications in Rural Development*. Norwood, NJ: Ablex, 1984.

———., ed. *New Directions in Satellite Communications: Challenges for North and South*. Norwood, MA: Artech, 1985.

———. "Access to Information Resources: The Developmental Context of the Space WARC." *Telecommunications Policy*, March 1985.

———. "New Television Technologies and Indigenous Cultures." *Media and Development*, Summer 1985.

———. "Mixed Planning Approach at Geneva." *Telecommunications Policy*, December 1985.

———. "Satellite Communications for Developing Countries: From Conjecture to Reality." *Space Communication and Broadcasting*, December 1985.

———. "New Communications Technologies: Policy Issues for the Developing World." *International Political Science Review*, vol. 7, no.6 (1986).

———., ed. "Innovative Strategies for Telecommunications Development." *Telematics and Informatics*, vol. 4, no. 2 (Spring 1987).

———. *A Bibliography of Telecommunications and Socio-Economic Development*. Norwood, NJ: Artech House, 1988.

Hudson, Heather E., Douglas Goldschmidt, Edwin B. Parker, and Andrew P. Hardy. *The Role of Telecommunications in Socio-Economic Development: A Review of the Literature with Guidelines for Further Investigations*. Geneva: International Telecommunication Union, 1979.

Hudson, Heather E., Andrew P. Hardy, and Edwin B. Parker. "Impact of Telephones and Thin Route Satellite Earth Stations on GDP." *Telecommunications Policy*, December 1982.

Hudson, Heather E., and Edwin B. Parker. "Medical Communication in Alaska by Satellite." *New England Journal of Medicine*, December 1973.

Huff, Laura A. "Developments in Satellite Communications." In *The 1988 Satellite Directory*. Potomac, MD: Phillips Publishing, 1988.

Hulten, Olof, and Charly Hulten. "INTELSAT: The Changing Pattern of TV Transmission." *Intermedia*, January 1985.

Humphreys, Peter. "Satellite Broadcasting Policy in West Germany: Political Conflict and Regional Competition in a Decentralized System." In *Satellite Broadcasting: The Politics and Implications of the New Media*, ed. Ralph Negrine. London: Croom Helm, 1988.

IDATE (Institut pour le Développement et l'Aménagement des Télécommunications et de l'Economie). "Growth and Telecommunications: A Summary of Research." Montpelier, France, 1984.

Independent Commission for Worldwide Telecommunications Development. *The Missing Link*. Geneva: International Telecommunication Union, 1985.

Inglis, Andrew F. "The United States Satellite Industry: An Overview." *FIBRESAT 86 Conference Proceedings*. Vancouver, Canada, September 1986.

Intelsat. *Project SHARE*. Washington, D.C.: Intelsat, 1985.

————. *Small Earth Station Symposium and Exhibition Proceedings*. Washington, D.C., May 11–13, 1987.

————. Intelsat Annual Report, 1977–88. Washington, D.C.: Intelsat, 1988.

————. *Project SHARE: A Final Report and Evaluation*. Washington, D.C.: Intelsat, 1988.

International Telecommunication Union. *Radio Regulations*. Geneva: ITU, 1959, 1979, 1982.

————. Extraordinary Administrative Radio Conference to Allocate Frequency Bands for Space Radiocommunication Purposes. *Final Acts*. Geneva: ITU, 1963.

————. World Administrative Radio Conference for Space Communications. *Final Acts*. Geneva: ITU, 1971.

————. International Telecommunication Convention. Malaga-Torremolinos, 1973.

————. World Administrative Radio Conference for the Planning of the Broadcasting Satellite Service. *Final Acts*. Geneva: ITU, 1977.

————. International Telecommunication Convention. Nairobi, 1982.

————. Regional Administrative Radio Conference for the Planning of the Broadcasting Satellite Service. *Final Acts*. Geneva: ITU, 1983.

————. *Information, Telecommunications and Development*. Geneva: ITU, 1986.

Jussawalla, Meheroo, and Donald M. Lamberton, eds. *Communication Economics and Development*. Honolulu: East-West Center, 1982.

Kaiser, Gordon E. "Developments in Canadian Telecommunications Regulation." In *Marketplace for Telecommunications*, ed. Marcellus S. Snow. New York: Longman, 1986.

Karunaratne, Neil D. "Telecommunication and Information in Development Planning Strategy." In *Communication Economics and Development*, ed. Meheroo Jussawalla and Donald M. Lamberton. Honolulu: East-West Center, 1982.

Kenney, Gerard I. *Man in the North: Parts I and II.* Montreal: Arctic Institute of North America, 1971.

Kinsley, Michael E. *Outer Space and Inner Sanctums: Government, Business, and Satellite Communication.* New York: John Wiley and Sons, 1976.

Kirton, John, ed. *Canada, The United States, and Space.* Toronto: Canadian Institute for International Affairs, 1986.

Lai Guozhu. "Development of China's Communication Industry Highlighted." *Beijing Dianzi Xuebao* (Acta Electronica Sinica), no. 5, 1983.

Levin, Harvey J. *The Invisible Resource: Use and Regulation of the Radio Spectrum.* Baltimore: Johns Hopkins University Press, 1971.

Lewin, Leonard, ed. *Telecommunications in the U.S.: Trends and Policies.* Dedham, MA: Artech, 1981.

Lipman, Andrew D., Alan D. Sugarman, and Robert F. Cushman, eds. *Teleports and the Intelligent City.* Homewood, IL: Dow Jones–Irwin, 1986.

Livingston, Victor. "Made in the U.S.A.: American Films Vie for Global Home Vid." *Television/Radio Age*, May 26, 1986.

———. "Murdoch's Media Reach Invites Global Advertising Schemes." *Television/Radio Age*, October 13, 1986.

MacBride Commission. *Many Voices, One World.* Paris: UNESCO, 1980.

Magnant, Robert S. *Domestic Satellite: An FCC Giant Step.* Boulder, CO: Westview Press, 1977.

Martin, James. *Communication Satellite Systems.* New York: Prentice Hall, 1977.

Martinez, Larry. *Communication Satellites: Power Politics in Space.* Dedham, MA: Artech House, 1985.

Matte, Nicolas M. *Aerospace Law: Telecommunications Satellites.* Toronto: Butterworth, 1982.

Matthias, Glyndwr. "The Monopoly Strikes Back." *Cable and Satellite Europe,* no. 3, 1987.

Mayo, John K., Gary R. Heald, Steven J. Klees, and Martha Cruz de Yanes. *Peru Rural Communication Services Project: Final Evaluation Report.* Tallahassee, FL: Center for International Studies, Learning Systems Institute, Florida State University, 1987

McAnany, Emile G., and Joao Batista de Oliveira. *The SACI/EXERN Project in Brazil: An Analytical Case Study.* Paris: UNESCO, 1980.

McKnight, Lee. "The Deregulation of International Satellite Communications: U.S. Policy and the Intelsat Response." *Space Communication and Broadcasting*, vol. 3, 1985.

McQuail, Denis. "Policy Perspectives for New Media in Europe." In *New Communications Technologies and Public Interest*, ed. Marjorie Ferguson. London: Sage, 1986.

Mody, Bella. "Contextual Analysis of the Adoption of a Communications Technology: The Case of Satellites in India." *Telematics and Informatics*, vol. 4, no. 2 (1987).

Murdoch, Rupert. Speech to the annual conference of the International Institute of Communications, Washington, D.C., September 1988.

Nakamura, Yuko. "Direct Broadcasting by Satellite in Japan: An Overview." In *Satellite Broadcasting: The Politics and Implications of the New Media*, ed. Ralph Negrine. London: Croom Helm, 1988.

National Aeronautics and Space Act of 1958. Public Law 85–568, 85th Cong., 72 Stat. 426, 29 July 1958.

National Technological University Bulletin: 1988–89 Academic Programs. Fort Collins, CO, 1988.

Negrine, Ralph, ed. *Cable Television and the Future of Broadcasting*. London: Croom Helm, 1985.

———. *Satellite Broadcasting: The Politics and Implications of the New Media*. London: Croom Helm, 1988.

Nettleton, Greta, and Emile McAnany. "Brazil's Satellite System and the Politics of Applications Planning." *Telecommunications Policy*, June 1989.

Newton, Harry, ed. *The Teleconnect Dictionary*. New York: Telecom Library, 1987.

The 1988 Satellite Directory. Potomac, MD: Phillips Publishing, 1988.

Nora, Simon, and Alain Minc. *The Computerization of Society*. Cambridge, MA: MIT Press, 1980.

Ogan, Christine L. "Media Diversity and Communications Policy: Impact of VCRs and Satellite TV." *Telecommunications Policy*, March 1985.

Oliver, Kurt R. "Is Your VSAT by the Book?" *Communications News*, March 1989.

Oslund, Jack. "'Open Shores' to 'Open Skies': Sources and Directions of U.S. Satellite Policy." In *Economic and Policy Problems in Satellite Communications*, ed. Joseph Pelton and Marcellus Snow. New York: Praeger, 1977.

Ospina, Sylvia. "Project CONDOR: The Andean Regional Satellite System: When Will This Bird Fly?" *Proceedings of the Pacific Telecommunications Conference*. Honolulu, January 1989.

Pal, Yash. "UNISPACE 82 and Beyond." *Journal of Space Law*, vol. 10, no. 2 (1982).

Pardoe, Geoffrey K. C. "The 'Other' Communications Satellites" in Pelton Joseph N. and John Howkins, eds. *Satellites International*. New York: Stockton Press, 1988.

Parker, Edwin B. *Economic and Social Benefits of the REA Telephone Loan Program*. Geneva: International Telecommunications Union, 1981.

———. "MicroEarth Station Satellite Networks and Economic Development." *Telematics and Informatics*, vol. 4, no. 2 (1987).

Parker, Edwin B., Heather E. Hudson, Don A. Dillman, and Andrew D. Roscoe. *Rural America in the Information Age: Telecommunications Policy for*

Rural Development. Washington, D.C.: Aspen Institute and University Press of America, 1989.

Parker, Walter B. "The Alaskan Satellite Experience: Lessons for the Developing World." In *New Directions in Satellite Communications: Challenges for North and South,* ed. Heather E. Hudson. Dedham, MA: Artech House, 1985.

————. "The Evolution of the Present Alaska Telecommunications System." In *Telecommunication in Alaska,* ed. Robert M. Walp. Honolulu: Pacific Telecommunications Council, 1982.

Pearce, Kevin. "SMATV: Still Kicking." *Channels '89 Field Guide to the Electronic Environment,* December 1988.

Pelton, Joseph N. *Global Communications Satellite Policy: INTELSAT, Politics, and Functionalism.* Mt. Airy, MD: Lomond Books, 1974.

Pelton, Joseph N., and John Howkins. *Satellites International.* New York: Stockton Press, 1988.

Pelton, Joseph N., Marcel Perras, and Ashok Sinha. *INTELSAT: The Global Telecommunications Network.* Honolulu: Pacific Telecommunications Conference, 1983.

Pelton, Joseph N., and Marcellus Snow, eds. *Economic and Policy Problems in Space Communications.* New York: Praeger, 1977.

Pierce, William B., Jr., and Nicolas Jequier. *Telecommunications for Development.* Geneva: International Telecommunication Union, 1983.

Plante, Jim. "Reporting by Satellite: A Challenge for the Networks." *Intermedia,* May 1986.

Ploman, Edward W. *Space, Earth and Communication.* Westport, CT: Quorum Books, 1984.

Porat, Marc U. *The Information Economy: Definition and Measurement.* Washington, D.C.: U.S. Government Printing Office, 1977.

Prenner, Angela. "The Ups and Downs of Third World Satcoms." *Developing World Communications.* London: Grosvenor Press International, 1989.

Primrose, Neil. "Australian Telecommunications Services: A New Framework." Paper presented at the annual conference of the International Institute of Communications, Washington, D.C., September 14, 1988.

Quackenbush, W. G. "Nation's First Two-Way Private VSAT Network." *Telecommunications,* June 1986.

Read, Paula. "Consumer is Ripe for Global Approach: Saatchi and Saatchi." *Television/Radio Age,* October 13, 1986.

Reinecke, Ian. "Satellite Broadcasting in Australia." In *Satellite Broadcasting: The Politics and Implications of the New Media,* ed. Ralph Negrine. London: Croom Helm, 1988.

Renaud, Jean Luc, and Barry Litman. "Changing Dynamics of the Overseas Marketplace for TV Programming: The Rise of International Co-Production." *Telecommunications Policy,* September 1985.

"Retail Chains Cut Customer Waiting Time." *Communications News,* March 1989.

Rockoff, Maxine. "Telecommunications Technology: Can It Lead to Health Care Delivery Reform?" *Hermes (The Communications Technology Satellite): Its Performance and Applications*. Ottawa: The Royal Society of Canada, 1977.

Rosenfeld, James H. "The Age of Abundance for Television Worldwide." *Vital Speeches of the Day*, January 15, 1986.

Rothblatt, M. A. "ITU Regulation of Satellite Communication." *Stanford Law Review*, vol. 18, no. 12 (1982).

Rutkowski, Anthony M. "Six-Ad Hoc Two: The Third World Speaks Its Mind." *Satellite Communications*, vol. 4, no. 23 (March 1981).

Sanchez-Ruiz, Miguel. "Key Issues in Satellite Communications: The Mexican Satellite Program." In *New Directions in Satellite Communications: Challenges for North and South*, ed. Heather E. Hudson. Dedham, MA: Artech House, 1985.

"Satellites: Flying Higher than Ever." *Broadcasting*, July 14, 1986, pp. 41–52.

Satellite News. Potomac, MD: Phillips Publishing, September 26, 1988; October 10, 1988; November 7, 1988.

Saunders, Robert J., Jeremy Warford, and Bjorn Wellenius. *Telecommunications and Economic Development*. Baltimore, MD: Johns Hopkins University Press, 1983.

Schaffer, Ken. "A Television Window on the Soviet Union." In *Tracing New Orbits: Cooperation and Competition in Global Satellite Development*, ed. Donna Demac. New York: Columbia University Press, 1986.

Sherrid, Pamela. "New Ways to Keep in Touch." *U.S. News and World Report*, vol. 100, no. 16 (April 28, 1986).

Simmonds, Kenneth. "The Third Lomé Convention." *Common Market Law Review*, July 1985.

Singleton, Loy. *Telecommunications in the Information Age*. 2d ed. Cambridge, MA: Ballinger, 1986.

Smith, Delbert D. *Communication via Satellite: A Vision in Retrospect*. Leyden: A. W. Sijthoff, 1976.

Smith, Ilene V. "Taking the Bull by the Horns." *Satellite Communications*, May 1985.

———. "Retail Gains." *Satellite Communications*, April 1986.

Snow, Marcellus S., ed. *Marketplace for Telecommunications*. New York: Longman, 1986.

Snow, Marcellus S., and Meheroo Jussawalla. *Telecommunication Economics and International Regulatory Policy: An Annotated Bibliography*. Westport, CT: Greenwood Press, 1986.

Sparks, Will. "Satellites, The Telegraph, and the Pony Express." *Satellite Communications: Developments, Applications, and Future Prospects*. London: Online Publications, 1984.

Srirangan, T. V. "Why Orbit Planning: A View from a Third World Country, Parts I and II." In *New Directions in Satellite Communications: Challenges for North and South*, ed. Heather E. Hudson. Dedham, MA: Artech House, 1985.

"State Regulatory Monitor." *Telematics*. July 1984.

Stephens, Guy. "Big Business, Small Dishes." *Satellite Communications*, February 1986a.

———. "Equatorial's Focus on C Band." *Satellite Communications*, February 1986b.

———. "Antennas for the Air." *Satellite Communications*, July 1988.

Stewart, Alan. "VSAT Technology Provides a Price-Stable and Strategic Tool for Handling Corporate Growth." *Communication News*, May 1988.

Stokes, Bruce. "Beaming Jobs Overseas." *National Journal*, July 27, 1985.

Stover, William J. *Information Technology in the Third World*. Boulder, CO: Westview, 1984.

Taylor, Leslie A. "Depoliticizing Space WARC." *Satellite Communications*, January 1989.

Telecommunications Reports. Washington, D.C.: Business Research Publications, May 9, 1988; September 26, 1988.

Tietjen, Karen. *AID Rural Satellite Program: An Overview*. Washington; D.C.: Academy for Educational Development, 1987.

United Nations. UN Conference on the Exploration and Peaceful Uses of Outer Space (UNISPACE 82), Vienna, August 9–21, 1982.

U.S. Congress, Senate Subcommittee on Communications. *Overview of the FCC*. 93d Congress, February 22, 1973.

U.S. Department of Commerce, International Trade Administration. *High Technology Industries: Profiles and Outlooks: The Telecommunications Industry*. Washington, D.C., April 1983.

U.S. Embassy, New Delhi. "Economic Trends Report: India." New Delhi, May 1986.

"USIA Worldnet Revises Game Plan at First Anniversary." *Television/Radio Age*, June 9, 1986.

Valaskakis, Gail. "Socio-Economic Implications in Canada of Satellite Communications." *FIBRESAT 86 Conference Proceedings*. Vancouver, Canada, September 1986.

Valaskakis, Gail, R. Robbins, and T. Wilson. *The Inukshuk Project: An Assessment*. Ottawa: Inuit Tapirisat of Canada, 1981.

Varis, Tapio. "Global Traffic in Television." *Journal of Communication*, vol. 24, no. 1 (Winter 1974).

———. "The International Flow of Television Programs." *Journal of Communication*, Winter 1984.

———. *International Flow of Television Programmes*. Paris: UNESCO, 1985.

Vicas, A. G. "Efficiency, Equity, and the Optimum Utilization of Outer Space as a Common Resource." *Annals of Air and Space Law*, vol. 5, 1980.

Wedell, George. "Television without Frontiers?" *EBU Review*, vol. 36, no. 1, (January 1985).

Weibull, Lennart, and Ronny Severinsson. "The Nordic Countries in the Age of Satellite Broadcasting." In *Satellite Broadcasting: The Politics and*

Implications of the New Media, ed. Ralph Negrine. London: Croom Helm, 1988.

Wihlborg, C. G., and P. M. Wijkman. "Outer Space Resources in Efficient and Equitable Use: New Frontiers for Old Principles." *Journal of Law and Economics*, vol. 24 (April 1981).

Williamson, David, Jr. "Changes and Choices in United States Space Policy." In *Canada, The United States, and Space*, ed. John Kirton. Toronto: Canadian Institute for International Affairs, 1986.

Williamson, John. "Telecommunications Expansion in China's Economic Zones." *Telephony*, April 22, 1985.

Wines, Leslie. "Business Tunes in on Telecommunications." *Crain's New York Business*, July 8, 1985.

World Bank. *World Development Report.* Washington, D.C.: World Bank, 1988.

World Teleport Association. *WTA Update*, Winter 1988.

Yurow, Jane, ed. *Issues in International Telecommunications Policy.* Washington, D.C.: George Washington University Center for Telecommunications Studies, 1983.

Zhang Yan. "Satellite to Broaden TV's Vision." *China Daily*, June 2, 1986.

Zhou Yougao. "China: Leaping Forward." *Intermedia*, July-September 1986.

Index